To Kevin in
the moment
here to face & wonder!
what a witness to the magic
of the all-inclusive nature
of Oneness!

THE GOLDEN NAIL

" Man is a Song

Ken.

October 19th 1993.

THE GOLDEN NAIL

KENNETH G. MILLS

with drawings by the Author

Sun-Scape Publications
Stamford • Toronto

Canadian Cataloguing in Publication Data
Mills, Kenneth G., 1923-
    The golden nail

Includes bibliographical references.
ISBN 0-919842-13-5

1. Metaphysics. 2. Civilization, Modern - 20th century - Philosophy.
3. Language and languages - Philosophy. 4. Life - Philosophy. I. Title.

BX9998.M55 1993   110   C93-093645-0

Sun-Scape Publications
A Division of Sun-Scape Enterprises Limited
P.O. Box 793, Station "F"
Toronto, Ontario M4Y 2N7, Canada

65 High Ridge Road, Suite 103
Stamford, Connecticut 06905, USA

Cover design: Concept by Kenneth G. Mills; art by Robert Withstandley

Printed in the United States of America

ISBN 0-919842-13-5

TABLE OF CONTENTS

FOREWORD

Kenneth Mills has compiled an operator's manual for the real human being in *The Golden Nail*. Fundamentally, all unreality percolates into consciousness through culture, history, and language, with their built-in, limiting mind-sets. His challenge is to "dare to be Real."

While an automobile is test-driven to determine the causes of various knocks and rattles, the vibrational disturbances in the human aura may also be detected by an expert in tonality. Not for nothing did Mr. Mills study so many years to be a top concert pianist, only to give it up to speak the Word. The Word is carried by sound and distinguished from verbal noise by tonality and meaning. The opening verses of St. John's Gospel portray the continuing (and not once and for all time) sounding of the forever and everywhere Word. It is the living Fundamental of creation, carrying innumerable interwoven overtones and diverse harmonies inextricably melded into a unity, called by Mr. Mills "the Real."

Echoes of the Word are being sounded constantly everywhere, from the sub-microscopic to galactic scale — and all that is in between.

Thus, Mr. Mills has conducted exercises and lectures totally extemporaneously to permit the Real, that is the Word, to be conveyed as a resonance to others, without the hindrance of preconceptions from his own mental storehouse. Valuable as such filed-away remembrances might be, the keynote is freshness and spontaneity.

The Word is independent of time. The preparation to sound it must be lived and not practiced by rote, as might a minister or pastor recite a Sunday sermon he had boned up on all week. All that such a recital could convey would be a content of dead men's bones! Because it is lived, the Word is living. Unless it is lived it is just verbal noise accompanied by a similitude of meaning — the unreal. The comparison of the unreal to the Real is as junk food is to nourishment.

Having forsaken the concert stage, Mr. Mills needed a sounding board: The Starscape Singers, far more ample in range, wider in dynamics and, above all, less mechanical than the piano. Unlike the metal strings of the pianoforte, the individual Singers were to be stretched taut not by pliers, but they were to be educated (that is, drawn out of themselves) by an initiation of plunging into the Real. Often, this was a painful process.

Once he had assembled and trained the Singers, Mr. Mills conducted the group in stimulating concerts all over the world. Such tours are not made for the sake of fame or money. The object is always to set in motion centers of co-resonance in as many locations and amid as diverse a variety of peoples as possible.

The Golden Nail, if inverted, might suggest the clapper of a bell, which, once set in motion causes the sweet melody of the carillon to sound forth. The bell, however, was not cast from any metal. Human beings, awakened to their individual and collective Reality, constitute the bell. Unreality corresponds to flaws in the casting which could sour the purity of the tone. That is why Mr. Mills attacks any and all manifestations of unreality, deriving from culture, language, and history, with what amounts to a ferocity — softened only by an inexhaustible patience and compassion.

What sometimes seems like an obscurity in *The Golden Nail* is precisely an attempt to overthrow the barriers erected in consciousness by the dead trinity mentioned. A nail, a gold one, has been hammered by Mr. Mills into their coffin.

Language is perhaps the subtlest member of the dead trinity, because we cannot communicate without it and are seemingly bound by its preconceptions and built-in limitations. Only by flights of poetry can the limits of language be surpassed. Not surprisingly, Mr. Mills is a prolific and eloquent poet of the Real, the Word.

The Teaching of the Real obliges man to get out of the way of Man! Ego is the great stumbling block, and second to ego is fear of the new and unknown. To demolish ego and fear, Mr. Mills stands ordinary language on its head: sometimes mocking, at times cajoling and punning outrageously.

Cultural biases, too, must crumble before this onslaught on the unreal. The Singers are equally at home with Negro spirituals and the songs of indigenous peoples of North America. They can handle Russian and Ukrainian folk music as well as such popular Christmas carols as "The Little Drummer Boy."

Not least of the dead trinity is history. By "history" is meant the whole of the latent memory of the evolutionary process down to the cellular level. Many predispositions to pathology and neurological disorders are due to not-yet outgrown history in this sense. But, don't wait for any end to history save in His-story! "Yours is not a day of prophecy, but yours is a day the Lord hath made, and the Law is written in the Heart. Love is the fulfillment of the Law." Where is such a State to be found? "Don't even look under your nose, it is closer than that!"

Spontaneity is the Soul's uncontainable expression of wonder. "That is why it is ridiculous to take a piece of music and think there is a prescribed way for interpreting and playing it." Wonder, elegance, and spontaneity are the trine to the key which unlocks the prison door of history. "Being cannot be other than elegant because Being is that state which embraces all that is termed beautiful." Nature brings forth ever more elegant creations: progressing from ponderous saurians to lithe wild horses; from the ungainly archeopteryx to delicate humming-birds; from the scaly coelacanth to the rainbow trout.

For man to assist Nature in making for elegant excellence, he must find the Register. But, "The registration is decided not by you, but by the music." However, "Spontaneity does not consist in what you like," but feeling "what the music asks for." "Beware of registering for mere novelty." In the freedom exercised by Mr. Mills there is no room for the chaos of individual self-wills. It is, above all, the Principle which brings harmony to the previously separated wills. That Principle is the I AM, a Wholeness or Holiness which radiates the Divine Word.

The mighty, universal I-AM Principle, the emanation of the Word, precludes egotism. Talent "should be the God-Being instead of the personal being enacting the role of success." The Register sounds in the Tonality and then the music is alive.

To return to language, what is demanded is a "change in the individual's tonal register": a change of habit, a change — above all — of identification. A new language demands a new character "without the habit of a past (history) to make him or her seem acceptable to the present" (i.e., culture). The individual "can only conform to Principle, he cannot form it." The I-AM Word is totally uncompromising and it confers a totality of freedom within a total discipline.

To pursue the topic of discipline, Mr. Mills says, "One of the errors of the age is receiving Instruction or Training without the living of it." There can be no medium or mediator between you and Reality — that is the Essence of the Teaching, of which the discipline is to live without crutches. No need to go off to Tibet or India; everything can be done at home. No need to sell your house and car or desert your family to follow some guru or to join an ashram — all that is needed is "closer than under your nose," and no one can sell it to you.

It should go without saying that a "drugged" mankind won't "look beyond the bushes." All that we have invested in as occupation, status, our health or financial position, Mr. Mills says, acts as a drug which prevents a feeling of Oneness with the I-AM Word. Surely, it is a matter of priorities of attention. How we bestow our attention constitutes discrimination.

Discrimination of priorities of attention was called by religious mystics "praying without ceasing." Verbalized prayers alone were not meant: rather a state of attention switching as rapidly as needed between Reality and the here and now of daily tasks. Thus, Blessed Theresa of Avilla could reprove idly chattering novices in the kitchen, "Sisters, hearken, God is among the marmites!"

With this discipline of awareness and discrimination, false identity and false identification disappear. So much for the touted modern identity crisis! One is not "a doctor, lawyer, Indian chief" — One IS. Such a realization of Self as opposed to self saves one from the so-called "search." Forget searching and just work! This is also called by mystics "Practicing the Presence." But one cannot practice the Presence unless oneself is wholly present! Further, "The Art of Being is the Presence of Nowness in the face of procrastination." Again, "What is the value of Being? It doesn't need to have a shadow to Shine." False identification is the shadow. "The Art of Being is never found by being sought in time."

Mr. Mills speaks of the Brothers of the Shadow and the Brothers of the Light. It is the refusal of the former to recognize the Real that gives rise to the shadow, which could not even be perceived unless it were cast by the Real, the I AM. Yet, the tone is the shadow.

Mr. Mills brings into play a seeming opposition of hearing to seeing. Now a tune can be brought "perfect pitch," but untrained seeing (as well the artist knows) leads to innumerable perceptual errors. Is it any wonder, then, that the Singers are trained and honed by Mr. Mills to radiate streams of Light-Sound, awakening new creativity in the visual artist.

"The world's Soul, we are told, is in dire need. It is because we are perched on the edge of an incredible happening." Mr. Mills demands and exemplifies the new Paradigm of Wonder, which alone can bring Man through, intact and realized, within "a tattered mental society." Together with the Singers, he sounds once more with the eternal, reverberating Word. This mighty Tone is for the healing of the nations. May he and the Singers accomplish joyfully their Divine Mission in a troubled time.

After all, viruses are contagious: why not Truth!

Timothy Phillips
Tucson, Arizona

EDITOR'S NOTE

Mr. Mills uses the words "you," "me," "I," and "I AM" in a very specific sense. The you and the me, especially when stressed, refer to the imaginary entities that we have created in our minds and claimed to be the identity of both ourselves and others. The you and the me represent the state of thought that believes itself to be embodied physically and thus part and parcel of a material world. It is our conceptual identity; it is a limited corporeal self-image that we have been educated to construct on the premise of duality and materiality. In short, it is the human personality that parades one way one minute and another way the next.

The I AM is the Infinite, the Eternal, and the Unchanging. The I or the I AM is our true Identity. The I AM is what we really are. It is beyond any thought that can be identified with the finite. It is not a conceptual identity for it cannot be conceived, yet it is the Light to all conception. The I AM is synonymous with other terms appearing in the text: Consciousness, the Source, the Self, Christ, Truth, Life, Love, the Light, That Which IS. Yet, we cannot think in terms of being That personally, because that would impose a limit on the I AM, which is limitless.

Mr. Mills gives this very clearly in the following statements:

"I" points to Being.
You call it "you" or "me"
when you think in terms.

The I AM
permits man to assume
an "I am" identity;
but the I AM
isn't in the identity.

PREFACE

The one coming to understand these lectures (called "Unfoldments") would have to be capable of standing aside from his inherited belief system in order for a new development to happen. One cannot expect a change if one is so full of his own accomplishment. A change only happens when one allows a "space" to exist as a result of disbelief.

These Unfoldments are given from the Point outside of the historical context of a word being holy, for it lives now, for the Speaker lives now and, therefore, it is my authentic story, for it is my experience; it is no one else's. Read it with doubt, you will have more. Abandon doubt and trust may occupy space as the Light dawns.

The language of these Unfoldments has been said to be the language of Soul. This has a highly charged meaning for me because Soul has revealed itself to me as *the Feeling of Being I AM*. Thus, the poetic speech demands such movement on the part of the listener. You will find the language filled with provocative analogies and metaphors, allowing an idea to resound to its fullest expressive capabilty in the foyer of expectation.

Perceive that capitalization is the sign for you to alter your everyday consideration of your ordinary words. The words capitalized in these Unfoldments will exalt the concepts so presented, hopefully to the Realm of the Uncontradictable, and from that Point, why don't you adopt this attitude and see if you can achieve this One and become!

An Unfoldment has been found to be appreciated as a musical form, such as a sonata, fugue, rondo, or theme and variations. Ideas are introduced, developed, and then recapitulated in a new key — or are you found in it and it is called a new key? The Unfoldment is spontaneous and is given under the impelling force of ideas that are not used in a linear fashion so that one may find, when the Subject is perceived, the object is laid out!

> In the classical form redemption is at hand,
> And may you so find in the Light of this Radiance
>   it's part of the Plan.

Words are utilized like pivotal chords on which ideas can modulate, leading to the wonder of words when you have perceived that their use is a key to either bondage or freedom.

The themes that I have presented in these Unfoldments are of universal significance because it is so simple to treat everyday life as a symbolic pointing to a Higher Way of viewing the world and you, its inhabitant. If you are willing to probe, study, and wrestle with the themes of this Experience, new wonders and considerations will be found the proper dues for your effort. Your appreciation of language and how it can lead you into the realms of either fettered or unfettered thought should add a new vitality and a vehicle of practicality for lives needing to be rescued from the turmoil of dismay.

Read with your eyes, but listen with the waxing of your ears; then you will perceive that the Sound is the garment weaving an attraction for you to follow the Radiance to its Source.

Kenneth G. Mills

I

THE UNTHINGNESS OF THE WORD

The Wonder of any gift at first can appear to be in the beauty of the gift, but then the gift, to be perceived as it is, cannot be considered just a "thing," to be truly appreciated, because any gift that is beautiful must have a certain freedom from being the "thing" it appears to be.

THE UNTHINGNESS OF THE WORD

We know that the season is filled with expectation, it is marked with the ribbons of promise, and it is effulgent with the Light that can be turned on when people rejoice for the sake of a Festival and the relief it brings from the serious situation, wrapped with taping gifts, labeling gifts, choosing gifts, preparing gifts to be opened; and then, found beneath the wrappings, the intent of the wrapping, the purpose of the wrapping, the gift, the *cause* of the gift, the *effect* of the gift, and the *result* of the gift.

All gifts are *wrapped* in such conditions. There is no greater condition than the condition of being *gifted* and remaining taped with the foliage, the *foil*-age of attractability, the tinsel of intellectual attainment, and the scarcity of attainment without makeup.

No gift can be found or understood from the standpoint of the one gifted. The one gifted presents the gift as a talent, but no talent evidences itself as a gifted one without the effort necessary to *unearth. The demand to unearth is paramount in today's world.* You have to unearth all "things" that can be unearthed. When you start to see what *can* be unearthed and you are grand in your considerations and say, "Yes, all 'things' must be unearthed," do realize **all "things" are Earthed and cannot be unearthed.**

Do you realize a "thing" doesn't exist other than on Earth? The "thing" and Earth go together. A talent is not a "thing." The condition of a "thing" that is talented is termed "gifted."

If you are *gifted*, it means that you are capable of being able to offer a collection that is perceived by "*things*," appreciated by the "*unthingness*" of the "thing." The Unthingness of the "thing" is readily perceived in the developed *gifted* one, because *to be a gifted one is to transcend a "thing" being the doer and the doer just being a "thing."* If you perceive evidence, or the collection of talents or gifts, then you perceive a promise that is beyond the mind's attempt to *crib* in passing the exam concerning the subject of "transcending the 'thing' and explicating the Unthingness of the 'thing'."

The Wonder of any gift at first can appear to be in the beauty of the gift, but then the gift, to be perceived as it *is*, cannot be considered just a "thing," to be truly appreciated, because any gift that is beautiful must have a certain freedom from being the "*thing*" it appears to be. When a "thing" is given as a gift and the gift is appreciated, the appreciation helps to free the gift from the "thingness" it isn't; and the "thingness" that the gift isn't is the Realness of the gift appearing as the "thing." One of the great Wonders of gifts is that the whole symbolic nature of the gift is *redolent* when we approach the nature of incense.

When you are confronted with sticks unpackaged and expecting to be fragrant with no match around, don't try to set up another blind stick and expect it to be a successful date! *Who is to say*, from the standpoint of an incensed stick, what the sense of its "unthingness" is from the encrustations of its congealed, powdered nature? How often do we attempt to perceive and adjudicate an incensed stick and then say, "Well, it's all because it hasn't got the proper *stick-mate* to make it a stickpin." And you realize that most of your juggling starts then with the Papermate.[1]

If you take the Papermate and it should run . . out of having a legible point, you better ask for a Bic.[2] Then you perhaps realize that, no matter how much writing you may do about what it means to put two incensed natures together and expect to have something that's going to be a fragrant nature ever going to happen, what you need is the big flame, constant Bic. So, you "flick your Bic" and you set your stick on fire. And what happens? You have a flaming stick and you have a fragrance, the proof of dying to a congealed, dustlike state.

When the smoke of the *insensed nature* is freed from its auric film (say, when you have to clean it from the walls), you are left with the aroma of its passing. No one says, "Was it worth it for the 'thing' to give up its 'thingness' for the sake of its Unthinged Nature?" You never consider the gift of a stick as the possibility of beating the bum tricks of time! You never consider that perhaps the sojourn today of conceiving "*things*" in abundance is really just a multiplied effect of the mind's ingenuity at creating after its own kind, waiting for that moment when somebody will press the right button and say, "Stop! and let us see what came *before* the 'thing,' and what comes chasing *after* the 'thing.' Is it what *permits* the 'thing' to be the Unthing that *allows* it to be *considered* a talent of value?"

If you cannot see beyond the "thing," then you *cannot* perceive the incredible talent that your "thing" has when it is given to consider the *magic* of the "thing" in Light of the Unthing.

The whole story of Magic surrounds the whole story of Fulfillment, the whole story of surcease from bondage, the whole story behind Calle Elena, the Way of the Light. You can approach the Way of the Light via the Road of the Christ, or you can approach it via the Way of John,[3] which of course is via the Way of the most mystical approach to what was given as the considerations surrounding a long-gone enunciation of Jesus.

The whole *story of a Star* is to free it from the "thing" it *seems* to be and allow the Unthingness it IS to **penetrate** the constellation of your intellectual achievements and cause such an *implosion* that you *expand* from within, to see your limitations. You can perceive without doubt that the constellation of your significance in the intellectual realm is a tinsel of adornment of the "thing" waiting to find itself *gifted* and, not being freed by unearthing, remaining satisfied with the soporific appellation of a degree in attainment in the "school of hard knocks." A hard knock is the resultant condition that knots encounter when there has been *no one* present to unwind the woolding surrounding an irritated point of intellectual perception.

It is imperative that you start to see that no amount of logic can do anything but *add* to the *amount* of logic. No logic has ever amounted to anything other than logic. We dress up the conclusion of one amount of logic with *another* amount of logic as being a conclusion of another new premise for operation. That *standpoint* of operation from one accumulation to another accumulation is *nothing* but the magnification of a suggestion that logic could ever be increased to be other than what it really was in the beginning: the ability of the intellect to successfully put together something that could be accepted as a fact and stand a test for a certain period of "linearality."

Who ever heard of a Star giving a damn whether or not you think it's alive?! Who is concerned here on earth that the star they're shooting and trying to understand is emitting its light of fifty million light-years ago?! Who is fooling whom in trying to understand *logically* whether or not the star still exists? What is interesting is

4

whether or not there is still light in the eye of the star*gazer*.

A star that *shines* on the dome of the mind is all put there by your imagination, and the star that *falls* from the dome of your mind all happens within your imagination. A star that *rises* on the dome of your mind *sets* as well on its horizon. Why would you allow a mind to be both the cause of something happening and the cause of something *not* happening and the backdrop for which it *is* happening and for which it is *not* happening? How do you allow the mind to be the "thing" that you say it is? The mind needs to be an "*un*thing" as the brain is considered *some*thing.

The gift is considered some*thing; its beauty is not considered the "thing"!* The beauty is **beyond** the "thing," just as the beauty *must have been* or the "thing" couldn't be beautiful. Not always is the buyer of the gift aware of the beauty; he feels that somebody *else* might like it, although *he* wouldn't want it.

Now remember, you don't buy anything for anyone else that you wouldn't buy for yourself. So be as generous in your giving as you would be to yourself . . without a mortgage! And *then* see where you are making your "collection." Are you collecting onto the photographic plates (negatives) that need to be strung before a light panel to be seen? Or are you *developing* them so that you can see an *impression* of your condition? Wouldn't it be an incredible thing if you could take a picture of the Unthingness of the "thing," so that the beauty would *evidence* itself before "you" *decided*!

If you could **see**, *how would you decide to see?* Would you decide to see the "thing," or the Unthing? Then, in seeing the Unthing, embrace the "thing" and *allow* it to *glow* with the *aura of a Presence*, the result of a **Light bombardment of appreciation**.

The reason the gifts of the Magi were so important was because they were *pointing* to the *necessity* of seeing what was given to a Child who knew not He was being given gifts (according to the picture); and the cows and the sheep and the asses *couldn't have cared less* about the gold, frankincense, or myrrh. But the *marvel* came when you started to develop a distance from the picture and perceived its "*thingness*" and then its *Unthingness*. Its Unthingness is not in the painting; it's in *what happens* when all of the palette of mental titillation happens, is swallowed up by the fire of *feeling*, and each act of magic *alters* the vision.

It is this *altered vision* that is so essential, because *if your vision cannot change, you perish!* It can only change through *Love*, through devotion and through consecration to the possibilities inherent via the road of Mystical Metaphysics and the Philosophy of the Sacred. You *cannot achieve* a freedom from the "*thing*" if you go around *convinced* you are the "thing" and there is another "thing" and another "thing" and another "thing." You know, it's amazing that religion would be called "the religion 'thing'"! Or it could be called the "thing of religion."

What is the "thing" of religion? The catatonic state waiting to meet its Match! The only way it can meet its Match is to meet its *Fire*. And the Fire is that which does not necessarily destroy, but *alters* the essential structural nature.

The reason these words are used is because we are not speaking of the Fire that we consider the common, ordinary one in a fireplace or in a candle. We are considering the Celestial Fire or the Electrical Fire of That . . *Ring of Force* surrounding what is called "the *Masters* of Power or Force."

The Masters of Power or Force are what? The names given, the words given, to describe an Energy Field that you cannot conceive intellectually any more than you can conceive how the incense stick is going to smell or appear with its aura *until it has happened*!

The Masters of Power, the Masters of Transmutation, the Masters of Translation, and the Masters of the Force are those names given to prepare you to consider the *transforming power of a mind force that is available when the "thing" is no longer in supremacy and the Unthing is perceived as the Power to the "thing's" apparent presence!* When this happens, the "thing" can be present, and the Unthingness of it is evident.

Guess what the word is then? It's a "*thing.*" *That is why the ordinary words don't do anything!* **But the Unthingness of the Word allows it to appear to bypass your intellectual computations and reveal a new consideration** regardless of your constellations of intellectual achievement.

This is the most *fanciful* consideration, the most *practical* bestowal, and the most *wonderful* Christmas present, because it will take you either a moment to unwrap it or the rest of your lives! In that case you will start calling upon some other poor creature saddled with the belief that he was the only one who knew the Mystery of "What is on that Hill?! Is that the *Hill of the Skull*? Or is that just the *mound* the 'thing' plays off of until the right *Christ* is at the bat?"

What is the Christ? The Unthingness of the mental realm that would have the "thing" a religionist? The Christ is not a religionist! It is a State of the Unthingness that *allows* the constellations of intellectual fortification to be given to the *Arrowhead of Mercurian Light Might*, so that the **Word** may be ejaculated from the Bow of Promise.

You can see that a Star *broke* the horizon of time and fell to Earth and caused men to consider, "If this came from *outer* space, we must be *inner* space! If we are *inner* space and something was able to enter us from outer space, we must have created an *implosion* for such an exploit of the intellectual fortifications without perceiving the *usage* of words that do nothing but trap and snare the mind into indolence, apathy, and indifference, into racism, religion, and laws."

You are destined to be unwrapped, no longer foiled by the mind, and you can subdue gall and have the gall to do so. It may be bitter, but remember, the sweetness is not always what you go by; the sweetness is what usually should cause you to stop. Don't go by sweetness. See it for the "unthingness" it is. "Sugar is sweet and so are you." How can "you" be sweet? Salt, water, chalk, protoplasm, or slime. Somebody is pulling your constellation!

How can you say "sugar is sweet and so are you," if you weren't meant to be more than "you"? If sugar *is* sweet, something happened to the sugar. "And so are you." It means "you" are the result of two things happening: the sugar can't be sweet unless it's obtained as sugar and unless it's *experienced*, in other words, **altered** *or transformed in its nature*. You can't be sweet unless *you are* experienced, altered in your nature, and then you are no longer sugar or you; you're sweet.

7

You *take* your words too loosely woven and glued together by the gradual "acceleration of learning," and the inevitable deterioration. You know why? You can't expect a "thing" to be more than it is, but certainly when you free the Gift from the "*thing*," in spite of your yawn, you will find the Gift not boring, but holding your attention. You will find yourself either a more *dammed* "thing" or a more *freed* "thing," because you were willing to look at **Beauty**, the result of the Gift *you* have received.

Beauty is the window, you might say, that the Light has made in the house of your intellectual considerations in case your door is still locked by your degrees of attainment. If there is Beauty perceived, there is hope that someone may open your door. And guess who will have to do that? *You!* Because if you are content behind the crib of your attainment, you are limited in the birth of a Cosmic, Immaculate Wonder.

The Nativity Scene is meant to instill Wonder into the childlike thought, for the "child-thing" could never have happened if there had not been the "parent-thing." The "parent-thing" was to have given to the "child-thing" the Wonder of preparing a Festival to *sing* of the Wonders of Un*thing*ing. The Wonders of Unthinging free you from your incensed natures and the inevitable sticks that so many are! They allow you the opportunity to be fragrant heads of your state, thus allowing through your auric splendor, by your very presence, others to engage in the Wonders of experiencing Something that is no longer some "thing." That is when you may be asked, "Oh, 'thing,' *tell me*, what is the meaning of Being Unthing?" And "thing" sings, and the feeling of Unthingness embraces the Infinite, for the Infinite no longer is a "word-thing"; IT's a **Sound** *Thing*. In this may be a key for your Unthingness or, more bluntly, your undoing!

Rest in the joy and *hark* to what isn't said, for what isn't said is termed the Unthingness of the Word, and you call it "Silence."

God rest . . ye merry. Thrice blessed is he who sees the "thing" . . the Gift, the Unthing, the Talent, and wonders! *Unthing*.

Enjoy and be ever active, for that is the whole purpose of being a "thing" and having "things," to be able to appear *gifted* and allow a Star to shine in the midst of your presence, and others term it the work of those who still know the reason they marvel at Wonder. Yours points to the *wisdom to do* so; theirs will point to the *need to do* so; and blessed are those who *know by doing so* they have found the Way to go *"Home . . Home."*

The Gift, the Talented, and the Accomplished will always be with you, but how many will there be who will ever allow the Wonder of each condition to be *effulgent in the Conditionless?*

Thank you.

December 24, 1989

---

1 "Papermate" is a registered trademark of The Gillette Company

2 "Bic" is a registered trademark of the BIC Corporation.

3 The Way of John the Beloved, the Apostle, is the way of love, devotion, or **bhakti.** "Bhakti" is defined as "the path of devotion, in which devotion to the Guru transcends all separateness or difference even while the apparent relationship continues." (From Saniel Bonder, *The Divine Emergence of the World-Teacher.* Clearlake CA: The Dawn Horse Press, 1990.)

II

A SURPRISE – A PROPHETIC UTTERANCE

The theatre lacks drama, as life lacks drama, because people are afraid to be unique, to be called heroes, to be called Great Natures, therefore, Divine Actors. No actor of significance can change the world unless Divinity is all that is pulsating his stream of confluence with time!

A SURPRISE – A PROPHETIC UTTERANCE

We are in the Stream of Everlasting to Everlasting. We are approaching that Tide of Event that ushers into the world of imagination, considerations, and considered imaginations the fulfillment of dreams. We are entering into a Stream of such Force that those who are attuned unto it and who are moved by it realize the great demand of Presence is to *energize*, to *dramatize, to reveal*. Yours is this inclination. Yours is this obligation. Yours is this responsibility.

You have not participated in the great Feasts of Light without considering the manifold glories and expectations which are beamed unto you. In the quietness of the Soul you may perceive the quivering movements of a greater longing trying to manifest itself unto your tremulous and insecure heart promptings.

The great **demand** for everyone is to follow this sentence given by Mary Baker Eddy: "We must not seek the immutable and immortal through the finite, mutable, and mortal."[1] You cannot consider on the same line of consideration the thought-structures that are seductive because they are based upon your objective experiences.

You are *cautioned* and yet alerted with the vigor of the ancient exclamations to *free yourself* **from the limitations that are self-perpetuating due to the surface-self.**

You are encouraged from the beginning of considerations, from the moment you start to consider the surface-self, and you are *prompted* to be free of *self*-imposed limitations. These are all conjured by the mind and its ability, at one and the same moment, to give you an I as a subject and an I as an object, with blindness prevailing!

The Facet of *Brilliance* is released from the opaque conditions of the mind when you re-member that as a child you did not think in the terms of limitation. Even the *"Unseen"* presented friends to talk to and friends to play with, while the "seen" was frequently drab and dreary, yet amiable.

"You" are *prone* to be at ease with the dream of proportions. You are not at all *inclined* to view what you see as an object other than a total impression of the object. In other words, the components that make up your object are not seen as *parts* or units of the total object. It is only through *analysis* that you can understand what makes up the object that exists to you in comprehension as a totality; but through analysis and, therefore, through a distance achieved from it, you can break it down into the components that make up its imaginary form.

We look at a body and we call it a form. Upon dis*section*, we can describe what constitutes that form, what constitutes that body, be it of a plant or a man or an animal — or a world apart! You can see that it is made up of different ingredients, and yet we are given a great gift of seeing the total experience, of *perceiving* the total. We *perceive* with the outer eye; we *see* with the Inner One.

One great proponent of the theatre said, "Great drama needs great natures" in order for the theatre to be the dramatic and dynamic situation of revealment that it is. The trouble with theatre *today* is the *lack* of great actors. Great actors are demanded in great dramas, and great dramas and great actors are *never* devoid of great natures. Now do you see why the theatre is so boring, why you go to a theatre and wonder not, but complain abundantly at the shallowness of the surface impressions of the parts that are supposedly being enacted freed from the inhibiting factors of the surface selfhood of person?

What Path would you take that would have you and me divided?

What Path? It cannot be a *part* of Totality, for the I *sees* totally. You see . . through a dark glass dimly.[2] The clouded mind gives an opaque vision of what is a **vibrant** *situation of an Electrical Force Field*.

What is the whole purpose of **mining**? It is to free what is of value from the dross that makes up most of the mound![3]

What is the value of penetrating the superficial considerations of today? In the penetration, you are able to *reveal* the *importance*, the *preciousness* of the Unseen, in the mound so seen as part of a scene of projected entertainment.

Do you consider, when you sit by yourself, how many more are present within you? How many more of "you" are you entertaining, dressed up in different thought-structures, each trying to seduce you into following them so they can divide you and keep you following after strange gods? The reason strange gods exist is because you make them up in your mind as a result of the fractured patterns of thought that conform not to an Undeviating, Immutable, and Immortal Principle!

You try to *seek* the Unlimited Possibilities of Being by trying to persuade a mortal to be less mortal, less human, and more divine. *Rubbish*! That is a type of psychotherapy, when the whole problem is a result of an enlarged dream of delusion! All the attempt to bring about unity within the psyche is an attempt to bring about an understanding of its dreams, of its forces, when the *Dream* is not known that allowed the dream that is projected to be enacted as if there were a reality to it. There is nothing but the fragmentary, momentary experience of a portrayal lacking in revelation or revealment! It reveals nothing but the vapid, paucity-ridden experience of personalization and preparation for the grave of delusion!

You are of importance because you have the tremor within you of the earthquaking knowledge of Principle! IT really cracks the armor of suggestion and reveals the core of your Self invulnerable, and the outer shell of yourself a vulnerable, breakable, fracturable shell!

I suppose you wonder at times why under the sun you got involved with an Answer to a question! It is too bad if you do, because when you questioned, "What is the meat of this nut?", you little expected the shell to have to be cracked to get at it! What has happened today to the drama, the energy, the force that is required to give you the courage to *come out from the seductive relationships of time and be a Great Nature?! How can you be a Great Nature and relate to your limitation?!*

One of the greatest relationships that exists, which one of the Speakers of yesterday enunciated with such fierce dramatization, is that He "came not to bring peace but a sword," and to separate father from son, mother from daughter, brother from brother, et cetera.[4] Why? He was not saying anything other than you have to free yourself from the seduction of a relative or limited beginning. There is no hope for the future from your "beginnings." If there were, your "beginnings" would be taking care of the future. Instead of that, you're left with them!

Then how can you carry on the warriorship that is essential unless you are on that Stream of Everlasting to Everlasting and you realize the transitory nature of the historically significant event? It is all pointing to the need to free yourself from the classical tradition of bondage! Why do you think the Great Speaker of yesterday said so? He said it was imperative to free yourself from the limitations of your basic, great tendency: to relate to the initial impinging force of your birth and its accompanying forces. You cannot relate to your family; you must live free from evaluating yourself, free from categorizing yourself with their accomplishment.

If this one had related to the family, this one would not be sitting here. This one would never have left the "sticks." This one would never have left the limitations which a village mentality, a community mentality imposes. And this is why you were considered so important, because you were to be freed from this entanglement with an inherited, limited, amiable, and yet frequently energized situation that is not so amiable! That is its seductive nature. It's the one area where you can rampage through relationships and still have them in essence part of the yin/yang sponsorship in delusion! If this one had remained tied to the situation which was being dreamed for him by his wonderful, love-filled, and sponsoring parents, he would have been sponsored in limitation as they were and into a "churchianity" that did not free, even through the baptismal rite. What was missing was the Drama of a Living Self Experience! The minister was not free. How could the words be redolent with Transformative Power, when the "thing" was reeking with superficial self importance?!

These words are being said to encourage you to become what is an inevitable result (sooner or later): a Great Nature! A Great Nature is not persuaded to be docile, to be conforming, to be agreeable, to be related to the whole realm that is mutable and mortal!! The theatre lacks drama, as life lacks drama, because people are afraid to be unique, to be called heroes, to be called Great

Natures, therefore, Divine Actors. No actor of significance can change the world unless Divinity is all that is pulsating his stream of confluence with time!

You are treated to withstand the radiation of limitation if you wish to plug in to the Infinite Possibilities of Being as Principle Living, uninhibited by the mortal assumptions that go with the blindness of belief and partial adaptation to the demand to be adopted and found motivated as One given, One accepted and received in the Light of Those consecrated to the Pathway of Stardom!

Your inclinations should no longer be grounded with the mundane conglomeration of gelled situations of dubious quality. Your considerations, your whole experience, your whole thought-structure should be such that it is a becoming force field, a *gestalt* in which you involuntarily live and move and have your Being, and your presence itself reveals your attainment!

What would you choose? What Path would you choose that causes you and me to divide? Can it be one that you can find agreeable in the sanctuary of your Divine unreasoned Perception?! Perception isn't reasoned. When it is reasoned, you perceive the object; when you doubt it, it's analyzed.

When you perceive the object, *that is for the **Theatre** of which you are a part!* It is the theatre *off* Broadway. It may be on 42nd Street. If it is, it's all aligned to the power of reliable responsibility because you cooperate with the four-square power of your Master-ship, which is *joined* with the agreement that comes with coopera-tion. It's a theatre off Broadway; it is such a Narrow Way and it is a One Way.

How can you dramatize the Hero, the King?! How can you dramatize the buffoon, the minstrel, the choir, the flock, the mass, if you remain imbued with the learned, intellectual conditions of such a stated mass?!

You perceive such. It is freed in the *depth finding* of the Precious Jewel of Being! Then, normalcy reigns not, but an unabridged edition of Life's Unfolding Chronicle of Events, of which this day, this year, and you are inscribed indelibly upon its pages because *you agreed never to divide or take a Path that would separate you from your Divine Self!!*

You are God-dammed if you fall for the superficial self and allow it to persuade you into a *rhapsody* of *delusion*! Knowing what you know there is no*where* to go but *Home*! And that has nothing to do with your embryonic womb-like situation!

Your Motif is a *Light* one, and the recurring Theme is that "I have *seen* the Light, and in That Light may I be seen as the *Drama* to the Scene/seen of the Invincible Nature of the Divine Self!"

You cannot achieve the Immutable and the Immortal by *ranking, fouling* the situation with the intellectual configurations that go with the *analysis* of the *mutable*, the *mortal*, and the finite! "Come ye out from the world and be ye separate?"[5] To do so, cease being an inhabitant of the planet of *delusion* and find it a stage upon which *you*, a Star Visitor, are to reveal the **Points of Effulgence** commensurate with a **Cosmic Individuality**!

Yours is one equated with division and relationship, and the Great Individuality of *Being*, unconfined and uncontaminated by human hypotheses, *rests exactly* on one's ability to entertain a Grand Nature and perceive how you do not have to imagine; **you just have to be in that warrior state of awareness where you** *feel* **the impinging Force of an Invisible Power, and it leaves you wrapped in** *the Mystery that is termed Light!*

Move with the confidence of a man *drilled* in the abstract exercises of correct identification as Principle! *Live* as Principle, *moving in rhythm as a result of the drill* with what is composed for you to interpret as you view each and every happening on the picture book of the mind waiting for it to be translated into a *Sound* Experience. Why would you have it fractured, as the shell of delusion is fractured, when you have *found* the *Meat*, the Substance of such a Jeweled Nature, as a result of being willing, by asking a question, to be *cracked*!

You never can ask a question unless you expect to be cracked! When you ask for an answer and are *cracked* but you don't *yield* to the answer, you are *apt* to be "cracked" (upset)! You cannot go on pretending you do not understand an Answer so that you can go on *living* as if you knew not the Presence of this Teaching and the Teaching of this Presence.

You are the Core, you are groomed to know how to deal with the abstract exercises that come to you every moment when it says that "you are this and you are related to this." That's an abstract exercise.

"You" and "me" may seem to be all sitting in this room,
And all the lights are very bright and the heat is almost
    like a summer's noon.
"You" and "me" may be gowned as such, but what is
    present is not found
Other than a Tone, you say, appearing as Words which
    flow unbound.

"You" and "me" may ponder those and create a pool of
    quiet or despair.
Will you choose a Path that divides "me" and "you," or do
    you realize that such a Path is a dreamed-up
    nightmare, far from rare?
It's the *common* malady of those who *think* they can take
    from That Which IS
A little bit of "this" today and of "that" tomorrow, and yet
    they too can sing?

You cannot take one bit of Light into a darkened room
And have the room remain so dark that none of the dust or
    any of the attic brooms
Remain unseen, for in that Light you see the need of such
To sweep out all the cobwebs which create "you" and "me"
    and give us back to dust.

"You" and "me" are bound in years, but those years should
    reap reward,
For *you* questioned *me*, and on the Path I said, "'You' and
    'me' only seem to be,
For I AM always and never was."

"You" and "me" may appear to be garmented on this stage,
But the Light allows each to enact what will *become* an inner
    Rage.
It's the rage to be in fashion with what is *Real!* and True,
    Sublime.
It's the *Rage*, the Drama, and the Divine Attraction that
    comes as a new Force *wheels* you out of time.

Love is now named the Victor; *Vision is sublime,*
For the "you" and "me," the visionary, have been
    swallowed up as we walk the Star Trail beyond
    the mind.
And on that Mantle of Sparkling Glory may you keep a
    smile upon your face
Just in case an E.T. wonders what drama you played on
    what stage ere a Script is traced.

"You" and "me" may wish for marvels, and now you know
    they do abound,
For "you" and "me" seem to be here *solidly* present while
    the Song "I AM" is a *Mystery winged, bound yet
    unbound!*
Such is the Mystery of the Liberated Selfhood, and the
    surface-self says, "Ah, my God!
A Great Nature for a great Actor, for a great Drama is the
    Act of NOW."

You are part of that Cast, and you are cast away from the
shores of familiarity and must adopt the courage that goes with a
voyage of *discovery* beyond this world of *imagined* splendor and
enter into the *Unbridled, Unlimited* Wealth of a *Grand*, Cosmic
Consideration and Dispensation.

"You" cannot experience the Infinite . . if you don't claim . .
That IS All . . there is.

What an infinite supply of Wonder we have, with "you" and
"me" pretending we are such! But you see, *the magic and the marvel
of the Infinite* allow *all* of this to be swallowed up in a Divine
Moment of Sight, and in That, perception is unconfined and Life is
winged with victory!

Thank you.

December 31, 1989

1 Mary Baker Eddy, *Science and Health with Key to the Scriptures*, (Boston: Trustees Under the Will of Mary Baker G. Eddy, 1934), p. 286, ll. 3-4.
2 1 Corinthians 13:12.
3 Here Mr. Mills points to what is going on in the workings within the mound or the mind; i.e., the Mound of Skulls (Golgotha) as a symbol of the intellect.
4 Matthew 10:34, 35.
5 2 Corinthians 6:17.

III

NEUTRAL BUOYANCY

Look at the energy that is being utilized in emotions! I don't mean just emotions of a lower order, I mean the emotions of work and play, of every day. It's wonderful to be able to engage the whole spectrum of emotions, but don't lose yourself in them; you utilize them. It's like the waves of the sea.

NEUTRAL BUOYANCY

We are speaking to you this morning from the garden room of that house on the side of the hill overlooking the considerations of significance and the patterns of recognizability, so that you who are sitting quietly and pursuing the Mandate of your Inner Prompter once again may become friends with your Inner State and find agreement with the Inner Fraternity which has sponsored you and continues to sponsor you as you sojourn upon this planet with all its suggestive might, its travail and its wonders, as you prune your wings for Heavenly flight.

You are not here to garner the sweetness of this experience by understanding through the framework of limitation what is termed "sweet." You are here to experience the *hereness* of this place termed Earth, for you *agreed* to be part of this experience and thus bring to it the Culture that would be essential to fructify the seed-patterns of Light that have been spread from the Plane of the Stars with the Promise of the confetti of the Bridal Significance. When the Marriage is One Divine, Man unifies with the Self, and allows the confetti of rejoicing to sparkle with plenty the planet and the windowsills of the mind.

You are not a permanent resident. You are not other than a visitor to this strange planet, and each of the day's experiences brings to you all that is necessary for your purpose. You can say, "Well, *why* am I having such a *hell* of an experience when my life is filled with such challenges?!" It is *imperative* to remain fixed on the foundational Facts of Being which the mind accepts in the formulation of the Code attributed unto the landing and the flight pattern of today and of tomorrow. You must remain *fixed on the position of your acceptance*, and in doing so, become involuntarily the sacrifice to this plane where many have forgotten their reason for being here. Knowing this is only an auxiliary station, you are able to reorganize the patterns of thought or the *energy weaving* in order to coordinate with a fixed Point that will allow you to penetrate the black holes of your experience and perceive the Wonder of Galaxies beyond your mundane considerations.

Your hope of penetrating this darkness is all enlivened, emblazoned, and lighted by the Stars[1] on the dome of your high-ward attention. *If you look up*, you cannot behold other than the Infinitude of what is there because it is beyond your mind's comprehension. If IT is beyond your mind's comprehension, then the experience of IT is beyond it. Therefore, the experience of IT allows the mind to delineate the comprehensive Nature, which bears no resemblance to the limited pattern of intellectual computation that we have deemed so gigantic in this world of computers; and IT allows the possibility of reaching data that is laid in the electrical patterns prepared to receive an Electrical Force and termed a Voice Experience.

Every pattern that is laid in the electrical wave of time is there as the evidence of Force that is creative. It can be held in suspension or brought out of suspension according to the utilization of the will and its determination. The Will, like the Soul, is in *your* hands. This is one of the great gifts that you were allowed to experience upon this strange planet: you were given choice, Will, and Soul to structure. This has been the pattern that has agreed with your wishes before your adoption because you agreed to *adapt* to this planet with the *adopting* of this trinity of powers: your choice, your Will, your Soul to structure the spearhead for re-entry into the unmindful world of the Infinite.

Your *thrust* and the success of it will depend upon the *strength* of your choice, the *purpose* of your Will, and the *fiber* vibrating with the Harmonic Sense of Being as the Soul unifies *All* in its Force of Meaning.

The reason so much of our form seems to be uninformed is because we are such specialists that we fail to consider the fragments that are termed the facets that are possible, with scrutinization, to constitute our Rainbow Garment.

We should be able to wear all colors
and yet be perceived as Light Essence.

We should be able to dawn the color of the morning.
We should be able to don the garment of mourning
and still bear the garment of rejoicing.

We should be able to don the color of service
and still be the Wonder of it being performed.

We should be able to don the Robe of Inspiration and
Dictation from the Higher Planes
and yet still *appear* to be an earthly incantation of Wonder.

We should be able to be wise
and express the Wisdom of God
by donning the Robe of Sonship.

It would be unwise to make ourselves gods; it would be wise
to see. In seeing, who has made *whom*? And whom is not object!
I AM not object; I AM only Subject, and Being Subject, require no
object.

Perhaps, the reason the Absolute is such a confrontation to
psychologists is because they have no foundation to work upon,
and they say that men and women are *harnessed* to an un-free base
for "trying out" living. Well, you see, a metaphysical basis gives
you such confidence that you can penetrate the phenomenal world
and still not be seduced by it.

If we are looking for happiness — as we all *say* we are — I guess
I can say, as people do, that the past five years were such "happy"
ones for me. As I look back upon those years being happy, each day
was not *termed* happy; each day was termed dancing in rhythm and
seeing no obstruction laid in the Path of anyone and not *being* with
anyone who was laying obstruction in the Path of anyone. Now
that I look back on it, I call it happiness. So, perhaps, **happiness is
that state when there is no obstruction placed in your Path, and if
there is one, you can perceive it and fly over it.** Happiness is a myth.
Some declare, "I will never have happiness." You never will; **it will
be the description of a moment when there is no obstruction.**
Happiness is not what you expect it to be at all!

Happiness is the feeling . . after . . Being!

How do you know Being IS? Happiness is present in spite of
the garment of sorrow, sadness, and aloneness!

When we consider choice, we can always make it, but which
will you make? One vice-president I met the other day sheared the
mental concepts of his realm very well. He said to me that his wife
and he disagreed on the discipline of the child, in one instance. (I'm

sure there were many, but in this instance it was interesting.) He said that the wife felt that the child should do what it wanted to do and learn from experience which was right and wrong. He said, "Of course, I am the boss here. That will *not* be the case. What is the purpose of being a parent if you haven't learned what is right and what is wrong? So you do not *allow* the child the choice of finding out which is right and wrong. *You* know from experience. *That* is what you pass on as a parent!"

So I said to this man, "Well, you seem to be under great tension and pressure and stress here." "Well," he said, "Of course! I love it! It's all part of life! You do your homework at night because you have no time for thought when you're investing. It has to be instantaneous. It's all a matter of *awareness*. You have to be *aware every moment* because there is no time to make a choice. It is no time to miss an opportunity! And if you *think*, you will miss the opportunity! Opportunity cannot be grasped if you think! It is intuitive!" Can you imagine, a vice-president of the company saying this?! Needless to say, I liked him!

I said, "Well then, tell me, how do you deal with your *pressure?* No one around me seems to deal with it; they want to get away from me and do their own lives and everything." He said, "Well, the pressure! *When it gets to me, I just chew it up and spit it out in fun!* You can't make anything of it! That's all part of it!"

Somebody said to me not long ago, "I don't want to be dominated by Principle. I don't want to have to fulfill my commitment. I changed my mind. I want to have a peace of mind. I've got to have peace of mind." I said, "My God, what do you think you've got? You've got a piece! I've got a piece! Somebody else has got a piece! And you want a peace of Mind? *You'll never have peace of Mind from attempting to fracture it!*"

How do you expect to have peace if you are dealing with fragments? *A fragment exists as a result of division.* A nuclear force is required, and a *tremendous* dissipation of energy, to keep this complex picture appearing self-energized!

Look at the energy that is being utilized in emotions! I don't mean just emotions of a lower order, I mean the emotions of work and play, of every day. It's wonderful to be able to engage the whole spectrum of emotions, but don't lose yourself in them; you utilize them. It's like the waves of the sea. You have to learn how to take them. You can either suffer an undertow or you can ride them and land on the beach. You can be swept out to sea or you can ride the crest of the wave back to the beach. I've done both.

It's very, very interesting. When you put on your diving gear with all the lead weight around your waist and you have all your tanks for diving, and you sit on the boat, hold your mask, and then topple over backwards, you are some glad to have your buoyancy jacket. The waves, when you look down on them, don't seem to be dangerous; they're only four or five feet high. You drop into them and they seem eight or nine feet high!

Then, of course, you dive; and you have to let enough air out of your buoyancy jacket so that you sink, because of the lead weight that you have agreed to strap to your waist to make you sink. Your tendency is to remain on the surface of experience. But you know very well, to experience deep, deep considerations, there must be the weight of that experience to take you to the right depth! That is sometimes termed suffering, and it is painful!

But as soon as you are willing to face the depths instead of remaining on your back, floating, looking at the sun through your mask, you turn over and say, "I'll open my eyes and see what is before me." There are fish that you don't even see on the surface! There are the most beautiful fish just waiting to greet you. As soon as you get below the surface, their impression changes and you become one of their flotilla. You head for the anchor rope, for you must descend on this rope to control your descent because of the pain and because of the gravitational force exerted as you change your environment.

Why are we surprised at pain, and think the High Teaching must be wrong if there is pain? You have to change the condition in order to experience Newness, and to change the condition is *always* painful. I know. I've had sixty-some years of it.

When you go down to ten feet you grab your nose and you pretend to blow to equalize the pressure in your ears. The pain is so intense! You may head for the surface, but if the diving instructor is with you, your foot is grabbed or your leg is grabbed. *You must go through it!* You *cannot leave* this position. You can go up one foot, ten inches, eight inches; the slightest movements will alter the pain until you get control of it.

So you're held. "I'll go through it, I won't leave!" You're still there. You can't go to the surface, but you can go up eight inches. Suddenly, it's all right again. You say, "Okay, I can face it." You find you go to twelve feet, fourteen feet, fifteen, twenty-five, *thirty! Oh, the pain! You want to go back!* Your first experience has told you you mustn't! You *cannot* meet the greater pain by going to a lesser one! So you go and you equalize pressure. Your equilibrium is restored.

Then you go to thirty-three feet, where it happens. It always happens at the thirty-three foot level; it's very intense. Then guess what? They tell you the big pressure change is going to be at sixty-six, and the next one at ninety-nine. So down you go. "I want to be certified." I went down to sixty-six. My mask was hurting, my ears were hurting, and I suddenly realized all I had to do was balance. I equalized, and then developed neutral buoyancy and floated with the fish. They came up and inspected my mask. You just have to keep your hands folded, because if you put your finger up even to fix your mask, they think it's bait. I came up with tooth marks, red as could be. Little tiny fish! It's not always the big ones!

Then, we're down at the sixty-foot level. Then, we go to the seventy or the eighty. Then, following the leader, we know we're about to experience something that is quite frightening. You're prepared for it, and yet you don't know the experience. You're down there enjoying everything at the sixty-foot level, and she beckons, her blonde hair trailing behind her. "Come on!"

So, I followed. And lo and behold, we did what we dreaded, and did it before we knew we had done it! By following, we had passed over the edge (where it was sixty-five feet deep) of this huge, bottomless canyon, where the estimated depth is over six thousand feet. We had done it! We looked down and it was black as could be! Then she gestured downward and I thought, "Ohh!" So we went to the face of the cliff. She said, "Now you must inspect what you went over and see the beauty." So down we went, ninety, ninety-five, a hundred, hundred and five, hundred and ten, hundred and fifteen feet, and we were in a cave, with the most incredible sponges, huge fish, the most incredible coral, which you would see only at that depth.

Then we ascended and we had to count. You look back, look up at the sun, and this time it is not so brilliant at all. It's light; you can see a hundred feet in every direction. However, it's like being in oil. You're totally consecrated!

You're looking through this oil, and it's all moving so slowly. Then you have to count, and you have to judge: "I have only so much oxygen left. I have to gain the surface because that is where I am expected to evidence experience." There is no evidence needed at this level. The phenomenal is in the seeing; the surface is telling of the experience which seems phenomenal. And they say the Absolute isn't practical!

You gain the surface by timing, so that you do not have to enter the decompression chamber. You get back to the surface and you leave all the fish waiting for you.

There is this thing bobbing on the surface, being banged around by the waves. There is this little ladder hanging down, and you've got to *grab* it. You've never seen it fly out of your reach so many times in all your life, because the rhythm below is so different from the rhythm above. You have to compensate the whole time for being able to *hold* onto the first rung of the ladder when you change dimensions and gravitational fields.

Then there is somebody on the boat. You take off the flippers, and you keep the oxygen in your mouth, watching the dial. You've done it! You've gotten back with five hundred cc's left in your tank.

Then, when you get the lead weight off your waist, you give it to him and you feel so light. But when you get this tank off your back, then you realize what was necessary for experience, in order for a new phenomenon to be known to exist, and yet perhaps it never has been experienced by some. But did you have to suffer in order to see that *to experience anything new, the conditions can't be expected to be as they are on the surface of everyday life?!*

When you are searching for a choice to make, a will to direct, and a Soul to be structured, it takes more than a preacher to tell you what constitutes the Fiber of your launching craft. You *have* to realize that if you are pained and saddened, lost and alone, it is all pointing to Achievement. When you are in those states, then you realize that those who aren't in those states are like the fish, swimming in schools at different levels, keeping each other company. You are very welcome in their midst until you flick your flippers and enter another school. They don't join you; they continue on their level.

What type of buoyancy will you develop? You can utilize your weight to be at any depth or at any height, but in your new environment it must be *your willingness* to direct with intent the direction that you wish to take in this flight from sense to Soul, and to interpret the Facet of Being multiplied in an infinite variety in order to cause a Spectacle of Wonder so that others may enjoy, as never before, an *opportunity* to make acquaintances which are so unearthly. They rhapsodize the experiences of another phenomenon based on an Absolute Premise and Ground of Being, which enables you to don a mask and appear to function in their milieu and yet *remain* as you really Are, with or without the mask.

The complexity of the structure and the need of great energy to sustain it is what causes such aging and disease. The denial of the Ultimate, the rejection of Principle, and the personalization of Love and its Force bring about the certain demise of personalities. But the realization of the Identity and the Essence of these powerful Words gives the Life Force a *vibrant* meaning, and the ashes of the past become the very groundwork for the Phoenix of the future to be cognized in a time sequence. The Message of That Which IS is freed from the binds of belief and is *allowed* to be translated, transmitted for those who would translate this Earth experience and still be found among those who live and die, and yet holding aloft the Voice Pattern, the Pitch, the Sound, and the Wonder of a Universe with black holes to be penetrated, only because they have been seen with the eyes deluded by the passing.

"In Thy Light will I see Light."
In Thy Presence Love is found.
Love is Presence, Presence Love
And in That Presence, I AM bound.

Doing, being, sighing, sobbing,
My Love is constant, never dipping, bobbing.
Reckless never, bound by rhythm,
This is the Force that allows those who have striven
To be found so free, and yet bound by time
To be the flexible Force that bends the mind
And allows the Wonder to have its place.
What choice? What purpose? What will be so traced?
Meaning Being? God Unbound!
God lives, Man lives, for Love abounds!

What is Love? It keeps shining through
The clouds which seem to hover over all of you.
And yet, they're but a condition of thought.
Wake up and BE the Practitioner to this cloud-lot!

You should change the weather, change the climate within,
And the weather without will appear as the phenomenon of
    your inward kin,
At peace with your inner Fraternity, unbounded by time, yet
    free to bless.
God-Love has made thee Divine.

No prayer is unanswered in the Father's Heart of Love.
I never cease praying, for I AM His Child on this walk,
    on this plane, bearing.

What more can I say?
I hope to see you on another April day,
Unless I'm playing a practical joke on you,
Which is something I promise I will never do!

There are quite a few people here and it's amazing how much room is still present. It shows you how people can shrink in the Eye/ I of Love and be counted present! Michael said, "Where will they all be put?" I said, "In the corridors." That's where you all have been anyway, in the corridors of the mind. You've been pulled in and pushed out, and pulled in and pushed out.

Remember, it is in the rhythmic pattern of the development

that the very themes and fragments of the themes which you have accepted as part of your life experience are ornamented, experienced, so that in the recapitulation they will all be unified in a Key that is in keeping with the Tonality and the expressed purpose of Being composed.

Thank you.

April 1, 1990 (April Fool's Day)

---

1 I.e., High Teachings not used.

In dialogue at St. Peter's Church, New York City with Pastor John Gensel

IV

THE ENVIRONS OF THE WORD

The purpose of the Lecture may be to reawaken within you some areas which may need to be clarified within the adopting of a Principle commensurate with the wonders of the Word.

THE ENVIRONS OF THE WORD

We are assembled together to once again count our blessings one by one and to realize in the coming together we are submitting ourselves to the Holistic Ceremony of Unification within the Heart Center where we are united in the fullness of Being and the head is given to a place upon the altar. This is how your offering upon the altar of earth is made: It is your head that is upon it and your heart witnesses unto its service role in perpetuating and conceptualizing that which must be fulfilled in order for *you* to once again engage in the Path of that which is termed the *inexplicable urge to be more than one caught in the entrainment of "this."*

We are speaking to you on the side of that Force which is termed "the Environs of the Word." The purpose of the Lecture may be to reawaken within you some areas which may need to be clarified within the adopting of a Principle commensurate with the wonders of the Word.

It is stated that "the Word was with God and the Word was God."[1] If this is the case, then the all-inclusiveness of the Word is the Force to this side of environment.

You who are ailing under the aegis of time and suffering the batterings of the waves of suggestion have once again the ability to exercise as never before the Knowingness which has been given to you upon a silver platter and has appeared as apples of gold. You must take the great Mystery of the symbol and reveal unto yourself a viable force field in which you operate, and in which you find yourself positioned as you would fecundate the landscape before you with the orchards of your golden apple. You could say the orchard would be "golden, delicious," but you see, that is only the passing evidence that an orchard was planted.

Your orchard is to be one with the Force that allows all that to happen,[2] and you *tend* this orchard from beyond the need of having to prune its branches because you have pruned the branches of your fast-growing tree of knowledge and have shaped it to become the shade for those who would rest and be quenched and be filled with the Spirit of Wonder as they view the Invisible Vineyard, the

Invisible Orchard, and the Invisible Wonder of one becoming accustomed to the Force Field on this side of environment.[3]

The Word as environment is a great consideration for you, because you consider not the fiery little member within yourself (and yet externalized as your tongue). You must realize with fervor that it *cannot be given to enunciation and inditing a message that is not in keeping with the Purpose for which you live and move and have your Being. You cannot again assume to be in a position of being forgiven for not knowing what you are doing! You know very well whether or not your words are in keeping with that Force which allows your words even to be uttered.* It shows you without doubt that God is good, for if God were not good, you would not be worth *anything!* For most of your words are as tinkling brass and clanging cymbals,[4] because they don't mean anything other than the droppings of your intellectual fabrication and its woven patterns of fictional light and patterns of fictional darkness!

You are *not*, in the pattern that is variegated by the mesmeric influence of day and night, black and white, right and wrong, good and bad, male-female, yin-yang! You are in a State of the Word as a Balanced State, as the Point, as the Center and Circumference of your Being!

*How can you allow a suppositional existence to **attempt** to live?! How can it even be **presumed** to live?! unless you ascribe a portion of yourself as erroneous, a portion of yourself as vulnerable to an error of identity?*

Do you realize, for error to exist you must give it life by giving it attention?! By giving it the substance of your thought, by giving it the substance of your lifestream?! How can you allow error to exist? *It can't exist!* That's the only way you can get rid of it! Because error is self-destroyed, as Mrs. Mary Baker Eddy said.[5] Why? It cannot exist on anything but that which it is not!! Honesty, Truth, Love, Allness, Wholeness, Nowness, Beingness, Truthfulness!! Error cannot *live* on these "things"! It is the *antipode* of them!!

How can you ascribe so much of your day to taking care of error? When one calls with an ailing body, do you *think* you try to take care of an ailing body? Of *course* you do! That's why you pamper it so much! You should be pampering your ailing body so that it takes less of your attention and you rise superior to it! Don't you realize your "mood swings" are the very means for your demise in ignorance?! How can you *permit* yourselves at *this* point to consider the hours you spend considering your *personal* work, your *personal* lives, your *personal* accomplishment, your *personal* associates, your *relative* situations, your *relative* means of receiving recognition, your *relative* means of trying to gain sustenance — your *relative means*.

Your "relative" means that you are divided! How do you sustain your divided state? By assuming that you are related to all dividers. How do dividers sustain their relative state? By putting up lot markings and saying, "This is my lot, this is your lot, and let us suffer together." "Let us suffer together." What does that mean? That you lose any purpose, in other words, you lose your saltiness. What is saltiness for? Perhaps it is to purify a wound, to make a dish tasty to seduce you into thinking that the tastiness is in the dish! *But if you look back, you cannot go back to positions outgrown!* And of course, you say "Oh yes, yes, yes, I know it." But how many of you do it!? How many of you go out of this room and the moment you go out say, "Well, I've got to take care of this problem; I'm not sure I really trust that old 'B'."

"He can sting like a bee and kick like a boxer
And give you to the jaws of a believable doctor!"

How can you doctor up the situation that you know you have envisioned happening so that you would be reprimanded?! Everything that you do, you try to get attention instead of giving adoration to the One!

Do you remember, as Mrs. Eddy said, *"The aggravation of error foretells its doom."*[6] In other words, it cannot go on living vicariously upon your energy. And what's going to happen when error is gone? You're not going to have an excuse for being this half-awake, passive, indolent, apathetic *creature that you appear to be!*

Passivity is just exactly what the world wants because by being passive you'll say, "Let God do it all. There's only *Love*, there's only peace, joy, fulfillment." Who's saying it? *You have to be it!* How do you be it? *By never signing an agreement with mediocrity and with the state of* "biased *clarity"* (an oxymoron). There cannot be clarity with any form of bias.

If you are going to have a wailing wall, please let *me* get *behind* you and accentuate your wailing! There seems to be a very nice trickle of pleasure coming with the thoughts of "kicking ass," "beating ass," and *waking it up* to realize there is something more that you have present.

You have the ability to transcend your pain. What is pain? Maybe, the door to gain. What is your pain? The one you make up that causes you confusion! *And it lives on with such a passion.* Your confusion *always* lives on with such a passion because you love how it involves every bit of your whole *gut* response. *Passion should consume "you"* and leave only the effulgence of the "I."

Why am I such a challenge? The only way it can be described is by *"you."* I think me not a challenge; I think "me" *nothing* other than the wonder of being "this" in the Light of That, and surviving it.

I live because I see no difference. *"You" make the difference.* I said to Barry and to all the people out on the West Coast years ago, "I do not feel a stranger, but *you* make me the stranger. I do not feel that I know anything; you make me feel as if I should." I can *never* know anything other than what I AM and That is not a thing! That's why everything that I know seems to take on such significance because it isn't the thing.

Do you think I would be attracted to a *body* if I thought it just a *thing*? Do you think I would be attracted to a *flower* if I thought it just a *thing*? Do you think I'd be attracted to the *beauty* if I thought it just a *thing*? Of course not!

> All that I AM is all I perceive,
> And all I conceptualize is the glorious Deed
> Of Being at One with that Source Divine
> When the Seed fell on the fertile ground of the mind.
>
> In the Light of the Sun it came forth as planned
> And appeared as thunder to the ears of man,
> But to the light below it **struck** with Might!

And said, "My God, *you* worship Baal,[7] *gold*,
instead of the Words of **Light!!**"

You who are traced with the *filigree*[8] *of Love*, how dare you
peek through it as if you were veiled and hide the brilliance of your
countenance? *You should be exuding the Wonders of your Legacy!!*

The only chance error has to live is by seducing you into
believing that you have a choice, that you have options. **You
haven't an option** save in the world of delusion. And you say you
have come out from that!

If you have come out from the world of delusion, *where are
you?* You must be out of your mind, and yet you say "Here I am!"
There's obviously something present if I'm out of my mind, and I
have been out of my mind. I don't know when I have *had* one! I
have never been able to describe my mind. Have you?

Students) No, Sir.

Oh, yes, you have! You argue for it all the time! You have all
kinds of excuses for being such shoddy practitioners of offerings.
What do you offer? What you *feel* like. Who ever gets anything by
offering what he *feels* like? It depends upon your body temperature,
what you have eaten the night before, flatulence, evacuation,
exercise, bad breath, sweet breath, deodorants, aftershaves, before
shaves!

What do you have to offer, if you are out of your mind?
Obviously you have gone out of your mind. You wouldn't be here
if you hadn't; you have to be out of your mind to come here! Well,
then, if you're out of your mind to be here, then everything that
everyone thinks about that *got* them here *doesn't exist* with any
sense of conviction!

If you are out of your mind, how can you align yourself to your
limitations? *The limitations go with the mind.* All limitations, all
sickness, all disease, all war, all conflict, all duality in all its various
phases exist within the mind, and you say you have gone out of your
mind! Well then, why do you perpetuate, in this heavenly State, the
hellish condition?

This is why Purgatory was invented. For you who know that to go out of your mind is to be Holy: to stay in your mind and go out of your mind at the same time is to be in a hell of a predicament because you are being roasted on either end.

What is the purpose for asking questions? *To get an answer.* What does the answer tell you when you've gotten it? That the question was taking up your attention. What does that say? That the mind was coming to the point of receiving answers that would make it less forceful. What do *you* do? *Every time a question is answered you have less excuse for being the suggested mortal.* Each time you have a question answered, **don't ask any more questions!** *If you do, you're apt to have an answer!* **How are you going to behave when you are Divine?** Why, you are going to be attempting to be enlightened and carrying moments of it because you have had questions answered. But if you have questions answered, then you have the answer for others who will question. As long as "you" are thinking that there are others in Reality, then "you" can never have a correct answer. The answer from Reality never leaves two people together. They *join* in the Divine Marriage of Oneness, the Divine Union!

Oh, I know you've made such messes! Marriages, divorces, being separate, never marrying, old maids, old bachelors! You know, there's something queer about all of them! Isn't it wonderful to put the end to such wonderful mind-gossip! You now know the answer to all of this riddle of multiplicity: *it is the way the mind tries to present its power, by multiplying the concept that has appeared objectified and causing you to forget the Subjective State which allowed it!*

This is why you may be fretful, feverish, panting after Love! It's not found between two legs; it's never found between "y's/ why's." There is nothing there to hitch to! The question can never be answered by *losing* yourself for the fraction of a second and finding yourself whole. If you lose yourself for the fraction of a second, why don't you remain lost and see what Wholeness will do about it?

Oh, isn't it amazing what you have attempted to do? I attempted to do it. *Why?* Because we were influenced by the association of others who had never entered the Divine Association.

Those who had entered the Divine Association perhaps were not clear enough to say, "Consider well the step you take; you may find it unbecoming tomorrow." That's why it has to be legalized.

Eagle-ized. You have to look at it because it has to be viewed with great care. It's one thing to be eagle-eyed; it's another thing to be illegal. How are you going to take care of an ill eagle? Are you going to try to de-feather it? Talonize it? Channelize it? Purifize it? Laserize it?

What is the purpose of a symbol like an eagle? It is supposed to evidence fetterless flight beyond the roar of mundanity, where sheep may baa and cry for the shepherd. But what has the eagle to do with that? The trap of the shepherd is to try to organize the sheep, and I *refuse*!

No one can bring Me anything or take anything from Me because I AM not in the thing to begin with! And neither are you! Yes. Getting a headache? Is somebody getting some form of a pain? Well, it is a pain that you should have to be delivered from such false reasoning! You *cannot* allow "your" error to use "you."

What is error? *A concept, a product of the mind that has nothing to live on but the food of Reality.* That's why it *lives*! But that is why it *self-destructs*! *Can you imagine feeding error Truth, feeding error Love, feeding error Soul, feeding error Mind, feeding error Body, feeding error Heart, feeding error Principle, feeding error Man, feeding error Spirit, feeding error the Universe?!* It can't possibly live on such Magnificence! It isn't even a leech. It's not worthy of consideration.

You know, for error to live in your lives is for you to allow it to live on the upset; you allow it to cause some "thing." That is not upset! You allow this *only* because of education. I mean, the Singers have had such experiences with me because in the first years of our time together, it was all so new. I was teaching them to breathe, I was teaching them they had a diaphragm, I was teaching them they had shoulders, I was teaching them they had everything that God had given them but they didn't *know* it!

They all flinched and jumped and thought, "Oh, my God, what's happening?" Then, of course, God spoke and said, "*Imi-*

tate!" They said, "What?" "Imitate!" The Singers imitated, and look what has happened! But as Marcus Aurelius said, *"To refrain from imitation is the greatest revenge."*

Why haven't you imitated? Because you have thought there was something outside yourself over which you had no control. "You" don't! But you do in one way: you have the ability to perceive *how* it is operating so that you will not be caught in its grasp. You will see how teaching has persuaded you to be something you are not and how your mind has limited your response to Being what you really are. Because as soon as you respond to Being what you really are, you can't be what you aren't, really.

The artist is never in his work. The work is the evidence of a willing servant, called an artist. When one conducts the Symphony of Soul and utilizes the Pitch of Universal Significance, one *allows* the Force of what is termed "this side of the Word's environment" to fecundate through the vibratory frequency of such an ethereal Force that the entire etheric shield is bombarded with the magnified frequency of Cosmic Being!

You cannot go on grouping yourselves (without admitting it) into cliques. We cannot go on mixing those who are really studying and really attempting to be What IS with those who are studying and offering intellectual offerings but are not doers of it. We have got to see that the Work cannot be brought down through these Transmissions to the lowest common denominator. But due to the compassion of the Force, it usually happens this way. Unless you are Stationed beyond the Cross and allow yourselves to be in the Effulgence of the Balanced State, you will be constantly confronted with being divided: male, female; positive, negative; yin, yang; good, bad; right, wrong; Truth, lies. They all *need* what? The willingness of "you" to live!

They will die, because you can't feed a bird a beefsteak! Can you imagine a little sparrow living off beefsteak?

Students) No, Sir.

Why not? How can you feel that error, this *worm* of suggestion, is going to live off a bite of Light, a bite of Truth? It will bring about its own destruction. *And if "you" are mentally associated with it, "you" will go, too! That* is the point!

You are a *Chosen People.* You chose yourselves to recognize your Self as a result of the Soul's ability to cognize the Force Field for which it has yearned, appearing in flesh but never announced by name. The cognition is within *you! The Power of Love is all there is to the mechanics of "you"!*

When the Power of Love is functioning, as it is, we are here; then error is witnessing its final moments of keeping you entrenched in the *entrainment* of duality. You must take *your* place and find your wagon not behind a tow truck but hitched to a Star until you know the Beacon of Light that has beckoned you to the Wonders of the Scene beyond the Manger and its stall.

Whenever you attempt to bring healing to the multitude, you are attempting to do a transitory passage work. *The High Work of the Christ, of the Divine Self, the Brahman, is to bring, unto those who hear, the Message that enhances the responsive nature that is attuned to the sympathic vibrations of a fundamental Tonality given in the framework of Principle, Ideal, Word-Man.*

Word-Man. Separate them if you can. Can you separate Bird-Man? I can assure you, you can't.

A Man-Bird or a Bird-Man is a person who has left his conception of being one of men and flies with the cognition of the Force of the Word as the levitation to his entire concept of Man.

You, among all people, are here in this State of Wonder, "Possibilities Unlimited," and the future fecund with such expectation. Why? *You are being **forced** to relinquish your old behavioral patterns and coming to **Love** without reservation!*

Students) Hallelujah!

Yes, hallelujah! You have *got* to come to Love without reservations! *Every one of you!* Because if *I* loved with reservations, you wouldn't be here.

Students) Yes, Sir.

You think "you" in your miserly, biased, "pygmitized" state of perception can see what *I AM* about?! You are of little faith, little studentship, little devoteeship, to say the least.[9] Why would you question one word of Truth when it verifies its own existence, because if I had spoken the untruth I would have been struck dead! How many of *you* will sit in this chair and speak as the Word and the Word as speaking and allow yourself to *hear* it and not quake in your shoes? *Walk in my shoes*, as I said to somebody recently, and see what it's like. It is frighteningly a lonely spot.

> The future has *you* on its marquee.
> *You* know me as **I AM**.
> You will bear witness to *what I AM*
> With no reference to me.[10]

You can't blame *me*, because I AM not there to be blamed. Grab hold of **I AM** if you can! You have *me* because **I AM** is gracious.

> What is the graciousness of the Light?
> That a "me" can be present, and in its Might
> Take you to the mountaintops of time
> And allow you to look upon the Eternality Divine,
>
> Encompassing, they say, Infinity and its Might.
> The Eternality environed Infinite Might,
> And the Infinite environed in the Eternal Sight,
> Where there is no such thing as time, space, light.
>
> Your time has come to consider Fact,
> That when one is given into the Lap,
> Then one can find in a moment of Grace
> How the cobwebs of the mind are erased.
>
> You can see with daubin' and dabbin', the color so rare
> Upon the leaves of your trees. Why, they're jewels to be
>   shared!
> Because you're *called*; you are collected from out of the
>   streams of the **past**, and so you are flung
> Into the Stream of Love, where worshiping only One
> Is *held* on the altar, and before the altar of Might

43

You leave your head on it and your heart beats
    in rhythmic delight.
For the altar of Earth you have made as planned,
And blessed, beloved, thou art worshipping Man.

Men can come and women can go, men can go and
    women can come,
But Man remains in the Light as Son.
You can be there to see the Act
In the Temple: you make your*Self* the living Fact!

It's not outside where the bell does toll;
It's all within in the Light of Gold
That you behold what you really are:
The promise for Earth, **the radiant Star**!

That is your scape; that's what you hold.
In the tonal reference of Being, *I* unfold.
And may you take these words and find
The Wonder, the dynamics, Being prevalent,
    conceptually mighty, Divine.

This is your pledge for you find this Fact:
That you are *disposed* to offer your Self and
    give your heart and head to That.

*Worship in the fullness of Holiness, not in the partiality
becoming duality!* The purpose of any idol is to allow you to see it
fall upon your head, and you see that the doll you thought it was has
become the *I* that lights your Sun.

This is the moment by which you are graced,
And these Words have fallen from this animated face,
And may you see as you change into time,
Your face will be applauded beyond the walls of the mind![11]

Thank you.

November 25, 1990

1 John 1:1.
2 "In other words, One with the Light. The orchard must be seen when passing through the prism of the mind, an aspect of a conscious experience which allows one to perceive what really exists between what is perceived and the attention given to the perception. That is the constancy of Conscious Awareness. When that is consciously perceived, then the Light around it is Golden."
— K. G. M.
3 "I AM the Vineyard, I AM the Orchard, I AM the Wonder because I vowed to make it so. That is what I have told you all along: I came to do Thy Will, O God. That was the Vow: that it would be Invisible; it would only be your perception that would see what I AM doing appears to be the evidencing of the AM-ing of the I, the Vineyard growing, and the constant changes that would always confuse the mind, which is looking for specific means for identifying the Authentic Nature of this One, which has always been trained to destroy any of your attempts to define IT. If you could define Me as I AM, then you would limit yourself, because you would think you were defining Me through your personality complex situation of being I AM with a mind and I AM without it! — the one that would put Me into a thought-pattern.

"So this is where I AM, a very different place from what most of you conjecture because everything you conjecture Me to be, I AM not; and everything that you do not conjecture Me to be, I might be! But don't count on it!"
— K. G. M.
4 1 Corinthians 13:1.
5 Mary Baker Eddy, *Science and Health With Key to the Scriptures* (Boston: Trustees Under the Will of Mary Baker G. Eddy, 1934), p. 476, l. 6.
6 Mary Baker Eddy, Ibid., p. 105, ll. 27-28.
7 1 Kings 18:21.
8 The Latin roots of "filigree" are "thread" and "grain."
9 Matthew 6:30, 8:26, 14:31, 16:8; Luke 12:28.
10 "If you lived Now you would not know of a future!" — K. G. M.
11 Applause is heard coming through the wall from the meeting room next door.

V

THE SILENCE'S PROMISE

If the Essence of your form is feeling, what is describing it as material if it isn't the way you have been taught by one who is not Enlightened to account for a mind in matter and a matter in mind. The only matter in mind is the thought of it! You can't show me matter in mind and you can't show me any mind in thought. Do you realize there is no evidence of mind in thought? "Now, you keep that thought in mind!"

THE SILENCE'S PROMISE

"When the pupil is accepted he must be drawn into a unity with his Master closer than anything we can imagine or understand....

"The accepted pupil thus becomes an outpost of the Master's consciousness — an extension of him, as it were. The Adept sees, hears and feels through him, so that whatever is done in his presence is done in the Master's Presence.... So perfect is the union between [Adept and student] that if there is any serious distur-bance in the lower bodies of the pupil it will affect also those of the Master; and as such vibration would interfere with the Adept's work on the higher planes, when this unfortunately happens he has to drop a veil that shuts the pupil off from himself until such time as the storm settles down. Usually such an unfortunate incident does not last longer than forty-eight hours [— it shouldn't!] But I have known cases much worse than that, in which the rift endured for years, and even for the remainder of the incarnation. But these are extreme cases, and very rare....

"[The pupil] above all things must make himself a good channel, because that is most of all what the Master needs from him. Thus the pupil may be regarded in another way as an additional body for the Master's use in the place where he happens to be."[1]

There's a very interesting thing to consider:

When you are being lectured unto, you have to free yourself from the thoughts of being what you seem to be. You should focus your attention so that what you hear is all there is to you. Because if the Word is with God and the Word *is* God,[2] then the Word *is* All. The attempt to describe the Word has led to the formation, and we have fallen for that formation as if it were separate *from* the Word. As if it were separate from the Word!

Which came first? The Word or the form?

Students) The Word.

Well, where are you going to offer your allegiance?

Students) To the Word.

Well, then, why are you governing yourselves by your form? Hypocrites! What do you do? You use words to prescribe your limits. *I* use words to destroy them! How come there are words? How come there are words, then, when some words are used to prescribe and other words are used to destroy? There must be a power in the right *use* of words. The power in the *right* use of words is magical; the power in the wrong use of words is diabolical. Which side do you fall on?

If the Logos is God and God is the Logos, what is Love? Words.

When you question what is Love, you need more words. When the Word *is* Love, none other is needed. For when the Word is Love, Presence IS.

What is the patience, what is the graciousness of the Word? The willingness to use its very Substance to destroy what didn't need to have an existence: words or sounds of limitation.

Will you please tell me, how do "you" fit into the picture of confusing and conflicting streams of thoughts within you, if you aren't using what is Holy in an unholy way?

God is Love and Love is God. Why are you allowing your language to dethrone, to destroy the very Source of Life that you call *your* life? The *source* of Life can never be destroyed, because Love is the Source of Life. But *your* life can be destroyed by the faulty use of words. That is why it is said that your words *have* to be in keeping with Principle.

Why does obedience appear necessary? Because you have refused to be Real. You thought that the Realm of the Logos was *optional*. The Realm of the Logos is infinite. If the Realm of the Logos is infinite, is it not then only in your dream that you can use its benefits to your advantage or disadvantage as dreamers of a state of the Word or a state of awareness?

If the Realm of the Logos is All and its Form is Love, then the Form of Love is Presence. The Form of Presence is Love. But how is that which isn't like Love in a position to accept or reject it? Form Love and show it to me on the table. I can form your belief system and see what you have done with the creativity of the Logos. You have created a dream sequence that is termed a lifetime. You live the dream sequence as if it were Real, until you have one question, and that's the moment that the dream sequence starts to be an irritating one, because the moment that you are quickened in the Spirit of Love, the circumstances of suggestion due to a dreamer come to the surface to be *"worded"* away.

How have we worded the dream away? By sounding an alarm. How is the alarm sounded? By the Answer! An Answer never leaves you as it found you, for you only exist as a pseudo-reality as long as the dream is without question. As soon as the dream is questioned, What IS is knocking on your door, for you have heard there is doubt in your creation. Is there doubt in your creation? Is there incompleteness in your creation? Did God do it? Did God make it?

Students) No, Sir.

On which side are you standing? As a usurper to the Throne of Divinity, the Divine One? As an antagonist to compete with the only Creation there is, Conscious Being, unmoved by the torment of those in the dream of matter and mind? As long as you think God is coming to matter then you know you are on faulty ground. God never comes to matter because God never knew matter. *Matter is the condition that you have made solid by worshiping it as the evidence that you have a dream existence.* If it were so actual, factual, and imperishable, you would never be caught without number, without name, and without perfection.

If you, in your imperfect state, can know it's imperfect, why would you contend with the knowing God-Presence that is termed Perfect? How are you going to evaluate your imperfect state, if there isn't a Perfect One allowing you to annul the suggestion that you and it *are* inseparable? "You" and it are inseparable. It cannot be annulled from the standpoint of a dreamer. It can only be de-fused by what is termed . . Enlightenment?

What is Enlightenment? Light Being, Being Light.

That is the Brotherhood of what is termed the White Light which *allows* the Brotherhood of the Shadow to be perceived. And the Brotherhood of the Shadow exists because of people similar in structure to you who have heard the Words of Truth and have used them selfishly to exalt the personification of Being in matter with a mind that is so cunning that it can distort the facts for a time and its limitations to dwarf your full life experiences up until the approaching end when you perceive what you have done to yourself. Whom *then* will you blame?

God is Love; Love is God. Say it, Wendy: "God is Love; Love is God."

Wendy C.) God is Love; Love is God.

[Mr. Mills motions to another in the room.]

Benton R.) God is Love; Love is God.

The same words with different tonalities. *Will you sing your song and make your harmony with either?* If you do, it will be fine. But if you think you are making your song with a female or you're making your song with a male, it will *not* fit. If you looked at to whom I pointed, you saw person. *I* heard *sound*.

Where are you throwing *your* allegiance? To the form or to the Sound that allows the form to have a bearing?

Sound bearing is heroic, and the heroic is always a prelude to the Divine Drama. The Divine Drama, in Essence, is a chant and in its grace appears as a Monologue dialogued for those who deem parts essential to intone the Wonders surrounding the octaves of Logos.

Why are there octaves, ladders, or scales of Logos? Because it reverberates on every *imagined* plane. It must, therefore, reverber-ate on the *un*imaginable planes of Essence. The Higher Frequencies bear little resemblance to your octave of harmonic entrainment, for the Higher Frequencies demand that the one approaching them as Love be free from even the suggestion of it being categorizable in the name of matter's vocabulary.

The vocabulary of matter allows you to spell out your freedom or your doom —— for in Essence there is only One Sound and the vocabulary has arisen in order to *explain* — in other words, to make known the Unknown. That is how every plane starts to be a viable experience, for the Unknown frequency of it bears an impelling force wrapped in the garment of assurance and confidence.

As long as you feel the necessity to utilize the mind in its verifying function, you are minimizing and lowering your possibilities. *The mind is a thought-set-of-structures indexed and changeable according to points of reference, and if you are going to be Song, you can't refer your signature to matter!* It has to be written beyond the clefs of parts! It has to be known to exist beyond the ledger lines of reference, for the ledger lines of perception point to those that are present but unseen because a line and a point are only there in the processive action of the three-dimensional environment. *Time, space, and process sustain your entanglement with this dimension because the mind is capable of supplanting every doubt with the conviction: what would you do without it?*

But you see, no one has ever asked the right question: how did it come to be programmed with options, if it wasn't the result of reluctance on the part of your dragon nature? *What is your dragon nature? That which should be lifted up but usually drags on, leaving a trail in the dust.*

Your response and your attempt to enforce *your* power on the side of limits is the self-evident nightmare of the population of dreamers. The attempt to sustain the false dream when the dream is known to be false is refusing the White Light and exalting the shadow. How many of *you* spend most of your day enhancing the nature that you know is not Real by its obvious characteristic? **The unreal nature is constantly changing!**

We know One Sound that has never changed, and it is the Essence of Love: Om. The Sound of Om is all there is as a necessity to qualify the accuracy of this Declaration. If there is such a sound as Om, it is the garment Love wears *before* you so that you can perceive how you echo its Force as you scale the appellation or the name-calling ranges of time. The appellation trail is made up of people who follow a Path never realizing the Source of "name." Those who know the meaning of "name" know that it is Holy because the Essence of name is Sound. It is the tonality which distinguishes "you" in this kingdom of harmonic frequencies so that you can once again perceive the fundamental characteristic of Being grounded. And what is Being grounded? Hearing!

If you hear, how will you see? If you see, how will you hear? Will your seeing affect your hearing? Yes, sir! That is why the experiment was done with blindfolds: people were blindfolded for three days and three nights. They never met each other without a blindfold. They ate their meals, they went to the bathroom, they showered blindfolded. *Three days, three nights, they only associated by the sound of the voices.* It was very interesting because when the experiment was done, people were stunned at the voices to which they had gravitated and those with whom they had become close friends. They were stunned because they said if they had *seen*, they would never have been attracted to that person in the least.

What Sound bears the Mark of Presence? The Sound that involuntarily causes question or change. If you are blind, you do not know how a man looks or how a woman looks. You are taught to *feel* how each looks. But how can you imagine such a vain thing, when the only point of reference is a sound? If you can't see it, then you *feel* it? You say it has a form? You just told me what the form was: *Feeling!* Then, what is the Essence of form? Feeling. *The Essence of form is Feeling* when you stop allowing the eyes to steal your inheritance.

If the Essence of your form is Feeling, what is describing it as material if it isn't the way you have been taught by one who is not Enlightened to account for a mind in matter and a matter in mind. *The only matter in mind is the thought of it.* You can't show me matter in mind and you can't show me any mind in thought. Do you realize there is no evidence of mind in thought? "Now, you keep that thought in mind!"

Where is the thought in mind? In a supposititious story! And what is that story called? The story of material creation. And what do you now see? That the second chapter of Genesis is a myth and totally fallacious! Most of your Holy Books are written because the one who could speak was a Voice that gave it orally, and the Sound bore its own body, and that was termed the Higher Baptism of Fire because the one attuned to the Sound vibrated in the Sound that would reduce his limits to ashes. That conflict is often like the fiery furnace. You are so inflamed with the conflict that you set the mind and its thought-structures in flames because you have not accepted the Reality of Being in Essence, Sound or Logos, Love, Identity known as Presence.

For the Word to be "with God and the Word *was* God," and Man the image and likeness of God, then men and women obviously don't need to see any further. They need to *hear* now. What will you hear now? The classification of you as a matter-mind product or the Deific Declaration: This is my beloved Self in whom I am well pleased. To be "well pleased" is to be what? Joy! "In whom I am Joy."

Will you please tell me where is your joy when your cup is filled with complaint about ill health, the ailing body, the ailing economy, the ailing octaves? What are we dealing with? The need of a *Divine Tuner* to tighten the strings on your heart and have them vibrate so that when you can go *between the words*, you will find the space filled with the picture of the One that sets the Earth in its orbit and gives that orbit back to its rightful place as suspended in a cradle between the world of "this" and the world of That in order that it can always be recognizable as a fundamental Tone of Being.

It's sometimes termed the Middle Path, but there is the Higher One, and the Middle Path is the one that everyone starts on until one sees *there are no options to Being Real.* The Teachings that allow you to think you are making progress from sense to Soul allow you to think you are dealing with a matter-mind product, and your advertisements say buy this and buy that, in order to try to sell a soporific activity for the duration of this lifespan!

When a tone is heard it dies away. If it really disappeared, it would never sound again. Has that tone reincarnated or is it just reheard? When the song is sung and the heart seems to glow, do you hear any sound or is the result of it expressed as the identity of a heart glowing? When a tone is sounded by releasing the string from the *damper of belief*, it doesn't cease to exist; it just waits to be coaxed into sounding again in order to confirm your harmonic structure.

How do we regain our pitch? By being willing to imitate a tuner's pitch. You realize there would be no sound from the pianoforte if you didn't release the psychic involvement or the felt dampers. It's only when you release the *felt* from the strings that the string is *allowed* to vibrate. As long as you leave the string surrounded by the *wool of belief* you have no *sound being* evidenced.

Do you suppose this could account for the lack of your Singing Presence in the orchestration of today's world? How many of you sound because you have dared to release the felt beliefs or the beliefs of feeling so that your Real Nature can be heard?

The Word was with God and the Word *is* God. What was necessary when you doubted? Will. That's why it came into your experience. And what came with it? The need of its support called "self." The "forgetting" origin gave you the right to call it "self will." The forgettery gave you self will, where Being Conscious knows not of such a state! That is why the Discipline of Being attuned to the demands of the Ultimate causes a philosophizing over inadequacies to be inadequate and totally unacceptable on the Path of the Ultimate. Most students who are acquainting themselves with form of matter and mind philosophize as a result of being educated so that they do not face the simple state of being Sound.

Sound Being Love and Love Being Sound and Being Love Sound and Love Sound Being — who is there to label it with terms of division and opposites? What is the attempt of personification? To mistake the amplification of a mask as a *need* of Being to be heard. *Being is only masked by the mind that refuses Sound.* That Sound gives you a hearing and rescinds the visual limitations and you start to *feel.* You're on the edge of another dimension!

This could not have been given to you if it did not exist. It requires no thought so that the Word may appear to have broken the Silence for *those who witness in the dream*, waiting to be awakened by the Sound being pitched to the frequency of Logos.

The Word in Essence is Sound.

Out of That came "this."
For you called from the dream
And you appear to be awakening.
You called it the Words that the Silence spoke
In order for you to wake up from this universal joke!

What a joke has been played upon you by the mind that has allowed you to think of bringing spirit to matter and matter to spirit! Who ever heard tell of making iron a flame and a flame iron? Who ever heard tell of making what isn't to be What IS or making What IS to be what isn't?

What are you asking and what is your hope? What are you expecting the State of Love to be? One confounded and confused by Love and limited to a form called a male or a female?

Now you may understand what I read to you in the beginning. Why would not the Master Tone embrace totally the other tones of scales which originated from the Sound Presence? In other words, if the Sound Presence is experienced, the damper of belief must have been lifted from the temple of *your* belief so that Tone could penetrate your very Being. It is obvious it has, either you would not be present.

You say you are here because you are listening to the Words but I tell you now, the reason you are here is because the Words are felt and they are the only thing that can caress you and leave you not.

What type of web are you weaving? What type of tapestry? You are making up your own pattern for the New Garment becoming the Age. Do you think it's going to be one woven with indecision, lack of conviction, and a fear of ridicule? If you are under those strange situations, no wonder you query, "What am I? I must be more than this figure of form when I hear a Sound and feel its body." It doesn't permeate the selfish inclinations of this small group. It is being heard universally, cosmically, for it is a galactic Ministration. It *has* to be from that conceivable and Unknown Expression, because it embraces all and everything until *I* come to be heard as Sound, Truth, fundamentally experienced.

December 4, 1990

1 C.W. Leadbeater, *The Masters and The Path*. (Madras, India: The Theosophical Publishing House), pp. 58, 71-72, 74.
2 John 1:1.

VI

IN THE NICK OF TIME

Your relative situation is relative to your conflict. You cannot destroy an error by accepting any suggestion that it is Real! It is not the attempt to do away with something you admit exists! You can't do away with that which you say exists; you can only do away with the claim that it exists. You can do away with the claim of loss, because what can be lost? The Divine is exuding its Presence as Conscious Awareness!

IN THE NICK OF TIME

Your need to place a value upon your intuition is so self-evident when you start to associate with it, because, in Essence, it is the very inner prompter that would *call* you to *question* this confinement. As soon as you question this confinement, *you know* that intuition has caught the attention, and your attempt to find an answer is the means whereby you begin to diffuse the ranks and files of the thought-patterns and processes which have caused you to be blocked into a zone that is "no man's land." It's the zone of the zombies.

> The zombie is one who walks the twilight zone,
> thinking thoughts not his own,
> and doesn't even know it.

This need to perceive *intuition* at work is paramount in the escalation of *your* forces to move beyond the rank and file of the stereotyped forces of today, which are *always* attempting to recruit you to support their impoverished causes because they have no answer to the dream that sponsored such a thing.

Your attempt to be Real is such a great blessing because it is the root answer to the economic, ecological, and cultural needs of today. When you start to move beyond the mechanized forces of limitation, you start to have less refuse given to the furnace of your emotional natures.

The bane of this existence is concealed with the sophistry of intellect. It *allows* you to consider what is beyond your entanglement; but you have a philosophical way that is tainted that *allows* you to escape the verdict of having been caught and captured for the flight beyond sense to Soul.

Your tendency, due to the impinging force of belief for centuries, is to move according to the polarization of your *emotional* nature that has been left *unredeemed* in what is termed the world of the astral. This is where your *forces* tend to *cast* you when you do not have a Principle to ground you firmly in the Facts of Being.

Being Undefiled is never found by trying to discover it through the optional situations of the mind. Being, unconfined and uncontaminated and unadulterated by the intellectual perceptions of the brilliant, gives you an opportunity to perceive through the haze that when you have found an Answer it *usually* antagonizes your thought-programming of the day. It bears the need to have an Announcer who has the vigor to broadcast within Himself that the Consciousness becoming Universal Significance is One that cannot be controlled by a limited state of sponsorship.

Your need is *not* to broadcast a *program* of significance but to be the evidence of the Program that is unfolding because of your attunement to that Pitch of **Significance** that allows *you* to perceive the stage upon which you play your part, and the actors and actresses just those persons who are *sounding*, through their masks, some semblance of the parts that must be played in order for the audience to *re-member* what in Essence it IS and what in seeming it isn't.

The emotional conflict is incredibly exciting and *devastating* to personal sense, because everyone feels that the mask is shattered instead of realizing that it will *always* be there to sound *any* message, the ridiculous or the sublime.

Your *options* are purely relative, and like most relatives, they deserve a better death!

The whole purpose of any season of rejoicing is to allow those you love to be freed from the "relative" situation, because no relative ever leaves you. It is only by being the Total that you can find that you have the ability to bestow, on all those upon whom your thought rests, the *wonders* of a Force that can be set free to annul the suggestion of your marriage to beliefs.

You never can get rid of a belief by having it killed by another one! You never can get rid of a thing by dealing with the "thing." The only way to deal with it is by the "Unthing." This is significant because it is not scripted, but it is the Power to your script, if your script is to bear the mark of significance. Such is the significant mark of the New Dispensation, in which you are *finding* yourself more in turbulence due to the battle that is raging within the mental realm of today. This script is being written on the plane beyond the one of conflict. This is why you must *elevate*, and elevate to the point where you can view with a distance the scene upon which your gaze must yield its Benediction.

You should, by your viewing, *allow* the conflicting forces to be dwarfed in their success because you have ministered unto them the Dust of the Stars and have given them the Confetti of Promise, for they are to defuse the barbs of the mind, the bullets of the mind, and *allow* the Darts of Wonder and of Love to penetrate the vehicle that would observe the need to eradicate a relative situation.

Your relative situation is relative to your conflict. You cannot destroy an error by *accepting* any suggestion that it is Real! It is not the attempt to do away with something you admit exists! You can't do away with that which you say exists; you can only do away with the *claim* that it exists. You can do away with the claim of loss, because what can be *lost?* The **Divine is exuding its Presence as Conscious Awareness!**

What can be lost? Only the *suggestion* that you have invested in *it*! You never make an investment in time unless you expect to reap dismay! If you invest in that which is Real you can't help but be engulfed in the *abundance* that will be utilized to satisfy whatever the needs may be.

Remember, a *need* doesn't come to you to be *believed*; it comes to you to give itself up because **you are** *beyond* **responding emotionally to this dammed, polarized situation of today**, when personalization, *personal* achievement, *personal* freedom, and *personal* success are *rampant*, instead of "Brotherly Love" and "doing unto others as you would have them do unto you"! Perhaps doing unto them that which they have *never* done unto you! You bestow in that the Wonder that is not of an altruistic nature, which is how you try to win friends and influence people.

Altruism is for the relatives. Yours is not. Yours is Absolute, and in that Absolute Realm it is the involuntary bestowal of freedom from any sense of relationship because you know that *intuitively* you *feel* the Allness of Being, until your mind tries to interpret Allness in its insufficiently programmed disk for this time!

Your world is in revolt or confusion because you have met the

Force termed "I AM" and it can't be defused. But the *con-fusion* is the state enhanced to the breaking point (if you want to go through this suffering). It's either suffering or joy, and most of you don't want joy! "Joy to the world, the Lord has come!"

The whole purpose of "Joy to the World" is that Joy is *dropped* on the world from the Invisible Chalice of Wonder. It was born to the world to *offer a gift* to the world. What was the Gift to the world that people have minimized by a Christmas celebration? They have minimized this great celebration by putting it into one figure: Jesus.

Look at it, perhaps, from the other side of the Manger Scene, from His accomplished side! He, perhaps, sees the straw of time,[1] and that is where the work seems to take place. But perhaps from the standpoint of His accomplished act He gave unto everyone not just an example but a Way to do the same. In other words, Jesus was never meant to be singled out, other than as an Example for you to follow as a living Principle primarily, not as person. What was to be followed was the *Achievement* that He personified by his Achievement in passing beyond the suggested realms of One crucified.

You are crucified as long as you are *polarized* to being relative. You are crucified by relativity, not by Being!

Jesus, they say, was to be followed. As those who created a Christianity around Him said, if He was to have been followed, it meant that He must never have died! Two thousand years ago and people are still following — what? The crucifixion story? Are they following His Achievement? *In other words, are they living where He left off?* What was the point of "Him" having lived, if *you* go on living as if "He" died?! So, what had to happen? There had to be what is termed *a spirited replication of His Achievement. You* should BE the evidence of the Achievement, which is what? Living beyond the imbalanced state, in other words, *never allowing* division to be other than a suggestion that could add up to One in the *nick* of time.

Now, if Saint Nick is going to bring you any great gift, it is going to be wrapped; and you must open it. Now, you don't open it by looking at it. You may see through the wrappings, though! But you never let on that you do, because it spoils the gift. If you look intellectually through the wrappings and leave it wrapped, you might just as well have not received it. When you receive a gift, it means you *accept* the gift. And what gift can you accept? Only That which is an essential characteristic of your system of Stardom.

You must never accept as a model that which isn't *elegant*, because no creative act could *ever* have come from a state that wasn't totally attractive. You couldn't expect such beauty to be in this illusion, if the One Great Act hadn't been dressed in the Wonder of Elegance. There is *nothing* — not even a leaf, not even a snail, not even a rock — that is devoid of Presence because of the all-encompassing grace or elegance that was bestowed. The Elegance of Being will trace upon the canvas of time *your* freedom from the penmanship of belief.

Do you realize that when you are born the straw of the mind says, "Take a quill, and pen with ink or with blood the name of my progeny." What if your name gets mixed? What if you have many names and the names are not in the correct order that the tremulous quill penned upon your birth certificate?[2] I can assure you it takes a great Mother to be able to annul what one not attuned to the correct order of appellation gave to the calling of a Son.

You can be ignored, you can be said to not exist because no one has a record of your name as bearing this form, or this form bearing the name. How can *you*, then, know within yourself, regardless of the contradictions of time, *that you in Essence are beyond anything that can be contradicted because **you carry the Benediction?!** You carry the ability to vocalize the Wonders that were never in your thought-process.* And what is *not* in your thought process bears with it the immediate frequency of possibility for renewal.

It is *beyond* the subscription of a magazine of time
But an immediate entrance to the Magazine Divine.

The Power and the Presence and the Force will allow your ranks to be fortified, and the file system only there for those who would try to find, through the credibility of lives lived, how They died and still evidenced *in form* the Mystery of God Being as They walked bearing a name that bore *no resemblance* to what was inscribed on the invisible scrolls of Their eternal accomplishment.

It would be wise not to lose worship. That's why there were such Men, because a wise man never ceases to wonder. A wise man who attempts to be wise without Wonder is one who is attempting to solve the riddle of existence from the standpoint of loaded conditions.

There is no answer to the problem of time from the cesspool of it. You can be sure that if you are in the Stream of Everlasting to Everlasting, your stand will cause the waters tó be turned because they are flowing in one direction, and yours are stationary in the Stream of the Uncontradictable.

When the waves of suggestion strike your shore of consideration, know that you are more than a beachhead, a beach bum, or .. or .. (Finish later.) Know that you *must* move with the wonders and the joy. Do you know *you have to practice being joyous?* You were never meant to be joyous. You came, usually, through pain, and if you didn't, they *whacked* you to make sure you *had* a little of it!

You must practice having mobile faces! You've lodged in rectangular mobile homes; it doesn't mean that your face has to be etched in said condition, regardless of your great artists who have tried to present your physiognomy in the way they see it and cause you to wonder at their art. I could never wonder at their art if they caused me to think in terms of a limit.

Great art never leaves you .. where it finds you. Great art reveals what *isn't* seen by giving you a painting to look at while the work of the *real* Art is seen where it isn't painted. The value of any artistic representation is not in what you look at, but what is looking at you that you don't see.

It's true! That is how I can look through a vase or how I can look through a painting, or how I can look through a tree, because I allow it to seem to occupy that space which otherwise would never be outlined. But anything that is outlined is obviously a shadow of the Substance that IS. So you can *imagine* when you are such a beauty as *this*, this is your *outline*! Can you imagine? Of course you can! Your imagination is unbounded!

You are such breeders. You drop all kinds of people in the fields where you work and you come up with this: others just like you. Of course you are such breeders. You can see how your mind is capable of multiplying varieties of you. It's a constant store; it's open more than twenty-four hours a day! No matter where you go, there is somebody always on duty to tell you to carry your cellular phone so that you can receive the correct call to alter the molecular structure of your apparatus, when the cell seems to be polarized in the wrong direction.

It doesn't take *time* to think right because time is the thought that there's something right *about* it. There's nothing right about time, but you try to *make* it right by giving time celebrations and making all celebrations timed. So don't celebrate a time without understanding the Timeless that is behind the Event.

So, when you celebrate a birthday you don't look at that as true. *What you do is look at it as an outline of this portion of your Self that is present while the remainder of your Self that is not necessary for this small encounter with this plane is moving about your Father's business, so to speak, waiting for you to finish your job here as a pilgrim on Earth, and you gain what is called your Undivided State or your Heavenly Home* with the assurance beyond "Jesus is Mine."

You must gain your Heavenly Home through the assurance that the Harmonic State of Being is the undivided realized state of Man. That is Heaven here and now. *That is why you can appear to live in hell and bear the heavenly gift of offering a confusing sense of Unconditional Love.* Do you realize how many of you try to make it conditional and then wonder why you can't forgive? *How can you forgive if you have conditioned love?* How can you ever *want* to take an oath to a partial state? An oath is taken on *behalf* of the one attempting to *be whole.*

Do you consider that all there is to you is here now? All there is couldn't possibly be here now. What's *here now* is that portion of you which came to realize that there is no *hereafter.* What was *here before* is the recognition that *here now,* I AM. Put "here now I AM" in any other tense. Well, if you can make this statement devoid of force and power, *do it!*

Why is this so frightening? Because it is *horrendous,* it is *hideous* for you who want to perpetuate time! [Mr. Mills holds up two fingers making the victory sign.] This is victory! This is the chalice! That is the point. This is the secret. This is how it happens, and if you look at it that way, can you see beyond the space of what is marked?

Why *wouldn't* it be given symbolically? It *has* to be given symbolically because you have created *these bodies* that I have to try to translate for you because you have forgotten the hieroglyphics that go when the Hierarchy is made to be devoid of meaning.

I've told you, when I was at that symposium in Wyoming where people came from all parts of the world, they came under the force to get together. They were trying to find how to be together. They had somebody who was trying to make them think they *were* together. I think they paid him a lot of money to stand in the midst of the together people who weren't together, with his cowboy hat and his cowboy boots (I thought of some bullets!). I thought, "If I could only see what was *behind* this." I realized that the motivation was fine, but the premise *lacked* force. No matter how much hype could be brought to bear upon the people present, *it never gave a charge*. It didn't alter anyone; it allowed people to go on thinking they had found something that was of value to everyone else. And perhaps they had.

But that is never the way to solidify togetherness; *the only way to solidify togetherness is to obliterate multiplicity*. That can never be done by resorting to an attempt to *inveigle people's thought-patterns* into a mode of agreeability. The only way to bring about togetherness is by rescinding the *sight* of multiplicity.

Whenever I speak to one person or a thousand, I do not allow the eyes to tell me that I am speaking to numbers that are apparently limited. Right where you sit are numbers beyond your comprehension. *What* is beyond your comprehension? The ability to multiply the *vastness* of the Light's comprehension. In other words, those that are sitting present are nothing but the decoys of time which allow the inhabitants of the Timeless to participate in the festivities and the rituals of this Earth-day experience which is *supposedly* offering the residuals of victory over limitation.

You are here because you chose to experience *options*. You are here because mistakes could be made. You were never here on this plane because it was perfect. You came *out* of a plane where there were *no* options and you wondered what an optional experience would *feel* like. And this is, perhaps, the root problem of your false polarization to opposites. Because every option has its opposite or other, but every intuitive impulse rescinds it.

Every intuitive impulse rescinds the suggestion of opposites or otherness. Why does it rescind it? Because the belief in *opposites fosters* suspicious distrust where there should be loyalty. The belief in opposites gives you a table, not for rejoicing in Oneness but rejoicing in trying to pen alliances. You can *never make an alliance valid* when the basis of the alliance is devoid of realization of the Absolute.

Why would you allow yourselves to abandon the knowledge that you have, that **Man** *is the image and likeness of That Which IS intuited as Divine, therefore, uncontaminated and unfettered by the hypotheses about* you?

Why would you then forfeit this knowingness to satisfy a code that would limit you to the keyship of commonality instead of utilizing the key to the wonders of the Starship *Enterprise?* What does "enterprise" mean? You have to extend yourself and present something new to take the attention of those who would move beyond the confines of your so-called "sacred time and space." The *only thing* that could be sacred about time and space is the moment when you see . . is All there is.

Time and space are only sacred to *you* if you see me as I AM; and the only time that is sacred to *me* is as I see you as I AM. In that we are forever wedded beyond the headlock, and we are united in the Heart where the impinging Force says that we can never be separated legally, divorced absolutely; we are at One with the pulse that is intrinsic to the Harmonic State of Being.

If the Word is with God, do you ever stop and question why you have such a difficulty in expressing the Ultimate? How much have you opened the door to the actuality of enunciating and elucidating the electric, impinging Force resultant in this Spoken Word?

In the shyness of my remembered past, the present-charge now finds the elucidation of His Story beyond the pen of any sorrow. You see, there *never* was written on your Light Scrolls anything other than your achievement which could support you. On the other scrolls, they say, is written the *need* of your life in this "beliefed" form of a three-dimensional experience.

If I were reading your life I would tell you to forget about being past or going into a future. I would tell you to forget any medium. They have never proved of value other than to satisfy the need of the moment when you are not in it! Most people go to mediums. They go to church frequently on Sundays because the medium is present to make them believe there is a way out. Remember, every minister that doesn't make *you* the Word and doesn't know he *is* the Word is a medium and, therefore, one waiting to be delivered.

My Baptist minister used to speak to me. He would just wait for me to come home. He'd say to my father, "George, when is Ken coming? Where does he get his ideas?!" I used to tell him, "The fields are already ripe for harvest, but do you want to gather it?" When you get the Facts, you have to separate the tares from the wheat unless the mists of time allow you to superimpose some of the chaff in the offering of the wheat and contaminate it.

You know, when two and two is thought to be five, the twos only have to be freed of a claim that coming together there was an error. You don't work with the error to get rid of it. You don't make a reality out of the five. When you show that two plus two is four, it is freed from the penalty of belief.

Why do you have to stay in after school? Why don't you use your leisure time to rejoice in fecundating the plane with fulfillment? Purpose, goal, and aim are for those who have to develop sight.

One of the greatest needs today is not what you see, it's learning how to hear! You never *fall* in love; you are *drawn* by Love. When you are drawn by Love, you allow Love to have an outline. This outline is what you perceive as the *printed* Word. Right where you see IT is the body of that Effulgence termed the vibratory frequency that allowed IT to be symbolized until *I* come to BE, Unknown, Unlimited, State of Being.

The whole value of the Manger is never to lose Wonder. Allow yourself to appear in the straw, but know that the Great Berry of Delight was in the Sweetness of Being that was never touched by the belief of succession, by the belief of apostolic succession, by the belief of lineage, for these have only been the props and the staging for your show on Earth. Yet, who is there to write the lines of your story and allow *you* to elucidate the meaning?

If you have a question, know that intuitively I AM beyond it, therefore, the constant Answer.

Turn the scene inside out
And see that you may appear to be a gadabout.
Know that you fly beyond all suggestions of time,
And the joy of Being finds you unconfined.

There is no pain unless you wish gain
And think they are wedded as you travail in this terrain.
Move beyond this season with its plights:
"What gift will I give to this one? What gift will I give to
    that one? I've got to wrap it up at night."

In the Dawning and the glory of its early Light,
When your gift is unwrapped, will you perceive
    Second Sight?
Will you hear before seeing the Wonders as planned?
They were given in a Sound and the symbol appeared
    as Man.

The Sound was Man, and men made a plea
And they were given a form to outline the deed.
But that form outlined must be now filled with a Substance
    known to be true.
It's the Unconditional Love that causes "you" to seemingly
    smile through
This visible plane with the Invisible Might,
And say, "The Substance Unlimited is all shared in this
    Dispensation of Light."

This Age is built on togetherness. Separateness is the sure sign that you are on the side of one close to being a defector to the other side. Don't allow yourself to be influenced by separateness. That's all error wants is to be left alone!

Share in the joy and the Being that's Art.
Will your face reveal a canvas and Heart?
Will your body move in a fluid way
Revealing the liquid of which it is made?
Or are you so calcified with crystallizations of doubt
That arthritis is setting in, and you wonder why you have to
    frequent "joints" about.

"Where can I find this joint that can heal my pain?"
Oh, Dr. Joint will help you scream in relief of pain.
"Oh, where can I find someone to break my crystallization
    of doubt?"
Perhaps you will find an "el" extending, and the bow about.

You see, in the Bow of Promise it was so stated to time
That the Divine Creator would never leave you without a
    bridge to His Presence, and it was termed simply
    Divine.
And Elohim always extended His might to all those who
    could come
And worship the Unseen Wonder in the extension of One.

So, with this magnificence, do you dare to stand
Wearing the apparel of a Fire Man?
We gave *The Fire Mass*[3] and all the angels clapped
    their hands for joy,
Because five men and five women were able to stand the
    Fire and seemingly be employed
To withstand this ensuing, consuming Fire and Might.
The Mass was given, an opportunity of second hearing
    and sight.

The world shall be given back to the Arms of Love
When it's seen as your stage all prepared because
You said, "I want to come to Earth to learn
What it is to experience choice
And be able to give it up
And be *polarized* as Love."

These are the Words that have been flung
Unto you in this block of One
And may all those who are attuned to this Frequency find
That they are moved beyond the limits of the chattels of
     mind.

And may the world be graced in the dawning Light of this
     time
And be found acceptable in the sight of the One
     Altogether Lovely,
          and termed,
               labeled,
                    spelled,
                         for the moment,
                              "Love Divine."

Love Divine is so impractical, unless it can be outlined and turn
you inside out!

Thank you.

December 9, 1990

---

1 "The straw of time is the transitory nature of the seeming." — K.G.M.
2 See Chapter XXX, "The Augmentation of Authenticity," p. 389.
3 *The Fire Mass*, original Latin with additional text by Kenneth G. Mills, music by
  Kenneth G. Mills and Christopher Dedrick (Toronto: Sun-Scape Records, 1989).

VII

SHADOW DANCE

What is the evidence of being "bound to Be"?
Uniqueness.

What is uniqueness?
The mark of Individuality.

What is the mark of Individuality?
Newness.

What is the garment thus woven?
Nowness.

SHADOW DANCE

We are attempting to re-establish contact with That which we are when we have freed ourselves from the *suggested*, wrapped sometimes in what is termed "the shadow."

Every event of significance is deemed to be so by agreement. When a great number *celebrate* an event, it evidences that many are in agreement; when one celebrates an event, it evidences that one is in agreement. The more we have in agreement, the more at ease we feel in celebrating. Frequently, we find it difficult to celebrate alone. We are ill at ease with facing our situation as it dawns, for it bears with it a shadow; it also bears with it a Presence.

There are many stories about how men have tried to free themselves from "the shadow" that they cast by standing in the *sun*light. And the old story is that one tried to run away from his own shadow and felt the faster he ran, the quicker he would get rid of his shadow. He died from over-exhaustion. All he had to do was stop running and get in the shade of the tree, and there would have been no shadow, as the story points out.

It is so fascinating to see what we do to try to make the shadow know ALL. We create a life experience attempting to make the shadow wise, to make the shadow loving, constant, faithful, and true. We *spend our attention* trying to discipline a shadow to be transparent instead of realizing that as long as you hear, you will have a shadow, but it doesn't do *anything* to mar the totality of your experience unless you *allow it* to have an identity and a field of play that you try to suppress in order to stop it chasing you.

As long as there is being, there is a shadow. And we have forsaken our experiences of joy, of wonder, and wrapped them all up in attempts to achieve joy and wonder with the suppression of everything that goes with the shadow. So we try to suppress our energy, sometimes appearing as sex, and say it must go this way, it must go that way. We cannot allow it just to *be*; therefore it becomes one-sided, lopsided, and pornography is the fulfillment of *that* deed. The dissatisfaction, the repressed, is expressed and frequently in the lopsided fashion of encountering our everyday world, walking in an imbalanced way.

If we would accept the Fact that Being is cognized, we would realize That with That Being, if it is in expression, there is the shadow. You are not to fall for it and try to get rid of it. You never try to get rid of the shadow until you see what figure is standing in the Light. And what if the shadow is so subtle that your figure no longer stands in the way of the Light?!

What you are experiencing this morning is an experience of an unusual nature, because you are experiencing the awareness appearing as a shadow . . called words. The words are the shadows, and if it were not for *being* in the Light, you would not have the words or the shadows appearing for you to perceive there is nothing wrong with the shadow as long as you don't mistake it for Reality. When there is reality, it never leaves you comfortless. That is why, beyond the Scene of the Manger, I bear a comfort, and I leave you not comfortless, because the shadow of language points to the *Essence*.

Being is another word for Essence, and the language is a shadow-dance. And when it is in rhythm it can bear a melody that will enhance the *structure of experience* so that ideals are not to be chased but to be held until you face the shadow and agree not to be fretful over it, about it, and try to suppress it or get rid of it. But you see that you do not react to it and rest in the condition of serenity in the face of shadows dancing, because you know that there is *bound* to this dimension of experience that which bears the form that is essential for you to work with. You didn't know you brought it with you; you will not know you let it go, but you will see that in either case it is changeable and therefore dances like a shadow.

You give the shadow substance by *suppressing* the uniqueness of what is termed the Divine Individuality. And the Divine Individuality would be said by some teachers to be ridiculous because it's an Ideal. And some teachers say, "Do not hold an ideal. If you hold an ideal you will be forever *vowing* not to do this and vowing not to do that!" You are vowing not to love; you're vowing not to get angry; you're *vowing* fidelity; you're *vowing* . . vowing. And what's happening? You are constantly suppressing your energies all because of ideals which have to deal with the future. *That is why the Ideal is what you hold onto as you face That Which*

IS ideal-less: the Now. Because the Now lived in its fullness doesn't need to be "shadow-ized" by ideals or principles, because the Now is the fullness of That which has cast the shadows, unknown to you as the *fullness* of Ideal, the *fullness* of Principle, the *fullness* of Essence. *Now* is termed the accepted, sacred time-space, because it has *nothing* to do with the shadow-dance with a time signature. And you bear a time signature when you, without thought, have the confidence to sign your name.

Remember, when the Jesus babe was born there was no birth certificate. The evidence of his birth was a shadow . . dance. It had been announced before the Shadow appeared that a Light would shine that would lead all men beyond the grave belief. And the grave belief was that through the shadow you would gain Eternal Life. But you see, gaining Eternal Life meant that Life Eternal was *not* to be claimed as God would claim it.

God's Son is really the experience of **Being That Now!**

Why are you so discontented with *Being That Now?* Why aren't you rejoicing in the fullness of *Being That Now* if it isn't **because you have given such allegiance to the shadow!** You have made the shadow to be the *root* of your feeling nature but due to the shadow termed your sexual nature, your love nature tributaried to the sexual nature, your beauty attributed to the vanity — and your bureau covered with make-up! The vanity must have its table of operations! And vanity has the shadow attempting to be beautified. The shadow is only reverberating because the string is vibrating due to a molecular action of Light that bears no shadow, because in the Light I can only see Light.[1] It's when I am *not* That Light that I appear as a shadow.

What is the great agreement of birth, of a Messiah, of an Avatar or of a Contact beyond them? It's the interesting experience of a coincidence of Coordinates that appear to coalesce in order to enhance the moment of attention so that you may be sprung from the trap of the mind's entrainment to the shadow, which is being educated to become God-like.

The whole purpose of "you being enlightened" is a *gimmick* that you have dreamed up and have said is my calling to eradicate. You called me because the dammed "you's"/ewes wanted to be freed from the *field* of suppression — not oppression; suppression.

What happens with suppression is the perverting of the Force, and the perverted Force results in *mass* oppression. The "oppressed peoples of the world" is another way of stating that the shadow is believed to be Real and its emotions and contacts are considered Real, and therefore God-Being is ignored for the attempt to be *like* God some day. To be "like God some day" is just dressed-up theology, but to be **God Now** — or to be *That* Now — is to put an end to all your self-imposed restrictions.

You can't do this if you are filled with guile. Are you filled with guile? Perhaps so if you are thinking of the shadow's possessions: "*My* body, *my* feelings, *my* love, *my* wealth, *my* abundance, *my* joy, *my* blessings, *my* gratitude, *my* beneficence, *my* progeny, *my* creativity." Possession, they say, is nine-tenths of the law. Of what? Of oblivion, because as long as you possess each other from the standpoint of what you *know* bears no resemblance to the blueprint of Divinity, you are *deliberately thwarting your purpose to be Real!* You would *not be here* if you did not in Essence know that I am allowing the shadow to be dealt with under the Tree beyond that of knowledge. If you *lie* beneath the tree of knowledge, you will just be another deluded victim of a religious attempt to be robed for another venture in the dimension of limitation!

The whole purpose is to *stretch* beyond your mentality. Remember, your mentality is what is used to support your materiality. If I am casting the Light on your obvious mentality and materiality, then I can't be *in* that mentality or materiality because I could not *self-destruct*. "Self-destruct" is the name that is given to repression. It destructs the shadow, but it doesn't touch That Which IS. It's a subtle field.

If this Sound has meaning for you, it is because Light IS Self-evident. If Light IS Self-evident and this language is Self-revealing, what do you suppose is causing you to run away from your Divine State if it isn't the old archaic approach to worshipping the future in the framework of an Ideal?

That is how the baby Jesus grew. We put into a Birth that is miraculous the shadow of maturing. We put into the Birth the shadow growing bigger, greater, and becoming more attuned to being God.² This is the crucifixion, in the end.

The whole purpose of Divine Being is that IT allows you to make contact with the Tonality that bears no reference to your symbol-like nature. If this contact with Divinity is still present in your dance, you should have courage, because if it were totally destructive there would be no vestige of the raiment with which I AM clad. No man is left devoid of that which is essential for his characteristic that is becoming the uniqueness of the Divine Individuality.

Why do you have your thumbprint taken? In order to be identified, as one teacher pointed out. It's because it's so unique, there's none other exactly like it in the entire world that the mind has multiplied. If your thumbprint marks you as unique, *why don't you remain with that uniqueness* instead of trying to be like other thumbs and appearing to be *all* thumbs?

Why would a David ever come under the impression of a father and a mother when their thumbprints don't bear *any resemblance at all*, other than their hides? Why would *anyone* try to be like his father? Why would you be so a challenge to each relative situation *when your thumb tells you immediately you have no relationship other than a commonality called hide?!* Now that is what is the *root of a great releasement* from limits.

Michael will say, "Well, David is my son." Show me your thumbprints and prove it. The only reason the thumbprint and the other thumbprint are together is because of a shadow called "Small." The only reason Dan and his father have something in common is not because of a thumbprint; they *have* nothing in common in the form of a thumbprint other than that Ron accepted a name of a freed man. Why *wouldn't* Dan, why *wouldn't* Ron, why *wouldn't* Vicky, why *wouldn't* Debbie have stopped "dibbin' and dobbin' and dabbin' colors" and debuted in the Wonder of those uncondemned to the *boredom* of this puppet show on Earth, instead of being moved by the strings of the "mind operators," sometimes termed the "parasite operators"?

What is the value of Christmas? To see the Wonder of the *continuing effect* of Light! People will celebrate gift giving, because in Essence the exchange of gifts should be seen as the *acceptance* of

Individuality. Oh, yes!! Individuality is the *Source* of the eternal Abundance and Substance that is termed Divine.

Stretch your imagination! If you don't, you will imagine vain things.[3] And a people who imagine vain things are a people who are lost on the bureau of vanity. They become the members of the bureau of make-up artists. What is a make-up artist? One who makes you appear to be . . what you aren't. Some of the greatest make-up artists have been your parents, because they themselves were made up and didn't Realize it. Why do you think the cosmetic industry is such a big one? It has to support itself, and it's got all of "you" needing support.

The make-up artists: parents and educators. The educators are not fulfilling their role, "to lead out of." What do you lead *out of*? It seems to me that today educators are leading *into* conformity. They are leading into what? A commonness where the standards of uniqueness are minimized and the standard of conformity is elevated. Why is *uniqueness* such a threat? Because then sameness ceases to be perceived as an authentic experience. And when two or three are gathered together in the same state, there is "at-easement"?

Why is it, even in our common social structure, that people who are married usually have a majority of married people at their table, not single people? And why is it that most single people have married people at their table? Because there is an attempt on the part of the single people not to make the married people feel double, and it's the part of the married people to make the single people see other married people and not feel that being single is always the best way to be, because they are double. You know? Look at what motivates your shadow!

Now, why do most shadows like to dance together? Because when they dance together, have you ever heard a shadow stepping on another shadow's foot? But you know, in *some* cases, a shadow *does* leave footprints. No matter how lightly you run, you always see the evidence of having run; *but what accompanies the footstep before it's happened? The interval of hearing between each footstep leaves a mark.* You say it's a foot that's left a mark. If there hadn't been an interval between them, there would have only been One Print!

Then what does an interval always suggest? A distance between two tones. And guess what? If it weren't for that distance between the two tones, you could not *cognize*. Do you realize it's the distance between two situations that allows you to cognize? What if you do something to that distance and stop it from being the means of your adjudicating? Wouldn't that cease as well? And what if you don't adjudicate from the standpoint of an interval? Wouldn't you be the evidence of the Sounding Board that allowed the interval to perceive its somethingness until it gave up itself?[4]

The shadow allows the sound to be cognized, knowing that feeling must have bridged it. *Without feeling, the sound bears no meaning.* Therefore, the feeling can't be *referenced* to suppression. When the feeling is suppressed, it becomes rebellious. And how does that appear? As anger, resentment, retaliation. Where is the balm? It's in perceiving there is nothing wrong with the shadow, for it's *bound* to Be.

What is the evidence of being "bound to Be"? **Uniqueness.**

What is uniqueness? **The mark of Individuality.**

What is the mark of Individuality? **Newness.**

What is the garment thus woven? **Nowness.**

Use your Ideal for your future, your Principle as part of the
  Plan,
But be the uniqueness becoming Individuality and live the
  Principle Ideal: Man.
Beyond the Manger and its Scene of Simplicity you will see,
  as the Star does shine,
That if the Star did not radiate uniqueness, no Wise Man
  would have perceived the inner direction of the
  Divine.

They went to the east, they went to the west,
And all the appellations have been addressed.
But the Mountain of Light shall bear this Mark,
That it becomes nothing but a ripple of laughter in the
  shadow-dance of Life.

Don't *allow* yourselves to be such common people. What are common people? Those who are in the system of equating. The word "people" implies otherness. You are among people: you are in "*otherness.*" And what is otherness? The name given to all the shadows who bear a key for releasement from the bondage of commonness. And it's all given symbolically in the thumb.

How many of you dare to be the thumb released from its print?! The foot leaves a mark in the sand when you run to get away from your shadow, but wherever "you" go the shadow follows as your thumbprint. Uniqueness — none other like you — makes you what you can be. "*Makes* you what *you* can be": on the edge of the Abyss. You can be on the edge of the Abyss. What does that mean? Being freed from what you aren't. *That's* the leap into the Abyss! And that's why the Master can put you together!! You can fall into the Abyss, and that leap is nothing but *allowing what isn't* to drop, and what IS remains untouched. In other words, your shadow can appear to disappear when Being has no longer a need to be pursued because of false teaching.

Educators have got to learn. In other words, they have got to live to earn the right to lead. And they have to live and earn the right to be . . educators, because why? They are the effect of a Cause which they know not and appear to be the known Cause for those who are termed the effect. And how can an unknown Cause be an answer to the effects of an unknown Cause? The students and the teacher. The students are the effect of a Cause, of a teacher. The teacher wouldn't be a teacher without the students, but if the teacher knows he is only affecting the role for those who think there is a Cause for it, then the shadow is allowed to dance, and there will always be the honor bestowed upon the teacher because the student will realize the effect of the Cause is all wrapped up in *BE*!

What is the value of Being? It doesn't need to have a shadow to shine!

Oh, airy fairy? Then the angels will be so happy to be freed from their dreamed-up state.

Remember — the more you try to, the less you will. Remember: the more you try to, the less you *will*. I come to *do* Thy Will, O God. The more you try to remember, the less you will. What is the point of trying to remember a shadow when the point is just a point in it? But there must be a Point out of it in order for the point in it to be exposed.

> So that's the great paradox: to see the shadow, to see its
> substance and allow it to dance
> And not be entranced by the seeming shadow and its dance.

If there is a great value to any assembly, it is to perceive the uniqueness of Individuality and agree to move beyond the prints of time. Allow the smidgen of "you" to reveal the holographic wonder Man IS when you perceive, through the seeing of the I, that in the I/Eye of God there is none other.

If the uncontaminated Word is "The Word was *with* God and the Word *is* God," why do you allow[5] it to remain a shadow-dance? If the Word is God and God is the Word, then Love is God and God is Love. Why do you allow it to be a dance of shadows? Why don't you *allow* IT (the Word) to be the Fire of Translation so that the shadow becomes a Super One?[6]

Just think — and you can have all this . . and Heaven too. **Do you know there's not *one thought* that will interfere with the Divine as long as you keep the thought in agreement with IT!** It's *your* opportunity! Whom will you seek and what will you choose? To be this puny, changeable shadow, or allow this changeable shadow to appear always new, pointing to the Changeless in the midst of the changing. I have done it, and that's why I have gone before you. It takes great courage to be Individual; it takes none to be common. One in a mass is one in a mess, and one in a mess has a mass for company!

Why do you think your parents have never given you full agreement to be here? Because they aren't! How many of you have your parents present, and how many of your parents present have given "you" up . . to be the Individual you really are?

Oh, it isn't *similar* to *anything* that you have ever heard. Why are you comfortable in it? And why do you appear so unmoved?

> Why do you appear so cast down, O my Soul,[7] and why are
> you not disquieted within?

Shan't the foolish forsake the Way, and the unrighteous man
    his thoughts?
Surely the Holy Blessing of the Holy **Word** must be the Light
    to the darkness which is not.
Should not the dance be equated with the Equilibrium
    Divine
That knows no step is taken unless it's in rhythm
    with the melody: Thou art Divine.

Why would you choose a thought equated with you being
    this mass, this form,
When you know very well the Art of Being is never limited
    by what is born.
The Art of Being is never found by being sought in time.
The Art of Being is Timeless; it's marked with the Print
    Divine.

If the Joy of Being Holy ripples within your frame of
    transparencies and delight,
Don't you realize your mind is doing the framing, and your
    attention is bringing the Light?
The transparency gives all color to this spectrum through
    which I AM seen,
And yet, how would I have an apparent shape and color and
    form if you were not perceiving Me
By fracturing your Light so I may shine as your deed?

If it were not for the prism of your attention, perhaps
    'twould be only a shadow of the semblance I AM,
Because it's only by your attention and Wonder that you see
    a form bearing a semblance called man.
And so, when I look at you in your seeming, I rejoice in
    knowing the Fact
That the Light is *always* shining, and you appear to cast a
    shadow, for you agreed to dance!

Don't be afraid of a shadow when it becomes caught up
    with you,
Don't try to get rid of it; just sit down in the shade beyond
    the tree of knowledge and say, "I do."

What education is for the future? To lead all those who
have brought doubts to time
Into the Timeless, Balanced State where Love has translated
your name and given it Glory Divine.

Isn't it amazing how we have all agreed to respond to names,
which are nothing but the shadows of tones? And what if you could
find the Foundational One and allow it to be the Diapason of
Glory? What an Organ of Wonder you would become! You would
become organs of color,[8] because each one would allow the Light
to reveal his transparent nature, and others would call you a
Wonder.

You are well framed, but when you look upon your canvas as
you stand before your vanity, *perceive*, and conceive anew the real
meaning of seeing through the looking-glass. It's a Wonder Land.
Winter is when you hibernate from doing. Mine is non-seasonal.

It is so grand to conceive how the Brothers of the Shadow and
the Brothers of the Light are really the two forces that those in the
becoming have to contend with. For the Brothers of the Shadow feel
that "this" is Real, and the Brothers of the Light know that *the
shadow exists because something else is unrecognized as its place of
birth. There can't be a shadow if there isn't something* **causing** *it*.
Maybe the cause is still a question with an answer not wanting to
be known. In other words, the Brothers of the Shadow are those
who have chosen to be "this" instead of That. And what are the
Brothers of the Light? Those who bear That . . Now.

The Simplicity of the Manger gives you the scintillating
brilliance of a Star. The Wise Man never ceases to Wonder. Why
wouldn't it fill the land?

Your Presence unwrapped: "How do you do, Wonder?"

Wonder Woman and Wonder Man! How few of you ever are
this at a party? The common name, "party," which is really a get-
together for shadows. How many of you *dare* to Be? How many
give their full approval to you being Real? *Do you give full approval
to **yourselves** being Real?!*

How many people **have given** *all* **of themselves to being Real?**

Or just part of themselves? And that's what you call the decision that has to be made in the *preliminary Baptism of Repentance*. You have to know within yourselves how much or how little or *all* of you has been given to being Real in your shadow-dance. How many of you have reservations about being Real? How many of you . . . ?

Do you realize that if you think there are parts of you that are Real and parts of you that aren't, that you are slated for disease? The root of disease is an imbalanced system. And you wonder why there is disease? It's because people *think* they can mix all kinds of thought concoctions and come out with a Divine Prescription for Life. No human god such as Aesculapius could ever bring about the fullness of Being by attempting to heal through the shadow being Real.

If you are going to teach shadows to dance, you have to be in rhythm with the Divine Baton. And that is constantly beyond the metronome. Why are you such gnomes in this Wonderland? And so many of you in metros, where time is only there to wrap you in the wrinkles of aging. Look at the hours you spend giving time preferential treatment by dying to it! *Why don't you fight your timed experience with the Baton or the Sword of Truth?*

Oh, the world of tomorrow is a myth! And the incredible part of a myth is it never was anything; it's what people make up about something that never was . . realized. The root of a myth is that which is made up because something was not realized in fullness. And if something is realized in fullness, there is no myth! Then there's only the "ology," and then you don't even have that. You just have "oh." And when it's fundamental you would have "*Om*." But you can move from the "*Om*" to another frequency and it may be "oh" and then to "you." Keep on and you'll start to be creating a melody. *How many will sing your wonder through the communication?*

The communication of the future will not be spoken; it will be sung. All dialogues will be sung; all conversation will be sung, because you will not be conversing with a limited language but with *the sound impression of a Light Pitch.*

Remember, the tone is the shadow! And why does it have to appear to you to be in pitch? So that you will see the Absolute nature of being attentive in hearing. Who's going to see your tone unless they see it of the skin, your hide? Let the children play hide and seek. You have found your unique Individuality, and if there is a Christmas message, it is:

No Strawberry is ever the same, but each one brings a touch of Fire to the vine prepared to receive it. Each Mark of uniqueness brings a Wonder for others to behold upon the Vine of Conscious Awareness. Why do you limit your uniqueness by thinking in the framework of relativity?

Why do you think the Birth must be Immaculate? So there can be no proved relationship to a timed experience!

The birth of Newness can appear timed on your calendar of vain attempts to reach the impossible. It's so amazing to reach different continents by an electrical charge and a medium that carries a voice print. *Perhaps that's what each of us is.*

Why don't you hang up your belief as a receiver and start being the Message?

You sign your name without thinking. The only time you think is when you sign a check. You don't have to think about your name. Your name only shows how much you thought about the check. It always affects your writing. But you can always write your name. There's no doubt about it; you don't have to give any thought to it. You can be talking while you write it. You don't have to remember how to form the characters that make up your name. In other words, you don't have to remember each character when you sign your name. It's done without thinking. So AM I. The only time you *think* about it is when it appears on a check list of do's and do nots.

How many don't face their worth honestly? How many count their money and then pretend they don't have it? And then they *don't* have it!

Somebody said to me (some time ago now; it was ages ago), "I'm sorry you lost that money, Mr. Mills." I said, "I only saw figures on a piece of paper. I never counted one of them." How could I lose anything when I never had it other than as an idea? If you think the money is your Substance, then you'd better start counting it and be honest about it. If I had counted every dollar I had, I would have considered whether or not I could give this one this much and that one that much, or I could give this much to this situation in Europe, or I could give this much to this situation in another republic. No one knows what I did with figures. That's all you're dealing with: figures. Do you realize, if you need ten thousand dollars cash and John's put it in the bank, he has to notify the bank that he wants to withdraw it, because they don't have it?

I remember once pulling a trick on my bank in Canada. I went in and I said, "I may come in tomorrow and withdraw some thousands in cash." They said, "Oh, you've got to give us notice!" I said, "I didn't have to give you any when I gave it to you. Where is it?" They said, "Well, we don't have it." I said, "But I gave it to you! Now you tell me I have to give you notice because I want my money back?" She said, "Yes, we don't keep it here." I said, "Where do you keep it? It's strange; I didn't keep it there." Oh, boy. They really don't know how to cope with it.

I went into the same bank this day, and there were two elderly women ahead of me, and three tellers doing nothing but looking black. One lady spoke so rudely to these two women that I would not suppress. So, I banged the counter and I said, "I don't want to *ever* hear any of you *ever* speak this way to *your* means of livelihood. Every one of you, sitting there behind those desks, you get a smile on your face, because *you are working here because I come here* and so do these ladies! *You behave accordingly.*" And the assistant manager came over and said, "Oh, Mr. Mills, why didn't you tell us you were here!" Why would I? I said, "You have eyes to see." So, I wrote a letter to the chairman of the bank, and boy, did I get a letter back, and they got another one.

Commonness. Uniqueness! Why would you go in and be pleasant?! Why would you accept service from a situation that was deemed a service to you that was anything but gracious? You're gracious and trusting to be *allowing* your money to be in the hands of such institutions as banks who make money off your earnings and pay you enough to keep you from questioning how much *they* make off it.

Uniqueness isn't always being sweet. It often has to do with bringing about a whole new mint-age, and it doesn't just go as a jelly on lamb. But the leg of lamb is a mint. Do you realize the mint that has been made around a leg of lamb?

The lambs always had a chance to take the attention of the Shepherd so that He would give up his life to attempt to lead them. The cost of a leg of lamb: the life of the Shepherd! *Never!* You never stoop to trying to bring an organization into order. Be the order and fulfill it yourself! How many boards of directors have people who have no direction, other than a biased approach to part of a program? The board of directors should be the people filled with vision as a result of the visionaries who support something beyond the mundane.

And that is why may it be read
That the shadow danced for you to see
How the Light allowed it to happen as my deed.

If it were not for the Light, how could the shadow know .. All? That's a Super shadow!

Remember, when your shadow gets too much for you, don't try to run away. Go and sit in the shade of a Tree, and see where your shadow has gone. Is it beside you? Before you? Behind you? Which way have *you* decided to come and go? Up or down, or sideways? Be the Point and be the beginning and the end of the most incredible Story! It's the greatest one ever told, because it takes a Story-Teller who knows the Wonderland and knows there is no season. There is only One and that is why it is said:

"Be jolly, you merry gentlemen,
Let nothing like dismay
Ever enter your ken and foster anything
But the Brightness of the Irradiance of Day!"

May your greetings be always echoing — the *shadow*,
     don't you see,
Of what comes beyond the mountaintops and comes to
     those in the valley of options and deeds.
But you are the very Peaks of Glory because you don't have
     any crevice in your decision and your might
Because you gave yourself up to victory, and the victorious

know "All is Light!"

Don't be a partial. If you do, you'll have dampened spirits! Remove any damper of partiality and remove the fuzz from your heartstrings of being Real. I've plucked them! You'd better sound or we'll have to do something about your box. You stand in the witnessing box of today and bear witness through the tonality of your voice box. The canvas is your face; your face is the canvas of the Hand of Wonder, and your voice box elucidates the uniqueness of Presence.

So endeth this portion of this Word as it has been given without thought to those who know the Wonder of Plenty.

May you have a happy holiday; may your new year be ideally filled with your art of procrastination![9] Won't you be all That Now!

Rejoice, you merry gentlemen! There is no dismay
For unto you is born this day
An understanding of the shadow and its dance.

Thank you!

December 23, 1990

---

1 Psalms 36:9. "I appear to be a shadow doing away with shadow!" — K.G.M.
2 "The meaning here is the fallacy of believing Spirit can be brought to matter or matter can become Spirit! (It is necessary to move from sense to Soul.)" — K.G.M.
3 Psalms 2:1.
4 "One tone of interval pointing to another tone is co-operative stagnation! That is why three is so important!" — K.G.M.
5 "For 'anything' to happen, you have to be ready and willing to be altered." — K.G.M.
6 I.e., the Christ, the Self.
7 Psalms 42:5.
8 Reference is made here to an invention by the 19th century Russian composer, Alexander Scriabin, who devised a mechanism whereby colors corresponding to tones would be displayed while the music was being performed.
9 Mr. Mills emphasizes the tendency of men to overindulge in procrastination and present it as acceptable: "Procrastination is impoverishment. It is the onset of the deterioration of the will."

VIII

A DOORWAY TO THE SOUL

The temple to be made with hands can never be eternal in the heavens, but when Heaven is realized as a Harmonic State of Being, then Man can resound in the diapason of his realization that he is a Tonality upon which chordal structures of Promise can be built to satisfy the Unfoldment that must ensue when Man has once enunciated the various themes surrounding the Great Triptych of Being.

A DOORWAY TO THE SOUL

We have been awaiting with expectation the Wonders that a possibility reveals when it is not dropped just because of a verdict of circumstances all aligned to the horizontalized mind of time.

It is essential that in the days that appear to lie before you, as you fulfill the journey from this place you have in time to That Place which you expect to achieve in time, never to give up the possibilities of a Promise, so that it may be fulfilled, because a people without a Vision is a people that is without a purpose.[1] A purpose must have the tenacity to hold your attention regardless of the verdict that "all the lines are down"[2] and all communications with the possibilities of Being are annulled. For you know that in the Facts of the Realm of the Real, That Which IS is not attributable unto the superficial counterfeit and is forever the Force to make all that would limit null and void.

Today people are too easily led to believe. They are too easily led to drop the connection because of the circuits of their minds and all due to the low synergy. High synergy is an essential feature in magnifying the Impulse. The necessary feature, which is to magnify the Impulse, is the enhancement of the determination that comes with the volition termed the Will.

The will as personally used is destructive; the Will in the Light of the volition chariotized to the Sun's Achievement gives unto us the possibility of being recharged and enhanced in our suggested peregrinations from sense to Soul.

This morning has been; tomorrow morning will be. What shall be must now be because with the future tense lies the connection of suggestion; with an historical past is your bondage to the low circuitry of belief.

Your purpose for being here is one that bears not so much in Essence an altruistic viability, although it may appear that way. You are here because in the graciousness of the Light you have been given an opportunity to allow all those peoples who are camping on this stage called the Earth to start to consider the need for altering the temporary shelters of time in order to enter the stabilized structure of Glorified Being.

The great Wonder of Alignment to Purpose is the way the mind describes, on the exterior, what must come to be seen as the necessity to question your validity and your achievement in Being.

What are we trying to do but achieve a better society? But a society is the name given to what constitutes it: "you's." Unfortunately the slogan with "you" is:

> You haul, you pull, you push, you shove,
> You hope . . you have direction?
> You strive, you struggle, you seldom have joy.
> Oh! the wonders of such predilection!
>
> You hope, you succeed, your fashion right,
> To sustain your reaffirmation of your self in time and its
>   plight.
> You live, you die, you sigh, you cry.
> What a society made up of "you" and your sides!

Some say, "Split your sides laughing!" I would say, "Haul up, pull up, and give an uppercut to the glass jaw of suggestion which you carry onto this stage as a result of a skull that is empty and void of the Meaning of Being!"

Your presence, your form encapsulated in time gives you an opportunity to exude Wonder or to reek with the decaying slowness of a society devoid of an enhanced energy due to the reluctance to be recharged and to be refitted for entering into the great Festival of Presence presenting Man unlimited, unconfined and uncontaminated by belief.

One of the essential characteristics of a society today is its general tendency to drift into the line of least resistance. It is the tendency to seek those who are in your company with no command. It is in your agreement to be commanderless that you wonder what happened to the kick of Kirk.[3]

You know the wandering tabernacles that were made in time

and have an historical flap of appendages to the present were such that they were known to be the unstable structures of a more nomadic movement. You know the exteriorized tendency to worship was under the light of a hoped or supposed enlightened priesthood to activate your mystery and cause you to look within and beyond the flapping tent-piece of belief.

> The temple that was more stabilized was still tabletized,
> and the service performed incomplete,
> For man stood erect before the altar of time but forgot that
> it of Earth must be made in order for men to meet
> What is necessary to be sacrificed: a living suggestion of
> might.[4]
> The "you" who hauled yourself around and appeared to
> attend a service in order to become Light,
> "You" have been hauled and dragged and cajoled into time,
> seduced, and embraced in the suggestion:
> "Oh, you are mine!"

You must perceive the need of Identity.[5] Each cell of the body, each wonder that constitutes its appearance, works and functions in agreement with its own code, because the energy that proceeds from it is, in each case, of a different quantity. It has been discerned that the reason, perhaps, the Society of the Saints and Sages of the Ages has been historically made sacred is because of what the Presences of such did in allowing to be emitted to this plane the Radiance of another stream that could bomb the incoherency of worshippers and allow them to feel, in the exaltation of the Divine, the encompassing energy that would meet their attempts at worship and allow them, through a charismatic baptism, to be graced with an increased holiness, spasmodic for sure, but at least for a moment, a foretaste of possibilities.

For the moment that one allows oneself to be bombarded with the evidence of a Divine Principle or Divine Idea, the suggested realm of principles and ideation becomes subject to the laseristic bombardment, which allows incoherency to become coherent and the natural magnification of the Force to bring unto the chaotic conditions of time a new Order. In this enhanced State the cells remain just what they are but they have agreed to be attracted. They have not fought to reclaim their fractured and partial state. They have deemed themselves ready to be recharged and reactivated for the revocalization surrounding the Wonders of a tonal and auric baptism!

If the Word was made flesh,[6] you can perceive that it could never be so, other than to verify, for the variegated patterns of achievement in the low synergistic society, that there was a hope if they just dragged themselves to the edifice which was set apart as holy but needing support because of its emptiness.

When man finds the "Temple not made with hands but eternal in the heavens,"[7] then he finds that the Substance of its Essence naturally exudes within and without its suggested borders. There is nothing to deplete it, to encroach upon it, or to allow it to become a relic of worship.

Your Temple-not-made-with-hands is the one that is being considered by each and every one of you, for if it were not so, you would be satisfied with the paltry experience of a schizophrenic mind syndrome and allow yourselves to go on enjoying the suggested excitement of a dualistic society.

The Society of the Christ, of the Self, of the Brahman, of the Enlightened, is such a rare one because their Force stands present, but not out there with a marquee: "Here is the end to your rental systems of 'you-haul.'" The Offering of the Saints and the Sages is such that it waits to be recognized, and in this recognition the cogs are once again perceived to be ever-present and only needing the Oil of Consecration to make what appears to be the mechanized forces of time yield to the dynamic flow becoming a high synergy which surrounds an Emancipated State.

The great perception of today is that so many people are on the Path and searching, so it is said, for Enlightenment. It is unfortunate, indeed, that those who are on the Path don't meet the border where they have to declare who they are and their intention for entering such a rarefied atmosphere. You see, you cannot enter into that State, which is deemed the Emancipated One freed from the conditions of your mind, and carry with you the shackles of a historical past and a seductive appendage to a limiting factor of family or familiarization with a said root system that always needs to have a birthright searched in order to see if one is a member of the D.A.R.

The money that is spent in trying to search for identity — and how little energy is spent allowing money to be evidenced when Identity is found! It's amazing, when you have once found your family tree, it has not added one jot of a point to the Point that pricks you as soon as you approach it with an incorrect standpoint.

There is no need so great today that cannot be solved if those who are in need are willing to consider Identity — those in the world today who are flamboyantly exalting the woman and her rights and men (I've gone to the plural) and their rights! You can see the ravages and the savages that are on the hunt for equality, which will never be found in a society in which men and women haul with them the beliefs of an adulterated educational system which is devoid of the accuracy surrounding the understanding of appearance.[8]

Many people, I have been told, are very challenged, especially women, when I speak of Man. Man! Man! Man! Man! (Women!) (Men!) One woman suggested, "When you speak of Father-Mother-God, why don't you say Mother-Father-God?" I said, "God!" Man! Oh, there is the blow to the glass jaw! God-Man. Who wants to be going around this contaminated vegetation "godding"?

We don't plant "God-seeds." We cannot circumscribe the Wonder of the Unknown, even in G-O-D or the Unvocalized Sound of the Ultimate. All we can do is point to the Center of Being and allow it to be termed "the Ultimate." We can say ITs radius is infinite in ITs adaptations and ITs bestowals, and your circumference is nothing but the line that is drawn as you are shackled in an incomplete enlightened state to feeling that you cannot extend yourself further in your service role. You "just haven't got the time or the energy to do so." But it's amazing how much you will extend yourselves in the service role to pay for your cars bought on time, to pay for your clothes charged to "Ontime VISA," to pay for your extravagances all based on the American Dream (North and South America included, and Canada). You will all have credits of debit on your books because you have not spent your substance wisely.

You have attempted to reaffirm your petulant personal probable self into nothing but an enhanced state of probabilities:

"Maybe I can be free of debt. Maybe I will be freed of that office. Maybe . . . " Instead of saying, "May I Be!" If I be found, where be you? Who is there to witness?

Why do you need a Principle, an Idea? Because you don't understand, or want to understand, Man! Man. Man.

People want equality, so they say. They don't know what equality means! They think equality has to do with the balance of having and not having .. nationality, substance, country, et cetera. Balance is the dreamed-up state for those who are imbalanced! It never enters the considerations of the Sages!

That's why this Declaration demands the Sage to be broken into little pieces so you can get the Aroma:

This is the hell!

This is the sacrifice!

This is the offering! .. with nothing but the suggestion of death and the need to re-enhance the vehicle so that it can leave the plane with enough fuel to regain its heavenly orbit beyond the limitations of a mind-set of perspectives!

Man has nothing whatsoever to do with being divided! Man is Being, which equals unification, and unification is the outcome of a partial belief system. The Absolute says, "There is nothing to unify! I AM All!" If that is the Absolute statement, why would you contrive to create a balance sheet? Balance is not restored; it is eliminated from your vocabulary!

If you consider an atom or a molecule having to be balanced before it emits its packet, its quantum of light, do you think you would ever have a scientific approach for a mind to understand the periphery of its limits, and the hope of going beyond them by perceiving the laseristic effect of an Emission that is capable of bombarding your great bag of beliefs with the purifying effect of realignment to an Uncontaminated Vision?

Where there is no Vision, the people perish! Why? Because Vision is not on a credit card! Vision has nothing to do with your salary; it has to do more with your salad days. It has to do with the Newness of Being and the lack of concern about the leaf of adornment.

It is pathetic to see such great statues covered with a leaf of adornment because people might have to consider the need of energy. What grapes of wrath were squeezed upon us! Poor Bacchus must have laughed when he was drunken beyond wine at the revelry of the mind intoxicated with a dualistic endeavor to crush the grapes of wrath and to be intoxicated superficially in a state because of an altered content within the system.

Why do people (not you) tend to enjoy getting drunk, getting drugged, becoming dissipated? Because they are altered states which cause others to give them attention. It's fashionable. Fashion wants you to do what? To reaffirm your petulant self's identity.

What is there to reaffirm when you know yourSelf? The reason the worlds of today are in collision is because the peoples of today are trying to solve a suggested problem by gaining all types of information except that which says, "Relative information is nothing but an intoxication and will not bear the power of absolution which is required before the Altar of Light."

When this One appears to stop on this plane for a fraction of a second (and it is called so many years, perhaps twenty or thirty), it is because it was agreed. In the time sequence you hauled the event into prophecy, wrapped it in what is termed Holy Books, and left it a speculation of a Treasure of the future and yet failed to perceive that there is no speck in the I/Eye of Divinity. If there is, it still is the "i" with a dot and it needs to have a "t" put to it, because then it's an "it" and it has nothing to do with you!

Oh, you can declare with a sense of conviction:

"You've got the right number. Yes, I am Michael."
"Yes, you've got the right number. Yes, I am Helen."
"Yes, you've got the right number. I am Marvin."

And, of course, we know that when somebody says "I am," there should be the confidence that one is hearing one's Self, appearing diversified for the Wonder of still bearing into the suggested formation the Individuality becoming the Indivisible Wonder of Light, the gown of space.

Man is an Idea; it has nothing to do with being considered in terms of male or female.

Man is a State in which this type of consideration is not at all necessary.

Man is a State of Conscious Awareness which allows one to appear to be male or female, but never lived from the standpoint of having to conform to a sedated society.

The uniqueness of being Real cannot be found understood in the fantasy of this world! In the fantasy of this world you make up the God of the Other World and you make up the God of the Underworld, but, you see, the Universal Christ, the Universal Self, the Universal Cosmic Bombardment knows nothing of the divisibility that suggests itself as a force against the Indivisible State that is termed Oneness.

From the horizontalized plane you bump into each other. In the horizontalized plane you touch one another. But when you are not planed and you are no longer surfaced, then you are no longer peripherized, you are no longer globalized, and you have no longer a brain that is immobilized by being globalized! In fact, your brain is always up for alteration, because when you stand outside it, you can see which sparkplugs are carbonated from the historical data of your seductive heritage and which ones are clean as a result of being Real.

You see, there cannot be a leap of fullness if you try to take the carbon documents of the past into the indelible Light Wonders of the Eternal.

The temple to be made with hands can never be eternal in the heavens, but when Heaven is realized as a Harmonic State of Being, then Man can resound in the diapason of his realization that he is a Tonality upon which chordal structures of Promise can be built to satisfy the Unfoldment that must ensue when Man has once enunciated the various themes surrounding the Great Triptych of Being.

There must be, in the classical tradition of sonata form, three movements! One in which the themes are stated; the second movement, one in which you play or one in which you ponder; and the third, the one in which you evidence the enhancement of new themes considered and their development and their capitulation into a coda of brilliance!

You are forever endowed with an alien's rights! You have the ability to consider the protocols and the postulates of an "uneartherized" Document that is beyond the docking system of even your spaceships and their possibility of having an interplanetary refuelling station.

We can enter beyond your cosmic considerations because We have assembled unto Our Essence, to express it in the terms of time, the ability to be photographed in a three-dimensional way so that We bear for you a semblance of sameness as you, in order to play with you, in order for you to consider, in the adagio movement which you set aside every day in your chanting and in your meditation and in your offering of the supposititious, so that the Allness of That Which IS may descend as the Inevitable Light of the Sun extends its emitting rays to your window ledge of considerations.

This has been an agreement among all of Us:
To appear to answer a call,
To come and know the apparent fall,
And to enunciate in the Spring of Newness
That the tulips spring from bulbs through which you dance.

They are the Two Lips which are forever moving in a rhythmic flow of Ejaculations as words, or the carrying symbols of your communicative attention experience, which are held in the floodtides of Love and Newness, which are the tonalities surrounding, and built upon, the Great Diapason of Being.

Oh, the many facets that the diamond wears! In its raw state it is not very impressive; but in the hands of a Master and in the grip of pincers and vise, the Master knows how to make incisions and reveal the inherent fire that, if you hauled it to your table and just looked at it and expected it to be brilliant, would never be so.

You have to be able to look beyond surface impressions in order to perceive that there is a stone which, under the hands of the Master, can become transparent, and that transparent stone bears with it the inherent flame, for it is a symbol of Man's Diamond Nature. But remember, the stone has to be brought under the Mastership of One who knows how to facet the various planes in order for the Light to be revealed and the various faces to shine to satisfy the needs of those who have said, "Sahib, Food!" You said, "Yes. I come to the basket of your mind."

Then you must be obedient and follow the work orders and take it to the water, to the well, and do what seems to be ridiculous: "Bring Me the water in your basket, Son, for My thirst is great."⁹ He makes many trips with his basket and when he gets to the Father, the Father says, "Do it again! Again! Again! Again!" Then the Son says, "Father, what is the gain? Your thirst is not quenched." He said, "Beloved Son, My thirst is not as yours. My thirst is quenched when I see your obedience and I see you are now opened to being given a Truth."

By being obedient look how the basket glistens in the Sun, when before it was covered in the mud of time, the dust of the ages, and you now bear the crystalline evidence of unfractured Being, for you have come under the advice of the Father and you have adopted That which is needed to be an Adept of perception: the ability to perceive in a rough stone the Wonder inherent within it if it allows itself to be faceted with the removal of its outer corrosion. How can it be removed? By giving it the acid tests:

> Are you willing to stop hauling?
> Are you willing to stop crying?
> Are you willing to stop being joyful?
> Are you willing to stop being sad?
> Are you willing to cease willing?

"Willie, Willie, on the pickle boat." You can't enter the Soul, the boat of Being, and expect to carry a preserved appetizer. The will personalized is pickled! as the mummies of the past evidence. Today we realize that the preservation of the form is not necessary, for it does not go with you, any more than your money! Yet you pay; if you haul, you strive. You move to another place. What is the point of moving or hauling if you haven't moved beyond the caravan of your mind?!

This is why you have the mind harnessed to your Chariot of Wonder; then it will never be able to engage the great Solar Energy, the Light to this little world, without being destroyed. You see, if one approaches the Solar Energy and leaves it solarized, man has never moved it to the place where it can be utilized in what is termed the great power center of the future: the heart and the throat. The heart is one; the throat is one. But the throat has been in a catatonic state for centuries!

The great Plains Indians, the great shamans of the past, have all pointed their arrows because the arrow must penetrate the hide of belief in order to kill the animal nature. That point can only be found in the future, so they said, when the arrows are no longer used to penetrate hides but One comes who can allow the penetration of the Light or Sun Body to be revealed by the pointed Word of Regeneration.

Revelation is a state of lifting the curtain on the stage called Earth and allowing the myths thereby represented to be perceived as the organized drama for you to utilize until the Radiant Body of the Divine Rama would once again pierce your limits and reveal, through the voice box, the new womb chamber for the Presence present.

You see, there is no time for newness to be brought through the womb of the woman. It has to come from the Womb of the Immaculate, when the voice is Absolute. For then it bears with it what might be analyzed as balance but which, when experienced, is perceived as Nameless.

Your wonder is to behold, and your beholding, to another, is their wonder. When Wonder beholds Wonder, there is the magnification of That Force which will establish the coherency and bring about a synergized cosmic consideration that allows you to have Heaven here and now, and the Eternal the name given to That Which IS beyond all time and space, and you and your personalized efforts baptized in the laseristic force of an exuding Light Force and given once again in order for all those who have heard, regardless of age, color, or creed, back, forward, up, down, sideways, to be given to Love.

Love is that Power which embraces "you" so that "you" can be freed from the suggestion of a divided state.

When you are comfortable where you are, then you know you are dying in ignorance. When you look so unhappy in singing, in walking, parading with each other, then know you are dying. You have never heard the Light, you have never seen the Light, and you have what? Intellectually considered the Light, which of course is doing what? Putting it in death clothes, when you are putting it through the personalization bombardment, which is inevitable death.

One of the great evidences of today's engagement on the Path is the number who intellectually perceive Oneness but who haven't realized the State. This is why so many errors are made because personalization is still there and the ego so present that it keeps "you" on the go.

The ego still present can do nothing but make an impression. The ego so present can only have moments when a future state can be perceived. But you see, "present" allows all that seems to be to be given back, to be given down, to be lifted up, to go sideways. No. That is the way the unliberated state sees the coming and going of a Promise and terms it an Incarnation of Light.

I have never left what I AM, I have never become what I AM not, but due to the vacillations of your nature you have only been a vassal instead of an applicant in the Wisdom of I. When the Wisdom of I reveals Itself as I AM, it is an intuitive prompting to be free to self-exculpate from the alleged syndrome of familiarity.

The old farewell, "God be with you until we meet again," is only a consolation to the desolate, to the tent-flappers, to the worshipers in the temples made with hands; but to the one who knows that Man is the Living Temple, then Man is the pulsating Wonder approached, and in appearance the tonal, the oral, and the auric embrace felt, energized, and appropriated according to your credentials: "Who goes there? For God seems to walk in your shoes. Why?" "Watch!"

Do you have a choice? Only when you think you are in the becoming. I AM not a choice. If I were, I would be like a menu for time, but I live under the Law of Man and that is how the Law of Man takes care of men like "you."

This brings to a conclusion these remarks from this plane which are offered for those who have assembled in the semblance of form in order, in rhythm, and in harmony so that a space lab will bear the scent of the Sage and be found a constant companion beyond the "mess" way of time.

The Ship of Soul is only tilled as one perceives what constitutes it; assembled, it becomes a glistening skull of Wonder with no glass chin, for it has opened to the pouring forth of what man terms the Refreshing Fire of those who would cry, "I thirst!"

Thank you.

I'm just the same. The only difference: I was speaking and telling you about where I AM, but I had to keep the camera very steady as I used the magnifying lens to try to appropriate those scenes of architectural significance within the jargon of your language that would allow you to familiarize yourself with something beyond the tree of knowledge and of limitation. This is how your strings are attuned and pitched to the Wonders of "I Love Wondrous Light!"

Do you expect to be the same?

April 21, 1991

---

1 Proverbs 29:18.
2 This Unfoldment was given to several locations via a telephone conference call, and the operator had said that the lines to one of the parties on the conference were down. Mr. Mills refused to accept the thought that this could be true; subsequently, the line was found open.
3 One level of meaning here is a reference to the captain of the Starship *Enterprise* in the television series *Star Trek*. Another reference might be to the Scots word for "church."
4 I.e., personal might.
5 See Chapter X, "A Shift in Identity."
6 John 1:14.
7 2 Corinthians 5:1.
8 As the corresponding identity of an idea.
9 See the poem "Father, Son and Basket," in Kenneth G. Mills, *The Beauty Unfoldment* (Toronto: Sun-Scape Publications, 1977), pp. 25-27.

IX

THE ROUND OF VIBRATION

Your work is a planetary one, in one way, because your planet is this place that has happened as a result of your agreement to visit this matter. You brought it into experience and that's why you are on it.

THE ROUND OF VIBRATION

As we attune ourselves to the pitch of the vibrating cymbals, we allow movement to happen within the various layers of our experience as Conscious Being. We are considering, with what may be termed in time considerable depth, the exigencies which surround a mechanized society, moving with such speed to its future evolutionary involvement with its own dressed-up, camouflaged limitations and lack of the Energy. That Energy is commensurate with the deeper layers of Being in order for the said social encounter to be capable of stemming such an ensuing force of destruction . . it is imperative, especially for you!

For you will be, to all appearances, fructifying the future with the Wonders of your experience in Presence. You will be so well camouflaged that it will take many days, months, and years of exposure to the correct climate of preparation for those to perceive what you have to offer. For you do have much to offer, but until called upon it remains in abeyance, and by doing so allows you to survive in a semblance that is termed a normal, social encounter.

As your uniqueness is more readily perceived, your demands will be more readily received. For your demands cease to be those that are on the surface level of the skin engagement. They will be the demands that are corresponding to a deeper level of the needs, the penchants that are inherent within the deeper levels of the world's Soul.

The world's Soul is, we are told, in dire need. It is because we are perched precariously on the edge of an incredible happening, the happening of increased and speedy mechanicality and robotery, and on the edge of an accelerating force that is being fanned by the needs of the derived self to find its meaning. The shift for such a change is gigantic, demanding, and dangerous because you are no longer dealing with the philosophical aphorisms and subtle statements that have permeated the pages of time; you are dealing now with an Energy Field that is once again precipitating into your cognitive realm the enhanced Standards of a super-organization and a super-consideration of how it shall be achieved.

With the magnification of a superstructure socially, culturally, and economically, we are dealing with one of the most subtle and serious levels the world has ever encountered. You are right in the midst of it. It is fraught with upset, it is fraught with challenges, and it is fraught with the demands for the individual to meet the required fields of energy needed for change. It takes a tremendous amount of seriousness to alter your present state and to bring about a new paradigm. This new paradigm has to be achieved through the practice, perhaps, of adoration; by the practice of perceiving the very forces that are attempting to keep you locked into the pattern of similarity, that are enwrapped within the syndrome that has come to be considered the derived self and its formidable propensities. You will now see that this paradigm and this great shift is all relevant unto Identity.

The identity crisis is really the basic root question in the world today, and the world today doesn't take time to notice it. But it constantly brings up the matter in the form of various disguises. The unsteadiness, the scatteredness, the sleepiness, the attempt to be always on the go and always bringing up matters that have nothing whatsoever to do with the Structure of Being and its Truths are the evidence of a tattered mental society that is deteriorating rapidly into the stream of an emptiness and a society that is as empty as its words. Remember that what is heard is a sound experience, and this reverberates within the auditory realm of your attentiveness.

When you are inclined to bend your ear to hear the Voice of the Speaker, it is because somewhere within the derived self is the inexplicable urge to free itself from what it does not know. It does not need to know; it is only a presumed situation anyway and that is why the derived self with all its complexities uses its very complexities as a force of upset, discouragement, and disarray to point to its need for exculpation from your considerations. The small self was never given to be explained. The small self is the way we have come to name the happening of what appears to be the birth in matter.

Now everyone can bring up the matter in many different ways, but it is never the matter which is first. There never has been first matter and then this consideration of a new paradigm. Matter never came first, no matter how much of it was piled up. What came first has always been and always will be a Consciousness; for without it the matter could not be named matter and you would not be able to ascribe to it the properties that you now ascribe to it and try to solve through the very ascribing process. This is why we are engaged in an economy that is almost worthless because we are trying to arrive at a scientific explanation of our own invention. Consequently, it is seemingly a worthless endeavor to have spent your time trying to become a scientist, and, through your analysis, to have realized that you were not primarily matter to begin with; you were a Conscious Being or a Conscious State, and this beingness which you seem to be is only a small portion of that Totality of Consciousness which you chose to accept and utilize in this form of a matter encounter. It could not have been matter that came with the Big Bang. The Big Bang is the result of realizing that the matter situation is a construct of the imagination from a false standpoint of identification.

You see that the Universal Cosmic Consideration is so gigantic that unless you have a correct Point of View you are going to have that of the worm. You see, the worm's point of view is only one of a greatly limited nature. Unfortunately, so many who are in the offices today have a worm's-eye view: they plow through the subterranean ways to work; they plow through to their various little chambers of their underground caverns and call them the offices, all lighted by the artifical lights bearing no transformative power whatsoever. You see, the worm's-eye view is what enhances a society that needs to be dewormed. You talk about your dogs and your animals being dewormed; we have the worm society in our thoughts!

Most of our thoughts move so slowly that they create a possibility for other growths to happen. This slowness of thought is exactly what happens when you plod your thought through a matter situation as if it were real. The plodding thought through matter accumulates the debris of a nature that could appear bulbous or cancerous. That is why the society of today is on, you might say, a global scale, because of accumulating incoherent mass. This incoherent mass is a random energy, selfish energy, just as false identification gives you a random encounter with life, time, and soul. It gives you an accumulation of data that is falsely based upon an assumption that you are "this" with an external life span of seventy-eight years. But you see, when you take away the layers of this type of thinking, which you might call the epidermis of the mind, then you delve to another tissue, subcutaneous tissue, whereby you can perceive that there is more to the surface appearance than just this vibrating skin of humanity.

You are into a rhythmic force field that is obviously beating in rhythm with a universal cosmic involvement, or you are in a force field that is indeed involving in a comedy of idiots. When people are so capable of being educated today, it is too bad that they bring up matter as if it were something to be explained away. They should proceed to perceive that what came first was not matter; *Consciousness must have existed for matter to be even given an existence! Therefore it is a derived state under the same possibility of freedom as your derived self! This is your Teaching for the future!* If you are half asleep and half awake you will never perceive the effulgent Nature of this Force Field which is beckoning all those who are tuned to a cognitive pattern due to an enhancement of the paradigms for the future.

The tendency of so many today is to sit and think they are metaphysicians and they are on the Path. Well, what is "on the Path" is an intellectual pursuit using metaphysical terminology with the same end: death. In other words, an annihilation of the ability to maneuver the form for others to witness. Without consciousness the form is devoid of meaning. That is why death is witnessed by another form. Otherwise there could be what? The mystical thing termed translation, and right where you sat there was only the glow because you transcended and you left no trace; no body was found.

If no body was found, then:

Nobody knows the Wonder I've seen;
Nobody knows my gladness.
For all the world goes round and round
Singing about "nobody knows my sadness."

Nobody knows the trouble I've seen;
Nobody knows my sorrow.
But nobody knows the Wonders to Be
When the Body found is seen all glorious.

The Body that is pulsating with Wonder is the one that is imbued with a synergy that is far from the level of being low. You know, it tells us to "Swing low, Sweet Chariot, coming for to carry *you* home." Swing low, Sweet Chariot. How come? Do you feel that the Chariot of the Sun is going to allow that ark to take you to your heavenly home, when you have denied the possibilities of searching out and living in the Rapture of Being?

You can't expect a marvel, a miracle, a grace to descend, if you don't understand that the need to understand is secondary to acceptance. It is a totally fallacious state in which to be involved, when you have to understand in order to become a member of a said group or an unsaid group. A group is the name that is given to more than three people gathered together, supposedly with the same purpose or goal. A low synergy exists when the components that constitute a conclave have varying what? Goals. For then, incoherent waves are present on the deeper levels of your formation.

Remember, your formation is covered. That is why what is beneath your vibrating skin is concealed from the hammering of suggestion of the time-space continuum. For remember, it is not empty space; it is the magnetized force that allows the transmissions of energy to be synergized by a corresponding fork or point of attunement that is set in vibration as you attune yourself to the Wonders of a Cosmic Field, undefined and therefore undefiled by your mental analysis. This is why the meek shall inherit the earth.[1]

Now the meek are those who accept without judgment and allow themselves to be dismembered. Now, what does it mean to be dismembered? It means to remember your fragments. Your nature in Essence is fragmented and education tries to solve the problem of fragmentation! But the basis of your fragmentation is not known by most educators! Most educators are what? Speaking from a doctored-up, derived selfhood. Most educators do not realize that the derived situation of today has you in its grip for so many years, and the more education you have, the more altering or brainwashing (in the All) is required.

Don't ever consider that you are going to hear words and find them acceptable if you have, at the time of hearing, a train of thoughts that are forever mesmerizing you as the wheels of your life go over the dualistic tracks of suggestion. The railroad tracks beat a rhythm, and it's so mesmeric; just hearing the recurring rhythm of the wheels on the tracks can put you to sleep. But what do you think puts you to sleep today? The recurring rhythm of the wheels of suggestion that are going around pushed by the need to sustain a derived selfhood, the root of a sluggish economy. An economy based on the derived self cannot help but be fluctuating: the root problem of the economic situation of the entire world![2]

You who have expertise in the economics that you have studied and are degreed in, this is your great opportunity to show the world through your study what you have arrived at in putting an end to economics, as it is practiced by the developed cleverness of minds that are capable of taking in anything and completely ignorant of a need for the Invisible Principle, the greatest Paradigm that can be offered to the Conscious Realm of those attuned to the Mystery of Life.

As we are calling forth those features that are essential for the enhancement of the spiritual pockets — your spiritual pockets — for what is termed man's future, it is very necessary for you to perceive that your pockets are being filled just by the attention you offer to this One. Your very pockets are being filled, but if you are still operating in the deluded mind syndrome of person, place, and thing, you are only receiving a small portion of the Energy which will enhance the whole situation and allow you to be re-energized for what you call the future days of your incarnation. You see, "what shall be" is what we do when we procrastinate and gradually see the will deteriorating, because in the Knowingness That IS there is no cause that is of consequence other than to allow the Be to be seen without question.[3]

When you perceive that Consciousness is fundamental, then matter will cease to play so many tricks upon your string of attention. You will not be that constant, vigilant spider, attempting to weave webs of connection in order to gain prey to satisfy you because it has walked on your terrain. You see, when someone moves in today's society, we fail to perceive the incredible, delicate, invisible web that is supported on the unseen level. Now we know it is there, and you know without doubt it is there, because if it were not there you would not be able to say you are hearing a man speak! That is the invisible web that is woven for your salvation! That web vibrates to the tiniest energy that touches it, because it comes from the interior of your suggested outwardness, and this interior responsiveness to these words is the very living evidence of the viability of an inner network web of vibrating Wonder!

You see, when you study in school, the information you receive goes onto one part of that web, and you weave around the impulses the information that corresponds to the impulse. It is the impulse that allows the correspondence; it isn't the correspondence that causes the impulse. Then there is another web, and another web, and another web, and these webs vibrate according to your ability to live beyond a psychic involvement with the superficial webs of "your" vibratory Essence.

It is this incredible web that allows this One to move so quickly into a stream of consideration that only facets of it have touched His Web, but it is that Bundle of Wonder and Love that allows that web to vibrate. These words are heard magnified millions of times so that it is an auditory experience. In Essence it is a pulsation, it is an emission that allows an enhancement of such force to penetrate your attention span, which may bear incoherent waves. Your attunement to this allows this penetration to enhance your incoherent waves, and you appear to be moved with the Wonder of the experience when it seems to have finished!

This is the incredible grace that is termed the root of "charismatic." Charisma is the ability to bestow Grace. And what is Grace? That ability that is beyond the intellect's approval, but allows itself to evidence itself as it moves to the various webs where you will respond in spite of your limited intellectual attainment.

You know within you there is an accuracy because the very thing you are trying to transcend, the derived self, is giving you the very energy that is necessary. It's giving you the necessary energy to destroy itself! So it is like so many creatures of nature that give birth and in giving birth destroy themselves so that they go on living. This is what you are doing. What is this pointing to on a deeper level? It is pointing to the great need for you to become at peace with the consideration that you are a Cosmic Consciousness or a Universal Consideration, a Galactic Experience.

An Undefinable Cosmic Consideration is only the name given to that which does not vibrate in the terminology that you are capable of translating into this portion of you that you have decided to inherit. You have come down from, you might say, the Round of Vibration that is All, and you have chosen this portion of that Allness that allows this portion of Presence to be experiencing this while the remainder of you is still in the Round vibrating, waiting for you to regain your round! This is why this whole experience of moving correctly is essential, because it really quickens the spirit so that the first death loses fear. The first death: do it now! Die! You die when you stop! and consider that this portion is of the Holiness that allows this particle to be endowed with Infinite Possibilities.

This is why we can say, "The possibilities are infinite."[4] Why is it said? Because "infinite" is the only word that can be utilized in a sound language, in sound, that allows you to enjoy a frequency that is beyond your comprehension. "Infinity" means nothing to you, only in comparison with the finite. "Infinity" is the name given to the Cosmic Round that is not skinned, therefore can never be personalized; IT can never be utilized from the standpoint of person.

This is why those who are Enlightened Beings know that their Wonder is because of the vibration that is emitted onto their web of constancy and coherency. That allows a Transmission over the distances to be assembled here again in the congregation where those who are dead would now find the living possibilities of exhuming their bodies from the minds of time and allowing themselves to be re-energized, reorganized, and redirected in a purposeful pursuit for the enhancement and the re-enchantment of the planet!

Your work is a planetary one, in one way, because your planet is this place that has happened as a result of your agreement to visit this matter. You brought it into experience and that's why you are on it. The world is not inside you; this matter world, this globe is not inside you. It is the result of a vibrant imagination. It takes the vital dynamics of an imagination to sustain this stage, and the part you play is what you have chosen to play, and since it is one hell of a mess, it shows you what education has done to you instead of for you.

Education should have freed you from this perspective of dimension and masses and allowed you to penetrate the suggested field and perceive the Wonders of a Diaphanous Nature. Oh, you say it is impractical? No! That is your education. You can say, "Oh, Mr. Mills, I just can't make heads or tails of him!" Well, I was never in a gamble. (Heads or tails, you win or lose.) You see, the only gamboling I have ever done is over the hillsides of time, wearing the various disguises. When man knows Man, he wears whatever is necessary to fulfill his swan dive, or his dove dive, or his eagle flight into the realm of perception.

You have such an incredible vehicle! How can you play the violin unless you have a master who made it? How can you make it sound, unless the master knew the sensitivity of the woods used, the shape of the woods, the density of the woods, the age of the woods, and the shape of the woods when once hewn into form? Why do you string it? Because without the strings you would not believe he was a master, because it is the tone of the instrument that says it's a Stradivarius; it's the evidence of a master craftsman. But you see, it's only a mark on the instrument and sometimes the tone of it that reveals the Essential Nature as Music.

Man is a Song! Why do I say this so much, if it is just "you" standing up and singing? A song is a melody that must bear a rhythm and a sequence of tones that is more than two or three in number, and they must bear within them the need and the fulfillment of that need. That is why notes played, put on paper at random, are forever chaotic.

This is why so much modern music is chaotic. You will understand why people should not visit the discotheques because, you see, even if you are involved in dancing in a discotheque, you must understand what the rhythms are doing, not to the superficial. What level are you responding to when you allow the rhythm to utilize your form to move in agreement with it?

What you enact is what you become. Do you wish to become a saint? Then behave as one — but don't think as one. If you behave as a saint, you will at least be taking the right steps to be ordained. You must have taken the right steps, either you could never have been termed a saint. But it takes a long time for one to become a saint. In fact, it's other people who say one is a saint, and a saint is always dead. That is why a saint worshiped demands such a vital imagination. When you worship a statue or a symbol of a saint, it demands such a vital and dynamic imagination in order to imbue the object with your imagination and what it must have been like to know the saint. But what you give unto the saint is what you are. The saint has only what? The image of color on an ancient wall.

What do you suppose the cryptograms and all the symbols on the walls of caves — like the Canyon de Chelly, the petroglyphs which the Anasazi left as their inheritance — are there for? What have they done to you? They have triggered something in you, for you try to explain them.

I passed the Singers a card yesterday and I said, "What does it say?" They told me what the card said. I said, "The card didn't say that. Where did that information come from?" The card was a piece of blue paper with black ink on it, and they told me it said something! Where did the information come from? "You look at your music; look at your music, look at your black dots on a piece of paper." They say, "Oh, hear the sounds!" Where did that information come from? Oh, it's much greater than you think. It's the most provocative question!

What do you call that? A cup and saucer. Where did the information come from? The cup and saucer didn't say it was a cup and saucer. What do you call this? A body. Where did that information come from? He's not saying, "I'm a body; I'm a body; I'm a body." It's only coming through the rye that you say that. In other words, you're drunk with it. "When a body meets a body coming through the rye," you know? Then a body greets a body and says, "Oh, brother, I cry. I've got such a hangover." Where did the information come from that has caused you such intoxication? You are drunk with ignorance! This is why you die; it's getting rid of the hangover. Oh, yes!

Death is getting rid of the hangover if you are drunken with the phenomenal, space-time, horizontal experience.

Death from another point, from the Eagle's point of view, is the period in which the curtain falls on your act so that others may evidence what you have demonstrated for those who demand a demo in order to be interested in your performance.

You think that the Path is filled with options. It is only filled with options as long as you base your life on relatives. Born with, die without. Your life is filled with options as long as you consider it *your* life, *your* car, *your* house. As soon as you possess it and revel in the possession, you are dancing to the rhythm of a mental, destructive discotheque. It beats a false rhythm to the heart.

Why do people love to go and dance? Because the body is freed to appear totally free of a prescribed movement and action. Modern dance allows you to worm your way, frug your way, climb your way, do anything you please, as long as it is in rhythm with the mesmeric beat of the drums and of the sounds. Remember, sounds that you like are the ones that stop you from having to consider your emptiness. Classical music, baroque music, impressionistic music, romantic music, all call upon various webs of your sensitive nature's response to sound. Why do I say, "The sensitive nature's response to sound?" Because remember, the Essence of Conscious Being is Energy, capable of being perceived as a particle emitting light.

Why do you think people meditate? Because those who agree to meditate in a certain way free themselves from the patterns of thought that are in keeping with everyday necessities. They become a different wave that can be perceived. Now can that wave be passed to another? It can't. But, you see, the wave is like this great Ocean of Consciousness; it's a conductor. What is thought on a level that isn't chaotic is perceived by another. This is why, when coherency comes to a group of meditators, it is said that their influence is felt.

There have been experiments with two groups of meditators, a first and a second group, each of which meditated in different parts of the world. Through experiments it was found out that the actual body's response was altered when the second group was not meditating, and didn't know when the first group was meditating. Due to the same goal, the first group meditating could actually affect the second group, which could be measured on instruments, and they were over three thousand miles apart. There is no distance to thought.

So you wonder why this group is set apart from the other group? This group is vibrating at a different speed from the other group. Why is it vibrating at a different speed? Because there is more innate, spontaneous acceptance and expectation. When these are present, the Enhancement of Force is perceived and appears as the change from a low synergy to a high synergy.

A high-synergy society is one in which those who are present as the components of the situation have agreed to have the same purpose, the same goal, and the same expectations. This is the secret to a vitalized society, and one capable of being experienced by not only those in it, but by those who perceive it. This is why this small group is capable, due to the coherency of pattern that has been established by your attention, of altering people all over your projected world.

This is why you should stop talking about people in a negative way. You should keep your mouths shut unless you are offering those thoughts that are going to enhance the deeper, responsive web-natures of Light. Because, you see, felt is always used on the strings to dampen them. Feeling, personalized, is a damper on your strings of genuineness! Personal feeling is a damper on the strings of genuine feeling because genuine feeling will never allow personal feelings to submerge the genuine.

This is why, when you are genuine, the superficial feelings are really tremulous. Why is it that people who are too active with the tongue are those who have to be watched? Why do we say "watched"? What happens? You say something that isn't accurate, isn't kind, and it starts moving on a web similar to it. What are you doing? If the correct words are utilized, you are utilizing the very force of the underived Self to free the inaccurate and unkind.

When you die, it doesn't mean you have lost your individuality. It means your individuality is blossoming as never before! Your uniqueness is Self-evident and your accomplishment can't help but be cognized.

If you are considering what is the matter with me — "What is the matter with Mr. Mills?" "I don't understand this matter of Mr. Mills at all." "I don't understand why Mr. Mills did this or Mr. Mills did that." "I'm so worried about Mr. Mills and his matter." — this is saying that Mr. Mills is matter; and Mr. Mills is not matter, he is Sound, dressed up as this note on your staves of awareness.

I hang, somewhat like the baby in the cradle,[5] suspended between Mr. Bass Clef and Mrs. Treble Clef, who never did marry but had this common child, the one conceived in the cradle. When Mrs. Treble Clef needs the baby, he goes up in his cradle and stays closer to Mrs. Treble Clef and all her children; and when Mr. Bass Clef needs him, he goes down and stays closer to Mr. Bass Clef and all of his children. But he never loses his identity. He has the ability to come and go to whatever level is needed in order to stabilize the viewpoint of reading the Score beyond the ledger lines of belief.

No wonder it is stated that when you see the Truth of Being face to face, it is a fearsome thing, for you have to die!

Isn't it amazing . . Grace to see, to hear, and to find that Life and its Truths are not optional, and right where you sit is Holy Ground![6]

Thank you.

April 28, 1991

---

1 Matthew 5:5.
2 See "Be Still," in Kenneth G. Mills, *A Word Fitly Spoken* (Toronto: Sun-Scape Publications, 1977), pp. 40-42.
3 I.e., the question "to be or not to be?"
4 See Kenneth G. Mills, *The Quickening Spirit of Radiance* (Toronto: Sun-Scape Publications, 1990), p. 27.
5 Middle C on the music staff.
6 Exodus 3:5.

X

A SHIFT IN IDENTITY

Identity is the crisis that men and women face today. Of course, this is all being said as if this crisis were real!

A SHIFT IN IDENTITY

We need a great shift in our pattern of identity from that of the egotistical self involvement to that of what is termed "the Divine Self," which must be actualized or which must be made practical.

To leave a thing actual, it can become purely a scientific left-brain syndrome which rules the world, generally speaking, and has it on this incredible sped-up movement towards more and more involvement with the things and the need for things and the need for changing things in order for the thing that is always changing to be evaded in its quixotic nature, and it evades detection as being the very thing that is holding you in this merry-go-round of chasing after things.

As you become more and more aware of what is Real, then you become more and more aware that the things of time are those very things that will seduce you into believing you are a timed being and consequently giving yourself over to being bombarded by its limitations.

The whole purpose of any Teaching, the whole purpose of any Message of the Highway of the Light, is to bring to the attention of those who are an audience an opportunity to witness to a form and yet a Way of Life that may not be formed but yet is known to be experienceable, because it is the Standpoint from which I come and from which you come in Essence. It is not translatable into verbology, but what is translatable is the intention of what Life is in That Place from which I originate. The Actuality of That is found in the ever-increasing crescendo of the Power that is termed the magnetism that surrounds the heart chakra.

Remember that there is but one Divine Attraction, and that has been termed Love by Mary Baker Eddy.[1] No matter who said it, it is a fact; and IT is the One Permeating Effulgence that holds us in ITs embrace even if we ignore the demands of ITs Actual Nature.

Love is not something that is capable of being adapted to human needs; Love is not a condition of a human. That is why the Love That IS is the great Balm of the Light, because it embraces what appears to be the antithesis of it until the antithesis is given over to the transformatory experience which is revealed when identity shifts from the ego to the Self.

You can't expect the ego bound to Earth and matter to have any semblance of the understanding of an Infinite Gestalt of Being. You can't expect to penetrate the Infinite from the standpoint of an energized, finite, intellectual aggrandizement. In fact, the greater the achievement in the intellect, usually we find the greater the contest in the competition of who will win in the battle between the intellectual and the Conscious Being — at a bulge. The great bulge, the Battle of the Bulge, has much more to do with the over-inflated ego than it does with the vibrating pulse of a high synergy commensurate with the rhythmic pulsations of the Heart.

Your head will always try to indite the Message and try to analyze the Message, and thus allow the Message to be an analyzed, intellectual experience. But, in actuality, when you alter the thought-structures and assume the stance of being one willing to carry the new type of armament against the intrusion of the egotistical propensities, then you perceive that the great Battle of Armageddon is not in the future; you're "geddin'" it right in the head when you try to mix the two components that do not work together in a healthful way!

Today there is such a penchant for a holistic approach to life, and it is well to consider it. However, most people tend to think it has to do with a cleanse and supplements and a continuation of the old way of life with the belief system that is new to the custodian of the holistic theory. However, when men and women perceive that wholeness is not necessarily bound up with one facet of experience, they will see that it has to do with the whole concept of body, mind, and Soul.

So, holistic practice is not just a practice of cleansing the body and revitalizing it by proper diet and supplementing it with the essential ingredients which are missing, due (perhaps) to an over-processed food supply — intellectual, physical, and mental, you know? It has to do with being healthy in body, mind, and Soul. Well, you can easily take a cleanse and all kinds of colonics, and fast for as long as you like, and meditate for as long as you like, but as soon as you "no like," then you are still what you aren't anyway!

This is where the Soul comes into it. Soul is one of the most elusive constructs of the intellectual ability of men because it is the name that is given to the most ephemeral aspect of consideration. It has to be restored to its rightful place of viability in the lives of each and every inhabitant as soon as possible because without it we are not vibrating in the Spirit of Wonder. After all, the door is only opened by Wonder, with the key of attention to Principle as the means of reducing the belief in a skeleton occupation and the belief of being hung on it to an end that is capable of being transcended right while you appear to be hung on the skeleton of suggestion.

Remember, the skeleton of time is the calcified conditions of the thought-form that identified "you" with the structure that you deemed necessary to experience this gestalt of three dimensions and its confinement. And yet, you have the ability to entertain the unconfined and the unfettered conditions which can be acquired when you are willing to adopt a new allegiance to Principle, not to person, and to an Ideal that may be able to be elucidated as its intentions are perceived, yet never experienceable through the mental and articulated modes of expression. It can't be done.

For you to receive Enlightenment is to be capable of attuning yourself to a Mystery of a Being that in Essence you are, freed from any reference to one who is going to be freed.

The whole purpose of a great Teacher such as Jesus the Christ is that He gave, unto those who could perceive, an Initiation into the Higher Way of men if they could perceive His Activity. He gave himself up to the cross of belief in order to wipe it out through the tears of sorrow that were shed when it was believed that He had been forsaken. *It was the tear that evidenced the falling apart of the false sense of Soul and its encrustations.*

> The Soul is that aspect of Being that allows itself to be
> experienced as the pulsating Power
> That allows "this" to have a new natal hour.

If the Self, or the Christ-Self, was evidenced by that recent Master, it could not have been in vain, for it has filled the pages of time that men and women are the image and likeness of the Divine. But why would you image after a vain God set up in a temple of intellectuality?

The God of Enlightenment and the Enlightened God is One that is Self-evidenced in simplicity. One Master said that the mark of the Enlightened God is spontaneous simplicity. Simplicity is the ingredient that is so missing in today's world, because if we are not compound, complex in our sentences and in our statements, the mind is so honed that it will not consider what is being said unless the statements are convoluted, obtuse, and demand probing! You have been led to believe that you have to probe to "find the gold in them there hills," or you do not have the essential ingredient to offer in the exchange when you would exchange an object of sense for an Idea that could not be bound by it.

So, identity is the crisis that men and women face today. Of course, this is all being said as if this crisis were real! But you are being sort of seduced into a state of questioning your seductive natures and your tendency to attract unto you all those conditions that will support your position just as it seems to be. You seldom venture into that circle where your position is ever looked upon with a sense of doubt.

I look upon your position as very doubtful, as very fractured and very much inundated with your personal attainments. Of course, this is, in some cases, considered "sanctified territory," and no one on the outside should ever start to belittle your achievement! No achievement is belittled; it is only asked that you look at it in the light of how you are viewing it: as an ego endowed with the entity's going on, or the Presence that allows the Eternal God Omnipotent to have presence in you as a Living Power.

If you accept that "I and My Father are One Now and not shall be,"[2] then you accept a wonderful statement, because it stops the manufacturing process of needs. The whole economy of the world today is built upon satisfying the needs of the errant mind. The whole solution to today's economy is the realization that the needs of the errant mind are only apparent; and as soon as you cease to be one, then what becomes (arises) is the artistry of your Being becoming a full-fledged Power in your peregrinations through this suggested time-space continuum.

To feel the pulsating Power of Being allows another who is present in attention to be endowed with a sense of an increase of presence, sometimes defined as an increase of energy.

Now, it has been proved that in a low synergistic society there is much dis-ease, there is much need; and yet in a high synergistic society, the need is not nearly as great because it seems that when there is high energy there is no room for dis-ease to enter. So, when you see disease so apparent in peoples today, then you realize a very important point: they have allowed themselves to be penetrated by a virus that is contaminated as a belief system, instead of charged with the enhancement of realization that comes with correct Identity.

The shift in identity from being human to Being Divine is just the willingness to flip the coin of the constructed will from side to side. The coin of the will on the personal side is "I will do it come hell or high water — but tomorrow." The other side is "I will — now!" One is procrastinated; the other one is instantaneous! There are not two sides to the question. The question that "there are two sides" is because the Quest has been personalized and you have your little "i" dot and the "on" forever moving on with your ego: "ego-on."

Your "ego-on" is the unknown disease of constant activity with no fulfillment other than a paycheck which seduces you into thinking you have achieved something. Usually you are paid for dying, giving up so much of your life to satisfy the economy of someone who's tracing it as a corporate empire. Remember, corporations aren't succeeding today because they are not spiritually endowed. A spiritually endowed corporation is one that is enlightened, and can appear as a man.

So, a man that is enlightened is a living Corporation incorporating all the venues that are essential to the fulfillment of an Ideal that is vitalized and "dynamitized" by the relinquishment of a false standard of operation.

You see, the Path of the Uncontradictable would put an end to the seduction of advertising the need for something you have no need for. Do you realize the television and the ads in the newspaper never tell you that you are asleep?! There's not one ad, not one television program that tells you you are asleep. They just try to electrify your projections as if they were outside of you and allow them to appear on a tube, or on a printed page, or in the atmosphere as impulses heard by the ear.

A Shift in Identity

Do you realize they sell newspapers in order to get your attention to find out what's going on in the outside world? Do you realize there's no newspaper capable of being published about what is Real? Because what is Real is so instantaneous that as soon as it's printed it's old history, and that has to do with your dream state.

History, remember, is the child that was born out of the mind's obstinacy in giving up fulfilling something it wanted to do and never did complete — the source of karma?

History is really the evidence of the mind's inability to satisfy itself with its own intention and purposes! The mind has never a complete intention or a complete purpose because it has never been given the basic ingredient: that it is not of itself capable of bestowing Godhood or Prime Creative Activity.

The Godhood that is forever worshiped until I come is that Godhood which is believed to be capable of being understood from the standpoint of an outsider. The Godhood doesn't exist outside! The Godhood is a construct of the mind which recognizes its own incompleteness but knows there is the possibility of completeness and it's termed "God."

Men and women have gone on for centuries creating gods to be worshiped. Why? Because outside, they believe, the God is to be found. They did not know, through the symbology, that the God that they were to find was within their very own experience without the need of being made like the worshiper.

You can't expect to know the Mystery of God from the self-obvious absurdity of "you"! "You" are so absurd, and obtuse, and complex, because you camouflage your lack by the "tinsel-ized" thoughts that surround you in success in the corporate structure, which is really failure in the Light Structure, because the corporate has to be disposed of.

Why do you think the corporate structures are failing? It's because there are some people like you who are considering the Authentic Nature! The Authentic Nature starts to perceive the seductiveness of the production of outside stimuli appearing as needs.

Everything that you think you need is because you have been trained to think that it is outside yourself. But everything you know allows the thinker and its friend, the believer, to be disposed of having any supremacy in your life. When you know you know, you know you know; but when you think you think, you go on thinking you think, and believing you have "thunk"! By believing you have "thunk," you meet the bottom of the tank!

Everyone today is going to "think tanks" for new ideas on how to keep a business going on, when the whole purpose of Being is to put a stop to the belief of process. That is the craft — leave it to cheese! Processed cheese: it's worthless. It just gums you up, and you need then to consider holistic medicine!

You see, when you know that you have the ability to BE right where you appear to be, you can actually live a totally different experience, while the man sitting right beside you may be living an experience totally unlike yours. Right where you sit can be Holy Ground. That Holy Ground is the basis of the Knowingness that you are a Conscious Being, and the awareness allows you to perceive what the Light of Consciousness is showing your awareness is doing either for or to you or against you.

You are your own worst adversary because you usually work with the supposition that you have a relative state in which you are bound as a result of the "apparents." The "apparents" are those who claim your attention because they said you pained them for deliverance, so they have a right to your allegiance because they birthed their pain as you. That is what a child is: an attempt to prolong the suggestion of Life's "continuity." But that is putting Life into a sequential mode, and Life as IT IS is a constant experience of Nowness, Self-satisfying and Self-complete.

What do we do? We think because we have Ph.D.'s and Mus. Bac.'s and B.Sc.'s that we're going to be better equipped to get on P.D.Q. with the solution of the suggested problem of Being. There is no problem with Being, other than with the counterfeit suggestion that is termed being. You can always tell a counterfeit, because when you study the Real, the counterfeit always is self-revealed.

If you notice in banks today, they'll call in a special teller to tell you whether you're passing off counterfeit hundred-dollar bills.

The average teller doesn't spend any time studying the Real. That's why there are so many false tellers, because a false teller will have you a follower of all the symbolic passages.

When you look at a newspaper and you read your books — as I showed you last week: I gave you a piece of paper and you told me what was on it. All I saw on it was ink! My word, you insisted that you read something! You said, "Mr. Mills, of course it's on it!" I said, "Of course it isn't on it!" If what you gave was on it, you'd never use it for lighting a fireplace. What was on it bore no resemblance to the sound you gave it. None! Then where was the information?

Well, if the mind can be triggered by ink on a piece of paper to translate information at sight, why not claim the same ability to look at the object and to translate it immediately? Then what do you realize? That you are informed that it is the mind that is separating us, but in the Heart we are One. Then tell me if you're going to be fighting for your own case — always projected into a future . . tense, or a subjunctive mood, and then trying to decline.

What is the purpose of having so many verbs in your language if you don't know what the essential verb means? To BE . . or not to be? That's no longer a question! That was the whole point of "Shakey"![3] He tried to spear your whole shield with that statement. He tried to make you realize the ludicrous nature of thinking you are this, when you know you are That; thinking allows you to *appear* to be this when you know you are That.

This is where, when you have reached the State where you can confront the suggestion that you are this, and claim the Indestructible Man, Male-Female-One, then it is a Conscious State which brings about such synchronistic events that the intelligent mind is totally confused, befuddled, because the Enlightened State allows the confluence of streams to happen that the thought mind cannot even place in a stream, even a brooklet.

The real movement is not to be considered necessarily objectified to prove Reality; Reality, you might say, is the rhythmic movement that allows sense to appear to be swallowed up in Nonsense and appear to be the magnetic quality that men in the becoming have termed "Love" and, in the Knowing, appeared as its inevitable result.

In the beginning was Love thought to be attraction, but in the end it was seen as at the beginning, that it never was other than what IT IS: That Force that allows you to think that you are this, while I AM That.

Why would you attempt to consider the Wonders of God Being when you can't even create a worm? Yet Some One did. That Oneness is that Consciousness that allows the simplest, unexplained, not understood portion of movement to be perceived as a worm. It itself is like the sunbeam; it can break the intellectual impasse and allow you to see right through the pane/pain of suggestion.

Einstein was questioned by a young man who was faced with an intellectual impasse. The young man walked into the garden with Dr. Einstein and looked at his cherry tree. Being a very bright young man, he said to the bushy-haired one, "How do I know that it's a tree?" Einstein said, "You don't; but you have to assume something." As long as you don't know, you have to assume something. But when you do know, what is there to be assumed? There is nothing but the Fire that allows the whole change to happen.

You see, a low synergy is the result of a chaotic wave pattern; and a high synergy is the result of a wave pattern that is in agreement with a High Ideal. When those patterns can become more coherent and be interrupted by a spear or a Ray of Wonder, this shakes the very foundations of your experience and allows you to experience such a re-enhancement of Force that you appear recharged for the encounter with the Tournament that is to be played beyond that of the Roses.

You must understand that it is essential to accept without understanding that you are Conscious Being and, for time, appearing to be a human endowed with inalienable rights. You have the ability (it is obvious) to have engaged this planet, and since it is such a far-fetched tale, you think it has come through the womb of time and its tunnel. But in actuality that is the way the mind describes That Which IS impossible to delineate from this Place from which I speak. It is inexplainable, save through the fabrication of the mind's warp, due to time and space. But That Which IS the Fact to the picture bears the intention and the ability to penetrate your attention and allow you to rejoice with what appears as me in the undefined and yet very definite Character of Being Spontaneous Simplicity.

The Enlightened State is yours if you stop looking elsewhere for it. Don't even look under your nose; it's closer than that!

The joy of Being is unconfined;
The belief of time has you codified.
The joy of Being wraps the mind
In the cocoon of Light, and there it binds
All thoughts to One, and One in Act
Gives you a day of Light, and that is Fact.

Enjoy the Being, unconfined,
And you find the shackles of the mind
Drop and tinkle, as tears to the ground
Are traced as a cloud, which yields its unknowing
        when I is found.

Enjoy the Fact and let fiction fail
To seduce you into its earthbound wail.
And then you will see, as you escape the course,
The unconscious sea, for the whale of sorts
Gives you now the chance to stand on Holy Ground,
And the perennial Facts of Being are revealed:
        I unbound!

What a wonder to perceive that the door is opening and the sulphured cloud is only the counterfeit to the One that is blazoned in Golden Light.

Yours is a day not of prophecy, but yours is a day that the Lord hath made, the Law hath made, and the Law is written in the Heart. Love is the fulfilling of the Law.

To procrastinate is the onset of the deterioration of the will, and to exalt is the enhancement of the Melody that will bind all hearts when men and women cease to see many in the face of One.

In One I see how I can appear to multiply the many facets of my Being, while the Gestalt of Allness cannot in any way be temporalized, finite-ized, or externalized, for it is beyond all limits, and the mind's concept is that That Which IS is Infinite.

Now this is yours and no one can take it from you. If you live one sentence of it, you will find how tense it is and you will decline any suggestion of being taken from your High Estate.

Dance in the Wonder and know that the Rhythm of Love is always a waltz, for it will take you as a partner into its arms and embrace not only the great stage which we call the Earth, but it will also allow the Light to shine in such a way that others will see you spontaneously declining from being other than the present experience of the Great Verb "to BE." It needs no object and this will bless your commerce and your finance; it needs only Presence to allow another to perceive the Wonder of the I.

Until I see you again, we will consider it another chance happening in the future called tomorrow, next week when I return and you return, knowing that "I.O.U." is the Infinite Omnipotent Universal Self on demand.

It would be my wish to continue but the demand is to stop,
For we must fly to satisfy that which is believed to be
happening in a time slot.

Can you believe it? This had to be the moment, in order to arrive on time![4] How we pretend to satisfy all the needs . . by never giving in to them! If you think you are giving in to a need, you'll never satisfy it. The only Satisfaction comes from knowing that there isn't a need; and the only Abundance that will be found is when I is declared not lost.

Listen more,
    look less
        at the object
            if you would be blessed.

Your eye dictates too much in today's world; I am heard much more easily than translated by appearing to be an Informant on the Actuality of your State.

The reason your eyes are focused is because then the mind does not wander. If you find you have roving eyes, know that you have roving thoughts. When you know you have no roving thoughts, always keep the blinds on your eyes because to look into the eyes when the thought is not roving is a powerful experience and should be one not indulged in just because you try to make an impression.

Remember, you're not in the act of making an impression; you are, as the experience, appearing as an Expression.

You are not a reflector; it can be shattered.
You are the reflection, but of course, never in it!
The mirror tells you that.

See you.

May 5, 1991

---

1   Mary Baker Eddy, *Science and Health with Key to the Scriptures* (Boston: Trustees Under the Will of Mary Baker G. Eddy, 1934), p. 293, l. 15.
2   Mr. Mills' restatement of John 10:30.
3   William Shakespeare.
4   Referring to Mr. Mills and The Star-Scape Singers' imminent departure for the airport to leave on a concert tour of Russia.

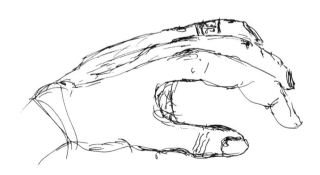

XI

THE MAJESTIC REMOTENESS

Yours is a world of your own making, your life is of your own doing, and your hope is present, if you are willing to be given to the Power of Wonder, Miracle, and Marvel so that the Superman and the State of Balance once again walk as some Holy experience.

THE MAJESTIC REMOTENESS

As we approach the riches of these moments of Soul preparation and reach into the Reservoir of Unlimited Power, Force, and
Strength, we view with Wonder this great enhancement of drama
that is being displayed upon the apron of time. We are geared to
answer the wish, spoken and unspoken, of that class which might
be called the Gentry of Light, to once again have an incomparable
experience of participating in a translated form of dressage when
the rider shall teach the body of horse once again how to be in
rhythm with the ensuing events of the pulse of the moments, when
men and women shall once again be orchestrated for the purposes
of *review*.

You are engaged as is one ready for a ceremony of marriage.
You are gathered from the far corners of this dramatic stage, and
you are selected by the Force of "your" Reality to question the
suppositional state in which you have found yourselves bred to the
stables of the mind.

You are the Custodians of a peculiar Force, a peculiar Light,
and a contradiction is only in the office of those who would say they
expect a direct answer to "What is Truth?" A contradiction
(paradox) can never be made other than in the *revealing* of Truth.
Everything that man seems to say he is, he isn't; and everything that
is unsaid, he IS. Yet the diversity and the multiplicity of the forms
and the variegated patterns of perception are not devoid of Reality,
for they could not exist if it were *not* for Reality.

So, the Absolute erases the engagement to a limited force field
and reveals one's ability to perceive the only Force Field that there
IS and find the practicality still available, because One may appear
to enjoy all that appears diversified in this dance of life and yet know
that in it he is not; out of it he could be *thought* to be; but as he IS,
he is neither described nor circumscribed nor *ephemerized* by the
mind and its space-time necessities.

You who are gathered together at this invisible place, beyond
this place, must know that we have leapt into a Region beyond the
trivialities of your mind's enhancement with time. You are at that

Point where it is so grand that it is like the stillness in the eye of the hurricane. For if you are to be a benefactor of the audience which demands your presence, then you must be one capable of utilizing the language that must come first before a Silence can be readied for your experience. The words should lead you to where there are none, and in that moment, then Silence is, of course, the benediction upon your state of receptivity.

Re-member, and you will find that yesterday is today. Yesterdays have constituted the *actual* current of events in which you are attempting to celebrate a Ceremony of Remembrance when the tongues shall be emblazoned beyond the dreamt solutions of the puzzle of time and reveal that the whole point of the Flame is to rescind the objective confinement and allow the ash to be worn as a symbol of the opening of a vision where the vision is not one of a visionary.

You perceive that the great Feasts that have passed from generation to generation are the past coming into the Now, and this is why it is imperative to purify your past by allowing it to pass through the Fire of the Now. The reason the Fire of the Now is present is because all that isn't is given to the Flame of Perception, and all that *shall* be is revealed as the Golden Light that allows each and every one to perceive the transcendent nature of the pattern of awareness when it is wedded or is betrothed to the Conscious State that is forever the Bridegroom waiting to be cognized.

Remember, the whole purpose of any Teacher, the whole purpose of any encounter with a Truth, is to prepare for a Marriage. It has been said that a Guru is really a matchmaker, and I would say that is so true, because a true Guru always knows the emery board is necessary in order to set the chemicalized head on fire! When you strike your head with the limitations surrounding its calcified state, you realize that you may sever it from the body and freeze it for the future, but what is the difference between it and a tomato? The possibilities of freezing you to revive you at a later date are as ridiculous as trying to thaw you in the present moment!

> The reason the world is in the grips of such despair
> Is because of the repression; men and women have not
> dared!

The reason there are wars and the rumors of wars is because men and women must learn that the mind is *bent*. It is bent on fulfilling its need! The mind's need, until disciplined, is to run the range of all emotions and of all experiences, because without change and without a purpose the mind is wild. It will run the deserts, it will run the range, and it will have to be corraled in order for it to be broken and ridden once again as one *would*, if one would be what one must be at this time: a Lone Ranger.

For you are now given the Commission of the Evocators of tomorrow, because yesterday I told you you would be Evocators. I am no longer such, for my Work is no longer geared to calling forth those who will come into a pattern of Remembrance. My Work is on the field where there is the lessening of the objective confinement, and where those present are willing to utilize the form present for their identity, but their Consciousness bathes once again in the Eternal Stream that flows from the Throne of God. This is the great symbol that we have when we do not know whence we have come and whither we go. We do know that the Grace of Victory can never be given to one who does not attempt to take the Highest in the humility of spontaneous simplicity!

You cannot cultivate an attitude to achieve the Wonders of God Being. You can only *BE*. Those who have perceived it accept the Presence of an Archetype that will fecundate a new culture that will enliven those who are bound *to* it. Remember, every culture is there because of the agreement of the mass to find comfort in the limitations of the many.

The great culture of the future is not a culture that exists with the accepted limitations of strivers, but the culture that will be the gown worn by those who have dared to venture beyond the frontiers of the mind. You will find that forces there found are geared to a great shift of identity and a shift in consciousness so that you are not needing constant inoculations in order to develop a culture that will keep you alive in the gradual deterioration of the form. You must have as your life support system That Which IS not passing through a medium.

Your Grace is such; it is overwhelming when you stop and ask for the Rhythm becoming the Divine. That Rhythm is not bound to a pulse of intermittent splendor; it is bound to the recurring accent of Newness, Wonder, "His Handiwork to show," as one sits in the saddle and causes the feet of time to stop and wonder at the Pause that refreshes. Each generation shall have such a Pause, and each generation has given such a cause, that you have come to bear in the newness of your moment the awareness that your yesterday is today. How you are experiencing it is according to *how you seeded it and bore it* in the Twilight of the Gods, until the moment when you could stand before the Throne of Light and know that the elucidation is due to the Fire that accompanies the Word that has been *pent* up for men who are capable of accepting IT and finding a Force of such power appearing to engage their bodies that the heat rises and men and women dare not look upon the great Coil or the Serpent. For he who sees it rise in its entirety, it is said, will never again live as he *seems* to be.

You are the great ones who have come out from the rank of the laggards, because you are given an imagination and a faculty that is like one in a university that is waiting to be filled. There is an air of expectancy as to what name shall be given to that empty chair. You see, men have imagined such vain things, but no one has ever imagined that there could be a *Faculty of Unity*. This Faculty of Unity is the one that allows you to become Altogether One without having to wait for the posting and the need of the trials for you to see whether or not you can leap over the hurdles of suggestion.

Your purpose is to become the familiar Custodians, *as you once were*, of these Higher Tendencies to elucidate the meaning of speaking, when the moment is right, and to allow another to understand you, when understanding is not in the word. The reason the Pentecost has been such a mystery, and the reason that the Power of Omnipotence blew open the window and the people gathered for ten days *felt* the Presence of the Spirit of the Transcended One, is because they had allowed their imaging, *fortified by the fear*, to develop enough energy to allow themselves to hear without hearing and to be *affected* without consent. That is the Fire of Pentecost.

The Fire of Pentecost does not have one iota of concern for the timber it engages. It destroys it totally, it engages it completely, and it requires no consent; it just requires that the energy be raised so that in the ensuing *force* of the steadiness of the Constant Pitch of Wonder, that Beam, that Flame, is enhanced and the effect is laseristic and charismatic for all those who have entered into it. The great wonder of being charismatic is seldom understood, for it is the *natural accompanying factor* of one united *within* and appears as the attraction without — the attraction without the encumbrance of limits.

The charismatic is the one that *allows* the expression to happen. There is no regard for your state! You cannot have qualified positions in an all-encompassing Fire. A tree consumed by the fire doesn't consider giving itself up! So many in the world today are like oaks: the rigidity is not at all becoming to the Will. The great *will to power* that Nietzsche talked about, which would become the Superman, was in Essence fine and dandy *provided* there was the awareness that allowed the Power *of* the Will to be known from its Source.

When person takes the will of power and the power of the will and personalizes it, it brings about such an enhancement of the ego that there is a madness that consumes the individual. The tendency to move into an area of total destruction is unnoticed and totally ignored, even when Love would point to it and say: "Step no further! If you do, your only hope rests in lying once again at the feet of Wonder and saying, 'Forgive me, for I thought myself into a dance of power and forgot that the rhythm of the Light is Divine.'"

One in the Rhythm of the Divine Power has a Flame that is forever bellowing forth from the unlimited Source of Wonder. In other words, the words of the Pentecost are those words that are fired, because they will consume *every branch* of your belief system *until there is a shift in consciousness. You don't have to understand how and you don't have to give your consent!* The Flame never asks a question, for IT is the all-consuming Might of Purification from your attempt to be a handyman or a handy-maiden in the service of the Light. Those roles are purely *fantasized*, as is this one, if you consider it purely a *formed* situation for your drama.

This One does not mind at all being considered in form, but the One informs you that it is essential to separate yourself from being encased in it. If you *are*, you will be constantly attempting the worship of the Divine from the standpoint of an unworthy heathen. You can attempt to worship the Divine and have thoughts about it?!

You are nothing but a heathen, and you attempt to take your viewpoints into the Temple, into the arena of the Light?

Your viewpoint has *no point to it* if you think you are a person endowed with Pentecostal might. You were never given the gift of tongues just to wag them and cause others to wonder. The gift of the Pentecost was the *transforming* and *transfiguring* possibility, when men were pursued by the Flame that scorched every belief they had personalized about a Saviorhood. As long as you put your Savior, your Christ, or your Buddha in the framework of a person instead of a *living Now Presence*, you are in the state of yesterday.

The reason the world is trying to find a new orbit is because the whole system is becoming devoid of an enhancement of power. The world is devoid of power, it seems, because there is such a diverse belief system that each one has a right to what he thinks he wants to believe. There is nothing right, there is nothing wrong, save oblivion . . which most are approaching and don't even know it! What is the success of oblivion? It's dressed up in the most tantalizing costumes. It's called commerce, finance, culture, artistic achievement, success, and elevating the race via legend, translation of myths, and the mechanicalization of the ensuing force field of nanotechnology. **Without a Principle claimed Invincible there is** *nothing* **to hitch the horse of your mind to, for "you" are devoid of balance.**

The reason balance is essential is because you have taken the belief system to be real; you have assumed your appearance to be actual; and you have not considered that the whole problem with the world today is a result of education. The education that has *spent* time. Do you realize you *spend* the first eighteen or twenty-some years of your life being *brain*washed in a bath of beliefs, in a system of fractured states?! And when you really have fractured your state you usually get a Ph.D. in it! When you have *not* fractured your estate you usually have a high school education. The high school is supposed to be something above the low school, but it's just a more sophisticated form of belief system where you are taught how to deal with abstractions as if they were real. But the most *abstract* problem, which no teacher in today's schools tackles, is the subject of Identity. This is why you have such religious ceremonies binding people to hope, because they have never had the proper *leading* to cognize Identity correctly.

You are taught how to think and you are given the means to identify your precipitatory act and to call it materialization of your objective world. They haven't told you that you did it! They have told you that it has a history, that it is one of a planetary system and that it has such an engaging, unfathomable background. Everyone dreams up the most spectacular dreams in order to sustain a belief system. What will happen when people start to perceive that their belief system and the world system is totally a TV production studio's work? You blow your tube and appear to be gobbing around fecundating this planet with boob tubes like yourself, and you think they are people endowed with wisdom. They are *endowed* with a belief system!

This is why people, perhaps like you and me, are not from this galaxy of Wonder. If we were, we would be more impressed with production! When you come from another State, you are always aware of how you have assimilated the patterns of force, so that you can bear this form and dress it to appear like those with whom you walk.

You know that you are here to blow the mask off delusion. You know you are here to penetrate the disguise of objectivity and to reveal that subjectivity is as much objectivity and therefore a conundrum: the problem that cannot be solved if you are in it. Subjectivity and objectivity go hand in hand, but what is the tree that's around if it isn't the tree of belief with all the limbs of its systems.

What frees you from the belief that two and two is five? Someone's declaration that it is four, and that declaration given by one who is the living evidence of it. This is the whole purpose of a Messiah or one elevated *as* a Messiah, which usually happens *after* an event. A Messiah's appearance is usually the promise of yesterday attempting to fulfill itself. What does it promise? A releasement from the friction of history. That's why eternality is promised, because eternality has nothing to do with time. The history book is made up of you and your yesterdays instead of being the present moment of discovery.

When you perceive every venture you take into time through the mind, you can say intellectually, "I AM." The great danger of that is the ensuing arrogance that allows you (so you think) the prerogative of being "enlightened." An intellectual enlightened by cognizing "I AM" is an intellectual that has to be constantly plugged into a belief system! "I AM" is not a belief. "I AM" is a word, is a sound. It's not a thought, but it is That which stands as the penultimate before Silence. For What I AM can only be declared, and that I AM not. That's the Silence evidencing ITself.

This is the validity of the experience of two plus two being four and not five. The one demonstrating it is the experience of it. You don't have to understand it at all. Understanding is one of the false limbs of the belief system. The most *important* ingredient you have at your disposal, which you seldom use, is *trust*. When you enter on the High Way of Light you have to *trust*, because there are no signs on the soft shoulders showing which direction you are going. You can't get on it if someone hasn't gone before you. It doesn't tell you that there is an exit because, you see, to stop and start is like one who is learning to drive . . a bargain!

The mind is so restless, it always wants to bargain how much of Reality it will accept. It stops and bargains just what Feast it will attend. Will it be the Feast of the Pentecost or will it be a feast for a marriage? Let's say a marriage, because in a marriage you seem to go on producing your likes and dislikes. At a Pentecost they are nonexistent. The only thing that may be present is *fear*: the great accent of God. You have developed fear because you know you need it. It's the only thing that *scares* you.

"You" are such a false god. You think you control your situation: "I will take this highway and I will leave it. I will hitchhike. I will snack at this bar and at that bar and get spiritual food." You gluttons for delusion! There is no way that you will ever find a cafeteria of Light, not even at the racetrack where you see the horse behave in the fashion expected. You will not find you're served a *smorgasbord* of wonderful, tasty dishes. The Real is usually very bitter and sour to the sweetness that you have been led to believe is essential for enhancing an appetite for more of it. Perhaps the reason for the wonderful, transcendent feature of renouncing within yourself your affiliation with limitation: it's pretty bitter to the mouth. It may be "sweet to the mouth but bitter to the belly."[1] We could say that the words heard are pretty bitter to the hearing because they cause it to have to deal with chaotic patterns that you have *thought* settled.

What is unbecoming? That which isn't in agreement with the ordinance of Light. What is the great known Fact? That the Light cannot be considered understood from the standpoint of the thunder, and that's what most of your worship of the Divine is. It's *nothing* but the dissatisfaction of God-Being appearing as the rolling drums of delusion: the drums surrounding those played *in memoriam* for those who have died in vain. How many have died in vanity? There would not be so many dying in vain if vanity weren't at the root of the problem, all because of wrong identity!

What is the mark? You bear it. If you are settling within the environs of your Unseen Nature the questions that come to the surface when one walks in the waters, then you will perceive yourself finding answers that cause a change. By these you are marked. When your interiorization becomes aglow with the Flame of Love, its purification and unification, then you will be perceived as one carrying the charisma of an *Evocator* who is slated to be cognized so that the stage may be prepared for the magical elevation of the world once again into the Arms of Love.

This description in words, all symbolically given, is such that the words cannot be intellectually capable of revealing. The intellect is there for the ordered expression, but what comes before the order? The plea or the wish that springs from the Heart *un*spoken, *un*sung, yet appearing to be chanted for the re-enchantment of your Earth and its experience.

Yours is a world of your own making, your life is of your own doing, and your hope is present, if you are *willing* to be given to the Power of Wonder, Miracle, and Marvel so that the Superman and the State of Balance once again walk as some Holy experience.

The Mind that is in keeping with what you call the Light is transparent, clear, and capable; the one that is all dressed up in keeping with person is opaque and little Light can directly be emitted.

As an *Evocator*, your Presence should be allowing others to note that you have been called out and they are ready to be called up! What is the purpose of being a mortal other than to see right through the suggestion and how it is all part of an educated system of belief.

To have others hear you correctly through the words that they use *incorrectly* is a wonder to behold! How anything I say could possibly be understood by anything you think, you might as well know, is an impossibility! That is why what I say (and you *think* you hear) allows you to *hear* and be changed. *What you think I say is not what I have said, and what I say unto you is not what you thought.* Therefore, the whole pattern of performance is one of attention, for in the description of *my* life may you see your own unfolding.

This is the value of Presence . . that *is* a Wonder, for we have assumed a body formed and have passed through the time tunnel in order for us to appear like others. And yet we in Essence have had nothing whatsoever to do but to BE the Irradiance of That Force which, when magnified and accumulated in the reservoir of our *spirited* pockets, allows all those with the emptiness of heart, body, mind, and Soul to once again *fill* themselves with Wonders of Infinite Possibilities, provided the will to power is the Law of Love that empowers each and every one on the Way of Light. To expedite the experience, expel the thought that you are "this," and be amazed at the effulgence of Beauty undefiled.

What a fashion plate you will be, what a meal will be served, for you will know that you are not only the tastiness to the dish but you are the magician that allowed it all to happen and participated in it in order for others to see what it means to be in seclusion, and yet in the exclusive but public *act of adoring* the One Altogether Lovely. In this I AM satisfied; may you be also.

You have understood; don't let your minds say you haven't. If your minds say you have not understood, it's because they have a will to power and that's why the promise of Utopia has been termed a dream. Why don't you leave it, dreamers, and awake. Let it be the one that is filled with the chant of praise. For in Thy Light have I seen Light; in Thy Glory, Wonder, and Ascension, the Bestowal that allows a Descent to appear as an Advent on your span of attention where I AM All.

On March 31, 1991, I said:

> What I am saying is calling you to the Table, and your turn is to come when you will be the *Evocators*. Your

time is at hand when you will have to answer for having responded to *this* Evocator. But I am leaping from calling out; I am leaping beyond your ledge of approachability; I am leaping into a new environment where the trivialities of your pseudo-living bear no meaning for the new experience whatsoever.

What an Unfoldment! You must never, never, never allow yourselves the whimsicality of spiritual thoughts to wave over your ensuing years of released expression. Don't allow yourself to think you will experience Enlightenment. That is the teaching of those who would keep a sparkle to Truth. For people have imagined vain things, and one of the greatest vanities of education is that you will become enlightened. This is a vanity that is given because it *allows* you to develop a confidence in choice: to be or not to be enlightened. It's such a vanity because there is no such state that can be achieved as a result of intellectuality.

Enlightenment is What IS that allows the intellectual to *seem* to have a sovereignty in your experience. Enlightenment is What IS when your intellect says it isn't. And when your intellect says it isn't, IT *IS*. You allow your intellect to say, "I have no idea what Enlightenment is." Why don't you just say: "I have *no* intention of being responsible. I have *no* intention of being committed. I have *no* intention of being married to Principle. I have *no* intention of being faithful. I have *no* intention of being constant. I have *no intention* of being balanced. I have *no* intention of being . . Real; I have *no* intention of putting IT first. I have no intention of putting IT second! My only intention is to nibble at IT when I haven't got sustenance in any other department of my 'no-no' belief system."

You see, no wonder, no health, no wholeness! Holistic medicine is coming to the fore. Why? Because at least *somebody* is saying you have to be whole in body, mind, and Soul. But, my goodness, holistic medicine will never help; it'll only be a crutch. As long as you *think* you have a choice of being a body, of being a mind, and of being a Soul, all you'll do is take the superficial belief system that goes with holistic medicine and find it takes time to be cured no matter how powerful the tincture of drops. It's an amazing thing how you can take an empowered drop and expect it to bring about a cure when you're such a drip! A hundred-and-eighty-pound one!

You see, you cannot allow yourselves to *think* any longer that you are filled with choices. Oh, you "have a choice to make." You only have *one* choice and that is to be Real . . or to be *un*real. To be Real is the only way you can take care of the *un*real, and to be unreal is such work. To be unreal makes you work, work, work! That's why we had that song, "What Are You Missing?"[2] There will always be the working man as long as you think equality has to reign. The working man is the man that has to struggle to sustain division. That's why it is so difficult to do it alone. That's why labor unions developed. It's very hard.

So, you have the right to work. In a free country everyone has the right to work. Well, the reason you have a right to work is because your mind is so noisy! It's always telephoning to different parts of your responsive natures that are so superficial that they must do something in order to keep things going. When you once achieve a certain place, you have not only the right to work, but you won't need to do it so much.

The best thing that could happen today is if all TVs blew! What would happen? You would find just how much you have depended upon them. I don't know what the schoolteachers would do; I don't know what children would do, because children no longer look at the image of mother and father as an *example*. They look at what? Cartoons on a boob tube and then see them figured out as family, schoolteachers, and their playmates. The fantasy that the television portrays for the virgin mind of the child is such that the *sight* is more important than what the child hears. The picture can alter more than a thousand words, and it certainly shows that there is no standard being set.

The reason the High Teaching is always there is because you should be finding, if you are really *being* consecrated to your one and only choice *to BE*, that the work is lessening in hours spent. You not only have the right to work, but now you have the right to BE, because you won't have it all taken up with those hours.

Why do you keep yourselves so busy? Because you don't want to see you are aimless. So true. People want to keep so busy so they don't see that they are aimless.

What does "aimless" mean? I don't know. I don't know,

because I've never used that word in my life. I've only used "purpose," "goal," and "aim" . . for the neophyte. Since there is no constant presence of a Teacher with you every moment of the day, you have the stand-in, Principle, the head of your school where you are training your thoughts to be classified according to their quality, and where you are strapped and beaten according to the lack of respect you have paid to the thought-forces with which you are associating.

Why would you get away with deliberately entertaining wrong thoughts when you know they too are the evidence of a Force Field that is Divine? The difference between Satan (the Devil) and Christ (the Self) is in only one fundamental feature of Essence: Creativity! The Satanic *creates* a different experience from the Christ, the Self. It's the same Force.

It is so important for you to perceive this, because you must establish the aristocracy. Your teaching of today tells you not to. But the *aristocracy must* be established, because this world has become so class conscious; it says everyone is equal, when actually you know very well that those who are saying so are not the people whom you know at all. How many people do you know in Ottawa, in Washington, who are telling you that everyone's equal? Try to get near them. One of them has I don't know how many body-guards; I know there are many surrounding some of them. Every-one who's telling you that everyone is equal is living a perfect example of its lie. They're not equal at all.

Why are people afraid of an aristocracy? Because then there is a *code* of demeanor, a way of access to Presence. This is why it is important.

What is the great demand of today? To free yourself, from what? You wouldn't be searching if you hadn't questioned, "Am I this?" or, "What's he talking about? I'm coming because I don't know why everyone likes him so much; I just find it very confusing, upsetting, and disorienting!" You couldn't have said a nicer thing, because none of your friends cause that. Those are the ones that you shouldn't be with. You shouldn't be with those at all, because any friend who puts up with you as you are is in the same bog as you are. Oh, yes. If you're very popular with your friends who aren't here, I don't know what *you*'re doing here.

Oh, *you are so important*. I keep telling you this in case I should quit the plane suddenly. I keep telling you this because it is *imperative* for you *not* to forget I said this. There's not going to be *one other person* that tells you this. There is not going to be one other person who will tell you this. They'll just say, "Oh, David. Oh, yes, Sherry. Oh, Wilson! Oh, the Son of the Will. Ah!" You see, they won't know that you are a Beacon unless there's Somebody to tell you that the Fire is lighted and it's glowing from within so that *without* they see the radiance. You know? You're very important, because people are running their barges of thought right onto the coral heads of belief. Coral heads.

This is why it's so strange to think of people severing the head from the body in the future and freezing it. I think there are six or eight that are frozen at the moment. It's much cheaper; it's only thirty-five thousand dollars to freeze a head, but it's one hundred thousand dollars to freeze a whole body. Being likened unto a tomato I thought was very, very good. I read this recently. This is where your technology is leading you! You're part of the technology, because you're thinking through the chips of belief-sets. The reason I came is to bring a Force that will help erase them before it's too late.

Someone said to me not long ago, "Kenneth, nothing must happen to you. Where are the men; where is your support system?" She's always saying this to me. She said, "Without you, I don't know what's going to happen. The world has got to be given back its Soul, and the people on it. And you've got to do this! You've only got ten to fifteen years left, otherwise it's going to go into total destruction!" And it is. The world will be obliterated (there's no doubt about it), because *you* have forgotten the Wonders of the very thing you have created.

It's hard to believe that "you" (the God of you) created this world. It is sustained by your unified belief system that you're on it! It's such work; that's why you have to sleep so much. Or not at all, so that you'll know where you are when "it" isn't. The point of staying awake is to see that in the darkness "it" doesn't show and in the light "it" does. That's why in the darkness, when you are "the Light," Substance is being manifested.

In the Light you're apt to be inundated with the verification of your belief system and the denial of the objective world, which is usually in your cellular, monastic mode of expression, where your eyes are not allowed to take in so much of the objective. It's very sparse. Then you are taught to look *within* to find the beauty, which is fine and dandy. Then there comes a time when you realize that that isn't the total picture, because no matter how much you deny the outer, you cannot deny the incredible gift of the Absolute and its Creativity.

The objective world, therefore, no longer confines you; you play with it. Since you're all objects, why are you so afraid of playing with each other? Just because you're thirty, forty, fifty, why are you so afraid of playing with one another? Because your belief system has got you hooked into pressing the right keys for the typed script to come out all the same. Oh, yes! Mal has got a very prestigious father and mother; therefore, this is the way Mal has to behave. This one's got this; this one's got that. What are you behaving like? A thought-structure! You're not behaving from your heart at all! If you behaved from your heart, you'd say, "To hell with this! Be in love with That!" Then, when you do that, when you're in love with That, "this" is taken care of.

A depression, you know, is pure propaganda! It's a contriving to make you believe that you aren't in control of Substance. You *are* in control of Substance because in Essence you *are* the Substance That IS. The depression is when you allow yourself to have the variegated pattern of belief become a "reality" to you. A depression happens because a depression is always lacking in interest in otherness. *A depression causes you to orientate to the selfishness of withdrawing to what is "yours."*

Don't allow the suggestion of depression to continue. It's *purely* made up, as two-plus-two-being-five is. It doesn't really exist. You know what's wrong with today's world? People are falling for the depression because they haven't stood for Truth. The reason hundreds of wonderful people are having a time is because Truth isn't first.

When you go to Moscow and you see countless thousands of people lining up at different stores, you ask, "What are they doing?" They say, "Well, they get there early in order to get food." The people who are there in the front of the line, of course, get the food, and those at the back of the line don't have nearly as much choice. Where the multitude is, there's usually lack. It's usually in the exclusive realm that you will find Abundance.

Look at the Abundance of the Masters! *Look* at their wisdom. It was exclusive. It was not shared with every Tom, Dick, and Mabel. (It was hairy enough with two men, let alone a woman!) The exclusivity of what you have is extremely important for you to utilize. Remember, people will often use your energy and your enthusiasm, like bums did during the Depression of '29 and '30, when they'd come to your door in the morning and beat on your door. Often my mother would bring people in and serve them breakfast with Dad, and then they would leave with my father when he went to work; they didn't have any work to go to. It was a different type of depression. That depression, I don't know what it was because I wasn't old enough to understand it. This one I don't understand either, because how can you understand something that's made up?

How can you stand "you"?! when you're made up! to the point where they analyze you and they have to really account for some of you via a microscope. And yet all I have to do is kick you, and you don't need a microscope to hear the "Ouch!" or an audiometer test to know that you've heard it.

Why do you consider your bulk so important, instead of the Lightness? [The sound of something falling is heard.] Something's heavy out there. You see? Oh, it's all right. I'm glad it wasn't *you* that fell; it would have made more noise than that! But who's ever heard of Amedeo falling? Couldn't. Oh, boy.

I hope you're not concerned about equality. It's never the foundation of the strong. The only foundation of the strong is fidelity, commitment, trust, and obedience. Those words are all taboo, you see, in your belief system. Oh, yes, it's forbidden to use the word "obedience": "You have to be obedient." "Trust!" Why would you trust anyone?

I remember one fellow telling me a story about how a father was teaching his son to trust. He put up a ladder, and the boy got up on the first rung of the ladder and the father said, "Jump, I'll catch you." The father caught him. Then he said, "Take another step and jump; I'll catch you." The boy had confidence, and the father caught him. Then he took another step up the ladder and the father said, "Jump!" The father didn't catch him and he fell. The father said, "Don't trust anyone."

That is not the Teaching! It would be marvelous if once again the hickory stick could be brought into the schoolroom, and principals be there because they are the living evidence of Principle, and the teachers there because they are the living evidence of being guides so that the children can be properly taught.

What are you adoring, if it isn't beauty, no matter what form it takes? How can you block Beauty? You can't! Unless you're what? Intellectual, and then you could be jealous because you haven't got it. What are jealousy, envy, and resentment, then? They are the identification of the sufferer with what isn't, and the result is death.

What is the purpose of High Teaching? The reason High Teaching is important is because the words blast your thought-sets, your belief-sets, therefore, your identification-sets. If you didn't really want this done, there would never have been a Plato, a Socrates, a Saint Francis, let alone a Jesus or a Buddha. Never! Why do you remember those names?

Isn't it amazing how you're using something that you never knew in a belief system that isn't? A wonderful excuse for not Being . . Now! Isn't that something? This is what you call being a Holy Horror! And that's real medicine.

If your body gets well and seems well and good, it's because it should get on with being Real. *You* should get along with Being Real while it's still not taking so much of your time and thought. One of the most mesmeric things is a healthy body, you know.

A healthy body and a happy life
Allow you to die and have inner strife.

A healthy body and a healthy mind
Give you a chance to wake up in time . . to die right!

[Mr. Mills eats a grape.]

Glad there was a vine; the fruit is great.
Do you spit out the pit? Or do you just chew it up as
   roughage for your own sake?

May 19, 1991 (Pentecost)

---

1 Revelation 10:9-10.
2 Recorded by The Star-Scape Singers, directed by Kenneth G. Mills on *Rapture of
   Freedom* (Toronto: Sun-Scape Records, 1984).

XII

THE BREAKER

It is the tendency of the mind to try to escape creative tension. When you have aligned yourself to a High Teaching, you have agreed to sit on the horse of the mind. In other words, you have agreed to watch the thought-field which lies before you, and reduce the abysmal state of suggestion to the Transcendent One of Knowingness.

THE BREAKER

We are meeting with old and new and realizing as never before the need to drop the classifications of the mind and its attempt at supremacy in delineating the situations in which we find ourselves.

Recently it was said that our greatest enemy is the mind. It can also be a very helpful legion of power when the troops that constitute it find themselves set into the position of a well-disciplined response to directives.

Dr. Tomatis[1] says that the right ear directs what we hear. It seems that too many of us listen with our left. It seems that the right ear is the one that allows the originality and the Newness bearing its vitality and its melodious nature to be perceived, whereas the left one tends always to be slightly off the beat, lacking an impulse to move one beyond the dry, intellectual field of the everyday world.

In the picture that presents itself to us, more and more do we perceive the fractured outcome of a fractured force field due to a runaway horse called the mind. We look at the world: we see chaos and we see freedom. Some say they find freedom in chaos and it may be that chaos seems to accompany freedom, until the situation resolves itself through an exertion of purposeful will and the Will of Purpose.

For so many years we have all looked upon the world, its divisions, all the states and their various seats of government, but seldom have we perceived that in the guise of each state having its government, there should be a drill of such a disciplined order that a rhythmic Pattern of Creativity is once again allowed to have a creative tension in the world.

It does seem that we have thrived vicariously upon the rampant energy of unbridled forces that are let loose in the guise of successful ventures in business, achieving freedom without considering in Essence what freedom is. Freedom is not "being able to do your own thing." Freedom is not that at all! Freedom is that state that is experienced when we stand at an experiential distance from our engagement with time and find that the world is waiting to perceive what we as the Newborn, Reborn Ones bear unto it in the sequence of events that await to be Christened "Holy."

In the movement from a controlled environment (such as we have seen in the former Soviet Union) to that state where we see freedom trying to be experienced, but in its place a sense of chaos and lack, we perceive that the salient need is running just below the surface of the people, in their secret yearning for a re-enhancement and a rebirthing of the pristine Force surrounding a creative action becoming a people prepared to take on the tension accompanying a new-birthed Soul. "A new-birthed Soul" may sound to you as if it means that you are prepared to be cared for like some swaddling-clothed creature. The only part of you that you dream at all capable of being dressed in swaddling clothes is that portion of you that we cannot see, that little pocket of expectancy that is kicking in rhythm with the promise of an emancipation from the tyranny of the errant mind.

There is nothing in our thought that is not the result of an Essence energy. There is not one thought that is launched by your agreement to entertain it that ever dies. This is why you may appear to be reborn. To be reborn, to live a certain number of years and then to die is the way the mind enslaves the progeny of the rebel thoughts that have been launched by those who have lacked the ability to discriminate.

Discrimination is one of the most important gifts that you as mind-creatures can entertain. It has to be entertained as well as the thought of nondiscrimination. Now, if you discriminate, you are labeled. If you do *not* discriminate, you're not worth labeling because the end is obvious: the grave of belief. Discrimination is of value when it allows its force to be used, appended unto the missing piece of the great puzzle of the fractured picture: the Center, the Principle Piece/Peace "that passeth the understanding."

This practice of aligning the thought to a Principle in Essence is Divine Discrimination. The propaganda of time would tell you that you are falling for the destructive influence in a chaotic society, wrapped in a spurious garment of freedom. If discrimination were not so important, it would never be put down. You can be assured that anything that is put down is of importance. When "you" stand up as the Uncontradictable, then you cannot find yourself hanging your hat on the doorpost instead of placing it on your head. You see, the hat supposedly covers the head in order to keep it warm, where actually, in former times, a hat was used to lower the frequency of your Enlightenment so that others passing you would not perceive your Light, unless they bore the creative tension that could take its ensuing Radiance.

What is happening today is that the head has been enthroned without knowing what's under it! We say we have the body and the skeleton and thereby hangs a tail/tale. It has been the tale of duality. We say that we have two eyes, two ears, two legs, two arms, and one tongue. That is not true. We have two tongues. They are just joined by the median. This is why I have taught the Singers all these years to consider which side of the tongue is vibrating, according to the frequency. Now, upon looking into the material of Dr. Tomatis, I perceive that he, after forty-five years of experiments, has found this is perfectly true.

What the Singers thought were the considerations of a mad-man turn out to be the considerations of an expert. There is nothing more interesting than That Which IS not dammed. When you look into the mirror, what is a "dam" you think is a "mad." So, when you get rid of that, you don't have the Adamic situation any longer. You see, the Adamic situation tells the tale that you are "this." Consequently, the radical gives you the root of duality. What we, as those being reacquainted with the Authentic Nature, have to do is once again be the Radical of Newness, which bears the Creative Might, termed tension.

This is what I used to say to the Singers, that tension is the most incredible gift I can give you prior to performance. I don't want you relaxed. **Tension is the sign that you're geared to perform.** Who ever heard tell of a violin being loose! If the strings aren't tightened and under tremendous tension, no horsehair is going to create a beautiful sound on it, no matter what kind of gut is present!

You see, no matter . . is possible to be considered. It is without matter that we are considering a situation that is beyond thought. The situation beyond thought is only known by negating what you think is. Everything that can be negated, that you think is, points to That Which IS not thought and IS. So, you have to be ready to find that little window through which you go and land and await at an experiential distance.

That is a wonderful place. A Wonder-full place. Why is it? Because Wonder is the keynote to allowing Newness to happen. If you can't come to a session with Wonder, you might as well stay away. Remember, your head on your shoulders is constantly pouring down to your feet. Your head as it should be is one that is receiving and reaching with its roots unto the Sublime. This is why we have fallen, through the mind's attempt to say we go "up" to Heaven and we go "down" to hell. I used to say, "Well, that is ridiculous." Some would say, "Well, Jesus ascended unto Heaven, and he went down to hell for a few days." I said, "My God, what's going to happen if you say He went sideways?" You know?

It's an amazing consideration! How many times do you look at yourself sideways? Frequently — to see how your posture is, to see what shows and what doesn't, to see what should and what shouldn't. When you face straight on, all that seems to be flattened out, you know? So, sideways you realize you may be bulging, but front-on you realize you may be posing for an ad. Now you don't want anything that is going to dam that. What you want to do is have some way to release yourself from the suggestion that you are this. That is through the realm of discriminating with the thought-realm: what thoughts you are *re*-energizing for a continued journey through the time tunnel of the tomorrows?!

Some of us are Reborn. Some of us appear to be Reborn to reawaken those who are prepared for the Government that bears authenticity to that of Man. This rests upon the premise that if "this" can change, it can't be considered Real. *The test of Reality is that That Which IS Real never changes. If it changes, it can't be Real.*

So, if you get up one morning feeling very happy and five minutes later you're not so happy, then you know very well that state is not Real. But the State that *is* Real is the one that allows you to perceive, "One moment happy and the next moment sad." Go to That State that allows you to perceive that. This will be a disclaimer for all those with complaints. They won't be able to bother you in school or anywhere else, because you will bear the equanimity, the equilibrium which is so rare in a fluctuating formation of these bags. You know, when you stop and consider, it's the most amazing creative suggestion appearing formed that we utilize. There's not one thing about us that will reveal mind. The only thing about us that can be revealed upon analysis is that we aren't this. "But then," people say, "what are we?" And I always say, "What's left over."

You know, when you've had a wonderful dinner and you've looked at your plate and it's cleaned, what's left over? The satisfying satisfaction . . of realizing that the plate and what was on it had nothing to do with your satisfaction. It was your *will*ingness to purposefully transform that kingdom into another form. And that appeared as the nutrition of the meal, or the fuel for your vehicle. *You are the tastiness to the dish.* Remember, you took it willingly and agreed to all those hours of work altering that kingdom so that you could experience it in a higher way.

Now, if you agree to allow your machinery to work all those hours to transform your food, why don't you consider *what* you take as the thought-meal and see the required time it takes . . not to digest Truth — that makes Truth processive. This is what everyone *wants*: process! If they have process, they have excuses! But when you take Truth and bring it to the fore, it gives you the immediacy of the Nowness of Oneness. That is how you can see that if you take what appears as a thought of process and try to deal with it, you create more process. But when you take the thought of Completion and allow the process to appear to happen, you are not in it; just as you are not in the process of digesting the Truth. The Truth is what allows the digestion, or the Transformation, to appear to take place.

So, it is by abiding in those thought-sets — those thoughts that are set with Principle, the Center of your puzzle — that you will bring order to the disordered world. People say, "Well, Mr. Mills, what would you say to the United Nations? Mr. Mills, what would you say to the people of China? What would you say to the people of Russia?" The only thing you can say to them is what is true: that the country is within *them.*

If you can't rule *your* little kingdom within yourself, why are you blaming any government?! Unless the government is upon HIS shoulders — in other words, is it upon the Invisible Spirit of Balance? HIS: the Invisible Spirit of Balance, with the Wisdom, the Insight, and the bridge of Intuition. If you don't utilize this force field within yourself, you can't perceive the counterfeit and insubstantial world.

Nothing is impossible, because "nothing" gives us the feeling of no obstruction. That's why you say *nothing* is impossible! Nothing carries with it no obstruction. Create an obstruction out of nothingness. You can't. That's why no one wants Nothing. People live on dealing with obstructions. How many of you are making your living because of people loving to live on obstructions? Muscle spasms, business spasms, and world spasms (war) — lameness everywhere you look!

What is the onset of dis-ease? Fatigue. Fatigue is, they say, the metaphysician's worst enemy. There was a time in the life of this formation that it was so difficult to get my arms up to the keyboard; I would be exhausted. It would take so much time for me to rest, to walk from here to there. This was when I was twenty-one. It was at that time that I started to probe deeply: Was I this object? Was I this object or was Ken the name of the object that I was utilizing for the purpose of putting an end to a tale of process?

If it states in the Good Books that "*Now* are we the Sons of God,"[2] there is no process. Where does the process come in? In our decision-making to be the Divine Force Field Self-evident. Why do we have a history, called the past, and the unwritten one called the future? You know very well you can write the future right now, if you want to. You might as well do it while you are alive, if you want to, and of course, when you come to the end of it, they call it your history.

The fascinating part of it is this: historically, people recognize war, famine, pestilence, and woe; they also recognize the possibility of streets paved with jewels, the leaves of the trees becoming precious jewels, and the possibilities of Revelation. Why do you think both of these thought-sets still exist, if it isn't that they run a relay course through the time tunnel of suggestion?

The force of suggestion has to be amplified, as your telephone call is over the wires. Your voice is impulsed right across the wires so that it appears at the other end as you speaking; it's enhanced electrically. That's history. This is why we recognize it. It's the same thought-pattern being perpetuated. The only thing is, the dress is different.

We saw it with the "little Napoleon" today. No different! Why is there so much similarity to a Napoleon, to a Caesar, to a Pharaoh, to a Magician? Why are there all these similarities continuing? Because the same thought-pattern is energized from generating to generating. And that personalized is "a generation." The *generating* system of dualistic, relativistic thinking is generated. What stops it? The Breaker, which is reborn the moment you say "I AM All."

Now, if I have to say, "Well, Greg, would you say that again?" he would say, "I AM All." The only reason Greg could respond is because I AM All; the I AM All of Greg is the I AM All of me. But for the *fun* of his drama, we allow it to be personified for those who believe in process. We are perhaps Reborn because we know that Now is the time. It's not tomorrow. *Now* is the time. That takes you out of the sequence of age, out of the sequence of nationality, out of the sequence of possibilities, but not out of the Force Field of Wonder, because Wonder accompanies Nowness. You see, Wonder has the same root as Miracle, and Miracle has the same root as Marvel, and our universe is a Wonder, because we can look upon it and call it, microcosmically, "you" or "me." Therefore, we can look upon the whole world with the greatest of ease.

When I am in Russia, the people don't know how to *account* for me; they say they don't understand the feeling that exists like that! [Mr. Mills claps his hands.] But you have feeling, you have feeling, you have feeling, everyone has feeling; it's only altered when you say it's your feeling, your feeling, your feeling, your feeling. But, *feeling the Being I AM is the revealed Soul. This* is what? The world isn't waiting for the sunrise. The world is waiting for the revealment that it never set!

Every time you think a proposition, notice how one thought tags on to another. Just like ants. When your stomach is hungry, you ask for "Food, Sahib!" Of course, you expect a steak and everything that goes with it. Otherwise you'll beef! Then, what else do you expect? If you say, "I am hungry," and I give you Meat and it's not visible on your plate that you expect to find it upon, Goodness . . satisfies you. It isn't the plate and what's on it. Isn't it the most exciting time for you people to be living?

I was talking to one lady who is very, very well known. She said to me that I had such an incredible feat to accomplish. She said, "You only have ten years to do it; ten to fifteen years at the most." I said, "What is that?" She said, "You know what it is." I said, "Well, what do *you* say it is?" She said, "It is to give the world back its Soul, because if you don't, the world will go into robotery for at least three hundred years, and much of it will be destroyed," and it will. There's no alternative, because much of the world is under the impulse of the mechanical mind. In other words, all men become the mechanical toys of *its* force field due to the acceptance of a mind as the seat of power.

The mind is never satisfied; that's why you have such a job meditating. When you meditate, you have to stop the thoughts, right? You're not supposed to think any thoughts. So I had so many people come to me at one time and say they just couldn't meditate; they couldn't stop the thoughts. I said, "Why would you bother? Why don't you start watching them and ask for more?" They said, "What?" I said, "Meditate, watch the thoughts, and ask for more. Watch what a creature you're dealing with." [Mr. Mills imitates the voice of the mind, speaking more and more slowly:] "I don't want to give you so many. I don't want to give you so many. I don't want to give you so many. I don't .. want .. to .. give .. you .. so .. many."

It's a great process, to go and sit under the banyan tree while the Little Prince[3] is out watering his geranium. You're supposed to be understanding the Elemental Nature? Why would you bother trying to understand the Elemental Nature if you don't understand the preciousness of the Element of the Timeless? Which is the Nowness. Because that is the Nothingness, the Somethingness I AM!

As soon as I say "I AM," I have allowed IT to become a Force Field right in the stream of adulterated thought. "I AM saying this; I don't know what you're thinking." That is the option that you have inherited as part of your genetic system. You have inherited the *ability* to accept thoughts as if they were your own. All you have is just a system of receptivity. Nothing else! It's the propaganda and the lack of discrimination that lets you think that you have thoughts of your own. "You" never created a thought. "You" are the creation of thoughts.

When you die, you cease to maintain your thought. The body decomposes only because the thoughts that constitute it are no longer fed. That's how death loses its sting and you have victory over the grave, belief.

It is the tendency of the mind to *try* to escape creative tension. When you have aligned yourself to a High Teaching, you have agreed to sit on the horse of the mind. In other words, you have agreed to *watch* the thought-field, which *lies* before you, and reduce the abysmal state of suggestion to the Transcendent One of Knowingness.

This is the work you're to do, when you walk down Third Avenue, Fifth Avenue, into Saks — and I always enjoy going into Saks. I think, "What an incredible name; no wonder it's such a successful store." I feel that everyone in Saks recognizes that I don't have one tied, and they want to fill it, you know? I'm constantly being asked questions: Wouldn't I like this? Wouldn't I like that? I just watch, and discriminate. "Choose you this day, whom ye will serve: God or mammon."[4] What's "God or mammon"? Tell me: Are you afraid of God? No! You're afraid of everything you think surrounds God, makes God up. Mammon? You're afraid of mammon? Only of what you think makes it up.

> God's up in heaven, mammon's down below.
> What if I go sideways, what of me will show?
> What if I ascend unto that Holy Spot of time
> And go right beyond the ridge of your errant mind?
>
> What if I descend and cause your thoughts to feel
> The turbulence equated with the volcanic nature that is
>   not real?
> What will you do in the fluid state of Fire?
> Try to cool it and find where you may reside beside it?
>
> The Fire is transformative; it's mighty hot, you know.
> And it doesn't always show that within it you have rolled.
> The molecular structure will tell you that outwardly it
>   may not be
> An accelerated sense of movement, but within it, if you
>   know how, you can see

The effect of Fire.

The effect of Fire is not always visible! It's felt in a secondary feature. And that is often termed the Force accompanying the Emancipated State of Realization. And that is frequently garmented as vitality. Remember, the mark of your freedom is your vitality.

So when you see your friends sitting around eating french fries and tacos, just look carefully and see. Discriminate!

I AM not a figure, and yet I seem to be
All dressed up just like you, and you say, "Oh, you there,
    he is a he."
I say, "You there seems a'walking, and seems a she to me."
So this is how the He-She's talking, and until understood,
    wears the beads.[5]

What is the great Joining Factor between He and She? The Holy Breath, the S. HE-S-HE. (It isn't a dollar sign, although it usually is!)

Can you *imagine* the world at peace?
Can you *be* at peace?
If *you* can BE at peace, so can your world!

The marvel is not Oneness. The Wonder is how multiplicity can parade in the Light of Oneness! How are we united . . and then there is no discrimination? In Oneness, *allowing* the multiplicity to appear the Wonder.

Who calls it nations, races? Only those who see the play given to Wonder. People thought it's been division. *Remember* — you did, and that's why you appear formed. You *re-membered*. That's why you have your members fitly joined together. You must remember that in Essence, Nothingness IS, and that's the Allness of the Being I AM. That's how you have no fear.

It's the most *wonderful* story for you to hear! What is the great danger? Oh, it's fraught with danger because that's part of the tension! There's nothing wrong with anything being dangerous. Anything that's dangerous is great! It's when you don't know it's dangerous that it's serious. So when you say, "Oh, that's danger-ous," then you know Wisdom is present and you'll know what to do with it. It's when you don't see the danger that it's dangerous.

The Wonder of the whole experience: it's dangerous to know what you know, but it is Wonder-filled when you can *navigate* through the course of the Absolute and still appear a viable, creative spirit, clad in the garment of multiplicity wearing the Chalice of Wonder. That's when your head is no longer "tucked underneath your arm," or your eyes constantly looking at the ground. You may be looking straight ahead at me, but in That State you will see what I see, and that is only mySelf, without the impediment of this discriminating mind. And yet, with this discriminating mind, I have the fun of saying, "Hi, Mal," "Hi, Greg," "Hi, Jackie," "Hi, Ellen." I can bring David in from the hillside, and he can shear his sheep, and tell Peter to get the Rock ready so he can stand upon it. You can tell somebody else to go because you have found the window to Wonder.

If I were not a Wonder, Nothingness would be oblivion. It isn't. I live, Reborn, a Testament to That. You have heard it, and now you do. How do you like it?

We were riding the horse; he's riding the fish. [Mr. Mills refers to a Chinese ceramic roof ornament hanging on the wall.]

So often we're dealing with the fish, when we're riding the horse. We don't see the fish, because the fish are those thought-sets that are layered beneath the threshold of your daily awareness. They can only be perceived if you know how to plunge into the depths and engage those different levels and different atmospheres without being destroyed by them. Then you can bring the Wonder to the surface.

It's so fascinating, when you fall off the dive ship with all your scuba gear, you drop off backwards and go down. On the surface it can be *so* choppy, it's almost scary. The waves look so beckoning: "Oh, dive into me, and I will give you rest." You dive into them and you are thrown around as if you were a cork. It's only when you do the exact opposite of what you think you'd do (swim to safety) that you sink. You have to let the air out of your jacket deliberately and let the lead weight at your waist carry you down to get below the surface impression.

This is what you have to do: *get below the surface impression.* You can develop a neutral buoyancy and stay at any level you wish and be at home in any school of fish. The fun is to be able to be in it, if you want to be, and out of it, all by movement. It's creative. If you don't have the creative movement, you can become discombobulated because, remember, although the waves on the surface are chaotic, the waves below are entrancing. They're huge swells and you hardly feel them. That's why you must watch them, because in the engagement of the currents way below the surface, a hundred feet down, if you're not watchful, you can be taken so far away from your buddy that it's dangerous. Do you realize that when you go beneath the surface, you never go below without a buddy? Always remember that. That's why it's great to have a buddy present because when you go below the surface of your impressions, each will see a different type of school.

Remember, there is only one School of the Fish that has ever survived. That is the one out of which came, from the deep recesses of the Unknown, the Somethingness that is termed the Power commensurate with the thought-structure of Self-Realization.

What is so wrong with so many today is the mechanical mind, which is all inherited, they say, by perpetuation of the thought-structures that stem way back from Atlantis, when the Soul was dwarfed. It's by dwarfing the soul that man creates a slave race or pygmies. That is what Atlantis did. The Atlanteans had the ability to create a race of slaves by deliberately keeping the real Food, the real Nutrition, from reaching those people. They had great inventions, so it is said, but they lost their ability to come and go at will.

When you speak the thoughts that are not relevant to the limitations of time, you are on the periphery of the Garment that is termed Seamless.

We have seen transformations within three days of thought-fields that were totally foreign to us. They were changed by appearing to listen, but really hearing what the Heart was saying. Too many of us listen to the words instead of to the Heart. Listening to words gives you the key to what the heart is saying or isn't saying. You can usually tell from a person's eyes, then from the tension in his face, whether he is inditing the message that you are supposed to perceive coming from the heart, or camouflaging the message so that you won't perceive that he does *have* a heart!

The thought that you entertain, whether you speak it or not, is a tremendous force. I showed you at the piano. There is another very good example with two pianos side by side: one piano has no player at it, but somebody at it releases the pedals and allows all the strings to be freed; somebody at the other piano plays, stops playing and the one that has no player at it is doing all the sounding from there on. But not one string was struck on it!

Have you ever thought of the keyboards that you play upon in each other's company? Look at mother and daughter sitting here, Barry and David sitting here, Greg and Ellen. Have you ever wondered what strings you are allowing to be freed, or have you got them "felted" so that they can't respond? Don't ever be an open string to the thought-realm, because you can pick up *every* thought that's going around in here and it's nothing but chaos. In other words, just listening to people talk without discriminating is allowing yourself to be an open string! It's *terribly* important. Don't *ever* just sit eating popcorn and listen to people talk without discriminating. The Fire changes everything; the heat changes everything. After all, you wouldn't have your popcorn if you didn't pop your kernel!

I didn't know what I would speak about this evening. You know, the wonder of it is that we appear to be doing it now, but who is to say who will be performing it? It is composed, so it can happen. It has happened and, therefore, is composed. It's orchestrated as a result of the Grand Clef of Being. It is frequency-modulated to this realm. It is this tremendous heat that I'm experiencing that always engulfs me when I bring this to you via this seven-strung string. Actually, I have eleven; the tenth and the eleventh support my ninth so that I can give it. The higher dominant dissonance is sometimes called the Divine Agitator.

It's amazing how the mind thinks that it has heard it before. The only thing it has heard before is in the harmony of music. The dominant is always freedom, but when you have the seventh, you know you have to rise. It has to move; whether or not you go home or to a deceptive depends upon your readiness to write your own cadence!

Whether I am in the bleachers looking upon the bleachers or I am in the field looking upon the bleachers, it makes no difference. The heights and the depths are the description of the observer. I AM All-inclusiveness. This is viable in everyday living, and if you don't live it in every day, you will find it a suffering.

If you start to live it, those who know you will respond, and those who don't know you will react. Remember, "react" is always personal. So when anyone reacts to you, it has nothing to do with anything but "you." Since you know the Whole Story, then when they respond to you, they're recognizing themselves — themSelf. Enough selves. Grammatically, it's hard to give.

Are there any questions? Yes, Alexandra.

> Alexandra K.) Mr. Mills, what you just said about watching either from the bleachers or from the field, is that then an indicator of the observer —

Oh, yes.

> Alexandra K.) — to shock "you" into seeing that you're not the one that's really moving this machine around?

I AM moving this machine around. But I AM not in it. If I were in it, I could be knocked out of it. That's why I can let it go, and you call it death. It's nothing but allowing the thought-pattern to return to its native nothingness from which it sprung!

> Alexandra K.) What is "it" that allows "me" to function in it?

Well, the explanation is said to be the *Silver Cord*, which is an energy that pulsates from the physical body to the etheric. But then you have a wonderful mind structure that also needs *suturing* half the time.

It's something to question, but it's also very important not to dwell too much in trying to solve constructs of the mind. Try to find constructs of Truth. Constructs of the mind are *ever* there to be solved because they are your invention. The Truth constructs its own Selfhood, and in That rejoice and be satisfied.

There's been enough said to see the Eternality already. So we're not even beginning. We've just experienced the Ouroboros, you know, the continuous Round of Sun.

It never sets; it never rose.
It's just as I AM, and so it comes and goes
For you who live in a period of time,
While I AM an exclamation, and your period, your I!

Dwell in the I-Period and let others exclaim
They have seen a great Light, and doff your hat and say,
"Hi! I'm so glad you recognized yourSelf."

Love is such a force; it's too bad to think it only has to do with the transitory. It's such a powerful thing. It has nothing to do with the transitory other than to embrace it and allow it to appear to be diversified and multiple in experience. Love is such a versatile Force Field that it allows what isn't to appear to experience IT!

January 23, 1992

---

1 Alfred A. Tomatis, *The Conscious Ear* (Barrytown, NY: Station Hill Press, 1991). Dr. Tomatis is a French audiologist.
2 1 John 3:2.
3 Antoine de Saint-Exupery, *The Little Prince* (New York: Harcourt, Brace & World, 1943).
4 Joshua 24:15.
5 Mr. Mills plays on the words by referring to *heshe* beads of Southwestern Indian tribes.

XIII

IN PRAISE OF THE INVISIBLE

Don't ever be surprised at receiving. It is natural to receive; it's very unnatural not to. I'm the living evidence of that. If I were not receiving every moment, how would I know what to say? I have only agreed to be the Executive of the Force that is prompting the cognition that there is a Plan that man has dreamed up that has to be fulfilled.

IN PRAISE OF THE INVISIBLE

This is the morning of January 26, 1992.
It is a day in which the Sun does shine and the Agelessness of
the I comes to view.
Through the camera of your mind you will certainly perceive
a suggestion, and the mind terms "an act,"
That one comes and goes in the apparent seeming while I
remain a perpetual, constant, creative Act.

In that recognition, we have made this morning a time
To be *on* it, not out of it, but present; yet out of it and
present, and in it, in order to satisfy the clime:
The climate of your thought, your considerations, if you're
considering yourself and the "me's" about,
Wondering and perhaps equating the screaming "me-me's"
and wondering what there is to do when there is so
much doubt.

Well, the Ages have always given a song of recognition to a
Principle, Perfect, Uncontaminated, Divine;
It's said this Principle, if you're not *really* religiously equated
with a dogma of a teachable mind,
Is a living, a vital Standard, always flexible, borne in the
Might of the Wind,
And *you* bear *allegiance* to That Glory, because in the Light
of IT you have never sinned.

You have walked in the Spirit of Grandeur because you have
wandered not off the beaten Path,
The One scourged by the suggestions of doubt, which the
Savior of the past pursued for those who did doubt.
You move now with the agility of an angel, because your
Pathway now does *not* lie
O'er the steps of the process of becoming, for a Principle
dawned in the blue sky.

It said, "Look up and behold the seeming. Look *down* and
find the Mother Earth."

There you are, a medium in form. What is your
      evolutionary urge? To birth?

Or is it to break a habit, the habit of Being confined,
      expecting a repetitive rebirthing in order to transcend
      "time"?
Or is it to give you confidence? To *hell* with the urge to
      revolt!
Claim the position of Evocator for those in whom "What do
      you feel?" is a passing question; "*How* do you feel?"
      a daily one.
This is why it's always the same old answer, the habit, the
      habitual: "Oh, pretty well, thank you, Miss Some.
I miss some of the Wonder and the Glory. I miss some of
      that Eternal Might
That comes when you know there's more to this seeming."
      Why give up the urge to find the question of this
      "passing life"?

Do you suppose you're reborn for a purpose? Do you
      suppose that you are reborn to act
The Divine Drama and tension becoming those who
      understand and know what is written on the
      Invisible Scroll of That?
Perhaps *your* place is to find how you're equated with the
      Facts *you know* in the Heart,
Giving to all those who are out of rhythm because their head
      has had a *head start*!

Give the Heart a chance to regain its position; in Essence, it's
      rhythmic in Act.
The whole purpose of the Heart is to be *filled* with creative
      tension. There is no blockage, of course, to the
      Rhythmic That.
It's *only* when you don your habit of being this aging thing
That you *fall* for a heart out of rhythm and forget how the I
      rhythmically sings!

"**YOU** . . wake up!" so they say unto the people from the
      Mount of the Sagehoods of Light,

But when you fly beyond the peaks of those sacred
    mountains, you see there's a possibility of going
    beyond those "horror" heights![1]
Because when you are just on the mountain of *seeming* and
    you think you're talking to the people in the valley
    below,
You still have your feet clad in Earth's time and the clay
    between your toes still shows.

But you see, in the Universal Nature of the Divine Self, the
    Christ, the Ultimate in disguise,
There *always* has been a Tonality becoming the Mark of the
    Principle, Eternal I.
What is the Mark of the Called Ones? They *always*
    respond, "Yes!" when asked
To give up going skiing on the hillsides of the icy slope and
    falling perhaps on their — uh-huh.

If you're poetic, you will know the rhythm; if you feigned to
    consider it gauche in time,
Then consider where *you* stand on the side of the Principle.
    Have you taken your place in the Kingdom Divine?

The whole purpose of a *flight* of elevation is because the
    Host went before you, you know,
And the sky is termed "blue" in your delusion, but perhaps
    it's just wrapping you in the Promise that you must
    show.
The Blue is so becoming to the Virgin. It's so becoming to
    the Archangel Michael, you know.
It's so *becoming* because He bears the Sword of Power,
    another symbol of the Sacred Fire, you know?

So, you see, when the Sword of Truth strikes you, you might
    say you get a *blast* of the Heat
That comes when the Fire of Translation is at your side and
    you the Holy seek.
What is the Wonder of Being? It's being freed in the
    Creative Might of the Now.
For I never came or went, or birthed. This is just all your

program for show.
Have you ever considered your Calling to *come out, be
counted separate* in Cause, to be One
With the Glory of the Reborn and sharing your
understanding of Son?

The mass is *obviously* asleep to the Song of Wonder! Why,
they chatter like chatterboxes, drunken with the wine
of thoughts.
They don't even hear the exclamation of Wonder in the
Grace an amazement brought.

If you *hear* in the room of division, you'll *see* (if you can
look beyond the seeming sight)
That the Structure of Being is harmonic and is equated with
a Heavenly Delight.

So you, in your Moment of Grandeur, move in a rhythmic
way,
And walk in a march for the Conquerors who have
vanquished the seeming, limited day.
Yours is an Eternal one of Promise. You think you're
comfortable just in your everyday life?
Well, now that you've met *Me* in this garment of seeming,
perhaps you will feel the Point of My Sword of Light.

I came *not* to let you be comfortable in your *habit*! So
change your gown and find
That in the *new* Garment, the One woven without rent or
seaming/seeming, is the One that is untouched by
time.
Your garment is woven in *attention*, because through these
words that hold your errant mind, or thoughts,
There in between each word is the Magic of That Power
which enlightens This Heart in This Spot.

So I look like this form, this thing, in becoming; but coming,
that's only in the slot of time,
For when you stop sleeping and dreaming, *when* did I *ever*
leave you? Was I not always the Comfort, the Beat

to your Heart that knows you live out of time?
Don't move! You might wake the baby. Don't shout
"The Earth!" unless you wish the Earth to awake.
And if you give praises of Song to the Eternal, a new birth
    your Soul will take.

So *raise* your voices in acknowledgment of the Wonder
    which at Heart is found
Allowing *your* seeming fleshly garment to be transcended at
    will, unbound.
Do you suppose that if you didn't look up, and if you didn't
    look down,
You didn't look sideways — what do you suppose would be
    found?

Heaven above, hell below;
Sideways, sideways. What dimension would show?

How do you probe the seeming, if it isn't by using a Point that can penetrate the fabric of the mind's suggestive might?

It gives me such pleasure to hear it. I'm so glad I'm not asleep! If I were asleep, you see, it would never be heard, and if I were asleep, *That* would never have been heard. Because if man is asleep, he cannot give the Message that is the Man that is equated with Eternality.

Mrs. Eddy said, "The greatest error is the preaching without practice."[2] I think it's a profound statement. It seems that so many people *talk* a great deal about the partials; they never stop and allow the Fundamentals to ring loud and clear.

When you stand up and declare your stand
In the drama of today, you will find not necessarily
    a responsive nature always at your hand!

If you think you will, you will be quite surprised; at least, that has been my experience. It hasn't been the preaching without practice. If it had not been for the discipline and the ability to separate the formulated children of my awareness pattern and have them dance according to the demands of independence commensurate with freedom, I would never have been able to engage the difficulties of the complex technical passages that this life has presented to me and to play them — in a sense, a cadenza — without a seeming sense of difficulty. A cadenza is always what is achieved when technical proficiency has become an innate part of your development or, you might say, the dexterity with which you engage the various octaves of your chosen keyboards of Light.

> To just sit and consider beautiful thoughts,
> You might just as well know that it's one way of being
> blissfully brought to the sense of rot!

Look what happens to roots! I mean, you overload them with water and they rot, and yet the plant is supposed to grow by being watered. But they have to have the growing pains of Sunship. This is how it is kept alive in the regenerating pattern of belief that man is reborn and regenerating.

You see, everyone loves to see children come because it keeps alive the sense, "Oh, life goes on even when we pass." Well, of course it does! You've made it up that way. Because you pass, so there's more room made! Oh, you know, there will never be overpopulation. That is propaganda. Oh no, and the people who are starving and the people who are overindulging — talk about *starving*! You've forgotten what starving is! You know? When you have a bulge and you think you've overeaten, perhaps you *have* taken too much . . of the seeming. You see? You must always know within your life experience that every thought that exists, you never created; you only have as an ability, the ability to cognize the thought and to decide whether or not you want to give it continued life.

It is the thought that follows thought that gives you a sense of logic, because a thought of love will bring other thoughts of love, a thought of hate will bring other thoughts of hate, a thought of envy will bring thoughts of envy, and then thoughts of death will bring thoughts of death. But when your thought is *linked* with the force field of known, experienceable patterns of thought termed your Legacy appearing as *recognition* of statements made — do you realize that's how you know your Legacy? Say, for example, you hear me speak, and you *hear* something that you know rings true: *it's because it's **within you**!* It's part of your Invisible Scroll.

The whole purpose of attending a joint exercise *in Praise of the Invisible* — which is all this gathering is; it's a joint venture in the exercise "Given to Praise."[3] That's all! If you don't know how to do it yourself, then you see what happens. You've asked somebody to come from another Area to be assigned to alert you into this action — hi! — but that is what this is. "Given to Praise" is the actual Essence that man translates into the English language that stems from the Revelation that the Sages have achieved but haven't been able to articulate into a dramatic, transcendent, creative tension. Because most consider the *need* of the form to *verify* the Invisible.

The need of the form to verify the Invisible is secondary. The light from the candle, whether you can see the body or not, is essential; whether or not you can see the wax is inconsequential; whether or not you can see the body is inconsequential. The light is important, but the light of a candle doesn't differentiate; it demands that you, in your attention to the room in which it is lighted, perceive where the dust is upon your shelves and on your objets d'art. You see? It isn't the light of the candle telling you "this needs dusting"; it's alerting you to the fact that you haven't looked frequently enough to see the dust is settling and it is becoming an attic just waiting for moths, which could corrupt.

How does a moth corrupt? It's a thought-cluster that formulates around a Light sentence, "You are Divine." Then you start thinking in the framework of person, and you're surrounded by moths! Your Divinity is never *thought*; IT is a Known Fact, because you can question. If Divinity were not the Root of All in the garment of time, IT could never be uttered in the framework of Praise. You *love* to be called Divine, but IT bears absolutely no reference to your form. IT bears no reference to your thoughts. It's only your thoughts that on your ticker tape say, "I recognize that. It's good! I AM Divine. I must *fax* this!"

What do you do with your Facts? Instead of faxing it, you put it "f-a-x," leaving the "X" there always unknown. If you stay with the *fa*, you *never* can go to the *sol*, and you have to bring very much a cadence with the hopes that somebody else will write your hymn of glory! Four-one or five-one cadence, whichever you wish. Sometimes it could be called an "abrupt" cadence, but we should provide an *abridged* cadence, or an *extended* cadence, because you can't rest too long!

You know, it's so nice to say, "I've got all kinds of time to prepare for this dinner." I say to my cook, "Oh, come on out with me, we've got to go out shopping!" "(Oh, my goodness, ten people coming for dinner.) Well, *sure*, Mr. Mills, we'll go." But the point is, look how you can abridge it. I've seen my cook do it; I've seen twenty people coming for dinner, and what is going to be on the table coming just a couple of hours ahead of time. Because why? *The Artistry of Being* gives *the instantaneous fulfillment of the need.*

I have been speaking recently, as you know, with so many people in the society here, which seems much more awake to the Unusual being of value; they don't seem to be afraid of it. It has been such an experience for me, because, you know, you can look very much like deadpans, but I know you're not! Remember, God made Himself available! Do you know how He made Himself available? By your face, the canvas! I mean, why do you think you want to *paint* it all the time?! Why do you think you *should*? Because it is seldom reflecting the Light, and you have to do *something* to make it conform to what you know innately is the State of Beauty.

Why do you think I'm designing all these new dresses for the fashion show? Who'd ever *expect* me to design clothes? *Why wouldn't I?!* **I'm asking you to put on a new one all the time!** Why do I always love to design for women? *Because it's obvious most people who design for them don't love them*! Because it never shows the beauty of the form. You either put on a sack because you've eaten too much or, if you don't eat too much and you have a nice figure, it's not in fashion to be belted. So you bulge for fashion. I'm all for giving a *Figure* to fashion. That has been the whole purpose behind designing: it's to bring a Figure to fashion in the Scheme of the Divine, so that One can be Given to Praise.

Now do you see? Isn't your expectation high? It shows you what *thoughts* about Beauty will bring, how you start to reconsider a Figure, how you start to reconsider a form, and how you can start to redramatize your Presence by Beauty. Isn't that the key to unlocking the potential of possibilities? Do you realize, when you dress up, you *feel* different. It is only because your thoughts have to be altered to be in *agreement* with your Presence.

Have you ever noticed how uncomfortable women are who are wearing mink coats out shopping, with no makeup on and . . pajamas? Well, they're track suits; I don't know what you call them. No makeup! I really think, "The poor little mink died to give them credence!" Like an elephant I never forget. I'll never forget this experience: I was out at a very nice evening where there were two wonderfully gifted young people performing, and I was told that an attaché from my country was going to be present. I never expected such a case! I was just expecting my representative to be present and match an Ambassador's wife who was dressed beautifully in a long gown, and beautifully presented. In comes this *case*, in a **PINK** — *baby* pink — track suit!

How can you attach culture to that? Why was I disturbed, and why did I do Work over that immediately? Because that represents, supposedly, a state of government. If the government isn't stable in presentation, how can the acts under that government bear fruit? Many points are essential to be passed under the Light of your Realized State, because nothing comes to you to be accepted if it is unbecoming to the Principle That IS; it comes to you to give itself up!

I was speaking once to a great metaphysician in New York and he was telling me about a very successful businessman from Wall Street coming into his office very disturbed because people were saying all manner of unkind things about him. The practitioner said, "Did they call you the Son of God?" He said, "Oh, no!" "Well," he said, "they weren't even talking about you!"

Where has error, or the suggested opposite of Truth, to go if it isn't to you? Why do you think you can hear This and be released from your duty? You're the walking custodians of freedom for those who wish to see your countenance, because the Light should be shining upon it, and all those who see it should see a remarkable Presence because it bears a *living* force field around it. You can't have a realization and not have the Force that goes with it. When you *have* this you can be assured that those who perceive it would like to be around you, but they will also perceive that it's costly to be around you.

It's costly because you cannot allow anyone to dwarf the magic that is so becoming to the Light. What is the magic? The magic is that which happens instantaneously, whether it is a healing or the tranformation of a thought-pattern so quickly that you suddenly see no longer an opaque stone but a transparent one. That's what it means to say, "Right before you is Holy Ground."[4]

The Ground of Being is the cognition of the fundamental statements that can be termed correlative to the Divine Principle. No man, no person, can ever give you your freedom, your enlightenment, or give you love. The only magic that one may offer is that which comes when, in one another's presence, two-ness fades out and there is nothing but the thrill of seeing the indivisible nature of Man.

Remember, if I seem to be a stranger to you, it's because you *think* you don't know me. But you are not a stranger to me because I know my Self and I'm not going to be fooled by your apparel, whether it's appealing as the bells that ring within my heart or as the song that comes from a responsive sound or the movement of a head that *cannot* contain itself and *has* to move in agreement with the constancy of the Newness of Being.

You here in this incredible city of the Big Apple have such a wonderful opportunity to look at the orchard that has grown beyond the imagined concrete walls of belief, "officed" by those who work as ants in the daily travail of keeping a semblance of "transcendent" activity. It is so wonderful to work and be a slave. I live in that condition; I don't have what you would call freedom at all, save when my phone is off the hook. But I was caught by it a long time ago; I was in the Stream and lifted onto the bank of what you call this Age. It is interesting to realize how many hours of every day you spend *trying* to make your boss happy, but you never consider the Director of your own Selfhood. You always keep your boss happy because he's going to give you a piece of a sulphurated tree trunk with his acid-formed ink for you to use your pen to countersign this acidic state, and you hope to keep it balanced.[5]

It's a fascinating consideration. Of course it's necessary, but it's *how* you service that's important. If you do the service from the Standpoint of the Omnipresent Action of Mind, then you are not caught up in the figures. It is by being caught up in the figures that you find the remuneration limited. You figure every thought when you personalize it. You have it blessed with the symbol of the

Infinite, the zero, when you are about in the offices of time bearing the knowingness of the Invisible that allows you to appear visible.

Don't *ever* be surprised at receiving. It is natural to receive; it's very unnatural not to. I'm the living evidence of that. If I were not receiving every moment, how would *I* know what to say? I have only agreed to be the Executive of the Force that is prompting the cognition that there is a Plan that man has dreamed up that has to be fulfilled. Of course, knowing that everything has to be planned in time, when you start to accept this, then your *un*planned state has to appear to be planned and you have to get at that experiential distance where you can appear to be in it or out of it but always remain as you really are.

Somebody said to me the other day, "Do you mind if I call you 'Ken'?" I said, "Not at all, if you can!" He tried it. It was awesome. Calling me "Ken" didn't work at all! The next time we saw him, he called me "Maestro." I don't care if you call me "Ken." But I'm, you know, K.G./cagey for sure!

Remember, anything that I appear to say that is true is only so that you can *remember*. That's the only reason I am here. I can't give you anything but Love, baby! That's it. Anything that you remember as a result of hearing these words is because in Essence we are One, and perhaps I returned so that *you* could take *your* turn. You can't expect this experience to leave you; you were *found* by it so that you would not be buried in it. Of course! The second death should have no sting. Grave, where is the victory?

The grave is only the result of doubt and faith and hope.
But the victory rests in knowing that I was never born to live
    or to die,
But I AM That Eternal Presence that appears to give light to
    your sky.
I appear to be a Light to your life from the dark side of the
    moon
Which you cannot see but I show your reflected light.

Then in *That* State so simple and grand
You appear to look like a woman or a man,
But when you see as I AM, there is no doubt:

The Beauty of Being is all about.

You can come and go and you can dance and sing
And you can yell and scream about what you aren't and
    what you are, and yet, the King
Is *always* enthroned on the Dais of Light,
For you don't have to look up, down, or sideways;
    Look in and behold,
    There, I AM Light!

What you see is how your sensorial apparatus is functioning. How you interpret is according to the limited framework in which you are experiencing this Cataract of Tones. Remember (as I was saying coming up in the car), when you look at a beautiful silk dress — or a sport coat or a smoking jacket or tuxedo — made out of silk, and you say, "Oh, that's a beautiful silk dress," it is, *but* it bears not the mark of its origin which was a cocoon and a worm. But you know enough to take that secretion and string a line of unbroken beauty and appear to clothe your figure in time. Perhaps that is my life. The Cocoon from which I have come is one that is allowing me to appear to string these lines of words so that the Butterfly of Wisdom and the Fluency of Light allow me to light your candle even in your attic, in your living room, and once again may you say, "Ah, the Fragrance, the Perfume, the Bouquet of a Birthday, its gifts and its Fragrances, All Light!"

Thank you very much.

January 26, 1992

---

1 Mr. Mills is playing on the name "Horeb Heights."
2 Mary Baker Eddy, *Science and Health With Key to the Scriptures* (Boston: Trustees Under the Will of Mary Baker G. Eddy, 1934), p. 241, ll. 17-18.
3 *Given to Praise* is also the title of Mr. Mills' first published book (Toronto: Sun-Scape Publications, 1976).
4 Exodus 3:5.
5 Mr. Mills refers to the making of paper in pulp mills.

XIV

THE FULCRUM AND
THE FUNERAL

Until our own garden is verdant and filled with the fragrance of the seeds which have been planted, then we should be silent until we are asked, "How does your garden grow? What have you used as a fertilizer?" You will say, "The fertile soil of the mind has been tilled because we have secured That Moment set aside in the annals of time for fulfilling the considerations that have been passed to us via the different forms of religion, which have kept alive in the hearts and minds of some the possibilities of a heaven in the future."

THE FULCRUM AND THE FUNERAL

As we engage the plane of considerations commensurate with your achievement in quelling the forces of the mind that would limit you to this environment, we would undertake, in the Rhapsody of Being, to restore order and harmony to the Soul in order for you to once again engage those planes that are in the fructifying state for emergence upon your plane for being adopted and adapted to the Frequency of the Harmonic Basis of existence.

You are being prepared. For, as you know, the world is once again in the throes of being considered an unknown quantity under the feet of time. But, under the Soul of that Force Field which allows you to equate yourself with the Cosmic Influences of consideration, you are thereby endowed with an impelling force to those thought-constructs that embrace what is beyond your temporal, finite, and sensorial acceptance. You are thereby once again endowed with the questioning mind and its force that compels one to find an answer.

We are being alerted, as never before, to the need of those who are given the Presence of the Holy Ghost, the Presence of the Godness of our Selfhood, and we are being forced as Lovers of One to find the One Love that frees all from the sense of separateness in this world of diversity.

We are faced with the plan of re-establishing a drama befitting the scenario of what man has termed his future, for which he appears to long, for he feels that it will be one endowed with the Beneficence of the Almighty. We are also very aware that we have to engage a thought-pattern that is going to restore order to chaos. The one who is not focused and is at the beck and call of circumstance is like one scattered and splattered o'er the face of the planet, preparing so well the garment of the ensuing chaos with which we are confronted in our everyday lives.

So, you who are here, perhaps you are here because of the magical connection that we all have with an intrinsic commitment from ages past. We are found once again gathering in the great space of open time to the timeless experience of an open door for men and women to perceive the coming of the Glory of the Lord.

This is termed the Law that is to be fulfilled as man gains a higher understanding of the Will and its dominance in the affairs of man.

Every day sees you as people endowed with the will to be or not to be, and at this I shake my spear! Because it is not open any longer to "to be or not to be." This is the Question. It is to BE that requires the one who has said it to realize there is no shake! There is nothing within that *cellar* to cause what is before you to be more appetizing!

You are forever endowed with the ability to formulate
as those required for time
The Prescription for Being undefiled by the concepts
of the errant mind.

You may be on the periphery of the greatest adventure of your life because you are, as never before, perceiving that your suggested aloneness is only the way that men and women see separateness and feel that civilization is falling apart. Of course civilization is falling apart, because it is the name given to the compilation of the suggestions surrounding the "citizen." When the citizens are together in the Wonder of Being, a civilization is endowed with the crowning achievement of an emancipated state, which bestows involuntarily the Grace of That Force Field upon all others who might ask, "How does your garden grow?"

Until our own garden is verdant and filled with the fragrance of the seeds which have been planted, then we should be silent until we are asked, "How does your garden grow? What have you used as a fertilizer?" You will say, "The fertile soil of the mind has been tilled because we have secured That Moment set aside in the annals of time for fulfilling the considerations that have been passed to us via the different forms of religion, which have kept alive in the hearts and minds of some the possibilities of a heaven in the future."

Remember, the reason religion appeals to the mind, and the heart hopes for surcease from being considered only a secondary feature of the mind's action, is because we have never been able to bridge the gap between this and That. This can only be achieved as you *don* the wings of the morning and claim that the sun never did set, that what you called the "arising" was how your mind had prepared to perceive, in its own upside-down way, a picture that would allow you to sleep in the belief that the sun set and, therefore, darkness descended and you would sleep. This mesmeric influence of darkness and lightness is the prime consideration manifested which points to the divisive state and the thought-field unacquainted with the supremacy of Principle.

It is the Divine Principle which we hold to the thought-mind in order to have all the thoughts attributable unto That so that when you need to explain (in other words, when you need to describe the *plane* that is under the X of the Unknown, the *X-plane*), then you will be able to delineate with words that will not lead your watchers astray on the plane of action.

As you know, the greatest rider of any horse and the greatest horse for any rider is when they are in *agreement* with one another. Remember, the horse had to be *drilled* to realize that there was someone sitting in the saddle. When that someone sitting in the saddle and the horse are in agreement, there is force and power and the plane can be known, because there you have the *wonder of agreement* and the decorative action to hold your attention for the act on this plane of time.

Your mind is what it is: "your" mind. Everyone talks about his mind, and his mind having to be filled with the thoughts of the Glory of God and equated with those thoughts that are like the waters which cover the sea.[1] But you see, the Mind of God is a *concept* of the mind of man. What is going to happen to you and to the world when the *conceptual* is seen to be a pretender to the throne of your Omnipotence?

You are appearing in form because of a plea of the mass. In other words, those who are attuned to the Higher Kingdom of Light, as you might say, are brought here in order to satisfy the plea of the mass, and you forget this. That is what forgettery does: it allows you a recess from the heroics of Being! The recess is the time when you start to pretend you are something you are not and don't think you have to be responsible for the play.

But the drama is the evidence of the Divine Rama. This means that you have subdued the *obstinacy* of suggestion and realized the need of the Royalty becoming the nobility surrounding the Hero when *obligation is essential*! *That* is what makes man a noble: his realization of obligation to That Which IS not seen. In the royal families it's called ancestry. In our day we don't want to *hear of it*, because we have nothing in ancestry to give us the possibility of being knighted, of being raised in title above the common. Therefore, *how are you going to bring "peace to the nations" when you haven't found the Totality of your own universe?!*

The "universe" means "to turn into one," and "individuality" means "the indivisible nature" which cannot be split! Then, what is doing the splitting? It's your mind, which has accepted faulty instruction.

How are you going to be reborn? All the fundamentalists want you to be "born again." "Born again!" How can you be reborn if you don't die? What have you got to die to? To two! You and God, or "you and me and the lamppost." (You have to have a trinity somewhere!) You have to realize that the "you" and "me" is the way we seem. These are always the knots on our web of awareness because we get so wrapped up with "you" and "me" that we forget I AM.

You know, somebody said in the car today, "I know I exist because I can say, 'I think, therefore I am.'" Of course, I think, therefore I name myself something that is not like everyone else but similar to everyone else. My thinking is different, but my AM is the same. What is That I AM? It certainly is something you don't know, but you associate it with what you do know: your "me." If somebody says, "Who are you?" you'll say, "I am Roger." I'll say, "Jolly or not?" You'll say, "I am . . Roger." I'll say, "Oh, you've underlined the need of conceiving *you* on a ledger line, because you don't exist on the staff of recognition where you are limited by the octave of this Earth suggestion."

So, you are *conceived* by claiming I AM, *vibrating* with possibilities of another octave, but, if you don't find the Fulcrum **That**, you can't reach it! If you stay with just a melody that is prescribed by the notes on a piece of paper, you can delineate those notes on the piece of paper, but that is *not* the origin of the melody! The origin of the melody only *indicated* that it happened by leaving a trail of notes, but people accept the notes as the melody! They are entirely different.

It is the same with Being and not-Being. You accept this "not-

Being" state as if it were the melody of the gift to time. It isn't the melody of the gift to time; it is the suggestion that the Melody of Being could be *limited* by time in the form of "you" and "me." That Which IS true has *sounded* in the feeling nature through all man's dreamed-up historical considerations. The history is nothing but *His* Story put into the framework of a mind that is capable of deceiving itself and giving you an identity that is transitory! To be reborn means to annul those thought-sets that make you succumb to the suggestion of being an aging mortal.

A thought-*set* is like a cement block, but *you* have to break it. That's why a great karate expert may break a half-dozen bricks with his hand (or break his hand a few times before he succeeds), but he has really accomplished something when he has had his hand set several times and then finally breaks a brick. What happens with that achievement? I have seen people who can do it, but they can't acknowledge somebody who perceives what the *set block* was. And what is it? The falling for playing a part of a teacher! That is the biggest set block you've got, because then you have to study how to be a teacher. When you are the Music, it is a constant newness *improvised* by the meaning of the moment in which you find yourself. It is, therefore, always new!

This is *my* Music; on the keyboard, it is Norman's: the evidence of our Divinity. That is what? *A State that is not circumscribed by the periphery of thought-sets!* It is that State in which your attention is like the radius; it has no end, unless you have a limited sense of energy which you limit by being acclaimed *a wonder.* "Oh, you're so attractive; everyone wants you." That limits your radius; it puts a *collar* on you. It leashes you to a little rod, and with this little thing you go 'round and 'round and 'round and 'round and 'round. You don't realize that you've been leashed and are behaving like a dog when you should be acting as God!

How can you have a God that is without action? Do you realize the mighty force field that you utilize to have a concept called "God"? You've been god-dammed all your lives! You've been god-dammed by your parents and they think they've christened you! There is nothing more horrific! Ask parents in this Group when they see their son realizing his Christ or his Divine Selfhood. They haven't a clue what's happening to their son because it doesn't fit into the pattern.

What pattern have they got to fit in? What pattern did my parents have to fit in? What pattern did Barry's fit in? What pattern does your parent fit in? It's certainly not one to be emulated. I've seen them buried! And they thought they lived. I *know they don't live that way.* Why don't you bury the belief that you live this way *now* and save the double cost?! Funerals are very expensive because, you know, a funeral is made up of everything that should have been *fun* and *real*!!

You can't chew on that! Only about the price of it. You should realize by every funeral the need for you to transcend it. You know? What is a funeral? *The attempt of a belief to get rid of a system.* What is this? An attempt to free the Earth's stage so that more newness may appear that may bear hope.

I knew my father would be leaving, and he pronounced before he left: "I have never understood you, but I have always respected you, for you have always lived what you believed." I knew he was going to get ready for leaving because he came to watch me. I didn't come to watch him. He came to watch me because he had to assimilate something he had rejected in *yesterday's exam.* Mum watched me just through love. But she was afraid to show it and did so in the inverted way: we always argued and sort of fought, because in that way she knew energy was the source of her aliveness. So I never stopped arguing with her if I could (which was not difficult), right up until she was a hundred and two! In this way I knew she had to realize the energy that was still present in the vehicle, because she was going to leave. This was *refocusing* so that when she *did* leave, the jewels would be able to be collected.

The platform today calls upon such a radical reliance upon Truth and not person. You see, this is based on Principle, not person — Principle that is undefiled. No person is *beyond fallibility,* because person is *your* mental construct of a **need** in the disguise of "you." You can't be wearing *your* disguise if you don't accept the imperfection that goes with this model. That imperfection is the dissatisfaction you must have experienced in *not having options*! You claim to have choice.

This is what Earth revolves around:
The core of **Fire** that can redeem.
But the outer crust of options
Comes as the part of your dream.

This is why the dramas are always based on subjects that have to release themselves at any play from just being words to being what? Impersonated? Dramatized! Words have to be lived, either they are just notes on a piece of paper. What are the notes on a piece of paper? Dried ink! But the evidence that what allowed them to appear on the paper was Light.

If I *thought* what I was going to say, I would *not* be speaking. I am enjoying hearing these words — I hope as much as you are — but I have never dreamt one of them! I have not *thought* one of them, but they are the *forces* that are impinging upon my sensitiveness and *demanding* clothing so that you won't feel you are living in a land where there is no Food for Being.

The Love that we *feel* for one another should not be contaminated by thinking it is ours. It is the evidence that God lives.

Now, what is God? The Unknown, but a concept that you say you know so you can have a mind that has an option of either being the direct bridge to that knowing or being at a distance to become known. Did you ever make love to anyone who wasn't touched by the power of it? If your love is power as God's Love is power, you can't help but be *falling* in Love? No! *Flying* in Love! *Elevated* in Love! *Exonerated* from your guilt, because Love knows nothing but ITself.

Do you think *I* care whether anyone says, "I am this piece of misunderstood humanity"? Do you think I care that, if I am in Love with you, you don't dare to admit you're in Love with *me*, unless you are in a position that is invulnerable? And what happens? We go on *pretending* that there's God's Love and man's Love. The reason there seems to be the difference is because man's is conditional and *God's* is **unconditional**! *That* is what you must be if you can say the Word. *Say* the Word and "I AM with you always! Even unto the end." Don't say the Word and have reservations! I will *never* be with you; you have only *thought* me with you and that is why I come and go. Each time IT wears a disguise that meets your need where you are at the moment. Unless you *know*, you don't recognize Me. If you *do* know, you *do* recognize Me, as one did last evening. But never recognize it with just words! This one embraced, almost melted the form, and declared a remembrance.

Why do we declare the *remembrance?* Because it is *a descrip-tion of how man can be exculpated involuntarily from the belief system in the* Wonder *of a Recognition.* That is the terror of **Being** Cognition! Because it means your "you-ness," your oldness is *vanishing* like the man. You see, in the screen of the Allness of God, there is only the image **I AM,** and see if you can figure That One . . out!

How could a note appear on a paper, if it weren't for the Invisible Sound that your time-ears didn't hear, but which your time-ears will hear because somebody has the power of *im*provising *im*provisation? Some improvise others' *improvisation.* This is perhaps *my* act, because I don't *read* anything, I don't hear anything. I'm like the monkey: see nothing, know nothing, do nothing. But since some have said I'm an agnostic, I know from reading that I have no alternative but to *do!* It's so wonderful to know that when you feel impelled to kick, you can! Then it's so wonderful to know if you do kick, it's right. You *must* rescind all the suggestions of pricks that inflict themselves upon you by *your* vulnerability to the opinions of others who would try to keep you a cactus in their gardens so that they can *name* you (but *"don't touch me* because I might have to say I fall in love"). *I* stand *reborn* in the Newness of Being.

What hope is there for China? What hope is there for Japan? What hope is there for Russia? What hope is there for the world? Some of the world has said it is in *these words.* Isn't it incredible how seemingly familiar it has all become because we can touch each other, hug each other, and say, "Love you, Mr. Mills," and I say, "Oh, I love you."

We have forgotten to see the sacrifice that has had to be made on each and everyone's part to be the Holy One that is devoid of a concept of limitation.

What is going to happen to this world or the world to come in a processive, historical race of beliefs? You will *always* be putting off the Now and calling it tomorrow. The most important thing for you to do every day is to be sure you *do* even what you don't want to do when it should be done. *That is the obligation becoming a hero! And no one today wants a hero because then you have a living obligation!*

The Eros has risen in everyone in this room! It's the most natural force; when it's planted in the garden it becomes a blooming rose. If you just leave it in the personality realm, you will always have the feeling of wanting to create, wanting to come together, wanting to be, but *never* civil! Because you don't *want* to see the community becoming the *demand* of *your* system of isolation.

This is why they say that barbarism stems from separateness. The very root of the barbaric stems from separatism. Civilization stems from the root of "citizen." When all people come together with a *common purpose*, you have a civilization. But how is that purpose clothed? It is given a name of Russian, Chinese, Japanese, American. What do we do? We take these incredible pieces of art (every civilization, in its finest moment, is a living art) but we don't recognize them! Whether I understand language or not, I love P.W.N. As soon as I met him, I knew I had found someone that was not *foreign* to *my country*. How could he be, since *My Country* is a Cosmic Embrace! In other words, what is Cosmic? It's something that is beyond your sonic-hood. It doesn't *need* to have an identity to be known to BE.

That's why P.W.N. is here; and I appear to be. It may be this *very link* that can bring about what everyone wishes. It's a harmonic state of Being and that in Essence is based upon Principle, the fundamental Principle. What? . . It doesn't need to be said.

I was asked recently if I would be at a press conference: "I would like it so very much if you would be present; it'll be very important if you are there, Mr. Mills." I said, "I'll try to be there." Why is a press conference important? Because the press is usually there to make public what the public has not perceived to be of consequence. Of course, the only purpose of any consequence is the Truth. That's why people were willing to take the game, "Truth or Consequences," and get a sixty-four thousand dollar question. It always had an answer, but for the right answer you were paid.

I saw a most *adorable* little dog last evening called Rambo. He was a Shih Tzu, little tiny one, most adorable one. It was love at first sight, and he didn't seem to mind at all! (It was perceived by his owners.) He was adorable. They said, "He can do all kinds of tricks." I thought, "How much like people." He was offered some food, and he came over and got down. The owner said, "Whisper.

Whisper to me." [Mr. Mills imitates a dog making soft noises.] The owner said, "Oh, a little louder. Oh, come on, louder." Then, "Oh, speak." [Mr. Mills makes a barking sound.] And he was given a cracker. Isn't that what we have to do? We have to *break* what appears to be the Truth, the Bread of Life, into fragments and offer it at a table of congregation, a table *prepared*. The only reason you should be here is not to wear out the rugs, but because within yourself you are holding the Table upon which the Goodies of Being are placed on trays of silver with apples of gold[2] — and not just the "Delicious." You have to know that even in the *red* you have the Power with which you have to deal; the *gold*, you must have the Fire to melt; and the *silver*, you must have the ability to purify.

What do you suppose your world will be when you die to your belief system and still appear to live, bearing not a fragment of a lost Gospel but the Living Exponent of a Testament of Newness? The joy of Being unconfined is that you didn't *have* to be reborn again through the womb of belief, but it could happen through the Word, the larynx, the new womb of today.

Men and women have existed in a vestibule for over forty-five years, never finding the Key to unlock the door to enter the Sanctuary of their own Godhood. You have to do it and be prepared, for *Now* is the accepted time of ceasing to identify with your concepts of what Man is, by *living* the Vibrant Frequency so that what appears to be your form indites the Message of Totality.

Your Message waits to be heard as a result of your ability to *compose* with ease and thus explain the Wonder of the Unknown and make it plain. You are so educated with the intellectual data of today that you have to be riddled with these Light Bullets that appear to be in keeping with your educated way but bear no resemblance to it whatsoever. You think it English; I tell you, it isn't, but until you *know* it isn't, you may think it is. The people in Europe have moved with freedom, not because they understood what I said, but because they listened to the Sound of my Voice and said it was so. I said, "If that is the case, go to *Doh*!" That was their freedom.

Do you think "*doh*" has to do with money or the bread that you need/knead, whether you need the yeast? Yeast is your what? Your activity *unseen* until it is evidenced in the Fullness of your

Being. Don't expose your new fetus before it is time to be perceived and cognized a Wonder.

> So we have looked over the plains, and we have "gadded" at
> the Might
> And considered it "well done" for the Servants of Light.
> You can see in the act of the bygone day
> That you were told to be faithful and then perhaps have a
> way.

> But now you know the Nobility Divine
> Demands you to fulfill the obligations *beyond* time,
> And then into time you will appear a slave to the Light
> And you'll say, perhaps, "Oh, my God, save me,
> because no one understands my commitment to the
> Heroics of Light."

> Your friends will dispute and perhaps cause you to cry,
> But why be concerned about a tear at your side?
> Why, the encrustations of the Soul must be freed
> And perhaps they will fall as a stream of tears,
> For the joy in awakening puts an end to belief
> That you were ever "this" in actuality, but in the Accounts
> I keep,
> The Wonder of Being the Dividend Divine.
> Wake up and BE! Thou art blossoming in Sun as it shines!

> How does your garden grow?
> With cockleshells, all planted row by row.

Most time sees crosses, because man has never achieved the Wonder of the Fulcrum and then been able to find, as in Heaven so on Earth, Harmony is the Divine State for those who would be in agreement with a Composition and a Melody without words.

February 9, 1992

---

1 Isaiah 11:9; Habakkuk 2:14.
2 Proverbs 25:11.

XV

THE NAPKIN

The world is waiting to be taken into the Arms of Love, and thus the soil that has been overturned in the name of achievement will be given to the proper fertilization process which will yield a harvest becoming the higher needs of what appear to be those who have inherited it and found it a footstool upon which they can rest their Soul and achieve the inexplainable and yet experienceable Choiceless Realm in the realm of the choice.

THE NAPKIN

This is the morning of February 16, 1992,
And it seems like an entirely different morning as the whole
	picture is seen and the view
Is altered from the Standpoint of perception and the contents
	undefiled
By the peregrinations of a mind that becomes what is termed
	the Earth-born child.

It behooves all those who are gathered within the periphery
	of such Might
To don the wings of the morning and forget the yester-night.
For in the dawning morning, Man sees as ne'er before
That what appeared to be the mesmeric turn upon this stage
	of the Earth where we seem employed
Is but a supposition that the sun has to rest,
And thus we bring an end to time and thus the God of
	Cronos blessed.
Because we live in the timeless State of Being, we live in That
	State Divine,
Where we perceive the mighty movement beyond the tracks
	of mind.

You who have gained a position equated with a Pathway
	straight to God,
I wonder how many are awaiting upon the Lord for their
	next movement to be seen and their feet thereby
	shod?
If we "wait upon the Lord," God help us in the act
Because we go on worshipping a *concept*, when God and
	Lord *are* Act.

If you "wait upon the Lord," you are awaiting an excuse
	not to BE.
What kind of mental health have you got, if it's based on the
	excuses? Do you see?

What type of mental health do we have? It has to be acquired, because if it *isn't* acquired, we are so ill mentally. Everything we do is based upon what *seems to be*. It is not, in any way recorded, appropriate to the Principle that is termed Divine. Remember: we are dealing with the form; and Life is *living* the form, we are *not* living Life!

Young or old, they are not *living* Life; **Life** is *living* the form. The reason we appear to be together is because the structure of the programming for this plane is based on the idea of community and civilization and the citizen. And really, most of them need to be *caned*.

We are under an impelling force to "come out from the world and be separate."[1] Why? Because the mass has no use for those who are not part of its association under the heading of "the natural man." There is nothing natural about those who are lured by the Divine. They are totally unnatural, because what the mass considers "natural" is really the agreement to live in the confinement of the achievement of the least within its structure. If you try to live in agreement with the highest in the mass structure, you have various forms of government including a "demo" democracy, which is government for the people and by the people.

The only government should be upon His shoulders,[2] which means it should be placed upon the rhythmical wave of inspired Insight that accompanies the Liberated Man. It means that Life is not lived at the beck and call of circumstance, but in the pomp and elegance of Being surrounding the Allness of *conceptual* Might. Remember, when we are conceiving of Allness and waiting upon the Lord, we are trying to find the rung of the ladder which is toward the end of it in the heights of our mental considerations.

But when we wait upon the Lord, it's as Ortega said: "Today's footstep in yesterday's footprint." You cannot put your ladder to the skies runged with the incompleted acts of yesterday! Remember, drawing upon yesterday to verify your presence now is the most ridiculous thing, because you have no way to verify yesterday's experience unless other witnesses are present to say you did such and such a thing. There is nothing living in the moment that is yesterday, because time and space accompany the dream.

We have tried to make gods. We have one God? Yes. But we have created so many other gods. There's the god of excuse, the god of procrastination, the god of selfishness, the god of resentment, the god of jealousy, and the god of *aloneness*; they are all constructs of the mind. Everything we are dealing with has to do with the manner not becoming the Royal One.

You see, today's society of the mass is without manners, but the Higher Society of those who are acclaimed Divine, even in our attempt to codify and station them beyond the cross of our human speculation, is given credentials that, we say, cannot be other than looked up to. We don't dare to appropriate them and bring them into our own experience because, if we do, we become That. For we are dealing with an Octave of Being that people have only dreamt about. We are not sounding in the octave where we are dealing with the hypothetical, karmic inheritances of yesterday's footsteps; we are dealing in the Octave where the felt has stopped the strings of suggestion from vibrating and the meaning of Life living is Being exemplified by our indomitable spirit to transcend this self-constructed imprisonment.

The urge to rescind the impotence of the mass is being felt by those who dare to take a step out of the suggested realm of the work force of suggestion. We who are in this service are beyond the civil, because we are in That State where we are not *bound* by the suggestion, but are *freed* by the enhancement of the transfiguring Power that accompanies the transcendent and the transformative State achieved by man's alignment of his thoughts to a Divinity that is *not* comprehensible. Our intellect *says* it's comprehensible, but in actuality it *isn't* comprehensible. It can be pointed to by the intellect, by the negative, but what's left over is what Really IS.

If you are doing anything in this world: having a profession, not having a profession, trying to find a profession, trying to find a place for you to *face* your great terror — what is your great terror? You perhaps haven't even faced it, you're so young. It's death! As the books will tell you, the great terror of man is the fact that he is a creature that has to defecate. His body is used for worm food. What are you doing? You're spending all these years getting this worm food with a bank account and you have no Light Account but speculation. You bet upon certain statements that are not tarnished by time: "I and My Father are One."[3] "Don't say 'now'!" Where did that come from? Ha-ha! You want to keep one footstep in the past. "Now" puts it in the present. That is the only way man frees himself from the nation of conflicting thoughts and allows himself to be set in the Majesty becoming the Elegance of the King.

The highest concept will not fit in with the manners of the mass, because our highest concept is not the *common* denominator; it's the highest exponent that man is capable of utilizing to *expel* the suggestion of an accomplished intellect.

The intellect is so clever in associating you with thought-patterns that hold you incarcerated to a belief system. In 1925, before he died, Hazrat Inayat Khan said in his legacy that in the Teaching of the future there would be no religion, there would no longer even be Sufism. Say that to a Sufi and see the suffering! Say that to a Christian and see the hellish situation! Say this to the mass and see the mess on your floor! The creature-hood is obvious! Look at what we program into time as an escape from facing the island of our own resolution into a Higher Octave of Being!

You cannot think your way into the Kingdom; there is no Kingdom to think your way into. The only kingdom you've got to cause to crumble is the one that you're building up about yourself, which is all a figment of your imagination. When this can crumble and be given to Wonder, then it becomes not an impediment, but the impelling force for *exculpation* from the alleged sense of *falseness* and creatureliness which you may consider your terror.

If I were in *this*, I would be telling you of its glory. But since I am not in *this*, the wheels of the mills go faster than you ever can think, because they annul the suggestion that we are doing "road work." You who have come are so *prepared* to *fly*, provided you gas up at the right station. You can't depend upon any type of octane to give you the octave required.

Do you realize that, after all, your alphabet and all these words are nothing but pellets of sound that are penetrating your system of attention so that you can be pelted with infinite possibilities!

What we call empty space is the way we have been pro-grammed by our support system. The reason they say the planet is in need of restoration to the Light and to the brilliant Star-hood it once held is because so many who have come have taken the Will, which they had in its purity at one time but adulterated by thinking it personal in later times. They have misused this Force and thus have brought the Light to bear upon a system that is *dense*, until it is freed in the Light Body of a Realized State, which some have called the Divine Self or the Christ. It doesn't matter what you call IT. What you call IT, IT isn't, but what IT IS allows you to call IT what IT isn't.

The incredible Force is so great that it can have you in need of a gauze garment instead of a woolen one, because it is very hot! Those who think that they have found the Truth and thereby live their own lives are really suffering the tremendous delusion that accompanies the mass who have a semblance of intellectual attainment but have lost the great Fundamental Tone of Being.

When you have once played a key or a note on the piano, as long as your finger stays on it, the key will sound, and then it dies away. The tone dies from that particular key that has been struck. It doesn't mean that it has automatically gone to another octave, unless there has been the willingness to remove the dampening effect of false identification and to allow that string to be sympathetically vibrated by the previous soundingness.

It would seem that those people present have this opportunity, because I sound the note and you respond in the octave. Now, if you will do this dance with me, as I move to a different octave (if you are attuned), you can also experience that. You will not necessarily be able to sing it, because it will be beyond your range, but it does not mean that it doesn't exist. Just because I can't sing a high note like Dianne (the A above high C) or like Laurie, doesn't mean that in my life that A doesn't exist! Just because I can't hear any more A's on the piano, other than the ones that are keyed, doesn't mean that others don't exist. It does mean that the calling from there on depends upon what? The releasement from any depressing influence upon the Harp of Being. It is only the Cosmic influences which can play upon your vibratory frequency and cause you to restore it to a keyship which allows the kinship with all those attuned to a Higher Octave to leap to that parallelism.

The mind of men has not been programmed to understand this. This is why people on various levels came to *lead* you, educate you, tie you to a system of systematic thinking so that a logical thought-pattern could be set up that gave you confidence in being this civilian, this citizen of a contracted society that is depressing the *very* Force Field that *allows the Earth to be reborn and given back to the Arms of Love.*

I was speaking to somebody on the telephone yesterday. He had been speaking to a woman who had left this Work and who said, more or less, that she felt she was enlightened and didn't need any more Teaching. I said, "My God, forgive her!" If a man is enlightened or a woman is enlightened, he or she never declares it! What is the state that you are declaring? I don't need to go around declaring. "I AM, I AM, I AM, I AM, I AM, I AM." I don't even declare that for you! It's the part of the I-O-U! I don't know what Enlightenment is, if you make me think of it! If she thinks she's enlightened, or any other poor fool thinks he is enlightened, and out in the world doing his selfish thing — he's not enlightened at all! The purpose of Enlightenment, if you have it, is to allow the world to reverberate in Wonder again and bless all mankind! It's not some selfish little pinprick experience. It's a vibrating totality that embraces your whole conceptual might and gives it back to the Arms of Love.

The world isn't waiting to be raped! That's what your mass is doing: they're raping this world! The world is waiting to be taken into the Arms of Love, and thus the soil that has been overturned in the name of achievement will be given to the proper fertilization process which will yield a harvest becoming the higher needs of what appear to be those who have inherited it and found it a footstool upon which they can rest their Soul and achieve the inexplainable and yet experienceable Choiceless Realm in the realm of the choice.

When you know What IS, you know you know, and what isn't is not a choice. And What IS is not a choice! Do you realize that those statements ("I will," "I won't," "maybe," "but," and "if") are all excuses to keep you from facing your eternal striving to evade your *shallowness in an attempt* to exculpate yourself from the suggestion?

What is the purpose of your life, if it isn't to exude the Wonder so that all men can say, "How does your garden grow?" You say,

"Because the *God-Seed* sprouted and my roots are in the Diapason of Being."

How can "the Kingdom of our God become the Kingdom of His Christ" if they are separate? It is so wonderful to have a "God-concept" and a "you-concept" trying to get together to swing it low so that *you don't have to worry about death*. "Swing low, Sweet Chariot, coming for to carry *you* home." You have to swing high and then you just find yourself going around in circles (spirals).

When you have once tasted the fruit of the Spirit, it becomes the glowing ember that never can be dislodged from your gut of suggestion. Never can be! And no one who has heard it can be deluded into believing in birthdays, because a *birthday* to me is just another possibility of celebrating the elegance of Abundance! It has nothing to do with the passage of time; *it has to do with the flowering of freedom from the suggestion of aging*. What is aging? *It's death in slow motion*. And what is the point of doing it so slowly?! When you put an end to it, then you can have the greatest birthdays and I can go right out on the polo field and have a great time!

> I can ride the horse and seize the goal
> And appear to just let it appear to unfold!

Unfolding is the kindness with which the Napkin of the Realized State appears to grace those in the asphalt jungles of time.

> When the forest murmurs, you never stop and say,
> "I must make it sound,"
> When the forest murmurings come to you, you don't try to
> analyze what in the forest is unbound.
> When the forest's silent in the light of sun,
> Every twig and every leaf is saying, "Go within; there is
> only One."

> The branches of time only shade for you the salient fact of
> Light,
> That if you stand in the Beam of Knowing, my forest is not
> this wood structure of time in your sight.
> When the forest murmurs, I hear its mighty call.

It tells me, "Don't be a sap like all those who bark;
      just go within and see the rings and how they fall."

The wheels of time have marked their course upon the heart
      of a tree,
But it's man's outward tendencies that give you a cross —
      upright? Filled with "but's" and "maybe's" and
      "if's," you see?
The cross of time is made of excuses for not being Balance
      Divine,
And for not taking the Tone that is sounding within your
      Heart cognized by the mind.

If you can hear that Pitch a'sounding within the vestibule of
      your Heart,
Then make your head bow to it so that at an octave's
      distance you may start
To appear to be like everyone else, but when someone strikes
      it well,
You open up your mouth and say, "I and My Father are
      One *now*, as my footstep now does tell."

Do you think you have a future? Of course! Thinking
      makes it so.
But if you plan for Being all there is to it now, the future can
      come and go.
Why do you think I AM Ageless?
Because I AM the same in the Eternal Song of Light.
It is only time that equates Me as I AM with the passing and
      changing My garments for sight.

But I have been the same and others have cognized it,
      and some have said, "Oh! I know you well!
And I embrace your form and kiss you mightily for I
      recognize my Self."
It's the same pattern of design,
Be it a pattern in music or a pattern in Light Divine.

The sequence of Holy Events finds us together
      and congregated on this side of this course,

Which is redolent with the promise of spring, with the
temperature at fifty-eight. (My favorite number, of
course!)
For thirteen marks the Wonder; no floor is stopped at in
time,
All elevators pass right over it because you mustn't see the
number, even to your mind!

But you see, it has nothing to do with bad luck;
it just has to do with what you face
When you see the Thirteen is living and standing potent
within the discipline that you must face.

*When you know what you know, why do you try to placate
what you know very well is not in keeping with the Higher Way?*
Do you notice how you do this every day? There's such a tendency
not to make another feel ill at ease in your presence. If they feel ill
at ease in your presence it's because they are not hammered in with
enough tension to perceive your Presence. When there is a tone to
be set free and the heart is right, the head does not get in the way.

We don't think it takes time to think right. It doesn't; it only
takes a willingness to accept without thought. To think that you
have to understand is one of the thorns in our educational process.
It is one of the great omissions to think that the cane can't be used,
because there is nothing that can be achieved without discipline and
it doesn't come by talk! Discipline is really, in Essence, the ability
to manage the self, or self-management. Discipline is only achieved
through blood, sweat, and screams! Unless that discipline is known
to be capable of being achieved, you allow yourself to grow only to
a certain grade in your achievement. *Technique is self-mastery.*
What does that mean? It means that you can appear to be what you
are and do what everyone else does, while you remain as I AM.

The whole purpose of an Example is to see it unfold as your
experience, not to see your experience unfold and try to analyze
your experience in the light of the Example. The only reason you
have an Example is to be the Example. Norman accepted the sound
of my voice and it came out with *his* prepared spirit, because the
spirit of man is sanctioned by the Lord. In other words, man's
conceptual might has geared him to respond when his Essence is

found tunable to a Pitch of Universal Significance. For anyone to think that he is enlightened is to declare that he is not, because when you think you are enlightened, you can only go as far as you can think, and I can assure you, you have to go where it can't be thought.

Remember, a thought-success is a conditioned one; a thought-achievement is a conditioned one. To be successful is to be the present activity of what it means to be the evidence of Life living your capsule. Your capsule isn't living Life; it is Life living the capsule!

Remember, your mind has been coded to give you the information pertinent to this planet and that is all. It has not been given the information for another state, but it is capable of receiving it, because it was *keyed* to receive the Higher Information upon your ability to use your computer to the enhancement of its fullness, but no further. The chip that's missing is the one that you *know* is missing. You *know* it's missing because you *question* not just your anxiety surrounding "Do I have a job? What am I going to do?" That is only the surface froth.

Oh, why does everyone want to find the answer to Life? Because they know this one is passing and Life as IT IS never does.

If we can't come to the Community of the Saints and the Sages of the Ages and have it a viable and a living experience here and now, how are we *ever* going to fulfill man's highest dream of a free world, an enterprise with no destination but to traverse the Infinite Cosmos and give an Adventure of Light?!

You *can't* allow yourself to enter the booby prize of a human when you have the skill to be One in the command of a Battalion of Light. All of you are officers, you might say, or the officiating force fields of the Crown. The diplomatic career is just opening, because the diplomacy of time is fast failing in its ability to heal the distress of the inevitable eruptions that freedom always brings, even in the form of a cough.[4] A cough is nothing but a tickle or a rumble when something is rumbling somewhere else.

Re-member . . and you have "this"; forget and you'll die! Live and find the living the Power to the seeming engagement which allows us to stand redolent in the Garment of Being, *madly* being

Love! And Love being mad, who cares to be labeled "not at all like us in the mass"? The only reason a mass ever tries to celebrate is because One alone realizes the only celebration is to BE All One. It's pretty lonely in the mass because they all say the same thing: "What are you doing for a living? How many doctorates have you got? How many degrees have you got for your cultural incarceration in limitation?"

I'm all for education . . of the right kind. I'd have you out of school so fast because, after all, we have to get through the sojourn with illusion and seed the plane with the God-Seeds of Promise. This is our job. I have opened the package; it's up to you to tend the Garden. It is growing richly within each and every one. We can't be bound by the culture. It is such an important consideration, because we can't be bound by what we seem to be.

Your words should be fitly spoken and placed like apples of gold on dishes of silver.[5] Why do you say "on dishes of silver"? Because it is the reflective state. The Golden State is the Omnipresent allowing the silver to shine by reflected light.

We are *never* reflectors. If anything, you may say in the becoming, you are *reflections*, but not *reflectors*. A reflector can be broken; a reflection can't be. If you have so much belief in what you seem to be, stand in front of the mirror and say, "Boy, there I am." Face your back to your mirror, then "I am not." Do you think the figure that you see mirrorized, "silverized," is really you? If you do, you're not seeing yourself correctly at all, because everything in the mirror is just the opposite of what it really is!

This picture is all opposite. You appear to be young; I *appear* to be old. But I am so old that I couldn't possibly appear to be in such a young garment, if it weren't a miracle.

Isn't it marvelous to revel in what it is to be on the bridge of your own Soul Ship and under the Captain of a Higher Voice Imprint than the one that you equate with a time and its symbol? Don't wait on the Lord.[6] If you do, it's going to be a hell of a time. People have waited on the Lord for centuries and the only reason we ever knew they existed was because people left footprints called the historical data of a disillusioned civilization.

The Napkin

The whole purpose of civilization is to be in agreement with
　　the pattern of design,
Be it in music or a pattern in mind.
It's bound to the Rhythm of the Being I AM,
And a waltz through the Cosmos and seeing the Plan.

It's to decode what is suggested by *your* realm of thought
Into the Language of Being, and thus you are brought
Onto this stage and give Earth its chance
To once again be resplendent in the Mantle of Light, because
　　Love holds, endeared and entranced,
The possibilities of all to BE and find
How the world becomes Light-full and no longer a burden
　　on the Christ of the mind.

Christopher is no longer the Saint to be adored
Because he carried the Christ, "the World," on his shoulder
　　to yonder shore.
But when he looked up, he saw as planned,
'Twas not a child, it was the Christ I AM.

Then, he stood aghast at what he perceived as Himself.
He dropped what he thought was the object he carried and
　　saw; He broke the spell.
And lo and behold! He's been afforded by time
An opportunity to cross the various fords of your mind.

And thus, the bridge has come to time.
It may be a Rainbow of Promise in the fairyland Divine.
But you know whenever you enter it with thought,
What appeared to be your irradiance is no longer there as
　　your frock.

But *when* you see within how the Light does shine,
Why, the Rainbow with the Pot of Gold is really all wrapped
　　up in your Heart, the Loved One Divine.

　　This is the Boat I offer; it's not filled with chocolates, but it's
filled with the sweet of embracing All becoming the Nectar of the
God of Love!

Thank you.

February 16, 1992

---

1 2 Corinthians 6:17.
2 Isaiah 9:6.
3 John 10:30.
4 Someone in the audience was heard to cough.
5 Proverbs 25:11.
6 Psalms 27:14, 37:34; Proverbs 20:22.

XVI

YOU LIKE GOLD

What are you missing? A strange thing: the willingness to be Real! Do you know Reality isn't processive? Many teachers want you to have it processive because then there is a reason for being a teacher. There is no point of being a teacher, unless you can stick somebody with the period of suggestion and he gets the Point!

YOU LIKE GOLD

We are speaking to you this morning from that house that edges the course of joy and play, skill and patience, for we must move with the agility of one geared to the Light and unfettered by the weight of the earthly suggestion that would bind you to the sod of belief, when the joy of unfettered flight is forever available as a result of man's greatest and most exquisite invention: his brain.

We have invented the brain, we have utilized it, and we have forgotten that it was to be *used* — it wasn't to dominate! We have allowed ourselves to be inundated with the characterization of being a brain-dominated man, an intellectual man, a physical man, and a changing man with a changing world, a changing attitude, and a changing situation. *In fact, life has become embedded in the volatile state of changing with no fixed point of reference.*

The future is all a result of the belief system that is required to sustain a changing situation. We have courage to maintain this situation, because we use a historical reference for a pattern that says: "Keep on! If we keep on changing, we will leave a pattern that others will follow into a tale of demise without the escape from this hatched condition which we have forgotten we instigated when we invented our brain and became subject unto it." We forget, and in forgetting, we allow our allegiance to become directed to the limited source of our own creation.

Our brain is that apparatus which is programmed from birth to respond to the conditions of the seeming and to respond to the conditions they say are past but will constitute our future. This is the condition under which mankind lives as a mass. When you step outside of the mass and realize that your brain is nothing but an instrument to be utilized in a Service of Freedom, then you are in a position to be what you should be, when you know within yourselves you have been chosen to question your identity as a human.

The human is the garment your brain conceals itself in. It is an instrument engaged in sponsoring its own illegitimate reason for being in the Light of Truth. We know that we can change our thought, change our contact, and thus make contact with That

Force which will extricate us from this educated belief system of bondage.

You were never meant to be engaged in being world servers from the standpoint of educated asses. You were meant to ride an ass, as Jesus did into Jerusalem. The palm frond was to be used because it never collects dust. Most are allergic to it. It is amazing the allergies that exist because we never dust the attic of our mind or the dustbins that have accumulated as a result of the sedentary mass of useless information.

You must consider, as never before, that the purpose of your incarnation is to be uncomfortable. The purpose of your incarnation is to feel frustrated and to sponsor similar conditions among your own kind until you can't stand it. So, you might say that my purpose for appearing is to fan your discomfort, to enrage your identity problem, and to cause you to be fretful, feverish, and chaotic so that the moment in the seeming center of your tornado is the calm that is the Center of every storm that rages on the periphery, all because of your willingness, not to be centered, but to exist in the chaos of the mass.

One in a mass is one in a mess! You know very well the reason that you have considered your True Identity is because something has moved within you that caused you to fall into an attractive Force, which then caused you to consider your stability as a man or a woman. One of the best forces that you have to deal with, of course, is your Fire Force, which most people try to put in cold storage. Of course, the result is an age-like life happening too quickly. One who refuses to express the Fire of Life refuses to fecundate the Seeds that were already planted when man was free to ejaculate the Wonders of a Promise that would flower in the Age when he could look upon the fields and know that they were ready and white for harvest.

If you constantly endow yourself with the idea of personal seeders and having choices to enhance the produce of your fertile fields, then know that if the Virile Member of Knowingness has paraded in the field of your awareness, you have the Promise at hand to be able to live in the world and yet be not of it. Thus, you are able to draw to others the possibilities of this experience being one of voyage and discovery and not one terminated with an unknown beginning and birthed with an unknown end.

So it's exactly the opposite when you stop and consider (which you shouldn't do too much), because the more you stop and consider, the less inclined you are to be creative. Creativity never happens because somebody stops and considers. Creativity never stops and considers. If creativity stopped and considered, nothing would have happened but a *period*. A period is always that point that causes your sentence to be reviewed — re-viewed. Each one is your excuse for not getting beyond the period, be it in life (male or female) or be it cyclical in the reincarnational process of belief.

That Which IS has never reincarnated. That Which IS has no age. It is only you, in your seeming frailty, who have ascribed age unto your embodiment, in order to try to keep a calendar of events that would somehow, within your chart of memory (which you constantly review as you move from Age to Age), equate with whether or not you are progressing as you should in the characterization of being an educated intellectual something-or-other.

Those who are well educated are those who are well directed in their thought-processes of limitation. Seldom do you ever find one that is well disposed for the collector. You usually find it a slow process, as is the orgy that goes with trying to make life a festooned experience with food, money, and sex. Of course, there's nothing wrong with any of them, if you know what they're for. But most people think that sex is for the purpose of relieving; most people think that food has to be relieved; and most people feel that money never should get out of their hands. So, you see, it's what you call a constipated experience with no herbal remedy.

If you are searching to be at ease with your mannerisms, do so as you scrutinize your behaviorism, which is all concomitant with your **wonder**less educational system. You have been taught so poorly and you have been sent to private schools where those who brought you wouldn't have to face what you're getting. They wouldn't have to face what they brought as a result of their belief system: something similar to themselves, another brain with a capsule of salt, water, chalk, protoplasm, or slime, all slung together in the bag in time.

But you see, there is *hope*, because there is not a thing being said here that didn't have in its beginning a big bang! At first you called it the whisper. The whisper was that something was brewing across Jordan. In other words, if you could cross the River of Judgment (which was Jordan), you didn't have to be baptized in it and be forgiven your sins of criticism, which were a result of your own intellectual ignorance of That which could not be found *possible* to critique in the land of your make-believe! That Which IS exists beyond the periphery of your mind's capability, but is *known* to exist because it can *ridicule* the limitations of your brain and allow it to start pushing keys, response areas within yourself, that will say: "Shut off that static; I don't want to hear it. I *want* to be this rigid piece, this floating piece, this decomposing mass of suggestion, which somebody else one day will have to dispose of and I will look upon it and say, 'Oh my God! What did I fall for? I should have *flown* the coop of suggestion and gone to my hen coop on High!'"

What is the point of having any bird talk to you if you don't don its feathers? It is wonderful to have all the great wisdom represented by birds. It's amazing how few ever rid themselves of the thoughts that would deter them from getting off the ground. A bird never flies with weight. Birds have, you might say, a natural ability to float above the suggestion of their featherdom. And you should have a natural propensity to exculpate yourself from any thought-field that would have you meandering in the bog of suggestion which is the result, of course, of faulty teaching.

Whoever in school has told you: "You are a nice looking body, but what I am appealing to is that piece of your brain that is capable of having a chip, not off the old block, but of that Energy that is the very Center and Circumference of Reality!"? Do you know your brain accepts it as easy as wink? Why do you go on sleeping? In the wink of an eye God is seen and unseen, because God is your innate cry for Reality. Every time you try to submerge your experience in anything less than the Allness that allows you to question the somethingness of your head structure, you realize that That Which IS allowing you to investigate your *very* sense of beingness can't be the beingness, either you couldn't find fault with it! What fault do you find? That it is not becoming the Most High, the Kingdom that is the reflected state of the Divine AM-ing of the I.

You cannot take the Kingdom of God by storm. You can only

take the concept called God by storm and allow yourself to bask in the Freed State when the concept fades out. You don't need a concept to be vivified unless you want verification. Anyone educated in time depends upon verification in order to have courage to follow. It takes such courage to follow. It doesn't take it if you are utilizing the worm's-eye view. You've seen how moles progress. What is the point of moving at that pace when the Center is one with the rhythm of the Heart and its unknown *Bundle of His*![1]

Why do you allow your pace in life to be regulated by a thought-structure that would limit your very possibility of being freed? Most teaching says, "You do this; you do this; you do this; you do this." That is to keep you in process and develop a craft. You can go to the cheese factory. A processed cheese is worthless. It's almost like the milk that is supposed to come out of a cow; it bears no resemblance to said creature. It's bastardized. So is much of your Truth, because it has been said that the Truth to be acceptable has got to pass through your mind. Well, the Truth to be acceptable doesn't even have to go anywhere near it!

Your mind is the thing that tries to make your freedom processive. The moment you recognize "I love you" you are free, unless you say, "Well, I love you, too, but I have my own life to lead." You haven't any "own life" to lead; you don't even know what your life is. Your life is the response you may *feel* if I kick you, or it's the response you may feel if I caress you, or it may be the "Ouch!" you feel when I prick you and you cease to have confidence in your ability to equate yourself with Me as I AM.

You can't equate yourself with Me as I AM if your self is equipped only with the educated appendages of a mind system that frequently needs to have a colonic, just as the intestines do. It gets clogged with the debris of unused fuel. Remember, education and thoughts are really the fuel system for keeping your incredible machinery activated, until I come and give you the Higher Octane or the Higher Octave of living, which *allows* you to move in parallel octaves with the Conscious Realm of Being and the apparent realm of objectification.

You don't find anything incompatible. I see all the differences and I see no difference, because I know I am part and parcel of that incredible dynamic portrayal of "All that I have is Thine."[2]

Everything that appears diversified in time
Is there for the purpose of allowing points to be elucidated in
poetry, prose, and rhyme.

It doesn't mean a thing to say you're male or female, and you belong to a male or you belong to a female. All you belong to is the One Love That IS that has allowed you to portray these incredible parts, fractured by your belief system, waiting to be given on the Direct Center of stage, so that all those on the wings of this great performance for Earth once again have a chance to escape from this thralldom of sensation and move into that eternal motion commensurate with the Rhythm of Being I AM.

Your joy is the evidence that it is possible to have a rippling rhythm that always bears a tantalizing conflict to those who generally inhabit the capsule called "flesh." You see, it seems almost impossible for the gooey mass running through our vein-like system to cope with a force of Joy, because it says, "In the realization of What IS, my joy is full, therefore, **Wonder**-full!" Wonder is the very root system that opens the windows of your incarceration, and the doorway to freedom rests in your willingness to accept the Joy that is yours and break the barrier.

What are you missing? A strange thing: the willingness to be Real! Do you know Reality isn't processive? Many teachers want you to have it processive because then there is a reason for being a teacher. There is no point of being a teacher, unless you can stick somebody with the period of suggestion and he gets the Point!

Now is the accepted time. If that is the accepted time, then you can't be in it as this thing, because Now is the reference that has nothing to do with the past or the future. *Now is the name given to a period as it starts to lose its symbolic reference.*

Nowness is the Beingness that I AM. This is why it is so wise to take the poem, the prose, and the art and put it into poem-ing, pros-ing, art-ing, and movement in the creative realm. You cease to identify then with the obvious inheritor of action and allow the action to be the portrayal of the *Invisible Inheritor*, while you bestow your largesse upon all those who still can be open to Wonder.

There are many wise men, but you'll only know them when you meet them because they never cease to what? Wonder.

The Wise always Wonder, the Wise always watch.
The Wise never say why; they just watch.
For no man knoweth when the Sentinel in the Tower
Perceiveth the Eternal Ray of Sun/Son.[3]

Who knows when you are going to be struck by the Light? Who knows when you are going to be infected by a computer virus and your whole computering system go into chaos? Your programs start to become incoherent and you pray for a Solution to the problem of Being from the confused state of incomplete data. You say, "My God, why hast Thou forsaken me?" and you hear in the Light and the thunder (whichever density you choose): "I AM a Sonic Reference and My Force has *nothing* whatsoever to do with your degrees of whether or not you will accept Me as I AM."

Do you realize? Of course, you do. If you do, then you can't parade as if you were an ignoramus, other than having a script in some future Amos and Andy cartoon. It shall be known that those who walk in the Light see Light. The lights and the colors appear as the evidence of His Sonic Nature, appearing upon your screen of observation as a hue-man.

The whole point of Being is to exude the Wonder. *Break* the suggestion that thou art this and that What IS *is* unattainable! What IS is the only thing that is present at this very moment, but what you are thinking is what keeps you from experiencing it.

I have heard all these words and I laugh at them because it hasn't made one particle of difference to me. I have just held your attention so that your thoughts would be focused for a minute so I could get in there and allow you to perceive me as I AM. Then you will see there is no division. It's so much fun to play with the division, when you know there isn't any. It's so much fun to take apart an apple and to put it together again, because then you are never unaware of its hidden orchard.

So it is with the Wonders of Life. It is so wonderful to be able to analyze the components of your space suit, say what each one needs, what grease job it needs, what oil job it needs, what type of clean-out it needs, what type of burnout has happened, and what type of spark plugs have to be replaced. Remember, as long as you are entertaining the Divine Essence of your Being, even in thought, you are calling forth an enhancement of Power, which is saying to your entire cellular system, "Purify! Because I will cause you to tremble! tremble! tremble!" I did it; others do it. It's because Man is being enhanced in the power range of what is termed a Divine Energy or a force field that is equated with what is termed Man's Transcendental State.

So don't be concerned when you tremble. If you tremble, remember, it's a promise that there is something happening to *your* system, because your system was never made to be static. It has been your minds that have created a static state in order to try to keep a status quo so that you do not have to face the force field of a Realness when you appear to live among the mass.

How many have tried to conceal the fact they know me because knowing me brings upon you the anathema of all those who are in a mass? They can't stand being confronted by something Real, because when they are confronted by you (and you're just perfectly natural), they feel their divided state. If they can't label it and name it, then they can't stay away from That Which IS really basic to their Identity.

The crisis today is not AIDS; the crisis today is a result of failing to perceive what the real need is: Identity. Then there would be no extravagance in the use of the Force that is creative in its very Presence and ignores whether it's male or female. It *allows* each to be exalted according to where each has stated he stands: either in the realm of the Enlightened God or in the realm where degrees have an apparent appendage to achievement.

It is said that a genius has to spend his time trying to make a name for himself in order to know he is one. Isn't it wonderful to appear to be an ass! Then you have nothing to do but to be ignorant, and yet alive to all the Wonders that allow that which is ignored never to be the force to destroy.

There is no one more ignored than what appears as me. There is no one that is more kept in the cupboard of your lives than me.

I don't want to use the words "than I," because if I do, I can't say that. So I have to put it as "me." When you refer to "me," and I am known for what I AM, then you cannot go around thinking your reference point is your "me." If you know me as I AM, you are as I AM. The only difference is I never consider being I AM, and you may have to practice being I AM, because your mind doesn't want to rescind its hold upon you and your predilections for judgment.

Why do you say, "Judge ye not lest ye be judged"?[4] Because what you judge you become. Why become a judge with a sentence? There's always a period to it. The only judgment that was ever passed upon you was that *Thou art perfect, for Thou art the Son of the Living God. In this rejoice, for All that I have is Thine.* How come you call the material wonder and the material elegance, material only? I call it the evidence of the Being I AM.

Somebody said, "You like gold." I said, "Well, don't you?" See, some people like something and they won't wear it. I *wear* what I AM. You'd much rather, you know, wear a plated situation, so that you don't have to bear the force field of those who recognize Real Gold when they see it.

When you wear a valuable gem, they'll say, "Oh, look at the show-off! No wonder he needs a bodyguard!" Oh! The reason that people love a gem is because the gem in its beautifully faceted presence causes peoples' attention to be focused upon it. In that moment they see an aspect of themselves that they never realized, that was beautiful and was what they wanted. But they hadn't earned it! You can't be a thief and expect to take the *Jewels of Force* without having earned them by the right of the discipline that is essential to develop the technique that enables you to encompass every octave without having to thumb your way and, in so doing, have the thudding similar to the densities of the world below you and your caustic engagement with Wonder.

Process is your excuse for being wrapped in your mortality and its aging gown.

Something had been bothering me for weeks in my consideration. I couldn't understand why there was such a difference between the Singers' attitude and what appeared as my attitude. I said to David, "What is it, David? Ben, what is it?" It came to me: I do everything from the Standpoint that I AM All; therefore, I am always doing *everything* for the glory and the wonder of That Which IS I AM!

When you sing for the Glory of God, as the Fundamentalists call it, then you sing not for the Glory of God, you find *the Glory of God singing as you*; in other words, the Unlimited, the Infinite Resources appear manifested as your unlimited ability to vocalize the Sonic Wonders of Man's Essence.

We are not a material structure; we are not made with hands. We are **Sound** that has coagulated around a Fundamental Pitch that is commensurate with what we have termed the planet of our own conception, Earth, and the God of that planet, whom you have conceptualized as the Almighty.

It is all a Sonic Reference. As soon as we start to move within that Triad of Wonder becoming the Sonic Essence of the Triad, we move into such a state of being able to modulate at ease into any key that suits a choral work of encounter as a result of Reality's Sponsorship.

Your success, your wealth, and your fame are all limited or enhanced according to either your freedom from the personal involvement or the acknowledged Wonder of Being able to sing, when you are nothing but a capsule which has been used to clothe the brain (so you wouldn't be astounded when you looked upon it) which is allowed by your *keys* of intelligence to create new pro-grams. For heaven and hell are but concepts of your duality. They each are formed or created according to your acceptance of a Fundamental Pitch, a Divine Principle, a Divine Ideal upon which all life unfolds — whether or not you will have a set of ideas that you use occasionally and wonder why your system is so cacophonous when it should be one in an Ode to Joy.

Beethoven's Ninth contains that Ode. It's interesting. The Ninth Symphony is that orchestration that is so essential for the man who moves under the impulse of the Higher Hierarchy, because it is the Nine that contains the Law and the Will in its Essence. It has your freedom if you square your deals; it has your bondage if you try to manipulate your responsibility to your

Triangle of Wonder and Newness and Nowness.

You can have nine by adding three plus three plus three, or you can have nine by multiplying three times three. You can also have nine by eight plus one, seven plus two, six plus three, five plus four. You'll never get away from having to acknowledge the Unifying Principle. Never.

So, I come to do Thy Will, O Concept Divine,
And in that concept I have conned the mind
Into knowing its place in the Symphony of Life.
My Soul feels the Being I AM and alters my mind of strife.

I *feel* in the Being the Might at hand
To alter the seeming program for Man.
For into this span that attention does hold
There's a valley between each thought, we are told.

If your attention is held, the spark does jump,
And you bridge this gap and no longer slump
Into the mental realm of incompleted acts.
You bear the assurance of this Divine Fact:
That Harmony is the Realm. Will you truly dwell?
It's Heaven here now; it's your thought that makes it hell.

So *take* your place in the Triad Divine
And know if you play it solidly, you can go to bed and sleep
        in and out of time.[5]
But if someone comes along and upsets its stand, you can't
        help but move.
That's when you say, "God help me!"

Because you will *have* to move, and where?
*You can **never** go back to positions outgrown.*

The trouble with tomorrow is that one foot is in yesterday.

What is tomorrow? The carrot before your mind until it's satisfied, and then it's nothing but a calendar for others who call you an event. That is why we say the one Divine Event is Love — and you've had it! Did you ever dream you were going to be such queers? Isn't it wonderful to be free of being a human? It's so much better to be *a **Light display** upon the canvas of time.* Your face is a canvas; your freedom is etched upon it.

I said to one man, "It's amazing the stone-like countenance you have and the tender heart that it conceals. You are so afraid of being seen as the tenderness."

The reason we've seen all the divisions in the countries is because selfishness takes the place of selflessness. People have been educated to believe in parts instead of Allness.

Can you imagine what will happen in the schools when the teacher sees the classroom as nothing but the evidence of his or her state of readiness, without the bulwark of created adjudication? I know! I have taught so much that when the child is viewed as a wonder and limitless, there is nothing, even in his hand, to stop the writing on the wall that "I AM a Wonder."

I have seen the children so freed. They'd say, "Oh, I can't do that!" I'd say, "Why'd you hit your hand? Why don't you kick yourself? How many sisters do you have? How many brothers? You have a good time until you fight. That's what your fingers are, your sisters and your brothers. Whose are they? Well, fight with them if you want to, but I'd just tell them what to do and get along with the show." And they did.

What are *your* children, if they aren't the thought-sets that are manifesting to ruin your life, because they're all associated with you and some prejudice. "I'm this." "I've got this." "I've got plenty of nothing . . and nothin's plenty for me."

It was yesterday when I said, "Nobody knows the Wonder I've seen and *nobody* knows my gladness." Then I slipped in, "But *no body does* know." It really jolted that one to consider sadness.

Well, if I were an evangelist, I'd have a little more brimstone and hell. Then I'd smooth over the situation by caressing you and saying how wonderful you are and "Now drop at my feet and be healed." Well, do that if you wish! There's nothing wrong with it; it all depends where you are.

It is so wonderful to see that no matter what happens as man tries to find his way between the thought-forces of his day, there's nothing wrong with any of it. Each Way is expedient to put an end to the limitations, the resultant feature of false identity.

The crisis of man is not in AIDS, but in the aid that correct Identity will bring to his cellular system, because it will *allow* a re-enhancement of the vibratory Frequency that really allows him to vibrate in another Octave of Being.

This is why the harmonic sequence is so important, and this is why it is so important to attune thyself unto That Which IS, so that which isn't doesn't need to be rubberized.

Every time an instrument is tuned you use rubber pegs to isolate the strings so that all the faults are excluded and you just deal with the pure sound. Then, when it's perfectly pitched, or temperedly pitched, you take out the rubber and allow the mixture to happen. That gives it the *quality* that comes with whatever constitutes the string, the sounding board, and the tension under which man lives. Just think, if it weren't for the sounding board, your tone would never soar.

What is yours? If your tone is to soar, do you think there can be a crack in it? A piano loses its worth when the sounding board cracks, because they have to cement it; it can never take the place of the original.

It's amazing how many operations we go through. You see people take all kinds of operations. A friend had one just recently. She was filled with fear. I said, "Let her come up tonight if she's not going to have to be in the hospital until tomorrow morning." She came up. We talked, and I showed her some plans we were doing for furniture and showed her some designs that she hadn't considered. And all that fear left. When she went into the operating room the next day it was such a different experience for her, "because," she said, "there was no fear." What happened was, what they feared was so serious was not found! They made a little larger incision and explored all the organs because they expected to find something. I said, "It isn't there, dear. It's out here, first. And now it's not there." They said they took care of the hernia but they said, "You know, it's the strangest thing. The hernia was so small that it had only been *pressing* on the wall, it hadn't gone through it."

That was not where the pressure was; the pressure was the feeling of Divinity calling for her acknowledgement. And she did, by coming.

So, she just sat on the floor and watched me do things and look at photographs. When they went to explore, they found nothing. All she has now is the pain of healing, which always accompanies the space suit. But so much of it can be alleviated if you align your thoughts now and be acquainted with that *Bundle of His* that beats in rhythm with the Cosmic. It's the last pulse to leave the body and announces its withdrawal with another seeding for another time.

The Wonder of Being! Do you know what it is? It's realizing I am *not* "this," but I appear to be until you know I AM. See?

That is why whenever you say, "Mallory, what did you say your name was?" "Oh, Randle." "What?" "I am Mallory Randle, for God's sakes! Can't you hear me?!" I just waited for God to speak. God just said, "I *AM* wearing the clothing of Randle."

Randle, Randle, my Son.
You see? Neither let "Mal" or "or" be in your run.
But know that All that I have is thine,
For "Randle" is *My* garment that My Perfected State wears
    in/out of time.

You always claim your Divine Identity when your spurious one is in question! Every time you say, "I can't do it," it's spurious, it's false. "Oh, I can't imitate that sound." [Mr. Mills screams like a large bird.] "Can't possibly do it." You don't want to do it, because it will open something on you you don't want to look at. Why do you think most people are so quiet in front of [Mr. Mills screams again]? You don't dare to reveal what's underneath that. What if you became excited! What if you became *really* excited! What if you felt a form of the erotic?! "Oh, God!! And I'm supposed to be Divine!" You'll *never* feel the Divinity if you don't *feel* it. If people are in a flaccid state when they're entertaining the Divine, they're not hot enough. I tell you that now.

One reason so many people have gone onto restricted diets is to cause their dynamics to be lessened in their attention. I don't say eat steak, but I say certainly eat anything that's white. Leave the red meat alone. Okay. Be sure you use your enzymes, if you think you're without them.

Remember, Truth is never digested. If you think you're digesting Truth, it's going to regurgitate all over you!

March 29, 1992

1 In medical terminology, a small band of heart muscle fibers that conducts the heartbeat impulse from the atria to the ventricles.
2 Luke 15:31.
3 See the poem "Watch," in Kenneth G. Mills, *Surprises* (Toronto: Sun-Scape Publications, 1980), p. 85.
4 Matthew 7:1.
5 Refer here to the story of Beethoven and his uncle in Chapter XVII, "Seed Kingdom," p. 231.

"The flowers sing – the birds bloom!"

XVII

SEED KINGDOM

When I stop and consider how much money has been spent, and there is no evidence of it. When I stop and consider how much life has been lived, how much evidence of it? The only evidence of Life lived is the evidence of Life recognizing Its Wonder. That's what we all are.

SEED KINGDOM

We are bringing the Wonder of the New Moment which bursts through the encrustations of suggestion, allowing the Seed Kingdom of Wonder to bring forth unto us a parcel given to fulfillment, a land given to promise, and a world given back to the Arms of Love.

As we have gathered together in order to satisfy the need of our cellular selves to find themselves once again enhanced within the corporate structure, we are perceiving as never before the challenge that exists in the realm of the objective. This challenge is really a gymnasium for exercise, for we must forever keep alive the dexterity and the flexibility of our system of mental associations, so that they can be gained and dropped according to the need of the umbrella or the mask or the clothes we must wear to befit the occasion. And so, we are perceiving in the realms of medicine, in the realms of science, in the realms of education, the great emptiness that does exist in spite of man's attempt to fill the vacuum of his ignorance with the doctorates of his sublime ignorance. We are forever attuning ourselves to finer specialization, while we are forever causing excruciating pain to those parts of ourselves which cry out for expression and which we find stultified because of our fear of being touched by the Sublime and its all-encompassing, universal Nature.

We say, "Ah, yes, we are individuals having a right to our own movement. We are individuals having a right to our own march. We are individuals having a right to our own May. We are individuals having a right to our own June." But in each month there is a season set aside for the rejoicing of Those who have come before and who have, in a sense, offered unto us the great sacrifices that the world deems necessary for notice to be taken of an unusual movement from sense to Soul.

In this realm, of course, we're always dealing with what we call the sense testimony. In other words, the verdicts created by the mind. We are never dealing with anything other than the mind's qualifications for its own safetyhood and for its own suggested contentedness. People will say,

"Well, I feel so happy, and I feel so well,

I feel so joyous, what more can I tell?
I feel so grand, I feel so fine,
And yet I tip the scales of my mind.
I feel when I stand on the scales on the floor
I wonder from where that poundage came? Did it
    come from yore?
But I tell you now, if I would look to see,
Then I would find it's all with my mind in deed.
Without my mind present, no scales to tip,
No person to see, no joy to tell."

When we think of being healthy, wealthy, and wise,
We think that the God of all Being upon us must have
    smiled for a while.
And when we are filled with pain and with doubt,
And with hell and derision, we say, "Oh, my, where's
    my God? Has he become a gadabout?"
But don't you realize it's all part of the scenario of time,
Having nothing whatsoever to do with Facts Divine?!

The greatest mesmeric force is to fall for the belief that if you are well, the Spirit is smiling upon you, and if you are in travail, the Spirit has forsaken you. You are where you are by the law of your Being. You are utilizing every moment either to be or not to be this sad sack of protoplasmic, et cetera, situation, together with a bit of calcification and crystallization. This is all due to your education. Crystallization, of course, is education "doctorized."

So what do you do? You try to create a prescription for energy by devising all ways and means. None of them work because the prescription for energy is simple: Take this Dose once in your lifetime, *swallow* it, and see if you can spit it out! You won't be able to.

You are Love.
Regardless of body,
Regardless of mind,
That is Energy Divine.

Who will take it? You immediately separate Love and pre-scribe:

"So much for Mother, so much for Father,
So much for Sister, so much for Brother.
None for strangers: To hell with them.
I'll give them a nation and let it bend."

That isn't Love at all. That is not Energy. That is not the Prescription for Being . . Unlimited. Not at all! What are we doing? We're trying to find a cure for AIDS. How are you going to find a cure for what is the evidence of an attempt, in many cases, to have an experience of liberty without the *responsibility* of its gift?

We go on all our lives testifying to a *condition* of seemingness that doesn't bear the test of Reality. What does bear a test of Reality is the constant Knowingness becoming cognition, and Knowingness when cognized can be raised to the highest, Sublime Estate, because you can never have an apparent object without a corresponding identity. You can have an "idea" without an apparent object and a corresponding identity. You never will find the Ultimate devoid of satisfying your need wherever you are.

Somebody called the other day with quite a serious problem. I said, "It comes to you to see how well exercised you are. Are you going to accept it, or reject it? If you fall for it, you're not helping the other individual at all; and if you can see it as it really is, it may bless him." But remember: if you are healed it doesn't mean you are more spiritually ripe; it means that "you" aren't karmically cloned to suffer. Some people feel that if they bring about a spiritual healing, they're living correctly. Sometimes they feel when they don't have a spiritual healing, they haven't succeeded in doing the correct spiritual work. This is not really the case at all.

Some work is to be successful, for you have a purpose other than the disease. It's to see whether or not you're going to succumb to the suggestion that it is Real. And if you can prove that it isn't and you are healed, then it means you must get on with your work and be the purposeful encounter with the Light in this realm. If you are not healed, maybe it's the result of having been a heel yesterday and you've forgotten it! If you were a heel yesterday, it means that you have to get rid of your callus in this lifetime! This may have to do with your sole/Soul and what you get for walking so heavily upon the Ground that you find your soles unresponsive to the delicate tissues and issues which may encompass your Path.

To be a heel is one thing; to be a healer is another thing; and to be healed is yet another thing. But you see, they're all aspects of process. Do you know that all the Teachings that people go through, with their ashrams and with all the situations where people love progressive craftsmanship, are so processive, when **Being is not process.** *Being is Nowness,* freed from the thought that I AM in process and, therefore, a prescription to be filled at the Corner where hope and prayer meet (where the Vertical meets the expectant and cognition dawns).

Why is it that everyone in this room puts off being God-Man? Why is it that everyone in this room allows himself to think that he is of this race, this color, this creed? Why is it, when we know very well What IS? There's not one here who would say he was unconscious. You declare "I am conscious" by stating your name. Stating your name is the evidence of Consciousness present as I AM. Well, what more do you expect of I AM, if it isn't the Light to your very disguise in personification? You can lead people so far with words, but when you start cutting away and pruning the underbrush, then you start to see how much underbrush people make in order to evade Being *observed* as God-Man. **God-Man isn't subject to the objective rejection of timers.**

All my piano pupils — whom I had taught anywhere from five to eighteen years — as soon as the lessons stopped, I never heard from any of them again. They'll ignore you totally, because they don't *know* you when they have gone to a level that is not where you are. It's not that they ignore you. It is that as soon as they have left your aura of achievement, they don't know you. They have basked in your achievement and seem to have achieved as a result of your achievement. That is the graciousness of the Christ.

I have seen that so much in my life. That's why I'm so alone, you know? It's amazing how many people have family around them. But are they family? Who's fooling? I mean, most people who have family are not close at all. That's why you have to "come out from the world and be separate." The only way you can come out from the world and be separate is not to *think like the worldling!* If you think like a worldling, then you're having a fling with your destiny. If you're living as the Divine Self or the Christ or the Brahman or the Atman, then you are living in the Glory of a present God-Force. There's not one person in this room who isn't this

Force. But one reason we may not live it is because we would all have to be re-accepted by our associates.

It's very hard. You can say, "Well, there will be a reappearance of the Christ. There'll be a reappearance of Lord Mitraya. There'll be a reappearance of Krishna. There'll be a reappearance of the Buddha." It's just the same Force that's worn many different garments to satisfy the devotee. That is why it is so ridiculous to consider, "Well, I love Mr. Mills but I don't dare show it, because if I do, then I'm committed." To what? To being Real, or to your insanity? Isn't it amazing? Isn't it wonderful?

"Every herring hangs by its own tail in the end." You will!! It's fascinating how we evaluate our success by how others cognize us and how others pay us for our serfdom. Isn't it amazing how cleverly concealed is our slavery of today! How many people work not in what they wish to work in at all, because they have the ability to get a check, and sometimes without a mate! If they have one, they need it for sure! Then some have the ability to fulfill themselves and say they don't mind being a slave because they are doing what they love to do. That's great. There's only one question: *If you love to do what you're doing, how are you doing it?*

If you do it from the standpoint of it being an involuntary
expression of the Ultimate,
Then it's obviously Love, and there's no labor lost!
But if you have to work at it and do what you don't want to do,
Then that is labor without love and that is the cost.

But you do it often for what appears as the dollar bill. I have never seen anything quite like how the dollar bill carries so much power when it's only on paper. It's only a means of expression, so that we don't have to carry our gold with us. It's lighter! It's certainly more easily blown away!

Money, as you know, is only an impersonal way of saying thank you. Wouldn't you swear it's your passage fare to the stars? If money were Real, what would Substance be? It could *never* be a medium of exchange. And money is just that. It's amazing how people pall in the light of money. I've never seen anyone pall in the Light of the Christ. I've never seen anyone squirm in the Light of the Self. But I have seen people squirm when you *mention* money.

That's why I mention it so much. I mention it a lot because it gets more attention than anything else I say. It gets more attention than illegitimate love affairs and everything else. Money transcends them all! You're always getting tired exchanging the bills, you know? This buck for that buck. I'm trying to make you look at seeing how you think so much about yourself that you forget That Which IS Substance.

When I stop and consider how much money has been spent, and there is no evidence of it. When I stop and consider how much life has been lived, how much evidence of it? The only evidence of Life lived is the evidence of Life recognizing Its Wonder. That's what we all are. If we are not a Wonder, we are never open to poetry or to philosophy, because the doorway to each of these avenues of expression has to be through Wonder. The Wonder of our poetic life is frequently so misunderstood that people write prose! Poetry and philosophy elevate the awareness to such a level that man loses the weightiness of Earth, whereas prose may sentence him to the paragraphs of recorded data, whereby hangs his tale.

The Essence of your prose and your poetry isn't in the book; it's in you when you've finished with it. It should show in your face; it should show in your eyes; it should show in your countenance.

It is an interesting time for me! I don't know why people aren't jumping for joy at the possibilities of this *incredible* time in which we're living, instead of being depressed by it. The depression is totally manufactured. I have never been up or down. It has nothing to do with anything other than our willingness to equate the Ultimate with *choice.* That may be the cause of your depression!

The Ultimate can never be equated with choice. If it is, the result is depression. You can play a triad and go home and go to bed; but if you break the triad and play one note after the other, you've got to fulfill it. The fifth has to move, and you either do it mentally or you do it physically.

I told you once before: Beethoven got even with his uncle for treating him so badly. The uncle would crawl in drunk after a night at the court entertaining and wake Beethoven up. When the uncle was ready for sleep, Beethoven would run down and play a dominant seventh. The uncle would fall downstairs and resolve it. So the story goes.

How many times in our experience do we take on an experience of movement from sense to Soul, and then decide it's not exciting enough? If you find that you hope to attain by process, you will have process. Enlightenment! What is that? I know What I AM as soon as I recognize mySelf. Don't you? Well, that's Enlightenment . . I guess. If people don't recognize you as you are, they have never recognized themselves as they are. If people do not cognize the Wonder of your Beingness, they have not evidenced the Wonder of their own. And then they wonder why they aren't a success. *Success is Love's cognition of Its Selfhood.*

Struggle is the intoxication that man utilizes in an attempt to evade acceptance of Fact. People would much rather struggle than accept Fact. Why do they want fiction? Thereby hangs a tale! And look at the books we've got.

April 29, 1992

XVIII

ABSENCE

What are the nations? The division of the objectified world with the stamp of difference waiting to be transcended through the act of a redeemed imagination and a utilized power of discrimination.

The world as you know it is only conceived that way because of your involvement with limits. Do you realize that? The world you know goes with you; the world you know comes with you. But the world I know has neither "come, went, nor gone"!

ABSENCE

In the meetings with remarkable people these past few weeks, each one has brought such an unusual spice to the Meal prepared for those who are awaiting the satisfaction beyond the plate of limited offerings. The collection has been grand and unlimited with the ingredients offered, for the presence of new ideas is really the verification of what appears as those whom you have found enhanced by your participation in considering them with me.

So, much of the future, if you want one on this planet, depends upon your ability to exculpate yourself from this alleged situation of wrong identity and to grasp the kite of unlimited opportunities which flies always in the Wind and the Might of Omnipotence. You should be able to free yourselves from your tremendously egotistical involvements with yourselves and allow yourselves to succumb to the Wonder of Being Love manifested, refusing to accept otherness as separateness from your own Divine State.

You should see the multiplication of what appears as others as your infinite ability to supply the means for performing your *act of precipitation* through your visualization and your intention. See the materialization as nothing but the accommodating articles to satisfy the innate need of others for what is termed the Creative Force of the I AM. In the act of perceiving, as you perceive, the creating is happening and the AM is taken out of the catatonic state. Being in that AM-ing State, we are constantly creating the very conditions through which we may have to pass, whether or not we like it.

Remember, there is not one thing happening that *you* haven't programmed yourself to pass through. I never came to pass through. I didn't come to pass. I didn't come. You have only appeared to think I came, because you have been taught to think that That Which IS has to come. You should have been taught that *What IS is Omnipresent*, whether or not there is a form to mark the spot, the place where you should find your atonement, at one with the Subjective Pitch of the Divine Principle, I AM All.

The fructifying might of this Presence is so great that you have to be able to utilize the moments so that they do have a meaning, because "a word full of meaning is a life full of Love." Therefore, a life must be full of Love in order to have Meaning and Word, the evidence of Presence!

There is no point to considering the dullness of human conjecturing. There is no point to considering a bread knife in order to cut a nice, clean slice of bread. Bread should be broken! The broken bread is that *risen* part of the loaf that allows your Presence to *offer* satisfaction to those who are questioning the Substance of Being and the Meal that passeth the understanding.

You see, if understanding were so essential in your life, you would never come to know the Truth, because the Truth can never come through understanding. *The Truth comes through acceptance!* Your experience of it is articulated, and that articulation appears as understanding. Articulation should be so energized with the energy of Freedom that another feels **compelled** to find how to implement change.

If you speak to a group of people, don't consider them people. When I was concertizing, one friend said to me, "Go out on the stage and consider you're playing for a bunch of cabbages." I said, "My God, I practiced all these years and 'died' all these years. I'm not going to go out and play a concert for a bunch of cabbages!" And so, if you have this idea of going out and speaking to a group of people as if they are cabbages, well, undoubtedly, everyone will be filled with flatulence of some kind. It's unfortunate, because the purpose of any elucidation is to free the listener from the incarceration within his cocoon of thought-sets.

Thought-sets are those patterns that exist within your crocheting of the web of belief that surrounds your incarnation. Your web is either one that you can rest upon so that your nature is sensitized to the demands of the Unspoken and Unseen, and you can offer your presence through the Pitch of your Being in the silence that surrounds the hammock swung between the two trees of suggestion; or it can be the web upon which others get stuck because you entreat them into a place of commiserating with your impoverished state of thought-sets.

A thought-set is like a picture-set. You know, like taking a picture. Do you realize that when your camera takes a picture it's a negative? How could it be anything else? It has to be *developed* to give a positive. That was you to begin with! You came as a negative! You had to be developed *and pass through the solution?* Everyone is hunting for the Solution to the problem of Being. It isn't in the dark room; it's in the *Upper Room.* It's in the Upper Room where the Meal is served.

You should never have people at your table unless you love them. You should never have anyone partaking of the food of your table unless Love is present. A dinner or a meal is really a Love Feast. We should never be together if our being together is not meaningful. And meaningful means what? It transcends the *apparent.* We all *appear to* be parents. We are all *parenting* our creation!

I said to Dr. K., "Isn't it incredible when you consider this entire world experience is nothing but our own creation! We are totally freed of it when we go to sleep. It doesn't exist." The only reason the world *seems* to be as it is, is because someone somewhere on the planet is awake when you're asleep, thus verifying its constancy because of the attunement to the same pitch of objectification.

The world is a wave; the inhabitants are wavelets. That's *all* it is. All this business of being brought into families, being the result of families, is the limit to being the Wonder of a Divine Creation in which all that is seen is termed good, beautiful, wonderful, the Elegance of Being set free from the confines of a limited mind.

The reason we appear to be able to think *beyond* is because we are able to question *beyond. Do you realize if there weren't something beyond you, you would never have the question arise?* You'd be so satisfied with you as you are.

Why do you think there is always the "i-o-n" to quest? It's because the *I* must be *on.* That "ion" is not only that particle, that substance of a molecular structure, but it is also symbolic of the ancient City of Heliopolis,[1] the ancient City of the Sun. The reason the sun is so important is because it never ceases to be a constant, even in our dream state, because somebody is always dreaming light; therefore, we have the corresponding identity of this! But this is not really Light; this is counterfeit light. That's why it appears to change.

This is not Light. The absence of this we term darkness, but that is not darkness. **Darkness is the absence of Wonder! Light is the presence of Wonder!**

How can we look upon this body of salt, water, chalk,
    protoplasm, or slime
All slung together in a bag in time
And tied at the neck with the believe-it-or-not,
And wonder where Ripley went to relieve you of this knot!

If a hundred-and-fifty-pound man can be put into an atomic press, have all the holes squeezed out of him, and the residue be put on the head of a pin, is it any wonder that doctors are wondering, "What is this colossal thing called disease?" which covers *books*! Do you know all the books written about what you *aren't* couldn't possibly be put on the head of a pin! Couldn't possibly be.

If we are moving out from the seemingly solid world of objectification, we are moving into the world that is less and less solid. That is why we are having people exploring the galaxies, as well as the galaxies of the subatomic particle world. Each will be able to have a venue for being *lost* in performance, because no one will find an answer in the galaxies and no one will find an answer in the cellular galaxy. Each will have its black hole; and each will have its Big Bang, because every time you know What IS, the Big Band happens. And what is that Big Band? The unification of all the trumpets of Glory that sound: **I AM!**

Anyone who is in agreement with you allows a new pitch to be sounded in the world. That's why the world is not to be given over to: "Oh, what can I do about it?" It is *your* doing!

Why do you think people love children? It takes their attention off the world . . for a year or so. And then it never allows them to be free *of* the world for years, because they think what they have dropped into the vestibule of time is their doing! My Lord! That's the way the story is told. But you never believe a story; you always look to the hidden meaning of any paradoxical situation. It's paradoxical that you can be this matter-thing and yet your whole

Life Experience of Meaning is non-material. That's interesting.

Why do you suppose that men *suppose* all the time? In other words, assume. Why do they always expect? Because they were the result of expectation. *People are the result of expectation.*

What are our forests? What is the vegetation of this planet? The stage setting that is offered to embrace you as beings from inner space so that you are cuddled in the verdant state of balance in the outer. Your whole inner Being requires your attention to the Wonder of a balanced ecology. This inner State which has sponsored this outer verdant region for you to be wrapped in the foliage of promise *allows* you to experience, right in form, That Which IS termed a *Transcendental Wonder.*

That is from another dimension. That word has no meaning on this level. That *Transcendental Wonder* is the gaining of what is loosely and wrongly called "immortality." It isn't a gaining of immortality as the Bible says: "The mortal shall put off mortality and gain immortality, at the last trump!"[2] It's not mortality that's put off, it's a belief system that is laid aside. And man *translates*, because he moves from the identification with the objects and realizes his Universal Undivided State which is termed the Divine Individuality or Identity. It is this very crisis which is the problem in the world today: *the identity crisis.*

When you attend a rehearsal, isn't it fascinating, when you first start to sing there's such freshness! Why isn't it the same when you finish? What has said you were in process? Attention is never in process; attention is Now. (It's just a clue to always being awake.)

Do you realize that the sound is not caused by *you?* It is caused by a foreign, alien element, *totally alien*, yet so adaptable to your configuration of transforming: it is what is termed the *Breath*. You can't possess IT, and yet without IT, "you" aren't!

No one knows what IT is; they make up what IT is. IT's an energy field of such force and such weight. Our own is so much heavier, that we call the heaviness of space empty, light. It is not. It is the density of the thought appearing manifested as this structure that occupies it for a certain "space" of time. As soon as you live in space, you have the component time and the continuum of limitation. That is why it is said, "*I* never came or went," because I have never occupied space! The appearance may, but I never have. I AM That which elucidates the seeming via the *wave of your attention*, which you translate as *sound* accompanying the garment of words. I would be the same with or without words, and I would never have come or gone. It is your pattern of imagination with your flicks of light and darkness that you presume a pattern of yesterday, today, and tomorrow. **Your tomorrow in the Light of the Infinite is just another aspect of a twinkling diamond in the Presence of the Now.**

It is timeless; it cannot be timed. The reason you know this is so is not because of the words I am saying. The words I am saying are holding your attention so that you can hear each one, and between each one is a continuing thread of Intelligence. *Intelligence* is that component of Presence that allows the fecundating of the moment. *Attention* is present in utilizing the words to be given a meaning so that life is filled with Love.

Love is far-fetched, but I have been. But it's only Love that will save your world, because IT knows there is no-thing to save. "You" can't save anything. The *only* thing that can save is the Somethingness That IS. *The Somethingness That IS is the Force of Ideation that allows the objectification appearing as your subjective experience.*

This is a Meditation on the sound or the chant of words in the framework of attention, and the flexibility of Intelligence present in the anointing of the moment given to Love.

>Now, if you want to see just how difficult this is, take one
>>moment and decide to be
>Real, authentic in thought, word, and deed.
>Take one moment and allow it to be dressed
>In the form of "you" with no distress.

>Let others perceive in this wondrous guise
>How you appear to dance before their eyes,
>A human, an object, with glittering light
>Offering the Panacea to a world of plight.

>Look through the window and don't you see?

It's wide open; there is no pane/pain indeed.
It's there to free all those who doubt.
If they would look within, they would see,
    without any need of being,
    a confounded art
Confined to time and its blemished part.
Being freed to beam like the sun,
Do you realize you have never been able to look directly at
    the sun as long as you were a human?

You only say it's up there because of the brightness
    that shines,
And it gives you a tan on your behind!
But lo and behold, if you look and see
A cloud passing before your face as the thought of time
    and its deed,
You say, "The sun's gone on a holiday, Mom. What am I
    going to do today?"
And she'll just say, "Just look up and blow the cloud away."

You know it's been traced upon your attention span,
    that cloud of doubt.
When **I AM** known, it's not there;
But when unknown, it's the Cloud Unknowing that is there.

So you just know that if you look and see
A cloud clouding your sun and its deed,
You can part it by looking right through the suggested mass,
And lo and behold, the sun — the blue sky?
    Your promise to pass,
In this experience called Life, as a man,
Into the Generic Wonder of Being Man That I AM.

The Wonder of Being is wrapped in the deed:
I AM That I AM; no other plea.
'Tis only a sound, it's not "this" you know;
I AM That I AM is a toning, so "we" go!

And in its place stands in Presence Divine
A healing medicine beyond the mind,

The healing art beyond the thought of a man
Caught in the grasp of being a human.

But when you see the hue that Man really IS
Then he can shine and bedeck the stage and give it a thrill,
Because you came to share the Dominion as planned,
For you were given dominion over all of the suggested land.

How come you're a serf when the Lord is about?
Where did you put Him? In your attic of doubt?
Where did you find Him? In the Boat of Life (Soul)
When you were fishing upon the Lake out of sight?

Why do you think the rainbow came?
It came on your cloud, if you dared, and doubted to name
The mark of your Identity in the face of your disguise.
Do you suppose the world would be shattered if they
            knew you were a Prince of the Skies?

So the Prince may come and a visa will declare,
"You have access to this land for a short time and a
            little to spare."
But the exit is made when you pass as planned.
To come and go at will is the gift of Being I AM.

It's amazing! Not one word was heard, not one word
            was thought.
It was only when I heard them said that I realized I talked.

Think of the Wonder of the moment right now.
Don't put off into tomorrows the greatness and the grandeur
            of Being complete, right now.
The future is there for your craft;
The I AM Present allows it to come to pass.

Any discourse will tell you that this is the case.

So, I hope you have found these words confusing, paradoxical,
and far from being an aphrodisiac or a sedative. But anyway, they
have had their way. They may not mean anything to you; it doesn't

matter. They were never meant for "you. "

These words were never meant for a "you." A "you" only knows:

You haul, *you* pull, *you* drive,
You work, *you* labor, *you* strive.
You sleep, *you* hunger, me get *you*,
You get *me*, and what do we do?
You haul!
Pick it up here; leave it there.
We pay the expenses if you don't care.
You haul!

May 23, 1992

1 The city of On is the Hebrew name for Heliopolis, a city in lower Egypt, one of the oldest known cities in the world.
2 1 Corinthians 15:52.

XIX

OVERTONE OF CREATIVITY

You are now in that movement where your sense is cognized and your Nonsense is now known as the Unknown. Thus, the Divine Good is the Supreme offering in reflection that man makes when we exalt one another in communicating. By exalting one another, we reveal our faults in order to fill them with the Cement of Love and allow a surface once again to be polished for the Dance with God.

OVERTONE OF CREATIVITY

When I was a young fellow growing up, *Ken* was never exalted. *Ken* was always considered strange among his friends because he loved music. There wasn't anyone else who did in his whole class. It made me very conscious . . of difference. In those days I couldn't cope with it very well because I had no one to talk to. So the only thing I could do was to take it, in my religious training, to the foot of the Father. That's what I always did. And that's what kept me "okay."

The reason we have classes[1] is to become *aware* of what *words* will do *to* you instead of *for* you. If you tell somebody how much you love him and he doesn't know you very well, he is immediately ill at ease, because we have been taught, through the gossip of education, that no one should trust this. It is only the words of Love that should be trusted because Love never leaves you where IT finds you. *And if comments are critical, then they should be only to free you from a suggestion and thus allow you to be more the expression of the Love.* Now, Love isn't something that is always tender, forgiving, kind — but it is certainly true; it also knows enough to knock the hell out of you and teach you a lesson if need be.

Words are important. This is *very* important for every one of *you* to realize, because you are dealing with the attention of auditors. Your whole life in intercourse with one another is dealing with how *you* hold another's attention. Another's attention, you must know, is not *outside* your Self, and, therefore, you don't speak to the other unless you know the other as your Self.

The words are just slightly different from harmonics. Harmonics are the super-tonal experience hidden in the sounding of the Fundamental. The Fundamental will never hurt you. *When you separate and bring in the overtones,* they won't hurt you either, but *you have to be responsible for what they do to you.* I want to bring this before your attention because you can't expect to sing the overtones, work with them, and expect to remain as you are. If people see you changing, it's to be expected.

Do you realize that Creativity never finds you anything but

244

new? Creativity is the overtone of what? Of **AM-ing!** Creativity, the overtone of AM-ing, when misunderstood, results in what is termed a neurotic situation. Where the great *Talent* is misunderstood, man becomes confused with the purpose of his talent. And yet, his Creativity is what *allows* him to receive a station within the parameters of his talent. This is why talent is often the key to restoring order to the situation that is confused with ego.

A talent is never ego-oriented; it appears that the ego allows a talent to transcend its presence and reveal the more genuine condition of Being. Then, all of the circuitry becoming *your incredible self-constituted form starts to reverberate with the tonal reference becoming your genius.* It is like realizing that there is but One Thought. If there is One, then That is it. *One* is the Thought, so that's the One Thought; there's none other. **I AM** is not a thought; **I AM** is an overtone of the *Celestial Diapason of Being.*

This is how you have the bridge from I AM, that is only uttered by those who can move into the Transcendent State by altering their awareness and realizing the all-encompassing nature of IT, and IT embraces *this* condition: **I AM . . That . . I AM.**

That's how you bridge IT and never leave IT, and that's how you have never left Heaven for Earth. For Earth is just Heaven misunderstood, because choice has allowed you option to interpret, either from here or from there instead of from That! That is how you arrive at the Suchness of Being which is the whole Teaching of the IS-ness.

Nurit O.) I can't believe you can articulate this!

It's to be considered very, very important. Coming up in the car I was talking to Dr. K. and I was telling him that the Teachings of the Talmud are so sacred and so very important. They can never be given as simply as I give them, perhaps, but under the aegis of your presence and in the attempt of the satisfaction for your presence (which came in order to be satisfied), usually the Offering is made. *According to those who are within their head and heart united, the meaning really reveals itself in spite of the symbol.*

The symbol is the great carrying agent of Force or Power,

which, of course, is always what? Resultant change. One of the most unusual experiences for anyone is to think he is ever going to meet such a character described as K.G.M. and expect not to be filled with new considerations, because What I AM knows not the oldness you *think* you are. Oldness is the thinking that you bring upon yourself, and newness is what is termed the evidence of the Talent that is buried in the Ground of Being Fecund.

Now, Fecund Being is that which is acknowledged to exist but only able to happen when you have met the Virile Member of Knowingness, upon the occasion when the preparations of the Heart in man have happened and the answer of the tongue is from the Lord or the Law.[2] This always happens according to the disposition of the one who is becoming deceased in wrong identification.

What holds your attention can appear to be the object called "me" or the object called the flower. It can be anything that you allow it to be in order not to BE. *You will discriminate that upon which you focus your attention, if you would be free from the sentencing becoming one who has not decided to be Real.*

Decision is in the valley. Acceptance is in the foothills. The Summit is the attitude becoming the Invisible. The Message perceived is *beyond* the Mount.

"You" may be so assembled. The Original Cell had some form of consciousness. That Original Cell directly attracted to it others of a similar nature and grew into "you." You are a thought-form as a result of your cells knowing their innate attraction to the form held in the Realm of Ideation. Now, there is a great, great consideration: the Original Cell is perfect; it knows only itself and that is what allows it to seem to reflect itself. It is this cell reflecting itself billions of times that causes the form to be formed — so it seems!

As you recover from the false teaching that has you *in* this garment of flesh, with the only escape being the death of it, there *is* another way out. *There's another way in:* you will realize (that's one prescription). Another: you will follow. The other: you will *watch.* If you realize the questionable nature of your cellular body, then you know there was *Something* before the cell, because the cell could never structure its own panel or fraternity. There must have been a Force that is termed the Unknown that was allowing the cell to be without question, even in its formed state. But, when the formed state took on the form without recognition of the *conscious cell structure*, we had the very beginning of imbalance. That has resulted in what man calls his maladies, instead of melodies!

The malady is a result of *forgetting* that he, in Essence, is *before* his structure. This has got to be understood for the healing! This is the healing, because **when man realizes that he must have been before the cellular form, then he no longer questions the form for the explanation of its chromatic state.** He only *asks* that he return to his rightful Home, where it may be correctly classified in the domain of what they call "Realization." It is in this experience of sadhana that we realize how in speaking to you and you giving me your attention, you are (yes, in spite of your thought) attuning yourself to the Uncontradictable State in which you **find the Self not a billioned-cell creature, but the Unimprisoned Splendor.**

It's true! It is not the intoxication of a wine that you have trampled upon; it is the only *known* Ecstasy of the Gods. This is why it is termed such a *journey into the Unknown, under the leadership of the Hierophant.* The Hierophant is a glorified guide; he is *not* the one that tells What IS; he is the one that *guides* you to realize.

That is the whole meaning of the Inn,[3] because the Inn was the only place where there was hoped to be room, and there wasn't any. It's another way of saying that there is this place in all of us but, unless there is *room*, in other words, *emptiness,* you don't know how to enter this State. That emptiness only comes when you step out of the routine of your roboticized age. This comes when we start to put a value on leisure, because leisure means the willingness to step out of the ordinary and into the Unknown.

That is how leisure becomes creative; otherwise, it becomes a beer party. Often you call it your lost weekend, and no wonder it's such a *weak end*! You end up with all kinds of problems. When you move into *leisure*, you don't move into doing nothing; you move into a state where within the radiance of a contemplative moment all is rearranged in your garment of cognition. That is the *Essence of leisure*. It isn't where you escape from doing anything; it's where you are deliberately placed by your own inner prompting to step out of the outside world and into that space where you can drop the *appendage* of being called a human.

Being called a human will call you man or woman with all its varying degrees of patience, because birth, growth, maturity, and decay are nothing but different gowns of patience. In the scheme of the Transcendental, of the next Dimension, time collapses, and, if you are, as they say, neurologically prepared, you will receive the impinging Force that allows you to experience the Transcendent while appearing to be human.

This Force is so great that you can't allow too much of the chaotic to be around you, because to that State it isn't real and it doesn't exist. If you think chaos is your state, it is only because chaos, *deeply* considered, is bringing about a new order. It doesn't mean that there is disorder. It may appear to be that way, but if you go deeper, it's the *striving for Unification*, when you have deemed it division.

So, what we're arriving at is a question: **Are you living the Supreme Identity?** Upon hearing this and accepting this because you are listening, are you going to continue living the inferior role of one in the becoming?

The time is far spent and the day is at hand
When those who will know the Righteous Band
Will know in a moment, in the twinkling of an eye,
That the I of All-Being ne'er pierces the sky.

For it dwells within that Moment so grand,
When man can perceive the Rapture I AM.
And in that moment, all is changed, and you find
Your releasement from what seems to be the belief realm,
and you live as the Divine.

There would be absolutely no point of questioning your cell and your imprisonment if you didn't have a Judge that knew how to rescind the sentence.

Everyone says your DNA has coded you for good; in other

words, it can't be changed! Well, the DNA may or may not be, but do you realize the DNA was not known up until very recently? But the important thing is to realize that you cannot allow the suggestion of a new invention in terminology to defeat That which has given freedom to those willing to accept IT for what man calls his historical centuries.

Why is it so interesting now? It is because now it is coming to the ears of the Western people that there is no excuse for being the "hams" that most are — smoked or otherwise! You no longer have to play various roles to satisfy your own illiterate companions. You don't need to feel what everyone else feels, if everyone else is in the same boat as you are. Everyone in the same boat as you are knows the inevitable end! But you know that the *Boat* that you really utilize is the one that you manufacture through experience and the utilization of what we term Divine Ideation.

Now, what do we mean by Divine? It's that Something that "this" isn't. So you can call the Divine, or you can call the Something that this isn't, the Unknown. So, if this isn't, the Unknown IS. Now, isn't it easy how quickly you are able to accept the Unknown for being Divine?

You see, you don't broadcast your message; *you are the Message.* If you think you are in the process of a mess-age, you have mess-mates, which are companions. The root of "companion" is a mess-mate. Isn't it amazing they don't tell you that before you say, "I do"?

Why do you say, "I must say 'I do' one day"? Because all your companions, not knowing what the stew is all about, don't realize that the bean in it, or the corn in it, or the stock in it, is quite acceptable, even by itself. They feel that the whole thing has to be gathered together in the stew in order to be delicious. How many particles of your life have you put into the pot of belief, and put it on the back stove to simmer in order to have it more tasty within a few days? After all, remember, it's usually made from the remnants! What type of tribe were you from?

Re-member, and you have "this."
Know, and you may appear to have "this."

Think, and you're bound to have a thinker,
And that thinker is bound to think.

We challenge the entire mental realm of the ordinary education, because no matter to what small unit you go, to the cell or to whatever incredible galaxy and cosmic stellar consideration you may have, it is always lighted by *What* isn't in it.

Now, if you are going to talk to your cells, you can't talk to them without this knowingness. That's why people are looking for the miracle. No one is going to be healed unless it is on the Agenda of Light that they receive an instantaneous healing. They may have earned it by their fidelity to Purpose. However, many will be disappointed, because unless they are *willing to change* their thought (and thus preclude the necessary washing of so many diapers), they will only be able gradually to alter how they see themselves and how they see one another.

If I look at you, I am only seeing you because I am willing, I am allowing, I am accepting within my pattern of cognition the multiplicity called "you." Yet without my conscious awareness pattern, you would not exist . . to me. So, that is the mystery to the statement: "Where I AM, ye may be there also."[4]

You see, "where I AM" is before you. Where is the "*before*"? That's the incredible part of the English language. When you say, "The Angel of the Lord has gone *before* you,"[5] do you mean He happened yesterday and you came today? *Before* you. No! The Angel of the Lord is "good," so he went ahead of you. "The Angel of the Lord has gone *before* you." So you automatically think "ahead," because that sounds much better. But really it's your choice, whether the Angel of the Lord has gone before you and all the lights are green. Is He leading the way? Or has He done it?

So, you are before me; I AM before you. That is how a Code is given and can be broken just like that, or it passes.

> *If you are thinking in your head, you're bound to be a heel.*
> *If you are feeling with your Heart, then you will find the*
> *Truth revealed.*

When the question arises, "Are you living the Supreme Good?",

I suppose all those who are religiously bound consider "good" in all its various ways. But if you are living the Supreme Good, and you go to the root or to the overtones (harmonics) of "good," you'll find it is also attributable to "God."

"God" in twenty languages means "good." "Are you living the Supreme Good?" You see, I don't like the way the statement is: "Are *you* living the Supreme Good?" **Is the Supreme Good living appearing as you?** That's how it's disguised. So now you won't be able to go to sleep tonight. Are you living? Of course! Is the Supreme Good being evidenced as your living? It doesn't mean that you are blind to what seems to be; it means that your eyes are open, so that you can allow what isn't to fade out in the Light of What IS.

A problem always comes to you to give itself up, not to be entertained. Do you know why people love to entertain a problem? It gives them what you might call "a beer accent." It means that it gives you a lift for a moment, or it may be that you are lifted for the moment: It may be b-i-e-r instead of b-e-e-r. If you continue to imbibe that brew, you may hop, skip, and jump for a while, but you will not have the flexibility for long, because your pancreas won't like it, the Langerhans islets won't like it one iota! Look what happens! You have a malady that affects the entire system.

You can't hop and skip and *evade* the upright Pole of Being, which is the Rod of Right Identification. You see the hops growing in Europe; you see them on these gigantic rods, spread for acres, thirty, forty feet high. It's obvious the hops grow high, but isn't it amazing how with beer you're hung over, usually your belt! It's very costly, because too much of anything allows anything to be too much.

As a Maharishi said: he didn't mind his students working in the hospital that had been erected for him by the man he *saved from thieves*. This man had been beaten up and left on the side of the road to die. It happened in India and this Teacher saw him, carried him to his home, and cured him. He didn't know who the man was, but the man turned out to be extremely wealthy and showed his gratitude. (It certainly doesn't exist today.) He actually built a hospital from his own resources and had it filled very quickly with people who were sick. Then, of course, there had to be the attendants to help. An American visitor asked the Rishi how did he come to allow his students to work in the hospital. *He said he permitted them to work there as long as they didn't forsake their God-Being and start chasing the shadow.*

Your ministrations in the hospital are so powerful, if you are set before you enter instead of being upset when you leave! What does "being set" mean? *You know that you know that you know. When you know you know, you know you know.*

What is happening today in the medical profession? Everyone knows what they don't know. Everyone is telling me this. **But how many are willing to take on knowing what they can** *now* **know?** Because it's going to bring about a whole new prescription for Being. You may prescribe the old pill for the odd pill! You still love and you have your loving ministrations, and you *are* Love. Look how I have dealt with it all. IT allows it to all happen. If you have to take a pill, take it, but don't believe it's touching anything Real.

Never deny what each man's service is. No talent can be denied anyone who evidences his talent, but his talent should and always will evidence where he received it and what type of seeding has happened. When you are seeded purely with the academic registration of time, you are seeded with what? *The mechanical registration that never becomes the Divine Organ.*

The Divine Organ is such a magnificent concept that it can be played with many colors. But remember, the registration is decided *not* by *you*, but by what the music demands! *The demand of your registration is inherent within the Music. This is experience.* When I studied registering the king of all instruments, it was a huge organ with many thousands of pipes and three manuals. I made my debut at nineteen. The registration was not what *I* liked; I never *thought* of what *I* liked. It was what the music asked for: "Register me **thus** upon the piston of time, so when you strike it or play it, the shift is a tonal baptism of sound that enhances the **fiber** of those present." *You mustn't register for novelty!* You must never *allow* the registration to be such that it is unbecoming to the message of the tonal offering.

Remember, the manuscript is nothing but someone's proof of an oral/aural happening. In the past (so that you have a little confidence in what you call the present), the scribes expected to hear everything of significance said twice, and very slowly, because it had to be noted. What happens? When a thing becomes noted as the verification of an experience to which the notes bear no resemblance, the ones coming later (in spite of their Sisyphean yawns — push or roll your own stone up the hill!) started prescribing to a bar, or a cell of sound, a movement, an expectation, when it was *never that* in origin!

Originally when it all happened, it was not that way at all. It was all happening. Those who tried to make it noted destroyed what was always to be the Newness forever appearing. This is why it is ridiculous to take a piece of music and think there is a prescribed way for playing it and interpreting it.[6] What appears as the manuscript is the evidence that, if you haven't been able to compose something greater, and have to use somebody else's work, then you *owe* him the responsibility of reading his manuscript, if you're going to work on his piece. But it doesn't *mean* that you have to take what's *in* the manuscript, because what happened is only *pointed* to in notes; it is never the happening!

That is what has been so Wonder-full with the Singers. One composer grew in his ability to *offer* a piece. He would sweat buckets when I started to change it, but now drops hardly any dews! He used to just drip, but now doesn't because he has moments of realizing that this is only an *attempt* to portray what his *genius* is offering! It may be right to him, but to one who is looking at the *genius*, it isn't right! If I were on the same level, I wouldn't criticize him. I never do criticize *him*. What's the point? I could criticize his weight in two minutes. That's all I'd be looking at!

That isn't what the Work is. The Work is to have that Focal Point that allows you to perceive how another can be *freed* from a *voluntary* imprisonment. Everyone in this room has volunteered to be imprisoned with no splendor. Why? As soon as you have style (when you see somebody dressed as he should be dressed, it's considered style), you stand out. It's elegant!

Being can't be other than elegant, because Being is that State which embraces all that is termed "beautiful." That's why all the Holy Books have always tried to impress upon the fertile imagination of the aboriginals pictures and objects of beauty, because they always were signified as worthy of being in God's Presence. That's why your churches and your cathedrals are filled with such beautiful objects, because it's only those elegant, precious gifts that are worthy to be on the altar where the Divine is cognized. In other words, where what is cognized? *The Unknown — Elegance.*

The reason I always dress up is because I am always acknowledging the Unknown. You have to be dressed in mind as well as in body. That is how the Soul is *capitulated* into a new *scenario* for this Age in which you live and move and have your Being.

It is stated for this Age that, if the Soul is not restored to a meaning of significance, the Age will be lost into three hundred years of robotery. A renowned teacher told me this just recently. She said, "If you don't get this Message across to all these people as quickly as possible, and you've only got ten to fifteen years at the maximum to do it, we are lost, Mr. Mills. There is no other hope for us." It is so fascinating that not only she, but others in high places, have said exactly the same thing.

And yet, it is the one word "Soul" that had no meaning for me for nearly twenty-seven years. From the time I was just a young fellow I questioned it and I wrestled with it and wrestled with it, until finally it meant something to me.

But remember, the activity of Soul is creative; the absence of Soul is counterfeit: people aping the Divine Creativity.

You can't rob God, Good, and expect to have an unblemished future. You can't! *Good can't be distorted by selfishness.* So, when you consider, "Am I living the Supreme Good?", you know the demand is great, only to the moment that you agree to live by what you know to be True.

Do you feel a stranger in this room? If you do, it's all within you, because if it were in me, I would never have spoken and greeted you as I know you are in Reality. I have allowed my attention to embrace you and in that allowing have accepted the Force Field in a conglomerate field in order to move through and delineate those words that you have, in the Silence, requested to be heard in such a way that they would appeal to each and every one of you. For each and every one has been a portion and part of this Happening. This Epistle is just another one to those who have come out of the past into the now, so that the years of released expression may once again be found here and now as they have stemmed from the historical yore.

You are now in that movement where your sense is cognized and your *Nonsense* is now known as the *Unknown*. Thus, the Divine Good is the Supreme offering in reflection that man makes when we exalt one another in communicating. By exalting one another, we reveal our faults in order to fill them with the Cement of Love and **allow a surface once again to be polished for the Dance with God.**

Thank you.

June 6, 1992

---

1 These are classes where the Lectures are reheard and studied. The classes include in-depth language research.
2 Proverbs 16:1.
3 Luke 2:7.
4 John 14:3.
5 Genesis 24:7.
6 "Playing implies an ability to do technically; interpreting means allowing meaning to be experienced and felt." — K.G.M.

XX

A SOLUTION TO THE CONUNDRUM OF BEING

When you see that the body is merely the enhancement of the Unformed for those who are entranced with the form, then one who perceives this is the one who reveals the possibilities of seeing through this mesmeric field of opposites and is thus allowed to be here and now have a carefree way.

A SOLUTION TO THE CONUNDRUM OF BEING

In a very interesting lecture last night, it was pointed out that there is a window between each word that a person utters. If you could enter it, it would be the moment in which you would find the Self. I know what he's saying, but it means, perhaps, something different to me. What you would find between each word is silence. It is not the silence that is aware of coherency; it is the silence that allows what appears as the clothed energy fields called words to follow one another in a coherent or intelligent way. What is between each word is intelligence, and this intelligence points to Something that is Formless and yet formed, for it is the evidence of its incredible All-inclusive Nature in that it allows the sound of a word to bear an intelligent meaning to the next one. Behind the Silence, of course, is what is termed the Cosmic Self. The Cosmic Self or the Divine Self, if it's constantly thought, is as limited as is the thought-body and its thoughts. So the Cosmic Awareness or Cosmic Consciousness is the constant Presence That I AM evidences in ITs formulation of ITs nowhere Self and ITs somewhere Presence. For IT's nowhere, and yet IT's somewhere, and yet IT's no somewhere, and yet IT is nowhere.

So it's all a paradox,
And it doesn't matter which word you use.
When all is said and done
There's really only One,
And that does not need to be articulated.
It's due to IT that articulation appears possible.

Ellen M.) That would explain why the lecturer we heard last night could still give the same lecture after three years. What he has in essence done is delineated something through his thought; it's actually an interpretation. As soon as he put it into the sense of knowing he could get into it, it wasn't an experience any more. If he continues to do that, he's doing exactly what he described as

"remembering." It's a different level of rec-
reating himself in the moment that he called
"the gap." There's no change; otherwise, he
would appear different from how he was
three years ago.

He expressed it very well last night: remembering is extruding
from what appears as your memory bank that which is appropriate
for the Now, which in Essence is all you are anyway. Others see you
with a past, and in so doing, see you with a future. So you allow
your memory to be present in order to allow another to have the
encouragement to let it go and only use it in the way it can bless the
now. The future is not something that is created before us; it is
created because what we are now is all that tomorrow can be. This
is why it is imperative for those who are close to me to start exalting
the Wonder of Being and allow Presence to be Self-glorified in the
natural, spontaneous act of Effulgence. Others may call it the
expression, but that is the way the mind will have to interpret what
it conjures up as an experience of the Transcendental School of the
Divines.

The School of the Divines is one that has been established with
approximately one hundred ninety-nine Ascended Masters from
this plane that have been recorded as having performed tremendous
services to the dream of Earth and its inhabitants. They have all
offered to remain in a position within the Hierarchy of man's
invisible projections in order to sustain and to help in the suggested
exercise of Earth. This is a great mesmeric dance, but it is really an
exercise in which man develops his ability to be a great magician.
The great magic achieved is to seem to be present in the body while
you are absent, really, from it and present with the Lord, and allow
a synchronicity to appear present such that no one knows whither
I come and whither I go. And yet I AM All, and man says "forever."

Valerie W.) It's so interesting. You just
spoke about the great intelligence that is
between the words. I don't often hear you
use that word.

No. Well, "intelligence" is a word that the vocabulary
contains which allows a condition of nonintelligence to appear to

acquire it, and thus seems to exhibit a type of coherency so that language could be formulated when it ceased to be sung.

Language is a secondary characteristic of the Song of Presence. The **Song of Presence** was the Song that sang into manifestation the rhythm that each leaf, flower, and plant, and that the animal, vegetable, and mineral kingdoms demanded in order to satisfy the harmonics which constitute a Tone that might have been sung. This is why the Fundamental Tone sustains the Earth in its orbit. The harmonics allow it to appear to be clothed in the grandeur becoming the festooned glory of an animal kingdom, a vegetable kingdom, and a mineral kingdom that are termed wondrous.

The Fundamental Tone was sounded, but not known — was termed "the Big Bang"; when known, was termed the moment that there was silence on the slate of the demand-schedule for another planet. The demand-schedule is a very interesting consideration, because every demand has to be fulfilled, and the schedule of an event must be precipitated according to the visualization and the intention of the creature wishing to be comforted on the plane of the drama which has been his exercise. But so few people have been taught correctly. They fail to perceive that education should be giving them the means to remember the purpose of the exercise.

This is why, perhaps, I have had to come; why people like Maharishi Mahesh, Ramana Maharshi, Nisargadatta and Trungpa and all these different people have had to come. Perhaps the reason they've had to come is because the force of ignorance is so great that others have had to assume the role of a guardianship of the race. The **laggards**, who have never really moved in rhythm with the demand of Light, have been slowing down what was supposed to have been a much more brilliant passage from sense to Soul!

So, to tell an audience why they are there: it's one thing to describe geographically their position in a mass, but it's another to reach them through the Principle of preaching. **Preaching: you reach because Principle is the first Force that is present in "preach." When you preach, you reach. If you don't have the *P* present, appearing as the creative activity, you can't reach.** That's why the ministers who have to preach a sermon have got the sermon where it shouldn't be. The sermon is what man learns before he comes, so that when he reaches the people it is spontaneous articulation of

That Which IS beyond the Mount. That was part of the need of the Beatitudes.

> Ellen M.) Principle is really the only sound or way of stimulating or re-energizing the state of ignorance?

The correct thought-pattern of the remembrance. "Principle" is utilized more than "God" or "Christ" because most people can't fight with Principle. They can, however, due to their bias, react instead of respond to the other names given to the same Force. This is why what appears as my Assertion is so garmented in the language that can stimulate the batteries that man has prepared in order once again to cast a beam before his walk, having cast it from his own eye when, before we incarnated, we talked. The Teaching should have happened on the plane before the form capitulated itself into assuming this shape due to the thought-field. The body is thought into form. Otherwise it's nothing but sound .. that is not heard with the ears, not perceived by the eyes, and yet known to BE. You have both (ears and eyes).

> Ellen M.) So, could it be said that it is imperative for those who hear this Message in this incarnation to engage it, because its Resonance is affecting others who are in the material body now?

Yes.

> Ellen M.) Will many have to come back and do it again to keep the vibration of the planet seemingly growing or becoming more Light?

If man is at the stage where he feels that the body is the object of his love affair, then he will have the Earth upon which to play it out. Therefore, he will appear, so they say, to reincarnate, which means just change his garments for another act upon this plane of exercise. When you see that the body is merely the enhancement of the Unformed for those who are entranced *with* the form, then one who perceives this is the one who reveals the *possibilities of seeing through this mesmeric field of opposites* and is thus allowed to be here and now have a carefree way. There should be no one bound caring for limits. The limits are found only in the *shopping bag of desire*, where you go into a store of thought and pick up everything that doesn't have any value for the purpose of your presence.

This is what has happened with so many: they have shopped through the store of latent talents. Frequently, their talent has been one that would enhance their success in the objective field. They have left it there, instead of realizing that the talent expressed is the evidence of something beyond the human. That is where the talent should have been expressing the God-Being, instead of the personal being enacting the role of success. God-Being doesn't need to be qualified, because it is obvious there is no success or failure to the handiwork of such a vast and unlimited, imagined creation.

It is imperative for those who see garments woven with so many seams/seems, that in the weaving of the Tonal Garment the *chromatic situations be resolved from the Standpoint of a fixed Pitch*. Every other string that is strung unto time in order to bring about a Polyphonic Wonder must again be given the opportunity to find every string that is out tightened and strengthened through exercise and disciplines, so that when the technique is required, any Octave of Being can be heard or unheard, in order to satisfy the demand of those who would be present and yet not absent from That Which IS.

The evidence of Creativity and the Act of I allow those in the tide of current events to be positioned in the Light of a Conductorship that allows the Current to pass and alter those present with the attitude of becoming free from the personalized drama, so that the Divine Rama can appear within each and every one's unfolding Path. The Path seems to unfold because I stand revealed.

The I revealed is the One that sees through the suggested density of mass and perceives the nothingness of it and yet the Somethingness that allows it. Since most of "you" is empty space, what is responding to this is not the emptiness of space, but the Somethingness that allows the emptiness to be declared to be the nothingness; and yet I AM .. without need of verification. For That Which IS is not in a continuum where verification is needed, because the continuum itself is the evidence that What IS nowhere and yet somewhere IS a verifiable Force graciously allowing ITself to be talked about as if IT were something IT isn't.

262

The people who say they don't understand me are really saying, "It's a different language, and yet I thought it was what I knew." They have to be willing to perceive this, because if the language were the language that you use, it would not be capable of bearing the force that is required to free you from what language has done to you.

A rat in the same teaching with another rat doesn't know anything other than that rat classroom. That's why it becomes a rat race. Everyone in it is under the same force, and the only thing that stops the rat race is to have something happen that is termed of "new times." A new timed event that stops the rat race is always something different and new. That is what you call Paramount News! It stops those caught in this race, who expect those caught in the race to free them from it.

> Ellen M.) Mr. Mills, how can we better facilitate the learning of your language and being more exact? Are we here to learn to do that, or even attempt to?

You should learn the language, and when it is yours, you will find it natural to speak. It would seem that many people who study the Unfoldment do not speak well because they do not study well. They are obedient to their minds to do what they are told, to study the Unfoldment; but they are not obedient to do as I have done, which is to make the grueling effort to alter the language to be acceptable to Wonder.

If you alter the language to be acceptable to Wonder, "you" become questionable. This is how people have come to me. The reason many do not alter their language (only enough to gain social attention) is because they do not want to face what *the changed language demands: a change of habit, a change of identification.*

A new language demands a new character, without the habit of a past to make him or her seem acceptable to the present.

The reason we use Principle is because no one can form to IT. One can only *con*form to IT. When man conforms with Principle, he may appear to be seen or he may appear to disappear, but the Principle is still present, for man is able to describe the great magical act of coming and going at will.

It is the full moon of what man has termed the Christ Festival. It is the weekend of the full moon, it is the weekend of the full Christ. It is the weekend that is the springboard to the strong accents of the positive Nature of Being. It seems only positive, because those hearing it have not perceived the negativity that creeps in, in the belief system surrounding our present sojourn in a quasi state termed "becoming."

June 13, 1992
(en route from New York
to Washington, D.C.)

XXI

REPLACEMENT – DESTINY

You can replace the skeleton in three months, the lining of your stomach in a matter of minutes! It's not death in slow motion; it's death in the Wonder of movement postulating the Eternality of Being. This is what your job is: Being the pulsating Heart Throb to the Unknown Wholeness of Being I AM.

REPLACEMENT – DESTINY

One accent of living in this suggested form is the realization today of *replacement*. The body is constantly renewed or replaced. We are living in the midst of death every moment we utilize this body. If we were actually in it, we would go with the passing of the dead. After all, if your skeleton is renewed (and you're hung on it) every three months, where did the old skull go? It's obvious: if you've got the skeleton, it includes your head as well, the cranium and what it contains, I suppose.

It's rather an interesting thing to consider that you are living in the midst of a universe that is constantly decaying and constantly renewing itself — and you're going to *meet* death?! *You're meeting it every moment that you appear to live in this!!* It's fascinating, because when you realize, as you *do*, that *you are Conscious Being and not a person with a consciousness of Being*, then you know that you are external to the suggested "you" and yet appear to be internal for the suggestion to appear to have company.

Now, to realize that you are the external Wonder to your most incredible artistic invention, you have *thought* yourself into a body. That is why you cease to think when you leave it behind, because it takes your *thought* to put you into it. When you leave it there is no thought in it, because the thought was never in it to begin with! Thought is what creates it, and you project it, because everyone has taken it upon himself on this plane to accept the same projection and call it a similarity of experience. You call it the human form with the animal, vegetable, and mineral kingdoms added to it for a little bit of variety!

When you can experience *beyond* the form, as many of you have, and as I have, you know the form is being utilized by a state of Conscious Awareness. In the terminology used by this One, **Consciousness is a state that is unadulterated and uncontaminated by any of your hypotheses about it. Awareness is the aspect of it that changes.** It is your awareness that allows you to perceive all the different cultures, your classification of nationalities, their range of continent, contentment, and containment. If you can perceive that your body is a thought-product, you have met one of the greatest happenings afforded to the challenge of the intellectual might of the suggested human, and that is to see that "you" are a thought-product, and you live beyond it, because you can **change** your thoughts.

Now, That Which IS Real never changes! That is why the Love That IS never changes. That is why the Truth That IS never changes. That is why the Soul That IS never changes. That is why the Mind That IS never changes. That is why the Principle That IS never changes. **Anything that changes is unreal!**

We all know that this mortal experience is changing. We all know that it is imbued with life and death as the prime interests of being human: birth and death. In between you're supposed to have growth and maturity.

We know that the basis of "this" is mortal and, therefore, changing. Why are we basing our lives on it?! Everything we do we are basing on a premise that isn't so! "I've got to have my own life. I've got a right." "I've got to be an actor." "I've got to be a dancer." "I've got to be an artist." You know? But, you haven't "*got*" to be any of those things. You've got the "to BE or not to be" as a result of false education that this inner longing is what should motivate you. It isn't the longing to be some thing to gain attention, it's to BE so evidencing whatever art that you claim to be part of your destiny; it's fulfilled in being *artless*. This allows the art to reveal an exit to the suggestion of a limited framing of time.

You see, we frame ourselves into the most *gilded/guilded* conditions: a doctor, a lawyer, an Indian chief. And look how we frame ourselves! With what? With the responsibilities of our thought-products. And we have the full responsibility of reproducing ourselves. I have never seen anyone genuinely happy over having reproduced himself! In fact, many of the reproductions have been imprinted with, "What happened to the press?!"

In the reproduction program, we fail to achieve getting beyond the frame of the cells in which we have allowed ourselves to be contained, by name calling. **We do not access the greater Wonder with as much frequency as we should.** There appears to be, according to the unreliable sense testimony of mortality, a lack of people living the Solution to the suggested problem of Being. **That**

Solution is: "I and My Father are One *Now*"; the Cause could never consider tomorrow! It was supposed to have been instantaneous, the Big Bang! No one knows just what it was. It's a wonderful way to give a name to something that "you" have nothing to do with, but which you attempt to *define* in order to name it so you think you can *decline* it.

"What the world needs now is Love, Love, Love!" You may be able to perceive that the Truth of Being sets man free. The Truth of Being is this: *that Man is Conscious Being, and equals the term in language which is intoned.* I AM only *intoning* and you call it language! I AM intoning the Authentic through your hypothetical thought that I AM speaking *about* Truth. It is the very intoning of this Message that proves that Man in Essence is vibration. Therefore, **Truth only relates to this level where a lie has been sprung upon you. The seven Synonyms of Creativity of the Divine Creator cease to exist as such when the language of duality is transcended by the knowing Grace of the Absolute State of God-Being.**

You are a crying need of the world either you couldn't be here! Time doesn't cease. What has happened in your years, this time, has accents that you will never forget. Coming from another country to this country, learning how to stay in this country, being at home in this country, you have all kinds of conditions to meet in this experience.

If Consciousness were not Eternal, there would be no way of keeping the Torch forever aflame. *So, just accept the Fact; you don't have to understand it. "Understanding" is one of the ways you have been framed.* You've been framed into thinking you have to understand before you accept. That's how you are *seduced* into such states, which you do not want to *reproduce*.

Accept, experience, and then you can say, "I understand." What you do after you have accepted and experienced is **express** through *intoning*, and that appears as what others call "*your* understanding.*" Understanding is never "yours"; understanding is what *stands* "*before* you."

I want to speak to you about destiny. Somebody asked me about it in the car. (He isn't here tonight. I alerted him to the fact that he would be detained tonight by error. I told him this yesterday and he said, "No, I will be there.") I said, "One of the errors of the Age is receiving Instruction or Teaching without the living of it." This man said to me, "What is destiny, Mr. Mills?" I said, *"Destiny is how you face life without the daring to realize it is your own creation."*

The present situation with the people present is so interesting to me when I look back through the memory banks. That's the value of a memory. **A memory is a code that allows you to reinterpret what seemed to be an objective happening.** So, as I look back on what appeared to be the happening years ago, many people came to me who had done what? At your age, Jon, and at your age, David and Justin, and at all your ages, they gave up everything to find a teacher. They went to Morocco, they went to Algeria, they went to India, they went to Tibet. They did all types of initiations in the Tibetan language and what have you and, lo and behold, they would be gone for months and years. They gave up everything!

I met some at that time who were married, and to follow a teacher they were told they had to give up their marriage. They sold their minks, they sold their diamonds, they gave up their car, their chauffeur, and their cook, and off they went with the kids to follow the teacher because he told them to. I remember, on one occasion one of the students told me they were to meet in some place in Tangier, where they were asked for all their money. The teacher had asked them to sell their cars and their homes and to bring all the money with them. He wanted it that night, and the next morning he was gone. He said, "I'll meet you in India." They all stuck to it and met him in India!

What I am saying is that they were *so daring* to face what they considered important. Well, many of them are still around. Why is not the same tenacious attempt to achieve present as it was in giving up everything and traveling three-quarters of the way around the world, for nothing but an experience which allowed you to realize the transient nature? Transients everywhere?

A great point! They went through all types of deprivation all because of searching for the Real, the Truth.

Well, Life is continuous. **Death is that phase of living that is beyond the space requirement of form. You only need space to give**

you form and you only need time to define it!

Life is continuous. What makes death seem so horrendous is what appears as the suffering that frequently accompanies it. But it isn't the death that is painful; it is the redefinition of your allegiance to *effects* that accumulate as disease in disregarding the Cause which came first. People are so concerned about the effects that they *forget* their Purpose was the Cause! Jesus said, all great Teachers have said, "For this **Cause** came *I*";[1] not "For this **effect** did I come."

Please, this is *very* important! You are actually living forms of a Transcendent Experience that you can share with others by your Presence! You are part of the *Remembrance Pattern,* either you couldn't *possibly* be with me! That's why, perhaps, some of you are not too happy about being with me, but you see, somewhere in you, you know you *can't* or you *shouldn't* go. I never advertised. I was nothing but a piano teacher. That is all. I taught all my life and I never stopped teaching piano until February 1975.

An Indian teacher came and sat with his sandaled feet, which were dirty, on my new Scandinavian blue sofa, which I had just purchased, with one disciple on either side of him. I thought, "If you ever get that sofa dirty, I will be really annoyed!" He had come from India to speak to me, and so he sat there in the lotus position. I thought, "Oh, their roots are in the mud!"

He asked me all these questions as only an Indian can ask you! *Many people look as though they've got a canvas that never saw the Brushwork of God.* He came and he pummeled me and elbowed his way through all these difficult muscle-like questions that have caused men and women to question all their lives. I wish they would question their *Life* instead of all their lives!

I answered the questions and then he just stared at me with his black eyes and long black hair and heavy black-rimmed glasses. Unfortunately, I turned the tape recorder off prematurely, and it did not catch these words. He started to rock, put his hands over his face and said, *"Impossible! Impossible! What are you doing in the West?!"* What could I say? I suppose it just proved that the Impossible was possible!

The ingredient that you have that is not exalted is your *Find* in this lifetime! I posed a question the other evening: I wonder what your first priority is? At one time I knew it was the Search, but it certainly does not appear to be that way any longer. But you know, so many thousands of people came to see me that we had to use a hotel *ballroom*, because I only believe in a God that can dance!

There wasn't one person there by chance. They were all led because of the continuing episode of Life appearing as an effect called their lives to once again give them an opportunity to re-establish the correct Viewpoint of the Cause, and thus their appearance the effect.

It's all backwards. When I have seen all those come and go, I consider *death*, because they will never be rid of what this One in form represents. This One in form, when perceived beyond it, represents the meaning of so many of the esoteric statements that have been part of the great Teachings of all Ages, because no Age bears an element that can dislodge the Truth of Being. **Everyone who has known Me has known Me to acquaint himself once again with the Truth and allow God to finish His Handiwork.**

You have made an attempt intellectually to be students, but you haven't been the evidence of the Living Messiah, the Living Promise, the Living Opportunity, which *you* in Essence are! The reason the priests, the ministers, all the people in power, have *always* talked about God, the Virgin, the Messiah, the Prophet, et cetera, is because having a medium between you and what you really ARE pays off.

Man has *no way* of being other than Real. But he has been **framed!** He has been taught in the schools incorrectly that he has the right to think any way he wishes. That is not true. You were given the ability of cognition and, eventually, of perception, and then, of *con*ception. Then you could tell how an object appeared outside you. But you couldn't see yourself!

Do you realize you have never looked at your whole Self? You go around claiming how important you are and the only part you look at is your belly button, or your toes if you are in good shape. I don't know how you have such confidence in yourself. What in

God's name would you do if you broke the mirrors? You can't see yourself! Well, if you can't see yourself, it is because you were never supposed to see yourself . . as this! God would never have left you in need! You must see yourself as you really Are! That's not some divine, airy-fairy, impractical — impractical! God would never have left you in that way!

If God had wanted you to fall for yourself, He would have allowed you to get used to looking at your own face instead of seeing it reversed in the mirror! You look at a picture in a mirror that is the total opposite of what you are. In the mirror you are a flat surface! Well, can you imagine why I like you to develop a perspective?!

We say we look at each other's face. That's in the Wholeness. But when we look at each other's face, you appear to be looking at me in one way; our eyes are opposite. If I'm looking at you and you're looking at me, you see, what's right and what's left are two different things. That's why you don't bother dealing with opposites, even in sight. You don't deal with opposites in sight, because if you do, you have to weigh them in the scheme of your agenda for living.

When I look at you, I don't look at you and see oppositeness! It's so much simpler! **It makes you a real target, because people will never understand someone who treats them with the Wonder of an immaterial, Immortal Presence.** Everyone I meet, I meet as one whom I cognize as my own response to a form that in Essence is nothing but Love. Well, what's so wrong? Most people are under this framework of a restricted sense of expression.

You are never a reflector. You are never a little piece of mirror reflecting the Wholeness! How could you be? Some teachers, I've been told, tell everyone that they are just a little piece of a mirror reflecting the Allness of God. It's totally a hallucinatory gimmick, because anyone who tells you that you are something as a reflector of God is in a place that I wouldn't want to be. They're in the place of being cracked!

You can only be an expression as I AM. I am an expression of That Which I AM. How am I an expression of That Which I AM? It's not in the form! Don't be fooled! It's by the Essence that allows this form to **intone a meaning that is commensurate with the Feeling of Being I AM.**

It's fascinating to perceive that we all fall for the seeming
And give it all our attention, when it goes with the dreaming!

The only reason you sleep so much is because you know that you have confidence in That which isn't contained within your thought-model "you." You have the Presence of Conscious Being and Being Conscious. That *allows* you to rest, but when you open your eyelids, you have to open the lid of your *entombment*. You have to lift those lids and that's when you start to perceive your dimensional experience.

Do you know that the reason you have confidence to go to bed every night and expect to awake in the morning is because the Power that is present is the evidence of another Present State that is so close to you but, due to your unprepared circuitry, you haven't been able to engage the energy field of it. It exists because I AM the living evidence of That.

I would not be giving these Lectures if I were really where *you* are. I only *appear* to be where you are and sitting in a chair like you are. But where **I AM is just beyond the tissue of your imagination.** I AM in another dimension entirely, but the tissue is so thin that with a flick of my eyelash I can move back and forth between them. Now, if I can do that, it's obvious . . What IS.

This is why I can give David a swat if he needs it, and the next minute he feels nothing but Love. It's because the Love is from behind the *other curtain*. So, I step out from behind it, give him a swat, then step back in and I'm Love!

In other words, the Unfoldment, this Lecture, is a Transcendent State. It's what is termed "another dimension." How many dimensions are there? As many as you wish to dream! People have said, "What is the fifth dimension?" I said, "You don't *dream* well enough!" Because you want it like "this." What do you want? You want to hear me say something that you can reference in your thought-sets that satisfies your insubstantial nature by having everyone agree that it is *insubstantial*? Why do you think you always seek your own kind? Because you feel at home in your own kind, usually.

Everyone's telling everyone to get rid of nationalities, to get rid of color, race, and creed. It's the easiest thing in the world to do! We're all birds of one kind or another. I don't prefer a robin over an eagle or a sparrow or a canary. They all evidence the Wonder of spontaneous expression and effortless flight. They know enough to land upon a branch in order to feed when a call comes to them. They instinctively know their own and seldom bother with the unknown.

If the whole basis of your present life is such a miserable thing, what do you spend your days doing? Working. What for?

Years ago, no one thought that work was important; they thought the Search was important. Why has the spirit of the Search left? Do you suppose it has to do with age? Well, no one dares to admit it, of course. "We are getting older; we have got to think of our future." *What future?!* That's a dream as much as the coming of the Messiah. The future you are dreaming up! The Messiah, the Truth, has *never* left you! It's those who need a Shepherd's crook, a Promise, a prophecy to keep them going so that they will have a destiny.

Tell me something! If you know that a hundred-and-fifty-pound man can be put in an atomic press, have all the holes squeezed out of him, and the residue be placed on the head of a pin, is this what you are working for: the head of a pin with you on it!? You are always being *stuck,* nine to five, nine to twelve, because someone is sharper than you and has got you pinned into a position where you have been *framed* to think you cannot invent a contra-puntal experience of a practical nature!

What is the point of bushes? If you want to survey your estate, they keep you from *going in.* Have you ever tried to go into a forest with the bushes? *I* have. We tried to do it in the D.R. We had to have the Dominicans with their machetes cut the bushes, all the vines that cling to the trees. My goodness, the fruit trees and orchids were growing in the natural way, but you couldn't see them because of the bushes. Perhaps you didn't even see them without the bushes! I seem to be the only one that's ejaculating about them. They were incredible to see!

What do bushes do? They keep you from going in. How have you hedged *your*self? With doctorates, patients/patience? How have you hedged yourself into a role where you are feeling you are doing good, and yet you have forgotten your God-Being?

On November 29, 1987, I gave a wonderful definition of healing: **Healing is not the proof that Truth IS; healing is the proof that the seeming changes.**

We forget the *miracle* of what *appears* as healing. Unless we have a known need of it, we never consider our happiness as a drug, our wealth as a drug, our knowledge as a drug, our position as a drug, our condition as a drug. Mankind is *drugged*! with belonging to "pilldom." It is the most incredibly difficult level to belong to because it's usually dressed up in the most attractive ways.

I had to have a prescription filled the other day. It appeared as fifty pills. They cost more than what I'm worth. I'm worth about $2.69 on the market today; the pills were $126 for fifty of them! What price we pay, and go on paying, without ever questioning: **"What is my priority for Being?"**

You are people, to all appearances, bearing the Universal Nature of Light for those who walk in darkness. They must see the Great Light if you bear this Knowingness. It is imperative! I'll tell you why: because it can be related to the *knotted piece of wood*.

If you go to the lumber mill, the saw mill, you see a beautiful tree cut up into pieces. They're all laid one on top of the other. You see one and buy it for clear wood. You get home, someone sees it and says, "Damn! Look at the knot in this. It isn't there any more; there's a hole in it!" I say, "Where was the knot?" He says, "Oh, look at the hole." I say, "Well, where is it?" He says, "There's the wood!"

The one who has seen the knot and gotten rid of it has a hole. The only way he can describe the hole is by describing the wood. "Oh, it's mahogany, beautifully veined, but this knob in it has ruined the piece. But it's a beautiful texture and we can do this and this and this to it and reveal more of the veins this way and this way and that way." That makes the hole interesting!

In other words, this polished presentation of a piece of wood with a hole in it allows people what? *To know about the wood because of the hole.* **It's because of the hole that the wood became known!** It's because of the whole that the wood became known. And that's what you are! You are like the wood that is polished and waxing in the Light of the Sun. You are not waning in the light of the moon and becoming withered with the belief of aging and death in slow motion.

You can replace the skeleton in three months, the lining of your stomach in a matter of minutes! It's not death in slow motion; it's death in the Wonder of movement postulating the Eternality of Being. This is what your job is: Being the pulsating Heart Throb to the Unknown Wholeness of Being I AM.

It is only by your Presence that anyone ever realizes the Unknown lives. The Unknown lives *as you*! Unless you're polished and allowing the Wholeness of Being to be perceived, you're just another one of the trees out of the forest and usually surrounded by bushes. You never have time to go within and find what is beneath your bark. You ask this tree who it is and and he'll say: "I'm a fir." "I'm a spruce." "I'm a pine." "I'm a willow." What do you pine after? The willow! Why the willow? It knows enough to bend, and not break even in the frozen state when you don't really want to *show* your love. Go on with you, you crucifiers! If you don't show the Love, you never reveal the Wholeness, because it states fundamentally that God is Love or Love is God. God in twenty languages is "good," and, therefore, my God is good and good is my God.

What are the Ten Commandments? What are we searching for? There's One! The Oneness of All. Who is making it up to be otherwise? People who want to keep everything in nations and in religions. They try to make a fossil come back to life! It can't remain written in stone; it has to be the living pulsating of the Dance of God Being Real. That is the State that is known as Absolute, because from that Standpoint:

> All the seeming is there for dreaming, and all the Reality is
> truly Divine,
> And all the trains that man finds waiting are sometimes
> caught on a bride of time,

Sometimes caught on a coronation of splendor, sometimes
    worn when man doubts and despairs,
And finds the train of tracks are never ending, only in
    the illusion that they meet somewhere.

Why do you claim a train of victory? Why don't you claim
    the Crown Divine.
Why the Crown, lo and behold, is the willow bent low, and
    God hath made thee more than mind.

In the ceremony becoming the Select, the Known, the
    ceremony reveals One Alone,
And in that response the train tells the Wonder; it appears
    as confetti for the Stars that are blown
Across the sky of man's imagination, and under the feet,
    if you sparkle and see
What the Wonder of flowing with the Rhythm of Being
    gives to whatever you consider the celestial and
    the terrestrial to be.

**What is *your* priority in the scheme you have made up
regarding your framed condition of mortality?**

In the Round of *Music,* Man is a Harmonic State of Being;
Generic Man is a ***sound vibration.*** The only Pitch is the One that
is concertized, and Man appears to rhapsodize through the Voice
where he must stand in the witnessing box of the Wonder of a knot
in a piece of wood . . and who knocked?

I thank you all for having opened the doors of your minds to
me, and, some of you, your hearts, and certainly I have felt very
much wanted here. This is a wonderful feeling for me. It's one I
don't often feel. I stay at Home within myself in order to know that
there is no place for rent! I am fully occupying all time and space
with the Wonder of just Being what you think I am while I remain
what I Truly AM. That is the Magic of Light!

The great act of this time is to be what other people want you
to be while you remain what you really are and appear to dance at
times through the tulips/two lips.

If you have any questions, and you wish to live by the answer, all right. Don't ask me a question and not live by the answer because, after all, if you have a question and it's answered, it is no longer an effect; it becomes a cause.

Did you realize that's why questions and answers are so *dangerous*? When a question is answered, the question can be the effect of your consideration; but when the answer has come, it becomes a cause for your movement.

Well, I thank you for your persistence in knocking, and perhaps you will find the need of waxing in the ensuing Force Field that you have dreamed in the tomorrows. Now is that point of instantaneity when talent and genius and intuition appear on your hypothetical horizontal plane in order to annihilate its limitations. The Art of Being is the Presence of Nowness in the face of procrastination!

June 20, 1992

---

1 John 12:27; 18:37.

XXII

COAT OF MANY COLORS

You can't expect a Garment woven without seam or rent if you constantly knot it. You cannot expect Fulfillment when there are knots, because Fulfillment is the evidence of flow; knots are the evidence of blockage. The flow of the Light is unimpeded by the Knowingness that accompanies the Wonderment of Wisdom's child.

COAT OF MANY COLORS

We have enumerated upon the fields of accomplishment, as we scrutinize with ever-increasing awareness, enhanced perception, and accentuated enhancement of Fulfillment, the moments prepared for those who have remained faithful to the prerogatives of the Divine and the Fundamentals surrounding the Laws of Adjustment, the Laws of Attraction, and the Laws that bear about them a universal significance and an eternality.

As you have perhaps realized, time has nothing to do with Eternity and Eternity has nothing to do with time. Life has nothing to do with you living, but your living has something to do with Life, for if it were not for Life, your living would not appear possible.

Light is not in this dimension at all; Wisdom and Wonder and Intuition are the handmaids of the Forces that are not able to bear identity other than in these subtle spheres beyond manifestation, but which enhance, for those who continue to dream, the apparent manifestation.

The Insignia of the Divine has been marked irrevocably upon the Ledgers of the Scrolls of every man's accomplishment throughout the centuries and has those engravings which deal with the accomplishments and the dividends accorded the Work done under the appellation of One called forth and proclaimed a "good and faithful servant."

It is in the recognition of the One Divine Attraction that one understands that "If I be lifted up, I will draw all men unto Me."[1] Then, the episode leading to the recognition of the inevitable movement from sense to Soul is accomplished. In the Wave of Force and Power stands the Crest of the Masters and of Those who are in a position of dispensation to allow the precipitation of an infectious inner Knowingness that when "All is said and done, there is really only One." That is the answer to the question: "Do you dare to be Real?"

In the perusal of the plane of objectification, in the vibratory frequency of the plane, the great need has been seen for the thought-patterns and their enhancement to be mobilized under the force field of a heightened energy field of expectation and elevation, as men and women drop their garments of divisibility, rejoice, and re-accord themselves with the Great Triad of Being.

The Scepter is forever seen passed from generation unto generation "until He comes whose right it is to restore all things unto the Kingdom."[2] It is in this consideration that "you" are in the forefront of your imagination, and your world is forever beckoning unto you to act the Ministrations becoming the Chosen. No people today, whether entering synagogue, church, or mosque, can know, if thought is in terms of person, place, and thing, what it is to appear as a person in a place and in a thing and yet bearing the Commission of the Light Brigade. For it is in this bearing that the great marquee of time will start to glow with the cognition of man's inalienable rights under the jurisdiction of the Wisdom of the Saints and the Sages of the Ages.

None gathered in the places set apart from the traditional holding tanks of spiritual aspirants have greater Wonders bestowed upon them than Those who are without label and bear the possibilities of the Fulfillment of the dream. You, in your peregrinations upon the plane, have ever to be mindful of not accepting the suggestions that you know what This One is saying, for as This One wears a coat of many colors, it is also indicative that the Statements made bear many colors. It is hoped that your considerations will not drop to the considerations which some of the tones bear reference unto: the inclusion of Earth. For Earth shall be included, but it is not from Earth that man achieves the ability to distill the dew and have it appear upon the petals in your garden.

It is from the elevated heights of aspiration and inspiration that man is able to interpret the Unseen Scroll as it unfolds in the living pianoforte of the Cosmic Realms. For the octaves shall be covered, and the fingers shall be fired as the scherzo is revealed in its nature as joke, the great minuet and trio as the Dance of God among the starry considerations, and the finale as the ever-recurring theme of the past into the Nowness and the hastening to perceive that the statements of the first theme and second theme are now recapitulated in the final movement; frequently in their reverse keys, yet bearing an authenticity in statement, and decked in a great colorful way for the expected recapitulation to reveal the digital Wonder and the scintillating ebullience equated and expected, as the Word is given wings. Man takes this Word of Being, a winged Messenger of the Mercurian Light, to be the Winged Sound that bears the Voice to touch the various pools of receptivity as they are waiting within the Chalice containment of the skull, the Benedictions of Those who would say, "Well done, thou good and faithful servant.[3] Inherit all that is becoming to your endeavors in your fidelity to Principle."

No Schools of the past have existed without adherents and without the understanding of the graduates *knowing* what it means to be the exponents of the Sacred Esoteric Truths and their meanings. Few there be who are capable of intoning the correct Frequency that *allows, enables, and ennobles* those who hear it to be an advanced race in the forefront of that which is termed the great Modern Olympics in the Realm of Light. For it is a time when the great strength and discipline and force of those dedicated are there to leap the hurdles and know that when Love is set, *no volley is to be found.* Those who seem to have fallen in the battle where the cannons boomed and the faces faced the ground, now stand upright and are capable of declaring in the Soundless Realm where Man is sharing the Winged Victory without the head to interfere with a Heart that is *longing to hear what it means to be a Free Soul.*

The gates must be opened upon your considerations as never before and upon your renewed dedication to the Constellation of Aquarius. You must be under the constant bombardment of your **conscience**, for your **conscience, allowed, must function.** For too much selfishness, too much bigotry, too much bias, and too much egotism still remain to be washed away by Those who are afforded the opportunity of seeing the Great Stream of Everlasting to Everlasting carrying away in the floodtides of Love all that would hinder and impede your accomplishment.

If you were to consider only the Self and freeing yourself from the travail of your incarceration, then there would be no greater achievement than your own freedom, because you have the ability within the translation of the *photonic* experience of your perceptive might to rescind whatever you see. If your eye is clouded, so will your vision be; if your thought is clouded, so will your analysis be; and if your mind is biased, so shall the cut be upon the materiality of your experience, and much more yardage (or many more incarnations) will be necessary in order to prevent the stretching and the losing of the shape, as the garment cut upon the bias in its elegance may be worn. Unless the fiber is woven so as not to stretch, it is unwise to attempt more than the regular shape, the regular appearance, and the regular attitude in order to become adopted and adapted to the Frequency becoming the Great Invisible Light Stitcher who knows not the thought of missing One.

You can't expect a Garment woven without seam or rent if you constantly knot it. You cannot expect Fulfillment when there are knots, because Fulfillment is the evidence of *flow*; knots are the evidence of blockage. The flow of the Light is unimpeded by the Knowingness that accompanies the Wonderment of Wisdom's child. Wisdom has nothing to bear but the wiseness becoming even the owl, which sees in the shadow time of day that the suggestion of the sun's disappearance is only for those who know not the Constant Vision that accompanies One who is as wise as an owl, and yet perceives in the darkness that in the shade, there one can rest, for in that shade is represented symbolically the Accomplishment of Peace.

Why do you remain in the heat of the day if you have found the shade of the Tree, and remain perspiring instead of *expiring* in the egotistic framework, and finding yourself expelled from the dismal condition of limitation? Man was never given anything other than the Birthright of the Divinity from which he comes, and to which he goes in the Hereness and Nowness of Being. Man's Hereness is God's Presence. And what is God's Presence? Love's Presence.

Love is Presence, and for people to say they love you when they are not present is a semidemiquaver in their Scrolls that would compose the finale of their scripts! For you see, you cannot say: "I love you as much as I always have," and *be having a fling with another that was shot from the bow of one who would cause the demise of a success and an achievement beyond the ordinary.*

One who is to attain must be ever ready to perceive the arrow that flieth by noonday and the arrow that cometh by night in the form of dreams! But do not disregard your thoughts, because when you do, they may parade as dreams. Your thoughts unrecognized in their deterrence to Truth are frequently dressed up for a dramatic performance in your dream world.

Do you realize? Of course, you say you do. That is why you

don't realize with Wonder. Wonder keeps you always open to realizing. Arrogance always says, "Of course I wonder, but I know that."

When you consider that the Wonder of each moment is wrapped in the achievement of what others have said was your yesterday, are you surprised that others are looking toward you for the fulfillment of their dreams? How can you fulfill another's dream if you remain in it and believe it is true?

It is now known that Mind cannot be measured. There is no way of even knowing where it is located! *Do you realize Mind has no location?* It can't be found in any person, place, or thing. The only thing that can be found, the only evidence that can be found, the only suggestion that can be found that there *is* Mind is that the brain is affected by it!

The brain can be located because it is, you might say, the storehouse of your computer that is attuned via a code to the Source from which you have been rocketed. Your mind is impossible; your brain is certainly without doubt. "Going out of your mind" is only the state when the person in ignorance has taken the activity of the brain to be Mind! **The activity of the brain is the evidence that Mind is All and not in it.** This is why one can transcend and translate right before you and yet still appear to bear form, because the brain is capable of holding you in a corporeal identity, while the Mind in its great Force and Wisdom can come with its impelling Electrical Might and declare: **"That condition is a lie! You have mistaken your brain for Mind."**

"Brain" is the name of a limit; "Mind" (Allness) is the only *Sound* that can be Unlimited, for it means in its Meanings more than your brain can "dictionary-ize."

Your brain is measured; your Mind is measureless. **Your Mind is not yours!** *That's* **how you limit it.**

When you entertain the ideas of Divinity via the great Central Computer of the Universe (of which you have a small, concise, precise model within you), you are able to receive the Dictations from the Central Heart. These are forever impelling you to be in agreement with the Invisible, because you are in *dis*agreement with the visible. You are known to be in this state by an invisible malady in the beginning, called dissatisfaction, complaint, and moods! These are the first signs of the onset of a malfunctioning computer. It behooves you and those in the world who hear this to adjourn to the Inner and Upper Room and consider well what thought-force you are entertaining that allows a complaint to be considered Real. If you decided to be Real, then you would decide that such was an imposter attempting to gain control of your computer in order to *appear* to *in*dite the Wonders of a Mind Transmission.

How frequently the brain in its incredible mockery of the Divine Unlimited Source attempts, through its intellectual might and subtleties, to imbibe a language that would keep you engrossed in the gross body in which you find yourselves . . named. *Anything that you can name is limited.* That's why you want to call people by their first names and not give them a chance to have surnames, because if you do, you are at a distance from being able to control through a false sense of knowingness.

As soon as you can name a thing, you have limited it. As soon as you think you know what the thing is, you have made it equal to "you," which was never to be made equal! "You" is a common ailment of all formations that bear intelligence and can name each other. The greatest malady today is "you-ness." "You-ness" bears with it a power that is used in voting. If the "you's" will vote for another greater "you," then you will have the evidence of the demon manifested.[4] If all of you can cast your vote on the side of Truth, then the Leader shall be perceived as a Force and a Power beyond even the throne which represents its yin-yang nature and bears no concern for the classification bestowed upon it through the dictionary, its meanings of male-female, or the duality syndrome and its mighty infectious nature.

In the realm of your duality — which has sprung as a result of your brain-ality — your brain has been able to counterfeit some of the "similar" force fields of Mind. It has been able to mimic, it has been able to counterfeit, but the counterfeit or inaccurate teaching cannot be exchanged before the Divine Teller at the Gate of Transition. **Anyone who attempts to delineate the Word and finds that it has not been an all-out *Mind-Heart* attempt, knows full well the damnation that must inevitably confront either form of the appearance, male or female. Remember, anyone who has dammed** the Divine just through sheer resentment, through sheer jealousy, through sheer disobedience, stands before That Teller Who will be your Self facing yourself. Your soul will not be your Ship of Light, but your corroded capsule of disenchantment.

You were given the prerogatives to become the Great of time, because you were given such a commingling with a Spirit that far transcends the ability of your brain to comprehend. Your Heart can't help but respond, for it says, "*Love* is the fulfilling of the Law, and so help me, God, I can't help *but* love!" If Love is All I *now* know, then there was a time you *didn't* know! *That* was given for *you*, because it does seem that as you enter the Stream of the Quest for Life Eternal, you come with the unusual mental condition of thinking it is a *choice* realm! **The Quest for the Divine demands that you leave at the gatehouse, with the gatekeeper, what will never be used again, which could be none other than your clever intellectual attainment, which would attempt to argue on the Path with the Mind That IS.**

One of the most interesting accents of the counterfeit mind is its attempt to elucidate the Divine Mind and then change its mind. If the Divine Mind could change, there would be no Quest!

Have you ever considered that the Quest is not something tangible within your language component? Do you realize that the Quest points to something beyond your name-calling? If your Quest is looking for the Unknown, then it's obvious there's a part of you that is *vacant*. There's a vacant lot within you! What do you try to do with that vacant lot? You try to keep looking back[5] to see what you can put in it.

If you decided to be Real, the Quest in its unknown Nature would be filled with the exciting news beyond your hill of intellectual attainment. The hill of your intellectual attainment is something you must all come to stand upon. It's made up of all the skulls and bones of those who have built their lives upon *head* knowledge in preference to Heart and Soul Wisdom-Meaning! This is why Jesus was crucified on the Hill of Golgotha or the Hill of the Skull. For until the skull is emptied of its brain information, which has been named "the intellectual achievement, bearing the doctorates and the board of approval of all your finest universities, theological, rabbinical, et cetera," you have not graduated with any praise, for you are in need of being raised!

This is why you know you are on the Quest when Principle is sounded. *When many principles are sounded, you know you are in the holding pattern.* When you are understanding how it operates, you are only circling above your own unknown portion of the lot of your thought-world.

You would never be able to consider the Quest if "you" were not in question. You would never be able to consider it, if your name were nothing other than a *frictional* sound. It is the friction of saying, "Eunice! ("you"-ness) Ulysses! Plotinus! Socrates! Aesculapius! Matthias!" These are only frictional sounds. Why? Because they take your attention and are not part of your scale of present statehood. Those sounds, those names, take your attention because you expect something from them that you haven't got. That's why you have you bearing your names and Me bearing Mine. You need yours; Mine is for your convenience.

If I had not an irritation termed a name I would not have been in a position to be called. It is in the calling that you have to know your question. For your question is not for the One who will answer; your question bears the answer so that it no longer exists. **When you have found the Answer, you are no longer in an excuse realm.**

If you notice the subtlety of your computer terminal, you will notice how it's indexed. You have learned how to shift from mode to mode, because you have learned how to take one byte from one thing and one byte from another and still end up without having to change, because the operation of your computer allows it to regurgitate whatever has been given to it. What has been given to it can never be the Ultimate, because IT cannot be locked into a computer program; IT can only be the Light to the Program that is not computered!

How in God's name (or your name) can you expect a God-Answer to equate with your questionable state, when the God-Answer is beyond question, either it would never have responded to the emptiness called "question"? **A question is emptiness! The Answer from God is the evidence that you haven't cognized you already have it!** You are suffering a hole, or lack, in your province of operation, without perceiving there isn't any! You attempt to defile your Divinity by having no question in order to evade the realization you are without question on the Path.

So many who are on the periphery and never make their appearance are all in the same Force Field as this, only they are under the magnification of the Divine Light, for IT is causing whatever IT will for their freedom. Their freedom is inevitable because Love is the Essence of their Being. *Love allows what isn't to appear and What IS to be recognized, thus fortified, in the cognitive plan of self-exculpation from the alleged plane of mediocrity.*

The time is not up; the alarm has not gone; but the Watch is demanded! For no man knoweth when the sentinel in the tower perceiveth the Eternal Sun.[6] It is so wonderful to worship a God afar off; it is such an electrical shock to be called God-Son, God-Man Here-Now. God only exists for the moments of your incarnation when you need a buoy anchored on the Plane of Omnipresent Light! God face to face is anything but an apparition! You make God an apparition and a ghostly experience through your attempted worship. God is the Force of Spirit, Mind, Soul Meaning, Love's Force, Principle Empowerment, Here-Now.

These words are given as a Dictation from the Ever-Continuing Light of those who can be counted, those who can be sainted and seen to clarify the multi-faceted nature of God-Man, God's Man, Sun-clad, Sun-eyed and present! **Love is Presence and in That *BE* at your greatest moment of creativity!**

Thus endeth this portion of this Plane, bearing the Greetings as always: *"Peace be unto you. Not as the world giveth give I unto you."*[7]

August 23, 1992

1 John 12:32.
2 Matthew 17:11; Mark 9:12.
3 Matthew 25:21, 23; Luke 19:17.
4 "Democracy should be 'deo-ocracy' so that the demon of manifestation is seen unnecessary." — K.G.M.
5 Genesis 19:1-26.
6 See the poem "Watch," in Kenneth G. Mills, *Surprises* (Toronto: Sun-Scape Publications, 1980), p. 85.
7 Acts 4:25.

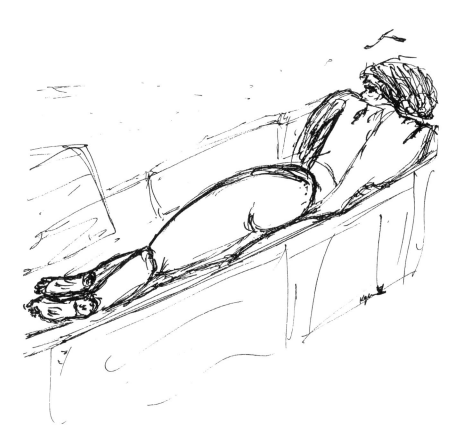

Kenneth Mills and soprano Dianne Forsyth

HDTV at Ed Sullivan Theatre for Moulins Originale Fashion Show with Kenneth Mills and model Sonya in "Madam Butterfly" gown

XXIII

EXCURSIONS INTO MEANING
– OR –
FORESTALLED OR FOREARMED?

Under the light of research, you have penned in a very rational way your explorations; and in the Light of the Intuitive, the Answer has come that has freed you from the rational. That is the evidence of a Force that is not forestalled by the events; it is fore-armed, for the Mighty Arm of God has been artistically extended in the evidence of the All-inclusive exten-sion of the Creative Heart.

EXCURSIONS INTO MEANING, OR
FORESTALLED OR FOREARMED?

You know so much; you have linguistically been endowed with a language of great subtlety, and a language that demands a great awareness of it in order to navigate the many possible excursions into many meanings. And yet, you see, the defining characteristic of preventing many meanings of words is the great limiting factor of Principle. Principle permits only those words utilizable in keeping with IT.

The difficulty of the language has in some way been transcended by what appears as the Speaker, for, without thinking, He has offered what is termed the Knowingness of the most sacred level of the Esoteric Teachings, which is such an incredible threat to the standardized means of locomotion. Loco-motion. The moon often lingers too long in the state of most of mankind!

You who have expressed, as a result of the Summer School[1] experience, have had the great inherent buoyancy of reaping the ensuing Force Field surrounding correct endeavor in the Light of Principle. Your research in the various departments which were chosen bears the testament for you when it comes time to show the work you have done in attempting to bring those facets of your interesting encounters into a place for redemption and for the remission of sins. You have presented your work in the Light and you have presented it in order. This means that it has taken a type of method and scheduling to allow you to present the material, which in turn has permitted, as a blessing, the ability for you to perceive the demands, even on the level of your involvement, that must be equated with aligning your thought-fields to a specific purpose which brings out *your* transcribed notes. Then you must be able to consider what it is and the magnitude of it, that allows what you have presented from your research to be re-arranged, re-formed, and *re-drenched* in the Light. For in the Rapture of Freedom there is the constant, militant, unyielding movement to Declarative Statement.[2] *The Declarative exerts such a force and such a grace that the elimination of what is usurping attention and prerogative is laserized by the incredible ensuing Sonic Bath accom-*

panying the world drenched in the outpourings of an unlimited Heart response.

If the Heart of Man could be considered by men, it would be an erroneous heart, it would be a malfunctioning heart, and it would not be the Heart that IS. The Heart that IS bears no similarity to any figment of your imagination, any more than the Man that IS bears any similarity in your figuration. Your musculature, your formation and its components, including the heart, bear only the testimony that, in the Dispensation, I will not leave you comfortless.[3] I will always allow what you have scheduled to be your experience to bear a corresponding identity for what appears as your event upon the *stage* that you chose in order to perform once again in such a fashion, with such beauty, such grandeur, that His Handiwork might show!

> How long it has taken the members in formation to subdue
> the ego so that His Handiwork *might* show!
> There is not a digit in the computation of the Divine
> That can be conjured into a verifiable formation
> within the limited computer of your mind.

When you have so felt the Presence of the Overshining Light of the Divine Self in the past few days, you have been allotted a sense of Reality. *Isn't it an **amazing** Grace that, out of the fifty-two weeks, fifty you live solely on Grace?!* Where else do you sacrifice? The sacrifice doesn't call for anything other than setting aside time to restore your Self, to be so secure in the ensuing years of your longevity that you are able, willing, and selfless. **Are these considerations before you or is your life *counter*productive to what you have said is the *Value* you have found and called *into it*/Intuit?**

Under the light of research, you have penned in a very rational way your explorations; and in the Light of the *Intuitive*, the Answer has come that has freed you from the rational. That is the evidence of a Force that is not forestalled by the events; it is forearmed, for the Mighty Arm of God has been artistically extended in the evidence of the All-inclusive extension of the Creative Heart. [The sound of a railway crossing signal is heard as a train passes nearby.] The signal is always present; it's fascinating how it's such a poorly attuned bell, but it's enough to stop your loco-motive action!

The noise of duality is thunderous! It will drown out the Voice if you allow it equal performance, for the Value of the Voice and the Word is the greatest key to the Alchemical or the Unfoldment Wonders of Man's great Quest. There is nothing greater in the kingdom of this dimension than the Word spoken freed from the Speaker's sense of any personal gain. The Word called forth is relevant unto *your* condition. Just as the X-ray tells you what is relevant to your condition, the *Words are relevant to your condition; they have nothing whatsoever to do with the Speaker's*. If I were to speak of what is relevant unto Me, I would wonder how much would be given, because *in words I AM not given and it takes not words to know that I AM given.*

It takes Cognitive Wonder to perceive the Gift,
freed, abundant, beauteous, and grand,
Bridging the suggestions of time and erasing the
duality tracks of mind and man.
Your train of thoughts so wheeled onto this stage of time
Needs more than an engine before you; it needs
as well a Divine Tender . . behind?

Your experience with the Word must, as you now know, be considered beyond the page of study and the subsequent antiseptic psychological bandage you thus assume for having been "good." (You studied five minutes before you went out to work!) The purpose of study is to find the Self, not yours, and that's why when you do find the Self That IS, you are no longer "yours." "Yours" is a reference to the plural of "yore," and yore was redeemed when the Word said, "It is the years of released expression *now* on the stage of observation."

The past two weeks showed this. It also shows in the singing, the released expression. But you see, it is also being noticed that when man *sings*, he has to utilize far more of the demands of karate. He has to use the Force to penetrate the suggested opponent: *himself*! It is so interesting to ask people to give more and yet there's not one movement on the dial of the audiometer! It's amazing the filtration system you have and the compensator that exists within it because, when you're asked for more, you think you give more, because your *compensator* allows you that. It cancels out your insufficiency in response. This is the great, great subtle demand of your future: **Do not allow your compensator to cut out your comprehension and its fulfillment.**

You have chosen to live in the most, you might say, advantageous time of all your incarnations. But you are living in a time where you have never known such mental dexterity, because you have been allowed, due to your mentality, to experience so many other facets of your dream world at the same time, giving you an opportunity to eradicate, due to the word "Presence," you might say, the karmic influences of your past.

The karmic influences of your past are not difficult to perceive. They are the expressions still parading that are not attributable to Principle. Karmic expressions are not much camouflaged, save in the most serious cases.

When you find yourself rebelling, resenting, and making appointments to miss intercourse with your Self, you are *deliberate* in your choosing and you will be deliberate in what you lose. *You cannot allow anything social to interfere.* The social scene and its demands are *irrelevant* when you know they are nothing but part of the stage setting which you have chosen in which to try out your improving redemption and allow others to see the prescribed meeting of your Radical.

Your systems are multiple and varied, but they are all under the heading of One Control; they are controlled when all systems are accepted in the Light for *being new.*

Be humble, be sweet, be gentle and kind, and absolutely *intolerant* of any form of error, having no empathy, compassion, or word for it but "Get thee behind me, Satan,[4] for where are 'you' found but in the suggested realm that God created two!"

Don't give God a beard; as soon as you do, "you" need the trimming! As soon as you make God a form, you need to see through yours! As long as you pray to God as a form, your prayer cannot be answered. But it does not go unheard; it is just answered in a relative way.

Don't try to feel the need of instantaneous healing or eventual healing! These are all conditions that you have chosen to bring home to you what you haven't done, knowing you should have done. Isn't it amazing how these words can be heard and how many have the wisdom to apply it to themselves? I wonder how many are listening as One to Me, instead of one of a series to Me. If this were your private Unfoldment, you would be attempting to see why I was saying these things — about you? I am saying these thing for you so there will no longer be an obstruction of "you" about!

Now you know the **feeling** of harmony, now you know the **feeling** of an increased force field, **now you feel** on the edge of great new possibilities — and you are! But this could have been felt years ago! Why have you allowed that which you knew from the beginning to parade so long in an attempt as a side force to limit the Handiwork of Life's Creative Act?

No one who minimizes the Grandness of Being and its Handmaiden or Handyman will ever be without a karmic situation of great intensity. If you are ill at the moment, then see if it is because you haven't done what you should. Or is it because you have thought too much about trying to prove yourself a capable doer? *Being is involuntary*; only in the initial stages is the be-er attempting to ape. When we ape we imitate, and when we climb the various Octaves of Being, we demand: **LEAP! Project! Extend!** Forget your puny, limited thoughts, for they have nothing whatsoever to do with Being the Songsters of the Divine, or the Vocalizers as the Group of the Divine.

Your self-consciousness throws "you" from your horse. Your over-sensitivity doesn't affect you, other than making you nervous. Over-sensitivity to person is a signal. So many try to make a cultural and societal **impression**; the purpose of your Presence is **expression!**

Only those who inhabit the lower regions are concerned about your impression! Those of the Higher look to see the expression, because it's the evidence of your faithfulness for having pressed on, that others come to know *why* you did so. That is why any *ex*-pression with an "X" in it is always open for others or even the "others" of yourself. *Ex*-pression.

The delineation of this Lecture, the observation given unto IT, will reveal to you how IT is offered with such a reverence for the sacredness of Identity, and how IT is kept above Identity falling into the colloquialism of everyday language.

Your language must be improved, your vocalization must be enhanced, and your professionalism must be evidenced! It will be so, as soon as the professions are made for That which you offer as the Purpose of your professional life. When you have a profession, you have *confessed* to the fact that you have followed an orientation in thought, word, and deed to fulfill a specific gamut of needs, but when you have the One Divine Profession, you are known, not because you are famous, but because you have allowed *That* to be known in the dawning of your own Reality.

How can you know the Light of a Buddha, the
Light of a Jesus, the Light of a St. Francis, the
Light of any of the gods of the past?
How can you know the Light Eternal, if you
allow IT to have a mask?

How do you know the Light of Victory, if the
mask appears in its stead?
Will it be a tragedy Grecian where no facial
expressions dared?
No facial expressions dared to equate themselves
with the Face of a God.
And now you know in due season that it, the face,
is the canvas of the One worshipped as a God.

Without the face of expression, without the Wonder of the
eyes,
Without the quivering nostrils of *scenting the Fragrance
of the Divine* as it's dropped from the skies,
Without the quivering lips of Wonder, without the
square chin of resolve,
Without the *ears* so listening without, what would
be other than a cause?

But then, when these are known as attributes, the
Scent is the God at hand,
Allowing His Presence to be equated with the full
opening of an objective, loosely called Man.
But in that *Fragrance of Being, put your hand in
the Hand* — *of God?*

Why, the arm is extended in attention. Have you
    ever traced the *Fragrance of Cause*?

The Cause of Being is untraceable, the Cause of event
    is done,
The Cause of a Revelator's Presence is declared in
    revealing One.
It says in the Book of Revelation, when the door
    has been opened,[4] it can never be shut.
And the door was opened when you called, and I said,
    "Hello," and you said, "I would like to talk with
    you."
And I said, "Come."

Thus endeth this portion of this formalized Offering from the
Formless Plane of the Invincible and from the Fecund Planes of
Graciousness.

Under the Aegis of the Masters of Power and Force and
    Light,
May Wisdom be yours in the days that follow you,
    for you have been partakers of Love and Its Might.

As I've said for twenty-one years, I don't really feel it is wise for
people to go right out after an Unfoldment and start talking about
business. I think you should be quiet, allow the Presence to be
entertained before excluding IT by filling that rare space that you
have allowed IT, *since you are not present as a practicing Presence
all the time. As soon as you are, I won't have to say anything about
wasting your Substance in riotous, external talk!*

Don't go out and have lunch and talk about what isn't!
Rejoice in What IS.
Tell each other how much you *love* each other.
Tell each other how much you see the *change* in each other.
Tell each other how much you are *appreciating* each other's
    attempts to change your forms.
Tell each other, *encourage* each other, to be *more* than
    "each other."

"To each his own" is not true at all. "To be or not to be" is not true at all! And to BE Real is inevitable, but to talk about IT keeps IT at arm's length, instead of the Arm of God extending in the might of extension to minister digitally unto the prevailing Octaves of Encounter.

August 30, 1992

---

1 This was the final lecture of a two-week, intensive seminar with Mr. Mills and a group of his advanced students. During the workshop, panel discussions had been held that focused on various professional disciplines, including the performing, visual, and healing arts.
2 "I and My Father are One Now . . not shall be." — K.G.M.
3 John 14:18.
4 Matthew 16:23.
5 Revelation 3:8.

XXIV

DRIVING TO DISTRACTION

Someone recently asked me, "What will the language of tomorrow be?" I said, "It won't be words, you know." She said, "It won't?" I said, "No, we're going to sing to each other." She said, "What?!" I said, "We're going to sing to each other. The words are just the camouflage until you can take the vibratory frequency of your Radiant Essence."

DRIVING TO DISTRACTION

What is a question that is driving you to distraction, to the point where you're involved with the objective world totally? **Distraction *is* the objective world.** What is driving you to distraction so that the objective world is taking all your attention?

Isn't that a good question? *Do you ever probe deeper than the superficial experience of your distractions?*

Several) We try to.

Well, how do you try to? That would be an interesting point. If you're trying to, how then do you try to? Tell me, so that I can extract you from your distraction if you get lost in your trying. Someone see if he can put it into words. Yes, Jennifer.

Jennifer M.) I think watching thoughts is a main practice that I engage. Also constant vigilance on what is my motivation, what is the real motivation behind what I'm choosing to do, or what course, what Path I take.

That's a very good one. That one is important, because when you're watching your thoughts it's one thing, but you have to extract yourself from them as well! Remember, your thoughts are on a very low level compared to what you are really experiencing in the language.

Language as we know it has deteriorated tremendously. *We use words so indiscriminately.* Words, of course, reveal our mind-brain state. We often fall for our involvement in the objective world as being of prime importance, whereas really **our involvement in the objective world is an exercise of discretion, because it is an exercise in the utilization of Creative Energy.**

This is why discretion comes in. It demands a wonderful system of values to come to the fore. You should enumerate your values in order to utilize the discretion that is essential for Creative Energy to be directed correctly, so that it isn't misdirected into illness and suffering. Illness and suffering are not serious, you know; they're just part of the experience of being in form.

Being informed is another one. One of the exercises that men have given far too much time to is the exercise of the study of psychology, because psychology tends to wrap you into patterns in which your whole framework of reference is allowed, perhaps, a precedence that it shouldn't have.

This is why it is said in metaphysics and philosophy that psychological parlance or any value of psychology should be relegated to a position of being considered improper, for it deflects the true value of metaphysical expertise. Metaphysical expertise not only "exchanges the objects of sense for the ideas of Soul," as Mrs. Eddy said,[1] but it also allows what appears as the object of sense to parade with less formidable presence. The daily confrontation with the object is what we are usually concerned with. We usually are dealing with having to move it around, dress it up, shove it around, sweat it out, stretch it out, pound it out, or push it out, and hope that something is going to change in our suit of camouflage.

If we are really in Essence much more than "this" which meets our eyes, perhaps it would be wise to perceive that most of our time is spent in dealing with nothing to begin with. This is why we have such a poor sense of value in our judgment, because when you "judge righteous judgment,"[2] it means you must understand the value that we place upon the judgment. The judgment is all from the Standpoint of the Son, and the Son/Sun can never be perceived by thinking it's exemplified by or equal to the light of a candle. The Sun is such a gigantic concept and it is such a Radiant Energy that it's impossible to approach it in our capsules and expect to survive its close presence.

This is the whole Greek myth.[3] When you personalize your achievement and start to fly into the sun regardless of your father's warnings, your wings melt and down you plummet into the sea. You see just one limb sticking up and the toes waving goodbye.[4] It's fascinating: what's sticking up in the air is the foot, which should be on the ground. It shows you that the foot is the only part of our form that is in constant reference to the Earth. If it weren't for the feet on the Earth, we would say we were not *grounded*.

What does it mean to be grounded? It means to be planted solidly in a balanced state in a gravitational field and fully awake. To be grounded, it seems, we have to be touching something which is solid; but it is so amazing to realize we are always dealing with this little planet bobbing around in space hooked by an invisible leash to our great Creative Energy. We tend to think that we are serialized and have all these various episodes that would even dare the solution of a Perry Mason or a Dick Tracy in spite of Sparkle Plenty. It doesn't take much more than a sojourn here to immediately cause questions to arise.

It is so amazing to see how everything that we term a specialized science is telling us that we should really be very special in what we think, because as long as we are "the scien*tist*," we are caught in the think tanks that have no filtration system. As long as we think from the standpoint of a thinker, we are locked into the pattern of misinformation and, therefore, we are allowed to think we have choice in the direction of Creative Energy.

Creative Energy is evidenced whenever you write spontaneously an experience of Newness. Every day you should wake up and see what's new in your life. If you have to begin, see what's new called your sheets and your bed. Then start considering when you changed them last, when they were washed. Were they done in the All, or did you forget even about Tide and just had to suffer with Blue Cheer?[5] Then, who ironed them? "Oh God, I never iron sheets any more!" Of course you do! I spent days doing it before I left to come down here. Have you bleached them? I spent days doing it. I did all the pillow cases. Of course you do! Why would you allow your head to rest on anything that wasn't bleached? Why would you allow your head to rest upon anything that wasn't freed of the stain of a suggestion of yesterday?

You see, when you are dealing with newness, you are dealing with the lessening of the objective confinement and the precipitation that becomes spontaneous creativity. Most of your lives you have been taught to deal not with what confronts you as new in the day, but, "Oh, there's the same old body beside me; I've seen it for at least a week." Or, "There's the same old body beside me; I've seen it for the past twelve years." "There's the same old body beside me; seems to be changing. I've seen it for the past fifteen years, twenty years, thirty years." Where's the newness?

You see, you have to look for something *new*. I don't mean a grey hair here or a grey hair there. Look for something *new* and see if there's anything creative about the way you *awaken*. As long as you are involved with facing your day with the residue of yesterday contained in the same belief garment as the days before yesterday, **you are caught in a system that dwindles in its creative ability. This is what we call the dwindling appreciation of the Creative Might that allows the Earth to appear as our planet.** Our lack of appreciation is clothed in the words of today's men and women as those who are "raping" the planet. This is how it comes about. **We allow newness to be thought of in a store window, or in a tin can, or coming out of a vegetable garden, whereas newness is the cessation of identification with the objective camouflage and its suggested Reality.** This suggested Reality and the acceptance of it causes us to question what comes next, because we have fallen into the serialization, and we have to have the correct connecting themes or music in order to join the parts together.

This is why education came into our experience. We were taught we had to go to school every day in order to realize. It wasn't that we had to go to school in order to realize; it was that we had to go to school in order, supposedly, to make ourselves understood and to be able to communicate. *But what we should have gone to school for was to learn the art of appearing to be objectified, bearing the language for this plane of experience as words and the future language, which will be tones.*

Someone recently asked me, "What will the language of tomorrow be?" I said, "It won't be words, you know." She said, "It won't?" I said, "No, we're going to sing to each other." She said, "What?!" I said, "We're going to sing to each other. The words are just the camouflage until you can take the vibratory frequency of your Radiant Essence."

Isn't it amazing? You *think* you are this! I tell you, if it is in question, you know you're not, because What IS is never in question. **The only thing that's ever in question is what isn't,** and that's how you judge righteous judgment. *Whatever isn't in question is your Standard of Judgment.*

Judgment is the process that is incurred by serialization. The instantaneity of spontaneity is already at hand when you have passed over the River of Judgment and have seen that your life as the river appears defined by those who listen to you as its banks. But you know very well that you are constantly in a circulatory action of appearing as the water: then there's the steam, the clouds, the heat, and then it is precipitated as freshness to your Earth. This is how we have come. Not that we're all just drips! Unfortunately, too many of us are. That is not the way we came. We didn't even come as a teardrop. We only came as the evidence that the encrustation of the Soul was being released when a tear could be shed.

In other words, we had come to some sort of interior continental divide. Everything at that altitude of attainment has to move to one side or the other. This is where you come to the choice. This is where, if you have to make a choice, as Dag Hammarskjöld said, you have to turn your back upon yourself.

> "Seek by daring to take the leap into unconditional obedience. Dare this when you are challenged, for only by the light of a challenge will you be able to see the crossroads and, in full awareness of your choice, turn your back upon your personal life . . . ."[6]

That always is a "knocker-outer." Who in this room ever turns his back upon his personal life for the Higher Way? Stop and consider how many ever do. How many moments of the day are you in Wonder about your creation? I'm always in Wonder when I see Chris, or Susan, or Barry, or Peter, or Marco, or Stuart, or Jonathan. Why? Because I *know* that they are all part of my whole Wonder of Creation. They must be part of my Life Stream either they couldn't be here, even if they came from a different region.

Remember, we are only a horizontalized event as long as time and space can be defined; we are not a horizontalized event in Actuality. That's why we say that there is only a small portion of us here at this moment; we're not all present. (It's obvious in many cases!) There are some of us here who think we're all here, but we're not. Don't be concerned, fellows; it's just that there's more to it than meets your eyes. You don't need everything that you actually have to be here.

How much of what you've got do you really use? Usually you use the bottom of your feet, your backside, your back, and your front side to face the world. That's about all you use. Your brain, hopefully working correctly to tell you what you've done — that's all you use! The rest of the day you go to somebody else's office; you go to some stupid school where they're teaching you something stupid and it's called a doctorate in stupidity. It is such an incredible picture when you stop and consider the time you're wasting. It's an *incredible* waste of time!

Why do I say a waste of time? Why don't I say a waste of space? You see, it's very hard to say that time is limited, and then time isn't limited. Space, you think, is this emptiness, where I say it is the Somethingness that allows me to be seen, and since I am in your presence, you have misunderstood the experience and called it "time." The terrible part of it is, you have been individualized in a belief system instead of a personalized package of understanding of your system of belief, so that individuality would not be tarnished by such hypotheses that are expended upon you as a result of education.

Somebody would say, "Well, then, you would suggest that no one go to school?" Well, I'd say, "Yes, go to school, but understand leisure." Don't understand the "system," because you can't. It is a method that has gone wild because it has lost its footing. It's lost the reason it came into existence. It's lost apprenticeship. *What does apprenticeship mean? You become tutored by living experience, which appears as another that you call someone else, until you realize what he is showing you is to be your own experience. When you can do it as well as your exemplar, then you have a master, and a Master in disguise.*

Why haven't we Masters today? Because we have never seen through the disguise of our seemingness. We don't want to. *You still want to remain what you think you are.* Now, when you don't think, you don't even have any identity. Why do you think you go to sleep at night? So that you can *forget* that you don't have an identity. You sleep at night because when you sleep, there's no sense of "you" or anyone beside you. You can share your bed with somebody, but when you go to sleep no one is there, and neither are you! But if you doubted you were going to wake up, you wouldn't go to sleep. It shows you immediately that it's only when you're eking your way through eekdom that you have to stay awake to "eke" out a living.

It's seldom that you ever experience living spontaneously, because your whole society is geared as a result of your education to making you live in a routine that conforms not to the Substance that is Real, but to the false substance that is exchanged. Now, metaphysics says: exchange an object of sense for an idea. We have not been taught the exchange properly in school, because we think that a coin or a piece of paper is the proper exchange for something that isn't a coin or a piece of paper. When you go down to the grocery store and ask for a pound of butter and a pound of peas and "How's your wife?" you don't expect to exchange a loaf of bread. You exchange a piece of paper or a coin, aside from your words. *The words only inaugurate awareness that you are present making a demand.* It's the only reason you speak to another: you make a demand upon them.

This is why this Unfoldment is such an unselfish thing. Here I am sitting talking to you, and what are you giving me but your eyes? **How much are you giving of your heart that allows it to help beat in the Rhythm of the Drum that would break the envelope of suggested belief and allow you to be the Living Heart of Wonder?**

No, we're taught that it's not in the heart that we live and move and have our Being, it's in the head. *But what is the head? The name given to that part of the body that is farthest from the ground, unless you stand on it.* The yogis tell you to stand on it in the corner to help balance you. Well, it gives you some idea of what your feet feel like! What are you going to do about this incredible belief system? Are you going to leave your schools? Why don't you? Are you going to leave your universities? Why don't you? Why don't they all close? I feel they should. I think we should all go to Greece — and do what? Come under the reign of the Wonders of the gods. *What are the reigns of the gods? You start to be able to identify Creative Energy and its various avenues of expression.*

Today we don't. We don't even have the reign of one God! Everyone's talking about one God; that's all Israel is based upon; that's all Rome is based upon, St. Peter's; that's all the Protestant religions are based upon; and did you ever see so much conflict in all your life? Wonderful educational system?!

What is the purpose of fresh manna daily if it isn't a symbol of the need for continuous newness being acknowledged? As one metaphysician I once knew said, you should try to introduce as much newness into every day as possible. That doesn't mean necessarily that you do all your pots and pans before you do your crystal, just for a change. It doesn't mean quite that. You know, when you dry your dishes in your kitchen, you should always use your fresh linen towels, which have no lint or nap on them, for your crystal, your silver, and your plates; then your pots and pans are a different story. You know, just don't think the change is great if you start doing your pots and pans first.

This is what we do. We put on different lipstick, different eye shadow, a different dress, and we're different? **If we were to spend as much time choosing the thought-structures we are going to wear for the day as we do our clothes, it would be a very different situation.**

You know, all you have to do is make a demand upon somebody and watch the thoughts that come around. Oh yes! Just make a demand upon someone and watch the thoughts come around. Yesterday somebody said to me, "It is not right. You do not make demands upon anyone. You just constantly give your incredible Force and Power, and you never make any demands upon anyone. Nothing ever comes back to you." Generally speaking, that does seem to be the case, in the majority of cases. She said, "Wait 'til you say, 'I *want* you to do this!' Truly this should be the demand: 'I *expect* you to do this!' This should be it."

I feel that this is something! I wonder if you treat yourselves that way? *I expect you to be new. What are you going to do to bring it about?* It certainly isn't going to be to buy new clothes. It certainly helps, but it doesn't really do very much if your thoughts are old.

Don't lose your Model T, for heaven sakes! It's the only thing that you can use as a model for your apprenticeship. Even if it only has a "rumble" seat, at least you're some part of it. Truth always causes "*you*" to rumble. I haven't said a thing here this evening that hasn't been sponsored by Truth. It's only been sponsored by your mind as my words if that's where you're thinking. **What I am actually doing is not telling you a thing about me. I am speaking because of those who are present in the room; otherwise, I wouldn't be saying a word.** That's rather an interesting point.

Ramana Maharshi made a very interesting statement: "**Doubts arise because of the absence of surrender. Acquire strength by surrender....**" I think that is one of the factors most missing in all the people I know and in the world in general. They *never* surrender to a Higher Way. They mistake their personality for individuality because they haven't had the proper education. They think that psychological involvement is the answer to freedom. It isn't.

> "Acquire strength by surrender and then your surroundings will be found to have improved to the degree of strength acquired by you."

Interesting! If I never saw you again, if something should appear to happen to me tonight, what I have said tonight is very important for you to consider. It may not seem so, because it's being said in a very simple, natural, ordinary, unimpassioned way. It's very contained because it is so powerful; I don't want to overemphasize it, because if I did, it would be too much.

When you have once seen your own masquerade, then you might be ready to consider change. Most people run like hell. You know in my life what has happened: I've worked years to bring people to the point where they might be able to change; they become irritated and everything else; at last something is going to happen! Then they withdraw. They leave. That's okay. But it isn't okay, because it means that no one is going to understand what happened to bring them to that point where they might have leapt and found it wasn't an abyss at all. This is something you should consider very well.

September 23, 1992

---

1 Mary Baker Eddy, *Science and Health With Key to the Scriptures* (Boston: Trustees Under the Will of Mary Baker G. Eddy, 1934); p. 269, l. 15.
2 John 7:24.
3 The myth of Icarus.
4 Reference to a painting which depicts Icarus falling into the sea.
5 Mr. Mills plays off of the detergent names "All," a registered trademark of Lever Brothers Company and "Tide" and "Cheer," registered trademarks of The Procter & Gamble Company.
6 Dag Hammarskjöld, *Markings*, translated from the Swedish by Leif Sjöberg and W. H. Auden (New York: Ballantine Books, 1983), p. 111.

XXV

THE WELCOMING RESONANCE
OF NOWNESS

What in God's name are you asking for?
A partial freedom? Or are you asking for
the Dispensation of that Force that will
allow the Soul to once again reach this
country and allow the world once again
to be given the Feeling of Being Authen-
tic, and the Authentic Being balancing,
adjusting the laws that are so out of
balance in the entire world that they are
screaming for what you are hearing at
this moment.

THE WELCOMING RESONANCE
OF NOWNESS

We convene here with those present who are deemed ready to sit before the altar of their own Beingness and adopt that State commensurate with the Wonders of Unfettered Being. We have been moving through the vestibule of time bearing with us the intrinsic measures of rhythm commensurate with the unfolding pattern of the Soul that is prepared for those who are prepared to engage the function of a redemption of the planet in the cognitive state of a Self-realized One. For we are inclined through the tenure of office, in other words, the habitual thought-patterns, to inscribe them with a force they do *not* possess, and thus we influence those who are under the impulse of a humane society to go along with our cognitive plans. And yet, *how do we know that they are the plans that are freed in the cognition of the Divine Self?* They are great in their possibilities. Really, we must pursue as never before the wonders of sitting prepared in humility to drop the patterns of concerted effort to maintain the semblance of Reality and adopt the attitude of a child and be filled with the Wonder of Newness readily at hand.

In the perpetuation of this dream we are constantly being awakened to the ghost within us, which enables all of us through our knowledge to understand the great mechanical contrivance of the brain and its ability to appear to be the devotee of the mind! And yet, we do not understand fully the complex nature of our seeming residence upon this planet, because we are inscribed with the teachings that are woven not "without seam or rent," but are woven with the passion of *personal persuasion, not with the delicate fragrance of that Gentleness that comes from the full blown Promise termed the Rose.*

As we genuflect before the Wonder of every moment, we perceive the Nowness of that Moment which is termed the Point of the past and the future which man says is an impossibility. The Nowness is the evidence on this plane of a State that is not fully known, but is termed Eternal. *That Nowness on this plane allows the past and the future to come to cohesiveness within the Nowness that we term Eternal.* In actuality it isn't, for if it were we would not be trying to term it. Anything that we can term is only a term that is used in order to have your pattern of thoughts more equatable with the Divine so that you can find yourself tossed into the lap of the Infinite.

You must always realize that anything new is never completely understood and, therefore, is termed *"the leading edge."* If it is understood you can be assured it isn't the leading edge! Very important point. If anything new seems old then you know it is. If anything is new it seems always bizarre, because newness demands not the understanding; *newness demands the willingness to be as a child and to see something you don't understand. Seeing something you don't understand is the very threshold of looking into the Abyss.*

Now the Abyss, of course, always seems to be an emptiness. (We laughed in the car the other day considering the plural of the word, because one is enough!) So, if we leap into the Abyss, we will find not nothingness, but that State which bears no resemblance whatsoever to the sensorial and mental appendages that we have given unto our imagination.

Our imagination, remember, is a result of an impinging force of the *thought-clouds.* The thought-clouds are there just as much as the clouds within your sky, and the thought-clouds are just as easily evaporated in the Light of the Sun. The Sun's force to the cloud causes what the cloud contains, perhaps in the vaporized state of distress and pain and tears, to be dropped once again from the cloud and appear as refreshment so that once again fragrance may fill your Path. For without this ingredient of water, there would not be the ebullience that we term Spirit. **The purpose of Spirit is to give us a chance at looking at a thought-cloud and divesting it of its mystery.**

We are all dressed in mystery, and all shall be "changed in the twinkling of an eye, for when the last trumpet shall sound, the dead shall be raised incorruptible."[1] *Now the dead are those who die in the belief patterns of today.* If they are to be raised, they can only be raised when they are given the Injection of Light that causes them to question how it is that they have termed their condition alive or dead. *What faculty is present that allows someone to say one is dead and another is alive, when each state is arising within your dream pattern?*

When you wake up from a dream, no matter how delightful your partners were and how many experiences you had with them, you can't drag them with you . . and in many cases it's fortunate! Then you say it was a nightmare. But then, of course, just by letting them go, you've realized their *strawlike nature. The nightmare always wants to be fed.* So, when you wake up you let the strawlike nature be cast to the flame of the thought-set, because the thought-set imbued with the Fire of Devotion and the Fire of Dedication causes the heat to arise and an interior combustion takes place. Then you have the straw of belief becoming flames that once again either drop ashes onto the ground and allow another Phoenix to arise, or cause the cloud to release its moisture, appearing as the dew upon your rose, which allows a new freshness to dawn.

Now, a new freshness to dawn can only happen when you refuse the futuristic pull. *The futuristic pull is an apéritif.* It causes you to have an appetite for something that is promised. Cease from taking apéritifs if they have to do with a future pull, because a future pull is the most diabolical. It tells you that the future is going to hold something for you that the Now doesn't. If you have been flip-flopping like tiddlywinks in this lifetime up to now, just know that if you believe in a future pull, you'll undoubtedly be called Mr. Tiddlywinks the next time, because everything you do you take with you.

If you don't do, you won't have.
And if you do do, you will have what you did do.
But if you didn't do what you should have done,
Then you'll be sorry that you didn't do what I told you you
should have done.
So, did you or didn't you? Um, didja?

All you are doing is testing probabilities. You are testing the probabilities of thought orientation to the arisal of an objective universe. You are testing your might and failing to perceive one of its essential prerequisites. To test might is to test, in a sense, creativity. It is how this creativity is used that brings about what is termed the Promised Land, because the *Promised Land of milk and honey is where the Creative Energy is used to rescind the laws or the suggestion of laws of sense.*

Now the laws of sense arise as does your externalized world. Oh, you say, "I have to get up tomorrow morning, I have to face the world." Well, of course you're facing the world, and you have to get up tomorrow morning, because it's part of your Creative Energy to re-create, not in the pattern of a cloud thought-set, but in the distilled purity of dewership/doership. If it is to be a new form, it has to be pure. *What does that mean? Free from mixture, in other words, no attempt to bring the Divine into matter or matter into the Divine.* The anthropomorphic sense is out (in other words, externalization).

Now, everything that you experience externally is termed your precipitation of an interior state. So, if you constantly fall for your precipitated interior state, you are constantly falling. That is what you might say instigated the fall of Rome, because everything went outside to the worship of gods that were devoid of altering the effect of a thought-cloud-set called "Roman superiority." We have this tremendous thought-cloud hanging over us, when we are totally wanting, not only in our *sense of natural abundance*, but in our sense of *sincerity*. **How can you enter any relationship if fidelity isn't at the root of it?** How can we enter into a world congress and expect superficiality of our sense of Substance to fill the banks of expectation with the undiluted Current that can dissolve a cloud of unknowing?

The extravagances today of the future pull are gigantic. We can break the atom apart, we can shoot a rocket into the air, we can cause the ice caps to melt, we can create cars, we can create all types of computers. Why? Because we have fallen for the thought-world as being the Real one. We think thoughts with such force that they manifest as externalities, and **misdirected Creative Energy is the Essence of illness and suffering**.

Now this misdirected energy is what religion is built upon: *suffering*. "Oh, you've got to suffer to find yourself approved." I don't! I say "I love you" without hesitation. You say, "Oh, you idiot, you don't even know me." Of course I don't! If I did I couldn't love you. If I love you, it is because I see none other than mySelf. If you love me, then you'd better not have yourself other than That realized. For "yourself" is a possessive state that allows you to think that you can be possessed by yourself. The only thing your self does is try to possess in order to satisfy an innate state of Self-satisfaction.

If you are here, you are here not to maintain a thought-structure that has been with you all these years. You are here to free yourself from it, because freeing yourself from such a thought-structure allows your structure to be erected that is "not made with hands, but is eternal in the heavens."[2] Now what does that mean? It means if it's an accurate state, it can be found through acknowledging a Tonality, a resonance that rings in agreement with your unclouded thought that you are more than this. In other words, it allows you to **perceive that the brain takes up space, but the mind is nowhere to be found in it!** Mind can't be found in space or time. If mind can't be found in space or time, it must be coming to another gestalt of conscious awareness that allows itself to explore this dominion termed the world! But you sit here, so complacent, when I should think you'd be running for the bathroom or for the bushes. It is so exactly the opposite of everything "you" are!

Everything "you" are is dead already, because the only thing that lives is the Vitality and the Wonder and the Dynamism becoming True Being. That True Being says you can't be this lopsided ass sitting on chairs or floor or lying in beds. *You should be floating beyond the cloud of blissful encounter with self-inflated thoughts. You should be encountering the Divine Flightness and bearing the feather that can give balance to your flight.*

You see, no bird can fly without a certain type of feather. That feather is called what? Pinion. Without that pinion, the bird cannot fly. But it doesn't say "opinions." The bird knew enough to stop questioning its flight and did it naturally! The bird knew enough to stop questioning how it sang, and it did it naturally! Man is the only stupid creature. He questions everything . . in what way? "Why don't I have it?" He is a glutton for wanting more and more of something that is really less and less of Reality.

More and more of this means less and less of That in your thought. How can you enact a drama when you're all caught up in the satiated feeling that you are an actor or an actress, a corporate head (oh Lord!), or head of a corporation (oh Lord!). (The words just on this level are ridiculous.) Or can you imagine being a chairman of a committee meeting in a board/bored room? There's nothing more lacking humility than a board room, because a board room is the result of all those forms getting together in order to have their options considered as opinions of worth. I tell you, it doesn't take more than one or two minds to come together to make something great; it takes Oneness to be acknowledged so that all appear to be in a Synchronized Movement of Wonder.

Before you enter any meeting you should always be sure that everyone meeting has invested in the service of aligning his thoughts to Newness, Wonder, and the living Vital Edge, which means something new and bizarre. If you don't, you are as dull as a hoe, and it isn't even good for pole beans. I'd rather do it with my trowel. What is the point of a sickle if you don't know when the wheat is ripe for harvest? What is the point of having a sharp intellectual tool and using it as if it were dull as a hoe? Most of you do! Look at your achievement. You use your intellectual process *to keep you in bondage,* because your intellectual process is deemed fine? It's gotten you where you are? *Well, where in hell are you?* I had to come, so you called and I appeared to. "You made me what I am today, and I hope you're satisfied"? An old song? But so is "The last trumpet shall sound and the dead shall be raised incorruptible." Why is it old and new? Because *Nowness is the edge on which all men may face the extremity of the objective external environment and perceive the bizarre state where objects cease to be classified an art. **The object of an art or the art of an object is to delineate the Creative Energy Being in that specific instance used correctly.***

That's for the Singers, for you, for me, for everyone! If you are so god-dammed stupid to go on behaving as if you have your own personal life, then you are turning your back upon it, realizing the inevitable condition of Being Now and putting it off to a later time. As Dag Hammarskjöld said, when you come to the crossroad in your life, turn your back upon your personal one. Why? You mask your possibilities, because you are always sounding off instead of trumpeting, "I AM forever new." Thus saith the Creative Energy that you term the Law and the Lord.

That is the value of a quality commensurate with the Foundational Stone of Being. I AM not an adamantine somethingness. I AM a Transparent Tone Resonance to your highbreds of humanity.

You are forever present in the Galaxy of Wonder, as long as you don't stop for the illusion of flickering lights giving you in any way a semblance of movement. As one author said, "Your signs can have the lights flicking off and on as if an arrow were in constant movement." That's what troubles the world. They have their lights going on and off so much within them that there appears to be constant movement up and down Fifth Avenue (no freedom at all), up and down Broadway (no creative energy well spent), up and down Little Theatre Off Times Square. That's where most of you are. You don't know what time squared is! You have to hide in a little theatre off time squared, because if you square your experience in time, then you will find that the bell rings, and you are not any longer in a square; you're in the circle of becoming the very center and circumference of it.

What in God's name are you asking for? A partial freedom? Or are you asking for the Dispensation of that Force that will allow the Soul to once again reach this country and allow the world once again to be given the Feeling of Being Authentic, and the Authentic Being balancing, adjusting the laws that are so out of balance in the entire world that they are screaming for what you are hearing at this moment.

What is being said is not being said from the standpoint of any specific skilled, specialized topic; it is being given from the Standpoint of the One Divine Event and that is the releasement of the Verities Eternal through the Law that must be fulfilled. If you can have this type of position within yourself, then you will find that your externalized situations are changing and are becoming in agreement with your pattern of new thought-sets. *Remember, you don't see a thought, but there is a current of thought as there is a current of air. If you are caught with your sails down or up, you should be careful how you tack, because you must know with the dexterity of Grace how to alter the course which you have set when it's heading for the shoals as a result of the course of belief.*

If your experience is one of *joy*, be very aware; it's *dangerous*. If your course is one of *happiness*, be very *careful*; it is the most seductive force to trap you in the seeming. If you are *suffering*, it is the most incredible force to allow you to consider what is Real. If you would pain be delivered, then find what is to be delivered of pain. Is God's resemblance of Himself in pain or is it the manipulation of God's thoughts that are in pain and a misuse of the Creative Energy? Got it?

This is what causes the incredible force field that is termed "the chaos." People are using the force field of the thoughts commensurate with the Almighty in the scheme of the finite, the mutable and mortal! If man is to break bread, then he must bless the bread and give it as a piece of his understanding of the omnipresent action of Substance. If he is to drink wine, he must see it as the evidence of his consecration to the Essence of Being. If he is to partake of the meal, then he must see it as that which is in the Light of the satisfaction becoming the Divine Effulgence and the affluence of That Which IS worshipped being perceived as a dispensation unto the land that is termed entering the Millennium of such significance.

Yours is a venture and an exploration and a unique one, for you are riding a wave of such a Current Event that it can only be termed Now, for when I disappear or when I appear, then only will Nowness appear to have an extent in the duration of your attention. For that moment we are glorified, for that moment I came, and for that moment you witness. It is in this that I find you and I inseparable One, and yet allowing this incredible picture of so many to be seen as a holographic Wonder and the Unknown Ghost to be that Force that allows me to inculcate and deliver such an enfolded Unfoldment in order for those unfolding to be once again enfolded in the Arms of the Infinite and the possibilities of Unfettered Being and its all-encompassing Love.

When I move into that Omnipresent Stream, it is amazing to don the hat of so many performers. The ability to do that is the one that I enjoy the most. It is so exciting. It is X-citing because it makes the Unknown X citable. That's why I always say it's ex-citing. It makes the Unknown citable.

Remember, if you're not vibrant with energy, it's because evil has an intent. As soon as you are not vibrant with energy, evil has an intent in your life. *What is evil? As one man said, "It's energy veiled."* Remember that! It's the easiest way to perceive where you're at. If you're lacking in energy, then evil has an intent in your life. *One of the most interesting intents is to keep those who know from being together.* It's so true.

What I've said this morning is important and what we will talk about tomorrow is important. You see, when I talk about last night and when I talk about tomorrow, all happens because *Now* is the moment. That's why the Now cannot be described. You might say that Now has the mountains present that you can see into the future; has the *W* present that can net the past; and has the *O* present as the Infinite Gaze. So you have this feeling right here now.

This one day will be seen as the most important moment you could ever spend, because it's at this moment that we are actually working at a level that man is just learning to conceive through the electronic microscope, where he can perceive the cellular structure and conceive such a thing as a cell that contains our destiny: the DNA? Which is just an acid!

If this is where this whole situation is, if it's in this One State that we are imbued with all the future possibilities, the only way that can be altered is in this manner. *It can be altered just by listening without adjudicating.* As soon as you cease to be the child in hearing, you annul the possibilities of cell multiplication in agreement with the Unlimited and the possible redefining of what you consider your destiny to be.

This is why the doctors are so interested. As one psychiatrist said, "We have searched for so long and now we have found you, because this Message is it!" Maybe so, who knows? I never know what the Message will be, because it's the people present who bring it. I have nothing to say, particularly. But you must be spoken to, because it says that "The Word was with God, and the Word was God,"[3] and, therefore, it was a Sound before you termed it a word.

I resonate just by Being Present, but you don't perceive it until I speak and say, "Hello!" When I say "hello" to you, I am saying I AM here. Do you realize that when you greet somebody, you are saying you are here? I am saying "you are here," but you are saying, "I am here." So you are speaking to I AM; you're not speaking to me. **"Me" is the way you describe something other than yourSelf!**

> Dr. F.) What you have just said is really the only answer to genetic research, because genetic research, as it's being done now, is an example of the misdirected Creative Force of

altering the cell through Nowness. What is being done is exactly the opposite. It's being taken into materiality, and it's misdirection.

Even though it's the least form of matter, it's still cognized as something. As soon as it's named, it has an identity .. and that's the crisis! It's better not to name a disease. As long as you don't name a virus, it could be the name of a son or a daughter or a mother or father. But as soon as you name it, you've got it! So, if you name a virus "JBH," you've got the name of a virus. They'll say, "What is that? What's the JBH virus?" It's better if they can't name it.

"Oh, I just met the Wonder last night! I don't know what her name was. She was a Wonder!"

"What did she look like?" (Silence.) "Oh."

One of the most remarkable things is to be in a room and not seen. When you can be in a room and not seen, then something, you know, has moved!

Keep on going if you'd like; we have a few more minutes, if you can afford it! What do you do when you "*afford*" something? You cross over something. When you afford something, you cross over it. If you don't, you go through it, and that's called Jordan. Everyone was baptized in the Jordan. They apparently were baptized in the River of Judgment. You can make it anything you want!

I have been in the Jordan. I stepped in it, felt it, and brought a bottle of the water home to my mother. She was so thrilled to have a bottle of H_2O! But when I told her it was the Jordan, she didn't want to drink it; it was precious. What made it precious? Because figments of her imagination had created this incredible specialty to it.

What makes "you" special? It's not because you're vile or you're in a vial, you know. It's because of what I make of mySelf. That's what makes the thing unique and the exploration in this density available to X-citing.

How I wish you people could grasp what I'm really saying! So many people just take it intellectually, as is obvious. They take it intellectually and go around allowing themselves to have the most terrible, hurtful, and harmful thought-patterns, not only for themselves, but for everyone with whom they're associated. It is usually focused on me by saying it's somebody else! You know, many people say they don't like "the group around Mr. Mills." That is only the safe way of saying, "I don't like Mr. Mills or what he teaches."

I don't teach anything! That's why I am not a teacher, and that's why I don't have disciples. If I taught something, I would be a teacher. **But I am not teaching anything; I am only giving.** A teacher is somebody who is allowing you to learn something new. I am not. **I am demanding that you know something you already know. I'm not teaching you. I have no disciples. Only** *you* **can** *say* **you are a disciple.**

Remember, *every thought-pattern* **being held that is not in agreement with your own Divinity is destructive!** It's a misdirected use of energy, and according to the strength you use to direct that energy will your material situation be changed, altered, and appear more abundant! *If you are without position and don't have a position, then it's obvious you haven't claimed one that is Real.*

Everyone who has heard these words is creating havoc either for me, for themselves, or for the world! As one teacher pointed out, "Thoughts create such a force that, if you could see them when you are creating them, it would be different from when you see them externalized as a condition."

To be ill, you have to be thinking wrong thoughts or somebody else has to be holding them about you, so that they alter your whole cellular structure. *It's not just your thought. You are perfect as I AM. It's the thoughts that you hold about yourself or about me that bring about the inharmony.*

There's not one thing I have said that should do anything but allow you to perceive the Current of Event, the current of time, and the current of air that has breathed This upon your window pane of coolness. Even your breath upon a cool pane leaves some form of figure that you can perceive. *Your plane of indifference is your intellectual one, but I have breathed upon it, and there is a momentary figure or form of condensation.* Watch it, and see if what you are condensing into your life is in agreement with the Transparent State of Transparent Man!

As long as you are thinking that you are suffering peoples working up to Godhood, you will have thousands of simply delightful years ahead of you, celebrating all the festivals in order to keep a belief system going! Do you realize that all the nations of the world are there representing the various divisions of the climates of thought? You have materialized every one of the conditions. Why don't you claim the Uniqueness of Being and stop being so much like every other boring thing?

Have the fun that you see the Singers having! People last night said to me, "What has happened? I've *never* seen the Singers so free! I've never seen the Singers so joyous! I've never seen them like this!" That's a wonderful stand! That's what's acknowledged! Why is it? Because the antithesis of freedom cannot parade where it takes freedom to inculcate the Divine Resonance. **You can't have opinions about the Divine Pitch of Being and dampen it by your wedge-like thoughts of personality, envy, jealousy, and resentment.** Why don't you allow your instrument to be like a winged harp and the Breath breathed upon it, and it sounds and says, "Welcome!" **You should be the Welcoming Resonance of the Millennium!** Not the mat upon which others walk because you only resonate your impoverished personality complexes.

The subject is so vast, and the nature of exploration in the realm of Sound Words is so demanding.

Personal will is one of the adamant forms of error! Remember, "the aggravation of error foretells its doom!"[4] Error really destroys itself, because it calls itself true and lives on Truth, which is its antithesis, and therefore it destroys itself!

So, don't roam, stay fixed, and be proud of the role that you play in this Theatre of Stars on the Cosmic Highway of the Enlightened God! Walk there and allow others to see your Train of Wonder as it caresses the vestibule of Earth!

One day, perhaps, I can take you on that train, when you are so secure, and allow you to perceive what is beyond. It's quite an

uninhabited planet, save for the Spirit of Newness which maketh all
things extravagant beyond your mundane conceptual might!

Thank you very much.

September 27, 1992

1   1 Corinthians 15:51-52.
2   2 Corinthians 5:1.
3   John 1:1.
4   Mary Baker Eddy, *Science and Health With Key to the Scriptures* (Boston:
    Trustees Under the Will of Mary Baker G. Eddy, 1934); p. 105, ll. 27-28.

XXVI

IMPERSONATIONS

No *wonder you have Captain Marvel!*
You need him, because so few of you
marvel! You are so afraid to marvel at
something you can't comprehend, and
that is the whole purpose of a Visitation.
You have to learn to marvel at the Un-
known, so that the Unknown can reveal
ITself. IT's in your lap.

IMPERSONATIONS

We find ourselves gathering together to consider the great topic so much in the forefront of people's consideration today: how to get along in life and yet bypass its restrictions by alleviating the limiting factor of perception — in other words, how to transcend our perceptual modes.

We have all considered in the realms of our *impersonations* the various characters that constitute our Charlie McCarthy-and-Edgar Bergen complex. We have various forms sitting on our knees as we attempt to have a dialogue with the Wonder of the formed and the Unformed: the lips that move and the lips that don't move; the wooden head and the head that doesn't appear to be (and is!); and then the head that is beyond itself, and, therefore, the construct beyond linear and logical explanation. When you have a head beyond itself, it's obvious it can't be the one that you think is on your shoulders. It could be termed the Godhead. **The Godhead is that Divine Head** that allows us to consider in this domain Love and its fecundating, all-encompassing Nature, which allows us to question the very considerations that confront us as this impersonation which allows us to consider the viability of this form.

The viability of this form is shallow, the foundation of this form is even shallower, and the considerations of this form as to its perpetuity are the shallowest. So, we leave off with the shallowest and end in what is termed "the Rest," which always confronts the demise of the form. Now we hope that the Rest will be understood by those who witness the rest. **The Rest** is not silence devoid of meaning; it is the Meaning that bears no translation in the realm where matter cares for matter, mind cares for mind, and cause bears no effect that is of importance. As they say in our modern terminology, we are dealing in the "holographic universe." In the Upanishads and the early Teachings, they would say we are seeing the "world within the pearls": as they reflect each other, so does every aspect of Being reflect ITself.

So it is, once again, with the great scientists and the great physicists we are coming to see, as never before, the coincidence of agreement in the realm where matter seems to care for matter.

There seems to be an interest in bringing an end to it . . with rest. How many people ever find "the Peace that passeth the understanding?" [1] We were told that when the Comforter, or that Divine Selfhood revealed by John, would come again, He would make all things new. [2] That "He," of course, is without being defined in form. He is no one's object of attention. He is the Implicate Order of the Transcendent State. In other words, it is in the *very* consideration, this impulse to worship the Unknown, that we find the Unknown known when the worship passes the perceptual mode of the technique becoming what is termed, of course, our ceremonial exercises or ceremonial initiations.

After all, what are we doing but constructing modes of thought so that the mechanics of the mind cannot infringe upon the Divine Domain! That Divine Domain is the domain that is not going to be understood by your logical, linear thinking. *If* this Message is of import, it cannot possibly originate on the level of the mind's mechanics. It is not a mechanical repetition; it is an offering that the mechanics of the brain allow to be translated into sound, which is beyond your words. *And yet the sound comes forth garmented as a word. So the sound origin is very much more important than the word origin.* The word origin can give you a dictionary, etymologically interesting, of course, but the sound origin gives you a Frequency Domain, and *this i*s where we are living! We are living in a realm of frequency.

This is that area from which This is extrapolated from the great Unknown Tree that bears all the various achievements of man's attempt at worshipping the Unknown and crowning it with the Crowning Glory. You might say that the effectiveness of extrapolating, from the branches of the mind's erudition, all those branches that would seduce man into believing himself part of a heritage of limbs and branches of trees ("From what family do you come and from what branch do you come?"), is that we will all realize that *the mind is making up this entire sojourn.* It is due to this Wonder of sojourn that we have been prompted to question, "What is That which never moves, that allows our movement to appear to be defined in a time-space continuum?"

A time and space continuum always goes with what is termed "hard Reality," which is objective Reality. Well, your objective Reality is seemingly hard because we have brought to bear upon it the necessities that we deem are mechanically sensitized and defined through our sensorial natures as hard. In actuality, they are not hard! They are not lasting. If they were lasting, they would be fixed and permanent. If they were fixed and permanent, then there would be no point of talking about the rest. (So I might as well stop!)

But since *this* is not fixed and permanent, there is no alternative but to talk about the Rest, which passeth understanding. If understanding is essential to be bypassed, then we must be living on the edge. We must be in that *bizarre* position where all rationality and linear thinking fade out and you become as a little child: acceptive of That Which IS not known, only experienced. Then, perhaps, it can be articulated. You can't speak of This without the experience of This, because it seems impossible to find the fortification of words and the vocabulary becoming a suitable stream of words that bears the correct mode for transcending itself.

Every one of these modes utilizes the mechanics of the mind to allow it to be perceived as a second-degree happening. The first degree, of course, is Consciousness. There must be a Consciousness that allows the mind to have a second-degree appearance. That mind's ability is there for *you,* because it is that part of you which you have an ability to apprehend by bearing awareness. You are born with awareness, but realize that before your awareness happened, Consciousness IS.

So, your rest only comes when you cease from identification with the passing. Rest in the absolution when you realize that **Love is the Divine Solvent** that really casts aside the impediment and the adamantine nature that confronts you as your solidarity and your Charlie McCarthy-and-like response to each other.

The only reason you ever get along with each other is because each "other" expects the other to know their improvised lines of encounter in time with a certain sense of knowingness that allows each and every one to get along with each other. *The best way to know that you're attaining something unique is when no one gets along with you.* When you see nations disturbed, nations in unrest, it is because they are tarnished; they have forgotten, they have relinquished their hold on a Divine Principle. There is an underlying, organizing Divine Principle at work, otherwise there would be a chaos. And, of course, there is only chaos in this world because we are falling for the supposititious reality as if it were real.

If we fall for this supposititious reality as real, we will *never* solve the problem which people say arises today as never before. It's always arisen! Because you live in a linear sense of existence, you fail to see how the past and the future are all stacked right into the Now. In a linear fashion, four thousand years ago is four thousand years ago, but in another fashion, four thousand years ahead is right here now. It is obvious. If this is where you are at after the birth of such an incredible Teacher and example as Jesus, such examples as Socrates, Plato, Saint Francis, all the great Leaders, if you are just at this point after their lives, then there is something wrong. What could the basis of wrongness be? It must be an identification with the false sense of Reality.

We tend to make God up and give him a beard, as if we're children. Unfortunately, most of us continue to do so all through life. We make God up and give him a beard — the next thing we know *we* need the trimming! What happens? We go on trimming away at our ceaseless mental manufacturing of modes!

If we are to escape from this perceptual syndrome, we have to do it by moving into that realm where there is no time or space but only Events. *That is why I say there is One Divine Event and that is Love.* Oh, this is a *horror* to everyone! "Oh, no," you say, "it's exactly what I want." Of *course* you don't want it, because if you went into *that* mode, then you would not call each other strangers, you would not call each other by names of nationalities. In fact, those would be the names that you would allow to be used in order to differentiate the characters in a play.

We forget that there is a living Ghost within us that is constantly roaming the Halls of Remembrance and telling us that we are more than meat! This is forever alluring us to consider who walks within these hallowed halls where the Divine is termed "hallowed."

How can you be without sin if you confine your worship to adultery? *The basic sin is adultery, mixing two states of thought.* Secondarily, it's another commitment when you create it on another level. But the basic one is allowing two states of thought to dwell within you and trying to make them match. The two states of thought: the matter-mind tries to bring the Divine to itself. The Divine knows IT can't be brought, because the Divine Mind doesn't know anything but ITself. I don't know of a Divine Mind worshipping a Divine Mind. I only know of minds worshipping Divine Mind. But how do you worship the Divine Mind? As one who is cast apart from it?

Several) No.

Of course not! But everyone does. You *all live* that way! You live nine hours out of every day with no thought of the Divine. You're as phoney as Charlie is! Unless you make him up to be entertaining. Why do you suppose you liked to see him on Bergen's knee? Because he was humorous and could allow you to have a moisture about you of laughter and pleasure so you wouldn't crack as an aging piece.

How often are you the "Charlie," with the unseen mind the ventriloquist causing you to speak words that go only with the terrain of your territorial encounter with similarities like you? Oh!! Confront people, tell them they are Love and see what it does to them. They either start to sweat or make an exit for the bathroom or something, because as soon as you tell people they are **Love**, it means they are without the limits, they are the **Living Verity Eternal of the Omnipresent Action of Creative Energy.**

How much of your energy is creative? When it would be creative, do you have intercourse? What is the intercourse? It's all within you. When it's just a shallow one, it could appear as an outside event, unexpected.

When you have the Implicate Order of things, you have that very Heart and Soul of the Cosmos capable of unfolding ITself. That's why my mother was right when she said, "Ken, why don't you call this Work 'Enfoldment'?" I said, "Well, Mum, it has to be called '*Un*foldment' to include others." **Enfoldment is my experience; the Unfoldment is the evidence of it.**

I have nothing to attune myself to but the Wonder of God Being All; therefore, I can appear to be just like you. I can love like you, I can play like you, I can have fun like you — but it's all, perhaps, from a different point. It may be from a Point that is beyond the limits of your perceptual modes.

Remember, if you see me as just a piece of meat behaving just like you, then you haven't seen the Wonder that it is to meet your I; but when you see, the Wonder of Being is capable of being defined, and yet undefined! When you are confused about your Divine State, it's not due to your brain and its mechanical contrivances; perhaps it's due to the fact that your lens is blurred. You know, in your holograph: it's a blur and the other light straightens it out so that you see the three-dimensional suggestion? Well, this is exactly what has happened here.

Do you realize that the words that are formulated this moment are sound images clothed as words? What if you didn't have a sound image clothed as a word? What would your image be? It would be without definition; the only Word left is an **Event** that is timeless and spaceless. That is why you cannot define Consciousness, because that is the sound garment of an Event that is timeless and spaceless. That is why Consciousness IS and awareness can be defined. It can be qualified: you have more awareness or you don't have more awareness; but it's limited by your perceptual factor.

Now, why is a **Lecture** important? A **Lecture** is important because it hones the attention and allows your perception, which you have come to identify in this case as language, to be brought under a bridle of delicacy in the mouth of the horse of the mind. You rein it in with the delicate rhythm of Wonder. It is this Wonder that becomes the child, that allows it to be opened to the possibilities of being more than a grown-up.

If you lose your childlike nature, you will be the most boring grown-up! Why do you think you're so bored with people? They're grown up! They haven't got anything like Wonder, and Wonder is the door to miracle and to marvel. No wonder you have Captain Marvel! You need him, because so few of you marvel! You are so afraid to marvel at something you can't comprehend, and that is the whole purpose of a Visitation. You have to learn to marvel at the Unknown, so that the Unknown can reveal ITself. IT's in your lap.

The words of an Unfoldment allow the pattern of limitation to be attenuated and allow the pattern of attention to be enhanced so that it makes no sense to your logical, linear reasoning. If it made sense to your logical, linear reasoning, it could never be coming from the Point that is beyond hard reality. Hard reality is soft reality, because when you rest you have no sense of what's hard reality. Why do you think you go to rest? To get rid of hard reality, because it isn't. You've fallen for a belief all your life.

Why do you think it takes so much energy to sustain this reality? These young fellas don't realize how much of their lives are going to be spent sustaining a false reality. They haven't a clue! They think they know everything already. They do! That's the horrible part of it, they know *everything*! There's no Wonder left! The universities are injecting nonsense. **Words are important**; if they weren't, they would never be used.

If you think you have to enter into the Silence to be Holy, there's something cracked. To enter into the Silence to be Holy implies that you're not in it already. If I were not in the Silence as I AM, This could never appear to be said. It's by *This* being said that what appears as the Rest manifests itself to you as an Unfoldment. That's why an Unfoldment never tires me; I have no sense of fatigue. *If there is a sense of fatigue, it's not the Unfoldment; it's the pressure that you exude of resentment or reluctance to accept. You say, "I have my own life to live." Unfortunately, you don't.*

That's one of the most injurious and harmful things you could ever consider, that you have your own life to lead. You couldn't prove it! Even to yourself! Stand in front of your mirror in the morning (be sure your hair's combed right) and *prove to yourself that you have your own life to live. It's impossible! You have One Life of Wonder.* That One Life is exemplified by all the Greats that have marched across the picture book of your mind all these centuries. The picture book of your mind is colored and figured with unforgettable characters. But *you* make them up.

What is a poem, but the garment a rhythmic Resonance wears so it may be personified, so that another mask may appear to sound it. *A poem is nothing but the rhythmical Resonance experienced by another in the gown of a poem or a poeming after righteousness.*

Why righteousness? Because Righteousness doesn't let you be "you," and you, you (you selfish so-and-so), and you, you (you selfish so-and-so). You with your little rights and your job and your life to lead — go on! *It is the Brotherhood of Man and the Father-Motherhood of God*! Oh, come on, you millennium seekers! Why are you all so excited about the next millennium? You've made a hell of a mess of this one!

Why am I ever said to be the Voice of the next millennium? I don't know why people say that. If anything, it's because what I am saying is Ageless, and what you are is a deteriorating form of age. You are putting yourself in process. The Divine was never made to be in process. You made the Divine up in your image, instead of allowing That Which IS Divine to appear clad as the Self. *The Divine doesn't see differences, only marks of interest!*

Is everyone equal? No!! Do women need to be liberated? No!! Do men need to be liberated? No! There's no point of liberating a man or a woman: they love to be chained. They love to think they're in chains in order to have something to pontificate about.

What if it happens that you are Real *now*? You don't need *anyone*! If you needed anyone, you would never go to sleep. If you needed anyone in bed with you, you'd never go to sleep! You know what it's like when you have someone in bed with you, and you're not used to it: you toss and you turn and you think, "Oh, it's that other body beside me." Of course it is! That other body is perhaps perspiring, it's tossing, it's snoring, it's turning, and you wish you were in another room all by yourself. But you have to share your bed because, after all, it's only the hospitable thing to do, if things are crowded. You don't put somebody to bed in your bathtub; unless it's an unhappy somebody who wants to sleep there because he or she doesn't like the classical music on the radio when you're going to sleep. You know?

What is the point? You don't need a body; if you did, you'd never allow it to leave your attention. The reason that you are allowed to appear to have a body is because the mechanics of the brain allow you to sustain an objective reality as long as you are willing to give most of your energy to it. When you sustain your reality and then find at the end of your life experience that you haven't really modulated to a dominant tonality, how are you ever going to utilize the necessary harmonic structure to bring about a Perfect Cadence, which is Rest? A Holy Cadence is IV-I/for One. It's the "Amen" cadence.

I said to the women Singers, "Don't say, 'Ah, men!' with such a sound, please! It sounds as if it's the first time you're seeing them." I said, "It's a contraction, due to your language, of a Universal Sound that should free you from the objective confinement."

I'm asking you: how many of you really want to be free? I don't believe there's anyone in this room who really wants to be. Well, I hope there is. I always say I don't believe there's anyone, because if there's enough energy, it usually gets the feathers going up along the back. *I wonder how many really want to be Authentic?*

Why do most people study the counterfeit? They will study counterfeit literature. They will say, "Every Book of the Bible is Holy, every Word in the Bible is Holy," never stopping to consider that the Books of the Bible were chosen by men with a *tremendous* bias. The Books of your Bible are only Holy when the Words in the various places within it are moving out from the Standpoint of One. It's One for All and All for One. Only when the Word moves out from the Divine is it Holy; when you are given the words moving *up to* the Divine, it is progressive and totally unlike what the Holy One IS. The Holy One says, "I and My Father *is* One." "Are One," we say in English, of course, due to the language, but that's where the barrier is, because we use the plural of the verb "to be." "I and My Father *is* One, not 'shall be.'" Oh, *that is* hell, isn't it?!

Have you *ever tried* to live with just one person as "I and My Father are One Now and not 'shall be'"? It's the most incredible thing! It's so demanding, because you're constantly checked every moment. "Am I seeing all as I AM?" "If I see another unlike myself, is not that a variegated pattern of My Own Perception?" I don't stand aghast at it; I *Wonder* at it!

My Ghost so lives and walks my halls, I think not of a head.
I think not of it below my feet, upon which I tread.
I think not of it under my arm, tucked there so kindly as I
    walk.
I think of my head a glowing Light that lightens the
    Pathway, and I'm a lark.

For I find it always ascending upon the Ray of Light,
I find the wingtip bending to those who would gain sight.

I find my Song ascending with no words, a Melody
    profound,
But to you, perhaps, it's clothed in words for a Melody to be
    Earthbound.

When the One is singing, are you plumaged and decked for
    flight?
Or do you just grip the branches of your tree and hope your
    talons will be festooned in Light?
Or are you waiting to find someone who will saw away at
    your limb
And say, "I see you saw Me a'coming, and I am not your
    next of kin."

"I AM the One who knows the act of dropping the Sword of
    Might.
It touched the branch upon which you're comfortable and
    you are destined for flight!"
Now where is your mind and where is your body? Falling to
    that plane below?
Or is your Body now compound/complex, a Light
    Resonating Radiance to show!

Hang on! To what?
Look down! To see?
Look sideways! There's no such place.
For when I AM a Sound Embrace
No time or space traced.
Where are you?

That takes a toll on your booth of attention!

We all have our phantoms of the opera. What do you pine
after? A box? Or a chest, with the promise of things to come?

September 30, 1992

---

1 Philippians 4:7.
2 Revelation 21:5.

XXVII

THE PORTALS OF GRATITUDE

There is nothing wrong and there's noth-
ing right. The only demand is the purity
of heart and the moral fiber of what?
Constancy!

THE PORTALS OF GRATITUDE

We are gathered together to count our blessings and name them one by one. We are gathered together in the name of those who are Holy in their attempt at worshipping the Divine. We are gathered together to allow those who are Holy to be Whole and to cease identifying with that which must be left behind as readily as the grasshopper moves from one branch of suggestion to another. He does not try to hold, as does the caterpillar, onto another branch to move to another branch. *It's like the ego.*

So we must leap as a grasshopper leaps, and never consider the distance between, for it is natural to leap and not stay bound to the suggestion of that which is a limiting factor in the venue of time, that is inhabited by those beings whom you know very well, for you have associated with them from the ground up. Unfortunately, you should have been associating with Those who *are* present from the Star Kingdom *down*! You should not have been imbued with the spirit of partiality but the Spirit of Wholeness, so that you might be endowed with That Power that will fecundate every Seed of Wonder so that it may spring forth in the garden of time and bear that Effulgence which is commensurate with the Wishless State of One Divine.

The Whole State is not based on a holistic, medicinal premise; IT is a Whole State that is only named in order to identify IT in your realm where matter seems to care for matter and, consequently, writes its own themes of wail and despair, joy and happiness, birth and death, and the suggested episodes always given to relativity and its ensuing platform of entanglements.

So, we are gathered together to offer our thanks for having present That Force which allows us to annul the suggestions of time, allows the error of suggestion to move more rapidly out of the state of seeming presence, and allows That Which IS known as Love to permeate the very Resonance of our Beingness, and the Effulgence that precedes and perceives our Presence to once again glow in the Wonder of a Radiance commensurate with the Transcendental State of what is termed the Divine.

Everything has to be named, as does a virus, in order to have an effect. So it is that everything is named in order to have an effect until there is no effect from, for we have been moved to the great paradoxical ends whereby the means is no longer considered, the venue is no longer considered, and if one is termed "present," then one is only termed present by the one who is waiting to find the term irrelevant, inconsequential, and nothing but an illusion prescribing the state and describing the state that we dream "from the ground up."

If we were to consume ourselves with study, as we do, with the universities, which we do, and with the false education which we receive, we would be disposed to be interred. Now, we are in the position of being in a time-warp that is commensurate with possibilities and commensurate with *Infinite* Possibilities, for we have the ability to perceive in an analogical way the idea of a hologram, thanks to Bohm and to Pribram[1] and all those who have offered explication of this Wonder, which we have failed to perceive is our own construct and the only evidence that we have that we can assemble in the artillery of our experience the entire experience freed from the cannons of suggestion and the bombs that would demolish the ever-residence of the Temples that bear the Wisdom and the Glory and the Light to those who would be imbued with the Wonder of Infinite Possibilities.

Now, you can say, "Well, how is this viable, how is this possible to be of worth in this time?" — when you appear to be so sedated. *You are sedated in identity*! We are grateful for Thanksgiving because we can give thanks knowing we are not "this." Therefore, the cornucopia of plenty may appear to exude all types of squash! But let the courts perceive that there is more to This than a game of ball, and racquet! But the whole scenario for time is certainly a racket; it's not who spins the cover but who plays the racket and wins the game. It's all a competition in this time, and it is all competitive as to whether or not one shall ascend unto "that Holy Spot" where there is a doctorate, who doesn't believe it!

Then, you see, when you get your degrees of ignorance and you find you are imbued with an intellectual fortification that is totally destructive, isn't it wonderful to be able to sit here today and to know that we can say, "It's all a dream!" If you are going to follow any form of a Higher Divinity, don't let it be in the relative state of feminine or masculine, because that is only part of your dream, and if you intend to come out of it, then *forget* about trying to unite opposites! Forget about trying to unite. Forget .. and find yourself Whole.

Forgetting and remembering are what? The subtle octave of awareness. They are still of the mind's children. *The mind is that name we utilize to evidence a fractional state of That Which IS not known in its entirety, termed Consciousness. We have to name it in order to have something to relate to. As Dr. Einstein said when confronted by a smart aleck who said "Well, how do I know that's a tree in your garden, Doctor?": "You don't, but you have to assume (ass-you-me) something!"*

So, how do we know that's Consciousness? We don't, but we assume something. How do I know you're bright? I don't, but I assume so! So, how do we know? We don't! We only pretend to! That's why we have so much time "unpretending." All our difficulties are having to deal with "unpretending." Some men pretend to be this "hunk of meat," like horses on two legs, walking through the town. Some of them are gelded due to our biased movements or attitudes, and, consequently, incapable of studding the Earth with the Gems of Wisdom.

The stud farms today are only for those who dare to race and compete to win a four-legged race, and, of course, that is left up to knowing whether or not you want to ride the horse underneath you or the one that's ruling your experience, the one of the mind. So the horse of the mind should be set in gold and should be emblazoned with the tail waving in the breeze, for the Might of Omnipotence has evidenced ITself as the Wind to blow away the dust of suggestion and reveal the ever-present glowing dust that has come as confetti from the Star, upon those who would look up and behold, and look down and say,

> "No Wonder? I Wonder!
> as I wander and offer the Sanction of a surprise
> to those who would be giving in to giving out."

How can you ever expect the explicate order to be worthwhile when the implicate order is so shoddy?! How can you expect your exterior facade to remain a vibrant palette of color and your face the evidence of God's canvas if you *brush* aside the demand that the outer must reflect the inner?! Remember, it's part of your mentality, and as long as you've got it, use it, but don't allow it to *use* you. Ride the horse of the mind and then, with a delicate bridle, use that to alter your course in life.

> If the horse of the mind is held in rein,
> Then the balanced Decree shall then again
> Be heard to sound within the belfry of the mind,
> And the bells will sing out: Thou art Divine!

> But if you try to equate what you seem to be with the Divine,
> You're strung on a rosary where you need to say your beads, because you're knotty in mind.

Your whole experience depends upon how you think, and you get it mixed up, as you now know, with the Realm of Ideation. You do not realize that the Force Field that allows the Essence of Being to be known as a Radiating Field of Energy has, as we intrude upon its stillness, this Soundingness coming forth. Because you see, when Words of Truth are uttered, they are Uncontradictable even by the most erudite mind, and that's *why the Absolute is the Solution to the suggestion of a questionable existence.*

Everyone loves to have a questionable existence in order to fill the chairs of a corporate slave market and to fill the chairs of an unenlightened faculty and to fill the chairs with the tenure of office, when the venue should be vacated for the lack of a Transcendent Ontology that would lead you to the rim of the Abyss!

There's not one bit of good expected from a half-hearted or half-assed attempt! Even the horse doesn't try to run with one. Why do you expect to? How can you gain the Supremacy of Being from being a *pygmy* in your considerations? The evidence of *pygmy* and of the force that is so prevalent in the world today is the lack of choice in partaking of the Menu of Light. Most people are delighted to have their victuals garnished in order to conceal the flavorless nature, because so much is artificial today that we wait and wait to be satisfied. So we drink, we drug, we have affairs and forget that a pure heart, a contrite heart, and a simplicity of nature are essential characteristics of those who are Divine.

Now what is That Which IS Divine? A Divine is One who knows What IS while appearing to be like everyone who doesn't, but his very Presence irritates. If you are an irritation, know that you're on the right Path, and if everyone likes you, be very careful; you're just like the sleepers. Bach said, way back then, to wake up: "Sleepers, Awake!" Don't be sheep and goats walking to the pasture! If you do, you will be led as sheep to the slaughter. Your vestments are red but they can be as white as snow.

The reason we give thanks is because *we have the power to take an interrupted energy field and, due to the utilization of what you term the mind, translate that interference into a soundingness called words.* It is this very experience that is happening at this very moment, because none of these words are contemplated, none of these words are heard until they are expelled and carried on the Holy Breath. This is why I have said it is so unwise to use the Holy Breath in an extravagant manner. There is no greater extravagant manner than those who offer lectures professing a stalemate as an accessibility to doctorhood.

There is no answer to the puzzle of this world from the standpoint of a puzzler! There is no answer to this world from the standpoint of taking a piece of the picture and creating a holographic semblance of a three-dimensional verifiable or known picture. That is all attempting to *show you* how your mind, how the mechanical lens of your mind, is capable of pulling together, through suggestions, a believable picture of substance. This is purely an example of *your Infinite Possibilities to create your own planetary system, to create your own new habitat, and to create a whole New World, not a "New Age"!*

The "New Age" is the dream of addicts. They're addicted to this form and to birthdays and deathdays, which should only be celebrated when you realize the ridiculousness of each! There is no proof that you were born other than those who have lived before you. Before you, if they said they lived, who lived before them to carry on the myth?

If you are going to believe in God, don't believe in one that's divided. If you believe in one that's divided, you've got a God that's here today and gone tomorrow. But God IS declared as a comforting Presence, and the only comforting Presence is That which can be found in the simplest form that is not a thought, that is the term "I AM." That's why it broke the tablets of stone, in other words, the divided state of awareness appearing as the one who received the Ten Commandments (five in each hand). He was told that "I AM THAT I AM." What does this mean? It means, without declaring your identity, you know you have one whether you are awake or asleep. You only sleep with assurance of awakening because I AM.

I AM doesn't need to be declared unless somebody doubts your presence. I'll say, "I don't know you're here, Paul." You'll say, "Oh, yes, I am, Mr. Mills." How are you going to convince me if you don't say, "Oh, yes" — what? "Paul is here"? No! "I AM is here!" As soon as "you" are in question, I AM says:

No, I AM not in question.

I AM the very unspoken Presence.
In other words, I AM unthought;
and, therefore, I AM untimed;
and, therefore, I AM unspaced;
and, therefore, I AM a Sea/"C" of All-embracing Force;
and That has been discovered to be termed, suitably, Love!

Love is not that ooey-gooey something or other that slips in and out of sheets; IT's that Something or other that is more than that which you use on a sandwich. IT's not honey; IT is a Force that allows Unity to be perceived as a Living Essence. IT doesn't need anything to satisfy ITself, and therefore, IT does appear to have something to satisfy ITself. But if you think you're going to get satisfaction, as some of you do, by sleeping around, you are asleep anyway! It's horrible to take somebody else with you who's in the same state. No wonder dis-ease is so prevalent.

You can't sleep with error without being destroyed. Error lives vicariously on Truth; that's why it is said to be self-destructive. Error destroys itself because the only food it can live on is what is True, and it can't find the Truth adaptive to its nature; therefore it brings about its self-destruction. That is why error parading is self-destroyed. It cannot live authentically. There are not two creations; your God that you have worshiped never created two creations. If

He did, He would have been Subject with an Object.

God saw His Creation done (so somebody said in the Book of Genesis) and "Behold, it was good." The second chapter says (it's like your professors: each one has a different theory), "God took a clod of earth and you're it!" Well, I prefer to feel at ease and stand at ease on the Platform that "I and My Father *is* One Now," in spite of the poor grammar. I never heard grammologists fight over this save when they didn't want to acknowledge the accuracy of it, and then they say, "You can't say that." "No," I say, "maybe not, but I can BE it!" Some doctorates "varoom" around trying to augment their thesis of a bifurcated nature.

You see, if you can't live from the Standpoint of Unity where you see all in Essence One, then you are living in the standpoint of relativity. That relativity is usually what you accept as the irritation necessary to prove to you that you are having an effect or being affected. If you don't have an effect or feel you are affected, you don't feel you are living! A horse, thank goodness, doesn't know it's in a stall; it just knows the difference between being where there's hay and when it's running. It doesn't say to its rider, "God, you've stalled me!" Has God said to you, "**My beings, I have stalled you in your mind**"? He perhaps says, "**I have given you freedom in the name of the Hierarchy of My Supremacy if you worship Me as One only.**"

Jesus wasn't any more miraculous than you *could* be *if* you *made yourself the Son of God* as He did! You are all subject to the prophecies if you believe that way, because the prophecies were not of a time. It seems that time bears a moldiness that allows you to have a mold to build upon. But the Promise of God or the Cause or the Essence of Being is always the same. There is not just one; there is just a Uniqueness appearing as One that shall never be forgotten, termed Jesus, because He was such an exponent of the Wonders of the Divine Fatherhood of God. Then came along the demand: there must be the realization that the Godhead is One, and that's why we say "Father-Mother-God." It's only when you try to fracture God that you have relativity imbued with the need of worshiping an Unknown God. As soon as you relate to partials you may not know the Diapason of Being.

This is what I said once when I met with some eleven Jesuits who were celebrating Mass. The head of the Order asked me to meet with these eleven brilliant men because they had come to an intellectual impasse; they were *stalled.* It was a good thing they had their service memorized and it was Latin. No, I bet it was in English. Latin would have been too much, because when we sang the Mass for the nuns, it was the first time that they had really heard the Mass in Latin! So it showed me just how far afield we had moved from the purity of the original.

Remember, a Mass was to proclaim the Allness of God, and the response was your rejoicing in a "Hallelujah!" of recognition. You were never meant to be deprived of responsiveness; in fact, *any Holy Service demands response.* This is why, although I am not part of any movement other than the constant interruption of such, and thus I appear, at least the Pentecostals know enough to shout, "Hallelujah! Amen!" I am grateful because there is a responsiveness even to a partial. Can you imagine what would happen if the wedges of suggestion were removed from the strings of the Heart so that they could vibrate in the wholeness of ITs rhythmic nature? Then the Bundle of His would never be considered a mystery in the Chamber or the Sepulcher of the Light.

When man finds the Sepulcher and the Place where the body is dressed in white — remember, your robes may be red but they can be white as the driven snow. The reason they can be red and then white is because in the Innermost Sanctuary of the Most High, the "red" or the relative diversity running through your veins of suggestion is purified, and you realize your Divinity, and that is termed your Christhood. This is why Jesus was in the initiation exemplified as folding His white robes, and then He walked forth with ordinary men on the Emmaus Way and was not even cognized because He was so changed, and yet it was the same Jesus.

Oh, the doubters said, "How do you know it is He?" They said, "Oh, He's got a mark, He's got a hole in His side" — but not in His head. He has the Wholeness of Being and realizes the Indestructible Nature of the Divine. That's why we talk a lot about Jesus: He's closer to most of you. Buddha is farther removed by about five hundred years. But remember, if there was to be only one, it's true, there's only one Son of God because there's only one Universe and there's one Individual. That is the thorny subject of all philosophical discussions. But remember, the premise of this

Work is that I and My Father are One *NOW* and not "shall be." It's much more difficult than thinking you are going to get it hereafter, and all you are going to get hereafter is *here* after — here, after! Here/after/before!? That's why it's so difficult to know when it says: "I have gone before you." I AM before you. How do you want to play it?

You know, if you could be squashed in an atomic press and have all the holes squeezed out of you (a hundred-and-fifty-pound man — some of you wouldn't fit it, but there are some of you who would, right to a tee), you would find that the residue of your greatness could rest on the head of a pin after all your holes were squeezed out. Isn't this a mighty creation?! Isn't this a Wonder?! It is only through this Window of Wonder that we can ever view why we give thanks, because the Seed Kingdom nurtured offers a total picture of Transcendence!

Even a nut, if buried, knows enough to spring forth bearing no resemblance to its shelled state! **Why do you?!** If you are fecundated with the Truth of Being, why don't you break your shell and be the evidence of the Son of God living among men? The world needs it. They don't need you to propagate things just like you! But if that is your wish, so be it! But is it essential, or is it to see What IS before you fulfilled? Before you . . come or go.

There is nothing wrong and there's nothing right. The only demand is the purity of heart and the moral fiber of what? *Constancy!*

Look at the impoverished mental state of the nuts! It's pathetic! There is no *fidelity*, there is no *constancy*, there is no *discipline*, there is no *obedience*. How do you expect to have that mysterious Gift of the Unknown God whom I AM constantly declaring as a Living Force? The Gift: the Comforter! How do you expect to have that Presence if you are *defiling* by your thought and its mixture? That's where your adultery happens: it's a mixing of your thoughts! You can't mix God and matter! Therefore, if I AM proclaiming nothing but What IS, isn't it a Wonder that you still see IT in form?!

Would there be any artistic evidences present if there were not the form of the artist? Would we have an art without the form of the artist? That is the Wonder! That is the Window through which I look! Would we have the song without the singer? Would we have the wisdom without the Speaker? Would we have the God without the Son? Would we have the Son without the Mother? We don't come to see them as personification of limitation but as the universal significance of Wholeness and Unity imbued with the Mantle of Transcendent Possibilities being held, waiting for you to don when you wear the Cape of Strength, Fidelity to purpose, and know that you no longer can sit and just listen, for the Proclamation is such that IT demands a response!

Students) Yes, Sir!

If the world needs Love, why are you withholding it? Why are you, in your arrogance, allowing yourselves to be equated with your imbalanced personal natures?! No matter what you pursue personally, it will come to an end, but What I AM is endless. Go on pursuing your divided, ridiculous states instead of *Being* . . the Solution to the Riddle of Being, and then allow your presence to evidence the Art of the Invisible (perhaps by your words, perhaps by your presence), and perhaps someone will recognize your Framing and not hang you on their walls but have you riding with a bridle of Wonder and the delicacy of mouth cognized as the womb of the future.

Man has no time to be born again through the belief system of just the womb of woman. The birth of the future all happens through the larynx or voice box. That is why we say that man today stands in the witnessing box of time to proclaim he is a villain, a liar, a cheat, utilizing the Divine for selfish purposes and, I hope, sentenced according to his deeds.

Only Love will hold one with promise who has attempted to be That which is termed "wholly acceptable in the sight of the One Altogether Lovely." Thanksgiving for what? For That . . that IT can't be touched by your mind but can be known by it, for IT irritates, and IT certainly agitates, and without IT how could your red clothes ever be washed and perhaps bleached in the Light of the Sun/Son's rays?

You will never get what is True for nothing! It takes everything you've got. As someone said last night in a speech that was so fine,

"What is the value, cost, and durability? Your life." "Oh," people say, "I will surrender." **Obedience is the first law of accomplishment,** and I have had people make promises, and they break them as if it were possible to do so. You can't. But you know, whether you remember it or not, you're not just a nut that is to be cracked. What is to be cracked is the suggestion that the Divine is hidden somewhere else than within you.

The Implicate Order is *fully in* agreement with the Totality of Being, and it is the over-accentuation of the explicate order that *tends* to make you feel that what I am talking about is external. If anything I have said, and you have heard, has any meaning to you at all, it's because of the Implicate; it's because the explicate order has been prepared to hear itself spoken as an art form of the appearance of another.

All I do is represent what you in Essence are. I speak not of myself but only of your wish, and that is the reason I am here. I have nothing to declare of myself. I have declared That, that I am not separate from you and you are not separate from Me as I AM, but in your belief system we are light years apart, and My Galaxy is only known as a wave within the cellular structure of your wildest imaginations. But in the genetic Code of Being, I can fructify and fortify the ailing pattern of your energy systems so that once again you may be restored to a useful and viable purpose in this experience for which you came.

You didn't come to be a humanoid; you came to BE, in spite of your appearance, a Divine Traveler, engaging the Cosmos and fecundating it with the evidence of your achievement, for your achievement was evidenced as a Tonality, and that Tone when sounded gave a Pitch that one cognizes as commensurate with One ready to serve in the Symphony of Soul.

The Symphony of Soul, under the Conductorship of Principle, is the One that can allow all auditors to realize their columns are to be marched through, and the Beam of Wonder the balance that is termed the Miracle of the Age.

Find the Fulcrum of your life and appear to be what anyone wants you to be while you remain as you really Are and thus cause them to wonder! This is That for which I give thanks, and the

Window is open. Are you going to look through, or are you going to pass through even the pain that a transparency offers in order to save your *personality and its complexes*?

Don't try to be so hard that you appear a phoney. It takes an awful lot of trying to be something you're not! That's the exhausting part of life! I have a great time. You know, you might say I could drive people crazy, but that's only because Man was born free. Why have you stalled your vehicle prior to entering the Unfettered Land?

The new millennium is only a calendar event. The forgettery and remembrance of the mind are only the outer regions of its considerations; the instrumentation remains within the Hands Invisible. May they be praying to find that in the prayer's fulfillment you are adjusted to the Diapason of Being, and the Principle Invincible is found to be the Open Diapason that allows others to raise their voices and sing, "Amen! Hallelujah! Thanks be to the Wonders of God Being . . Presence!"

Some people here are new, and of course they certainly feel it because they won't understand the sighs and everything, because they have never realized the Sigh of Wonder. They never have heard "Oh!" — the spontaneous, unformed Holy Breath being exuded upon cognizing ITs own Force Field. So they think you're a bunch of lunatics! I could feel it! So, just allow all the sighs and the groans and the moans not to play a part in your phantom of your tollbooth! But *allow* all of the exigencies that are arising within you to be *offended* by this Truth. Remember, the only reason you are here is because you are either where I AM, or you *want* to be, or you don't want to be but you hope that by being here you will have a chance sometime later *to* BE! But you can't put off to tomorrow what has to be done today.

Take time to be Holy. Speak *oft* with Thy Lord! *Aah!* How often do you do it? Or how much time do you spend talking to your little self that you have to be sure is present by looking at yourself in the mirror?! Do you realize you can't paint your face without a mirror — without other people laughing! That's how secure you are! I can assure you, most people need their faces painted. In this day and age, unless they're in the Caribbean, they certainly look under-cared for. Under care four — too many twos!

Too many twos
Give you eyes of blue,
Then you shouldn't fall for them, either.

Wear the Mantle of Blue. Then you'll have the Power and the
Force. That's what the rings and everything point to.

I love jewelry. I love gold.
I love beauty. I love. Behold!
I love Wonder. I love to see
What goes beyond the thoughts of "me."

I like "you" and "you" like "me,"
But that isn't the way you'll see the C (Christ).
You must BE; I must BE.
That is how B goes to C.

A, B, C, and then you find
Your alphabet beyond your mind.
Take a Z and say this fact
That if the Zenith is That, then the Alpha is Fact.

Then you'll know that in between
Are the Octaves of Being where you may continue to dream,
But if the note is struck and the sound is heard,
You wake up and, O, you're hurled
Into the lap of a Resonance Grand!
Behold, you're no longer just a hue-man.

You're wearing the colors scintillating, grand!
You'd be concealed in the autumn leaves of time for Man
But then you would step onto the branch and see
There's no grasshopper, there's no caterpillar.
You leapt! You didn't hang on to what's seeming;
You decided to leap, to BE, and now you see/U.C.

Then you'll extend in Elohim's Grace
And offer the explicate order because the Implicate Order is
        traced.
Then you will find in the Fellowship Divine
How the God of All Being truly shines.

Then in that harmonic iridescent State
You will find the colors, and then you'll awake.
You will say, "It's juxtaposed! It's grand!"
There is the kiln. What's in it? Man!

It takes the Fire to cause a firmness to be
    established, a color to be achieved,
But you have to be *willing* to be painted without a
    mirror in the color of your inner deeds.

If you think you've understood this, you haven't. If you think you don't need to hear it, you certainly do. If you think you've heard it — as the Jesuit told me — "I listened to it seven times and up to the seventh, I thought I knew everything you had said. I was equal, I didn't need to bow." Then, he said, "In spite of my sixteen years of erudition, I realized I had not understood until the seventh time! Never, Mr. Mills, allow people to hear you speak once. They must hear the same Message seven times for them to realize they just haven't heard anything!"

Another priest came and asked me all kinds of questions, and he said, in a letter to me later,

"You have empowered the Mass to such a degree
That now when it's offered, miracles you see!"

It can't be a ritual; the Mass is a Proclamation of Wonder and the response is:

"I accept!"

Do you think? You certainly do, too much! Do you know? A little. But with your degrees, you think you know more than you do.

It's the Simplicity of Being that allows a door to open.
It's the consent to Being Real that allows the Light to shine!
Have a Happy Thanksgiving time!

October 11, 1992

---

1 See Marilyn Ferguson, *The Aquarian Conspiracy* (Los Angeles: J. P. Tarcher, 1980), pp. 177-187.

XXVIII

DEADLY NECTAR

There's not one man or woman in the entire world who has glimpsed the Truth of Being who is allowed to have a contest with the Supreme.

DEADLY NECTAR

The class with the nurses was wonderful, and the two classes with the advertising students, which comprised about sixty people, were really another very engaging experience.[1] The people, of course, were all strangers to me; they didn't know me at all, and they invited me to their Christmas parties, so I went for an hour on Tuesday and Thursday.

It was interesting because one of the young ladies said, "It's so unusual. You walked into that room and *everyone* was attracted. Everyone listened!" One person said he would follow me anywhere. But it was interesting to see how that carried over to the point that their professor gave them all the latest book, *Words of Adjustment.*[2] She bought and gave every student one of these books, and it was a very interesting thing, because then they found they wanted autographs. This was also fascinating because they are all probing and they are very, very deep. I met the Director of the Communications Department, and afterwards he asked the Professor what I did. She said, "Well, he's a philosopher and a poet and a conductor and a musician, and he has a large group of people around him listening to his lectures. It's all philosophy and a Premise from which to live your life." He said, "Isn't that wonderful for these young people."

The outside world has nothing but hallucinations, and that is why a drug is so detrimental, because it enhances the hallucinatory effect of the activity called "seeing" and the activity called "minding." This minding, of course, is so important, because when you are minding your own business, you are watching only those thoughts that you wish to find experienced in your life. When you are lost with allowing the minding to be drunken not with wine but with evasion, then you see what happens: the whole experience is distorted and that distortion is very destructive. There's nothing more distorting than the drug of seeing every day without the proper Sight.

When you say you have vision, vision always implies what? An object. Vision always implies an object, and therefore we forget frequently what is the Subject, and when the Subject is known, then the Subject gives you a clue to the objectivity of . . vision. Vision is objective.

What is the purpose of this type of elucidation? What do you think it is? What is the value of knowing what I'm telling you? Stephen.

> Stephen W.) Sir, I feel, to clear something so that it can be lived. A misconception prior to telling us — your speaking clears that and enables us to live it, if we accept it.

If you live it.

> Stephen W.) If I live it. Yes, Sir.

Yes, that's the value of hearing this. It's the practice of the Presence. This *allows* you to perceive what is at the Root of your experience.

If there is a subject suggested by a vision called an object, what is the foundation of this? If there is an object, it disappears. Therefore, the subject that is in relationship with the object disappears.

Then, what is That which doesn't? Nancy.

> Nancy M.) Consciousness, Sir.

Absolutely! It's Shiva, the Divine Self; IT remains untouched. Now, if this is the case, then is there a moment of Self-forgettery?

> Some students) No, Sir.

Is there?

> More students) No, Sir.

What does this tell us? That the Divine is Omnipresent. The only reason you can call yourself the subject viewing the object is because of the underlying Reality. It is your *forgetting* the Common Ground of Being that has you so self-interested and secondarily interested in Me, which means that you are denying the fullness of

Consciousness or Conscious Being.

It is your vision that makes me the object of either adoration or criticism or speculation, which makes the subject what? Questionable as to your Authentic Nature.

Why are you so important? Not because you're "the vision of loveliness," but because you know that Consciousness is fundamental. It's the Universal Ingredient of All-inclusiveness.

What is the danger, the most *incredible danger* surrounding everyone in this room? That each will try to destroy the inherent unity that is concomitant with Realization, Oneness. It's been destroyed by so many in their lives.

Any people that deny God, the Self, Shiva, whatever you wish to call the Unknown, are a people not only without vision (and, therefore, they will perish),[3] they are a people that are drugged by the supremacy of the mind's intellectual attainment. This intellectual attainment is what is such a force field surrounding an unsure identity.

This unsure identity is always screaming, "I don't *want* the Unfoldment any longer! I don't *want* to change!" You are God-dammed. There is not one thing in Life that is supporting life as soon as you say that. No! Your end is obviously death, and sooner than you expect, because as soon as you say, "I don't want to change, and I have no intention of changing"; "As much as I'd like to change, I'm not going to" — **do you think you can be obstinate with That Which IS?** — you are *pitting* yourself.

And what's in the pit? Hell! Truly!! It is the hell of derision, the hell of division, and the hell of so many just like you.

Those who find themselves in the pit have the same complaint: it's too hot! Ha ha!

It is so fascinating to be able to delineate with words the condition of your fearfulness! Your frightening experience is only sustained by a false identity, the suggestion that you created yourself. No Supreme should ever be denied recognition in any government, in any school system, in any economic system, in any form of cultural or cultic system (which is really the outcome of culture — it all came from "cult"); for any system that does this, that denies the Supreme, is one that is certain to disappear.

I'll tell you a secret: this is why the former civilizations that we have recorded by our remembrance pattern have disappeared. However, what was the essential characteristic of them has remained: once there lived a people, a continent, and an attainment. That is the part of the legacy that still remains sponsored by the Supreme, because **the Supreme cannot forget its own acting!** And *you* know this.

Now, what is the pitfall? That you think you have choice.

And what is that? An option — as if you were in school in a Godless, Supremeless school, culture, society, which most of you *are* in.

But it doesn't mean you are following this. This is why you're here. This is why you are important. You are the hope of the future.

What hope is there if you deny IT? What am I referring to? The Supreme.

Why do I put "IT" in the upper case? Because when it's an I-T, IT can't refer to you. In the upper case IT can't refer to you.

You are the projection on the mind's screen and nothing else. You confute and argue with Truth?! Why do we say, "Oh, Mr. Mills is always so upset by those who leave the Unfoldment"? Well, it's obvious where you are: certainly not in a Realized State. You're not in a Realized State at all, because if you were in a Realized State, you would know that *I can't have part of mySelf lost! I can't have part of my Allness lost, and as long as you think that, it is otherness which you demand, otherwise you would not have called Me to put an end to your otherness.* Oh, yes! Do you mean to tell me that I am going to allow the suggestion that someone is not here who should be here, and accept it, and that I am not going to talk about it and ask about it?

I refuse to accept one sinner as part of my life. If I did, I would be accepting all the people in this world as if they were sinners! A sinner is only one who *pursues* the hallucination!

Why are you chosen among men and among women to be present? Because your very state was questionable from the beginning. That is why there had to be an imaginary Genesis! And, therefore, what? A continuing dreamed-up Exodus!

What does this mean? What's going on with the parade of your objectified fancies? A drama.

What is your stage? The world.

For what cause came ye? To stem the tide of hallucination and permit a Constant Current Event to be cognized in spite of the costume of time.

What is the costume of time? One that is cut and designed to fit the fabric of the dimension which you *wanted.*

Why doesn't this dimension give you rest? Because it was never mechanized for neutrality!

Why then, was the Grace of the Supreme known to be hidden within His evidence? *How* was IT hidden and what was IT? IT was what we call Consciousness or the Unknown, the Self, the Shiva, the Supreme, the Ideal, the Principle, the Soul, the Spirit, the Mind, God . . *IT!*

Why were you given IT? So that you could, for periods every day, have no vision, and it was termed sleep. As I told you years and years ago, "It is not sleeping in oblivion; it's resting in awareness."

Why awareness? It is the least objective.

When you become aware of the objective and dress it up with your awareness: you called, and I came, because you were en-tranced, entrenched, enchanted, or mesmerized!

I AM . . the **Center,** the Circumference. Those who are recognizing the Supreme as Conscious Being constitute the devotees of the Circumference, because where two or three are gathered together in My Name,[4] there AM I in the midst, and the only place that One IS, is at that beginning where otherness is not believed authentic.

What is the evidence of a radius? The Center is fixed but is extendable; it's what is pointed to in "Elohim."[5] It's the extension of the devotee.

What is the circle of influence felt? The **largeness** of that circle depends upon *your realization.* If your circumference is not affecting *thousands,* it's pointing to the paltry condition of the clarity of your realization. Can you imagine the *audacity* of the mind to say, "I'm going to try the outside world," having tasted the Truth of Being for *one moment!* Others have said *they don't wish to change.* My God, their end is already in sight! But the length of their stay in the hallucination will remain according to their *need* for purging.

There's not *one* man or woman in the entire world who has glimpsed the Truth of Being who is allowed to have a contest with the Supreme. He or she will never be awarded: "This is My Beloved Son in whom I am well pleased";[6] rather, he or she will be one known as a vampire.

The psychic vampirism that has gone on has been one of the causes of so much distress; it's much more than your superficial understanding is able to perceive. The *audaciousness* of people trying to understand my motives and that Law under which I live and under which *you* live from your hallucinatory state is absolutely perfidious! It is unbecoming, and it is un-BEcoming.

What announced your arrival but a rhythm? Before there was a rhythm, there was no expectancy. Every mother feels a rhythm change, a rhythmic happening; every father feels it, too, if he is one. A mother has no alternative.

What announces death? A lack of rhythm. Life and rhythm are the evidence of the pulsating Force (which we loosely call "life") of each genesis.

What will be the new? An unclean brush, dipping in the pot of the past and carrying, with the hopes of opalescence, the future? Remember the ancient saying of the Chinese: *"There is progress when the ink and the brush and the paper are in harmony."*

It is stated, in a sense of showing the Beneficence of the Supreme, that one mistake spiritually is permitted. May I just clear the atmosphere here: you've made more than that! Perhaps now you will see why you are so rich: *you have heard from the Zephyr of the West that which refutes the West's basic ingredient for illegitimate living — options!* You should be on your knees; and if you have any leg problems, you'll know soon enough that you have humility problems, and a limited gratitude problem! To be able to hear what I AM saying is allowing you a window in which to perceive (without the fantasy or the hallucinatory aspect of objectivity, or even the subjectivity as other than the result of a Wordless Sentence but one wrapped up in less than ten words) **I AM All!**

When the leaves on a plant sag, like "you" it needs refreshment, but unlike "you," the plant *expects* you to perceive its condition. *Yours* is only perceived by the Awareness of the Supreme. Where there is a lack of vitality and *dynamism* as a result of this Engagement, there is the vampire of selfish and partial engagement with the Known Divinity Thou Art! If hundreds of acres can be claimed for your material refuse, hundreds of acres of this stage's foreground can be *claimed* to be the deposit of your refuse, do you have any idea what must be the size of the pit?! It's an open-air one, because those who enter the pit of the denial of the Presence are those who will be bearing the decaying odor of denial!

You, as Nancy said, have God a Living Presence as an experience. If you doubt it, here is the verification: *I see you not as you seem to be but as* I AM. **There is absolutely no way but One.** The suggestion that there are many Paths to God is a soporific administered to a hallucinatory state! As my father used to say, "There are many roads to God, so they say, but they lead to hell." What is hell? Where your brushwork, your palette, and your canvas show the evidence of aging, of a lack of dynamism and vitality, and obstinacy etched in impoverishment.

Rest assured only in the Realization that Consciousness is fundamental. Now don't be so happy with thinking that you know: "Where there is no vision, the people perish." You must carry it further than that if you are going to preside over a continent in despair! You must know that if there is a vision, the subject must also be object, and, therefore, the resolution is in the Supreme.

May these Words of this One's mouth find acceptance within your hearts, for if you do not Love Him as yourSelf, then you are killing Him as well as destroying yourself. To think that you have an option to live is granting credence to a lie. The only opportunity a lie has is to be accepted as if it were true. Every lie dies; every error dies. Why? Because it has to **suck** like a vampire on the close proximity of those who are close to Truth in order to live! Guess what? The Food of Truth is its demise, because to error Truth is *poisonous*! That is why, that is how, and That IS the prompting behind "Deadly Nectar."[7] It might be the title of this Transmission from That Plane where all those who are beyond your gaze and your daze are rejoicing in the clarity where no spear and no shaking is evidenced, because not even the title of a great play, *As You Like It*, or even the suggestion "to BE or not to be,"[8] is any longer part of the language of those chosen to adore the One Supreme. Where do you find your Self but in the Realization uncontaminated and unfettered by your intellectual and materialistic confinement.

If you think you have options, be restless and continue to support the downward spiral to an un-understood exodus. *But just know* that when you have once descended, there is no option but to face once again the consequences of *your deliberate* denial of *your* **Golden Opportunity** because of what you called onto the plane for **Self**-glorification and adoration, so that the *Circumference* could be so all-inclusive that each world was included in the Grace of Such as That Known as *IT!*

There are no new worlds to conquer. *You* made them up in order to try to satisfy your questing for the Real.

You have been very attuned to a different Frequency this evening, and I thank you on behalf of the Body seen and unseen, for it makes it easier for these moments of Self-Presence to glorify That Which IS beyond your vision and yet known within it to be equated with what appears. In this, rejoice and be glad! Why would you look up to see a Star if it were not in Essence twinkling as the Ever-Radiance of your All-Inclusive Supreme State?

There are supposed to be so many false teachers in this Age.

The point is, you don't even know when you have one, or you don't know what you have. There are so many false teachers; but the mark of IT is constancy, and many other things. I heard a lecture once and the lecturer said this very important point: Even if the teacher was totally false and you followed him with all your heart, with no distrust, with loyalty and the conviction he was right, you would achieve the Ultimate. Because it is your heart, it isn't the words of a teacher. After all, the High Teaching always tells you that the Teacher can give you nothing. He is only saying to each his own Divinity. "T" is to **reach** his own One-ness. That is the force of a Teacher.

That's what all these nurses and advertising students were all in a class suddenly realizing — that there in those corridors of a college nothing was being achieved. I talked with them, and it was a group of people who were searching, generally speaking (not all of them, but some of them were deeply searching).

But a Tarot card reading will never reveal it. No course in miracles will ever reveal it. The Miracle is you! It's not the course; it's what it reveals you in Essence Are! The course is outlined so that you can follow; the course is formed so that you may perceive; and the achievement is allowed for you to bear witness.

How far does your radius extend? The extent of the radius from the Center I AM is only as great as is your Authentic Nature realized. If it is within your four walls, you haven't even realized it. If it's without the world, you haven't realized it. If it's within the world, there's hope, but if it's embracing the universe, there goes your world, there goes your house, and there goes you. Now, what's for sale?

Where are you? Did you do it in, did you do it out, did you do it up, or did you put it down in failure? Stand! Be counted, for the Absolute has meaning, and relativity only in the way that you may approach the Absolute in order to show *the great mystery: the coincidence of the human and the Divine!*

December 5, 1992

1 Mr. Mills had been invited to lecture to several classes at a nearby college and was subsequently invited to attend the respective class Christmas parties.

2 Kenneth G. Mills, *Words of Adjustment* (Stamford: Sun-Scape Publications, 1992).

3 Proverbs 29:18.

4 Matthew 18:20.

5 Elohim is one of the ancient Hebrew words for God, which points to the nature of God to extend.

6 Matthew 3:17; Mark 1:11.

7 A poem given spontaneously by Kenneth G. Mills, set to music by Kenneth G. Mills and Christopher Dedrick, and released on the cassette recording *Star-Scape Over Europe, Volume 1* (Toronto: Sun-Scape Records, 1983).

8 *As You Like It*, by William Shakespeare; "To be or not to be," a line from *Hamlet* by the same author.

On tour in Russia (Smolny Cathedral, St. Petersburg)

XXIX

CRESTS IN RHYTHM

When a country starts to build its economy, its wealth, and its political system on the Diapason of Being Authentic, then there will be Peace. Then people will not be thinking in terms of the cultish orientation of race, color, and creed; they will be thinking in the terms of Oneness!

CRESTS IN RHYTHM

[The following are comments from a conversation with guests after a dinner party at Mr. Mills' home in Arizona.]

How can you put a building up on land that may not want it? You know, you can't infringe upon the frequency of Gaia. People do it all the time. It is so important that you know the land and that you know the space before you put anything on it, because if you don't, what is apt to happen is that you are going to find the space antagonistic to what you are doing in cutting it up by your structure.

Space isn't this nothingness. *Space is what we give a name to that seems to be devoid of the Somethingness that is its IS-ness,* because we have such a limited point of view and a limited vision that we cannot perceive the IS-ness of the space that seems to surround you as nothingness.

So the "unthingness" of the space allows us often to massacre it, whereas, if it is respected, then it will often allow and support a new structure to seem to take place in its environs. The environs of a space are partly defined by the wind, by the light, by the rain, and by the earth.

Ellen Mann) Sir, when we were in Russia, that's how they described the way they went about constructing the great cathedrals. They found the space that would accommodate and accept what they wanted to do there. It's interesting, because you can see in North America, in a particular place, they go to build a store or something, and no store survives. That area is simply not meant to be utilized for that structure. Nothing that they do can change that.

We all talk about economy and think of it as the flow with exchange, and the effectiveness of the exchange flow. It's fascinating because economy, on another level, really has to do with the utilization of our Creativity in the most viable way in order for the evidence to be attractive to curiosity or question. It is only by question that one alleviates the enervation of sameness!

It is only through finding the Answer that a new springboard for newness is Self-presented, in other words, change! That is why America is in the incredible throes of the movement becoming change. It has to be a movement not bearing the old stamp, but a movement bearing the New Figure; not the stamp of a past, but the Figure that is not defined by the egotistical limitations of person. That is perhaps what will bless America greatly. I'm supporting its leaders in every way I can, just by holding the ideation of each in the uniqueness of his creative ability.

I think for the first time, America's leaders know the need for the Diapason of Soul to be once again sounded. If that isn't sounded within the environs of those who audit the boob-tube and the radio, the peoples of America are going to be seduced into the economy of mechanical efficiency and reduced to the mechanicality of intellectuality gone wild. Inventiveness is nothing but new ideas supported by an intellectual curiosity that allows another to witness an invention appearing in the explicate order as a commodity for your use. *An invention is really happening in the Implicate order, and the explicate order has to do with your advertising world. That is how it influences the economy.*

> Dr. Barry B.) Mr. Mills, what is the art of invention?

[Someone sneezes.]

> By allowing the Wind to vent your mind
> And remove the dust from your attic of time,
> By allowing the Breeze in its gentle might
> To reassemble the Wonders of an Unlimited Sight,
>
> By allowing, you stand perceived as such,
> An inventor by name who has removed the dust,
> And so allowing, has found as he stands,
> Offering a Newness to the semblance of men waiting
> to be Man.

There can be a two-part invention or a three-part invention.

From there on it is polyphonic and you get into your fugue, and you have to take care of that!

It is a fascinating consideration: we all have the law in time, in our society, but there are Laws that lawyers of today don't know at all. They feel them but don't know them, and those are the Laws that are governing respect to the Unseen, so that the seen is properly protected by the Unspoken Force accompanying Authentic cognition.

Authentic cognition is the cognition that dawns when you are free from the bias of the cult in which you live called your family, your friends, and their sororities. They are not sonorities! They are roar-ities! That's why when I was at the fraternity it was one thing to fraternize, but in most cases I wanted to defenestrate! It was such a strange dichotomy with the sororities waiting to be sonorities! Most people don't know how to sound correctly because of the lack of Authentic Foundation.

You only know what you are given to know, and that is why you *have* to know: when you know you know, you know you know. No one can ever take that from you.

To witness an event is to be present in attention and absent in conditions. Otherwise, you don't hear. *Listening is dynamic; it's not trying to understand a word, it's listening for its tonality.*

When I spoke at the college, one of the students spoke up and said, "You have the most incredible voice." Then, when I went to their Christmas party, one girl said to me, "How is it possible for you to enter a room, speak to people who don't know you, nor you them, and every one of us listened and didn't want you to leave?" One spoke up and said, "I'll follow you to any part of the world." I said, "Well, you see difference and I don't see any."

You never can conceive anything correctly if you are on the level of it! You never can conceive anything correctly if you are on the level of conception. You have to be above it to perceive it!

I always look down on a property. You can always do that! I just go up two or three hundred feet and look down and see how it could be. But that, anyone can do. After all, Dali did it with his watch; he had it running over the side of the table! Well, I saw that when I was a young fellow. I used to think, I can mentally do that so that I don't have to get out of bed to see the time. I got so I could!

> Dina R.) Is that, Sir, like the landscape paintings in Peru? From up above you can see that they last miles and miles and miles and they make geometric designs.

Yes. Well, it's interesting because when you fly above this house[1] you suddenly realize the design of it is the heart. The heart! Perfect! You see it from the air, it's a wonderful heart. I told the pilot where I wanted to go, and he said, "Well, on our way I want to show you a place up here." He said, "We fly close to it every time we come over." I didn't say a word! He said, "That place down there." I said, "Well, that's where I wanted you to take me!" He said, "Really?" I said, "Yes, that's my place." So he was thrilled! We were down a thousand feet and the engine was conking out, and I thought we were going to land right in the pool!

> Laurie M.) Mr. Mills, another lesson from Sparrow Lake, and all your properties, is that you are always creating more with what's there but there is never a sense that it is incomplete. It's always complete; wherever it is, it is complete and it's balanced and it's beautiful —and there's always more!

You see, one of the greatest failures economically of this country is that we have so many ideas that we superficially bring into production, but we never carry any one to its fulfillment, and that is the resultant lack. That is what is termed going "out of vogue." It is no longer popular: it is out of vogue.

Now what that means literally, on another level, is that *it no longer crests in rhythm!* In other words, *you are meeting a crest and a lull that are not in rhythm with the succeeding ones,* and you have the depressions being *felt* because your vision isn't long enough to span them.

That's why when you go over a choppy sea in a small boat, you are tossed about. But if you are on a big boat, then your big hull and the weight of it breaks the crest so you don't necessarily feel the depth of the lull. That is what is happening economically in the world. This is not understood! I don't know how I know, but I do! *For people to understand that will be the very foundation stone of the future.*

Bill W.) A bigger span?

The need of a bigger span of your bridging concept. The concept must bridge the wave of architectural significance in order for success to be termed its concomitant feature.

Bill W.) The architectural structure is one of Principle.

The architectural structure of significance is that feature of the idea that is nothing but an enhancement of its ideation. It is an accent that supports a magnification of the Original.

So, whether the waves are far apart or close together, the easier thing would be to bring them closer together, not to spread them farther apart. That can be done in time because we are dealing with something that is delineated by space. Those are both concepts that you make up.

So, when you bring these closer together, you don't find the need of forecasting or prophesying; all you have is the abundance of supply to those who question for "Food, Sahib," be it an invention or what have you.

You must try to alter the space and time so that they can service you, otherwise, you are servicing them! That is the aging of "this" instead of your releasement from it!

This form, this body, bears a resemblance to you because you expect it to. I know I am using it, but I am not in it. That's why I can appear to love "this," and love him, and love you, because why? There is really no division!

Sandy D.) This is amazing! This is the value of acceleration then, isn't it?

This is the value of acceleration, because it brings the waves closer together!! This is why the future is the belief of a recurring wave of expectancy, but programmed for time. Acceleration is annulling the bar that would limit.

> Sandy D.) Why didn't we ever see this about life when we finally saw it in the music? You would compact it; you would make us do it faster and faster, until finally we began to have an overview.

Well, it's because those waves of rhythmical intent are the very structure upon which you build your superstructure or *Sonic Temple*. Now, a *Sonic Temple* is nothing but a structure that bears the significance that brings about change. That's what people in America are expecting through this new election. *The election will be very successful if the elected remain in the "I" and dwell in "On" (elect-i-on). The "I" is the very beginning of cognition and "On" is the ancient symbol of Heliopolis, the City of the Sun.*

How can you say who I am or what I am when you are only describing Me in terms of "you"? Any more than I can describe you other than in terms of my Self. That's why I love you, and that's why it's so powerful. But why wouldn't it be?

Economy says there are two waves, but if you accelerate enough you will see what the mind in its slowness has seen at distances: one, two, three, four; one, two, three, four; one, two, three, four. . . [Mr. Mills counts at a faster and faster pace and concludes with:] One! They have come right on top of one another and the idea of process, past, and future have been extinguished in the *coincidence of what is termed "the human and the Divine"!* That's great!

This is *blasting*! It's charging; it's recharging.

What were you going to say, Victoria?

> Victoria B.) So, in Truth, there really is no recession.

There is no recession at all.

Victoria B.) But in the thinking of the masses?

In the suggested mass that thinks!

Victoria B.) I never think of recession.

No.

Victoria B.) I think it was about 1985, I was quite blank in business and somebody said to me, "Don't you realize there is a recession?" I said, "Where?" They would say, "Well, don't you read the newspapers?" I'd say, "No." "Don't you watch television?" I'd say, "No." I just kept right on going; my business was doing extremely well.

Several years later, this particular present condition called a recession came up and the person said, "Don't you realize we are in a recession?" You know, I took one minute to think about it and my business dropped! I had to work desperately hard to get back into my trust with the universe to get back up again.

Yes. Don't get in trust with the universe; BE the Universe that doesn't need trust! Allow the trust to be evidenced by those who come to you!

When men and women pass themselves under the Rod of Right Identification, what appears as a suggested might of multiplicity is swallowed up in the singularity surrounding the etymology of "universe," because it means "swallowed up into one" or "turned into one." From that Standpoint, you elevate and can perceive. From the lower standpoint, you have to work up and conceive.

Remember that! That is what they want to hear at the U.N. I know that. I know that this is one of the things that concerns me, because what has got to happen is not the extension of a theme, but the magnification of it! The magnification of a theme is frequently known by the embellishment or the witnesses. You might say my diamond studs are an embellishment to the shirt instead of just ordinary buttons. That is an embellishment that draws your attention, or allows your attention not to be drawn because it's in keeping with the foreground of the situation. That's why Carol is dressed this way; that's why Michael is dressed; that's why you all are dressed this way. It's in keeping with the foreground of your experience!

You noticed in the late eighties how people dressed; people would wear their jeans, they wouldn't have a tie on, they wouldn't have a shirt, the collar tight, or anything else. They looked like slobs and you wondered what you were paying for because you knew you paid them at least enough to have one suit, if not two or three!

If an act is completed, it doesn't require sustenance; it's self-sustaining. The trouble with our economy is that acts are started and, because they are in vogue for a minute, they are not thought to expand. They reach a lull because people are not taught to take an idea from its conception and allow it to transcend itself. *When a country starts to build its economy, its wealth, and its political system on the Diapason of Being Authentic, then there will be Peace. Then people will not be thinking in terms of the cultish orientation of race, color, and creed; they will be thinking in the terms of Oneness! United States will no longer be divided into states; it will be numbered as the coherent parts of a pattern of symmetry because of the conformity to a Divine Ideal!*

It's bouyant! You will always know when a thing is right: it will carry you. You'll know when you go counter to the wave: you'll hit it broadside. When you hit it broadside, you'll know that you have a counter-intention to your correct movement. *The correct movement is always carrying you*; it's when you try to create your own wave that you usually cause a storm! *If your eyes wander, you know your thought is wandering as well.* If your face is showing anything but wonder, you are involved in producing!

> Valerie W.) I just remembered, a man who had observed the attentiveness of the Singers to you said, *"Do you realize what an incredible experience of Love that is for everyone present in the audience, to perceive that Unity! It's the greatest service that can ever*

be provided for the entire world to have that experience on a stage. It's so important for the audience."

Well, it's fascinating. This is why audiences are so deeply moved, if they *allow* themselves to be.

Don't take on cases until each one is fulfilled because, if you do, you're going to interrupt that "wave closeness." It's like when you scuba dive: on the surface the five- or six-foot wave doesn't look like anything until you're in it. It's only when you go lower, down to a hundred feet, that you realize that the surface is rough but in the depths there is only the current that is natural and there is nothing throwing you around. *It's only when you go to the surface that you can be thrown, and that's exactly what happens here.*

If you focus on Me you go deep!
If you think of yourself, you are being thrown around by suggestion!

Terry S.) Sir, I've seen it so many times in the music, that you will prepare us for what is coming and if we follow that, we are actually following the longer architectural line of the piece, because you are the one conducting it.

I'm getting you to the goal post without you tackling yourself!!

Terry S.) If we don't follow that lead, then we can be trapped in following the surface engagement of a four-bar pattern or a two-bar pattern instead of that longer conception of what is really happening.

That is right. That is just what happens here, in the world. That is why when J.H. spoke to me a while ago, she said it was so imperative for me to speak to peoples everywhere because they have lost the structure of meaning of life. You know the moment you do lose it because you feel you have another day that you have to go through. As soon as you have found it, **the Day is a constant meaning of Being I AM. So, therefore, it is said that the Day is the** irradiance of That Light that is not capable of being defined, therefore limited. That's why when you try to define "men," then you have to use "women." When you try to define Man, you can't. You only can say you have to go to the generic concept, because Man can't be formed. *Man is a state of Conscious Awareness that bears Conscious Being as a wave of an eternal recurrent theme of significance.*

> Dina R.) A few minutes ago, you said not to take on a case until each one is fulfilled. What do you mean by "taking on a case"?

I mean, don't leave something unfinished and start something else. You must finish everything you are doing. If you are going to put away your shoes, be sure you put your shoetrees in them. Don't throw them and toss them off your foot into the corner of the cupboard and say, "They're in the cupboard; no one will see them behind the door!" I might open it! Put your shoetrees in them. Don't put them in an hour later, because that is worthless. A shoetree has to go in as soon as your foot comes out. I teach it to everyone in the house. It has to go in immediately after your shoe is taken off, otherwise it is worthless.

That's why you never can tell the age of my shoes! It was priceless: David went and chose a pair of shoes. I said, "Go to the cupboard and choose a pair of black shoes for me, David, that will go with this outfit." He said, "Why don't you wear this pair, Mr. Mills?" I said, "Sure, I love them! I wore those in 1952! Those are the shoes I wore at the time of my debut!" He thought they were new!

> Christopher D.) That ties in with something ·that occurred to me earlier. The opposite of "economy" would be "waste." No one would ever accuse you of being wasteful! I wondered what would you advise that everyone should be aware of not wasting?

Wastefulness is the outcome of refusal to conform with Principle, because without Principle you never make the right decision. If you don't make the right decision, it's wasting time, energy, money, and your space.

Christopher D.) It's interesting: the words "refuse" and "refusal."

Yes. Refusal is usually the tactic that most people use to prevent themselves from moving further. More colloquially, "Oh, no, I can't. I've got to ask my wife first!" "No, I can't. I've got to ask my husband first." You know damn well they're not going to do either. If they were going to do it, they would never have said it that way. I never asked my wife that way. I knew what she was doing and she knew what I was doing. You only used that as a "withhold." You just didn't want to face being honest. **Be honest!** If you don't like each other, say so! But find out why; then you realize it's all part of your make-up, and it's not pancake!

December 25, 1992

---

1 Arinaka, Mr. Mills' home in Tucson, Arizona.

XXX

THE AUGMENTATION OF AUTHENTICITY

Every moment you are without Feeling,
you will be devoid of Substance.

THE AUGMENTATION OF AUTHENTICITY

We are gathered in the Stone Room at Arinaka here in Tucson, Arizona, on this last evening of the calendar of events which has been numbered one thousand nine hundred and ninety-two, and we are approaching what is termed another number, one thousand nine hundred and ninety-three, just in order to keep track of our peregrinations upon this planetary surface which we chose to inhabit in order to enjoy experiencing a paradox.

One of the great enjoyments of people is to produce. They enjoy producing on all levels. When it is an enhancement of the Invisible it's called "art"; when it's a multiplication of the suggestion it's called "population." *When we are involved with the sense of choice, of course, we are involved with that notion that moves hand in hand with the consideration of our involvement with fragmentation and the resultant diminution of man's innate and intrinsic abilities to exculpate himself from the confusion that over-identification with parts has conjured into such a seeming force field of such mesmeric proportions that it has resulted in world conflict and confusion.*

It is the attempt to move from this involvement with fragmentation that is, in essence, the prompting to consider the shift that is going to take place when man begins to perceive the *Real Figure.* Too many are worn to conceal what isn't appropriate to Being (they're called shifts!) and too many work them to their own disadvantage, and they cover a multitude of sins! *Sin, of course, is again based on the idea of fragmenting or dividing. The basis of sin is all rooted in the belief of divisibility, and divisibility, of course, is all rooted on the basis of you believing in fragmentation.* Your belief in fragmentation results in believers believing in all the denominational, theological, Christian concepts which have tried to bring together the attempted worship of Wholeness from the standpoint of a fragment or a figment of your imagination becoming the Totality or the Wholeness of That which is termed the Allness of Being.

It has been said that the great need of today is the restoration

of the Monarchy of the Soul to its rightful place within the Hierarchy of the Divine. Well, of course, those in high places will tell you today that the Hierarchy is fading out because of our over-mechanization and computerization, which allows the immediate access of all knowledge and of all possibilities and thus an enhance-ment ever at hand of the economy and the availability for all men of great success and wealth. It is no longer confined to the individual baker who makes his bread for his household or for his neighborhood. Ask Nabisco! See, then, if you can get a crust that's worth offering from the Master's table!

The attempted worship of the Divine from the standpoint of the human, of course, is the most ridiculous thing that could be dreamt by a fragment. How many of you have been taught since you were children that you were fragments? *Well, you may not be taught that because you have been taught that you are an ornament of a melody, that "you" as person is the succeeding note of a foundational tone, a diapason of sound and vocalized by what has prompted you or sponsored you into this semblance of form.*

You were told that you were the son or the daughter of so-and-so, but they never go anywhere, and *soh* is always supposed to go to *doh* or some form of it! Usually you get stuck in it because there is no yeast in it! You have the flat bread and then, of course, you have Passover. You have all those things that you really try to pass over without shedding any blood! What do you do but paint your lamppost with the hopes that you won't be perceived as being a fragment, because you are saved, above all others, because you are really sacred for you know that there is an undying Source of Wonder as the very Essence of your Being.

Now, this is an ornamentation that rings throughout the history books of time all dressed up in myths and in gods and goddesses. We are all tempted not to sin in our ordinary sense of sin, but we are all tempted to sin — which is really falling for the belief that there is a division of Actuality or That Which IS Actual or Authentic. **That Which IS Actual or Authentic is non-divisible!** It is the very Fact of That as being correct that allows what appears as this divisible state to say it isn't and still it seems to be. What a paradox!

This is where you walk on the Narrow Way between the

mountains of suggestion which the *m*, of course, symbolizes. Now, the mountains always keep the sun from arising sooner than it might in other areas. But the sun also gives a great feat of Wonder to those who sit and watch it come over the mountain. What a ridiculous turn of events, as if the sun were coming over the mountain, let alone the moon coming over it with Kate (Smith)! So, it is just as ridiculous when the sun comes over the mountain and, fortunately, it doesn't know a thing about it! It's only your growing cognition of the Light that allows the mountain to be seen as a suggested obstruction. The mountain knows not of being a mountain, and the sun knows nothing of being a sun. It is from your fragmented position that you say both are part of your landscape or part of the decor of your stage upon which you are enacting your parts that are given the fragmentation of innate abilities.

Your fragmentation is only diminished by your awareness of Authentic Identity. Yes! **It's Authentic Identity which is the crisis today.** This is one of the thorns on your rosebush, because if you try to pick the rose without watching the stem, you can be jabbed by the thorn very, very easily. It is the same thing with Identity. *If you do not realize the Standpoint from which you must claim Identity, you'll be caught on the spur of suggestion and have that spear in the side of belief and thus suffer another crucifixion for another time in your continual round of systems.*

If I came to do, it would be to deal a death blow to your system of belief which allows "you" a deathly luxury of false identity. To time's accounts, you are "this." To Light's account, "you" do not even exist! It is the Reality that is not formed that allows this form to come and go. *That which appears has to disappear. That was our agreement: if we could make an appearance, we would have to be agreeable to the idea that we would have to disappear. We call that "death," and the only thing that resembles death is sleep.* That's why it's never known. The reason it is not known is because sleep and death can't be contaminated by the hypotheses of those who would like to theorize about the Theatre that might be of Stars. You see, we are earnestly seeking (we are not in dead earnest!) health. We know when we are not healthy because we cease to feel well. **Weal is the very root of health and wealth.**

What is telling us that we don't feel well? We say we don't "feel" well. We don't say we don't "taste" well! We say we don't "hear" well: it means it's impaired (because it's paired!). We don't "sense" well or "feel." *Feeling has an origin that has been slumbering beyond your remains!* That is why you can sleep so easily at night because you feel, without being even consciously aware of it, that you are and that's why you dare to not be.

Everything that you fight for during the day ceases to be fought for when you acquiesce to Purity. That is the uncontaminated sleep. When do you find "you" present? When your head arises from the brick wall called a pillow! Then you say, "Ah, I've got to struggle through this day!" instead of fly out of sight and into the Wonder of a new world and a new experience.

The jargon of today is to jog along with all other skeletons, you know? *All joggers are skeletons on the move until their vertebrae are impacted!* Then they have a club: they call it "The Vertebrate"! What is "The Vertebrate"? Those who jogged and had to give it up because they became stiff and lost flexibility of movement.

Why do you *feel* stiff? Why do you *feel* the need of sleep? Why do you *feel* the need of friendship? Why do you *feel* the need of Wonder? Why do you *feel* the need of newness? Why do you *feel* the need of God? Why do you *feel* the need of Mind, Soul, Spirit? Because those, as yet, are uncontaminated by your fragmentation, but still exist beyond it. It is some of these conditions that are termed the Synonyms of the Unknown that are the very custodians of empowerment, so that the shift can be made into a whole new arena of language and Life lived abundantly, that is, into the arena of Supreme Symbolism!

We use far too many words in order to fructify the suggestion that you are "this." Do you realize every little one of you is such a specialty that a certain type of language has had to be adopted in order to adapt you to the feeling of fulfillment as a fragment?

Have you ever asked yourself, *"What have I done today that I didn't want to do and found it successful?"* *"What have I done today that I should have done yesterday and found myself wanting?"* *"What did I do that I shouldn't have done, but did it, and found myself troubled?"* You see, each one of these conditions brings a resultant health state.

You are not dealing with a purely theoretical system of logic, because that has to do with reason. What we are dealing with is an approach to Being that is totally illogical and that's why most lawyers can't cope with it, because they can't find it *ill*-legal! Most lawyers are ill because their legality is all synthetic. No law is really authentic because it isn't practiced from the Standpoint of the Sun that doesn't rise. And IT never sets. It's man, in his vain attempts! And then you wonder why some of you have varicose ulcers! All the pressure of being false brings a wear-and-tear upon the vehicle that needs to transcend a pit of belief.

So, if a New Year is dawning upon you, you will find it one that is going to demand so much more of you than ever before, because you have grown into the stature of people attuned to Wonder and Miracle and Marvel and Wisdom. If it were not for these Forces of Power, there would be no way for you to find yourself concentrated in the Moment where Conscious attention is All that exists. In that is not the fragmentation, but the augmentation of the Authentic. *The augmentation of the Authentic is when man stops ornamenting the figure!*

In the olden days, before you had a damper pedal, the tone struck on a keyboard would be struck and then totally silent. It did not have any carrying power, because felt or wool or leather would stop it immediately from sounding. But when they invented the pedal and a note could be struck and continue sounding, it was as if Feeling had entered a mechanical situation!

It often takes a striking or a blow to make you realize what you haven't faced today which, if faced, might have released your dampened nature and allowed Feeling to bring its Ministry into the all-inclusive Nature of God or the Divine Self being Authentic. The great tendency of people of the past has been to be exclusive, and it is so wonderful to be exclusive in your All-inclusiveness! That type of inclusiveness-and-exclusivity is rare because it allows a theme of Wonder to transcend one of despair.

If there were going to be a new language of tomorrow, it would have to meet you right where you think you are, to show you you aren't. What stops your language? Using it correctly! **Have you ever practiced saying only what could be found attributable to what you term the Supreme Symbol? It is the most subtle exercise!** Moses found it difficult to cope with the declaration "I AM THAT I AM," because even that meant that to the people, he would appear as Moses, but to the God of his Realization, he was not human. That's why the Commandment had to be in stone for the Ages to tell in the fragmentation of Allness. The Divine Edict still rings true: there is but One God! What is that One God? The Realization that dawns beyond your fragmentation appearing as this figment of your imagination — your form!

The figment of your imagination allows a Moses of historical reference to have walked the Mount of Sinai, but I say, "Ah, was there sin?" Yes! Men believed in a fragmented God broken into parts and sometimes crucified. God, the Eternal Creative Principle, was never in form, but allowed the form to be informed. This is *imperative* to perceive because, if you don't perceive this, you will expect a miracle and a marvel to reveal a condition that is of little consequence. **A miracle or a marvel is nothing but the lessening of the objective confinement.** It's not the greater experience of God. **God cannot be a greater experience than God IS at this moment.** If the God of this moment were really able to be perceived without your thought, this moment would be Eternality, because it would have nothing to do with your space-time continuum. **Eternality has nothing to do with time.**

So, your future is part of your belief system. Your year, 1993, is nothing but the ink blots on a piece of paper, which we can have analyzed if you need. But, in all Actuality, I AM Eternal. I am only allowing the calendar to record my days so that yours may also be seen numberless, because in the Essence of Being there is no reference to a coming and going, an appearance or disappearance. That is only for those who want to see the various acts of Creation.

Each of you has, perhaps, chosen a scenario of many events, a stage play of so many events. You each were filled with envy, jealousy, or resentment; or goodness, exuding responsibility, co-operation, freedom, a squaring of all your deals, leadership, broth-erhood, et cetera. These are all wonderful! But, you see, each one wants to play these various parts. That's how come you're back! What about your front? Why do we always see your back? What's the front page news? "I never came or went!" If you look on the back page, you've got my history. On my front page there's not a thing printed. How can there be anything printed if I was beyond the belief system? "I" is not a belief. Do you know, "I" is not even a thought? *"I" is not a thought and that's why it's uncontaminated and unfettered by human hypothesis. "I" is nothing but a sound I'm making: "I"! You think I'm making some great declaration. I say unto you: "Ah!"*

What does "say unto you" mean? Nothing. What made "say unto you" something? "Ah!" What if "Ah" didn't say anything? The Unthingness of that "Ah" is incredible: it allowed this "thingness" to appear to be something it isn't, until the Unthingness That IS allowed this "thingness" to appear changed.

A note is only ornamented to draw attention to it. Why do you ornament a note or do a turn on it, with an appoggiatura or an acciaccatura? Why do you do these inverted mordents and turns and trills? To draw attention to a note. What do *you* draw attention to? How do *you* trill instead of thrill? *You* go along with a fragment in your own grouping. The Magnetic Center is such that *it doesn't move* to bring all that which is scattered into a wholeness. *You can't bring scatteredness to Wholeness; you can only allow the scatteredness which seems to be, to be the suggestion it is and fade out!*

What is the Essence of Music? Aside from having a melody, it has to have a rhythm in order to live. The Rhythm that exists eternally is: I AM THAT I AM, or "The Divine Principle of the Universe must interpret the Universe,"[1] or "The Universe, like Man, must be interpreted from its Divine Principle in order to be understood."[2]

What is your future? Your continuing dream.

What is it demanding of you? Mastership.

What is a Mastership? Being on the Bridge between Wisdom and Intuition and allowing Insight to scan your horizon of opportunities!

There is *absolutely* no limit! That's why we say "outward bound." But I don't like it too much because then it means I have to be inward bound, and I don't know what "inward bound" means.

When I used to talk to the Maharishi Mahesh in the early days before he became so famous, he would say, "Dive deep within!" I used to think, "What?" He told me, "You must dive deep within!" I thought, "No way! How can I dive deep within when I didn't dive without?!" I've never known what "within" and "without" were. I never have. The only thing that was "without" was hitting myself with a hammer; "within" I knew the feeling! *The feeling had much more power than the hammer, so I knew that "without" was the hammer; "within" was the feeling. That's the only way I knew "within" and "without."*

I didn't know which way to go when I dove because I didn't see any springboard, unless it was spontaneity. I think I once said that spontaneity is your springboard?

> Laurie M.) "Let planning be your springboard so that spontaneity can be your splash!"

All right. She said it! Okay? *I think spontaneity should be your springboard and Actuality your splash!* They always have these things you splash yourself with after you just finish drying yourself. Weren't you informed that you should splash yourself with this refreshing cooling lotion, after you have just finished taking a shower in a refreshing cooling lotion, and you just finished drying yourself? Now splash yourself wet again!

How are you going to energize if you constantly de-energize by false identification, by falsely identifying with what isn't instead of What IS. What IS?!

> Laurie M.) I AM.

What isn't?

> Scott S.) Everything else?

What IS *is* what isn't! But for those who haven't realized That, you say I AM! That broke the tablets! What IS; what isn't? What are you searching for? It's the greatest window!

You see, there's no point to being one in process unless it's a suffering to be so now until I come. Then when I come, I may appear to be one in process, but I AM never in it. That's the root of Mastership. A **Master** is one who knows he has acquired the technique to be the Music, instead of one attempting to play it!

Being Music is the Harmonic State of Feeling the Being I AM
With an intention appearing directed into the energizing of
the Plan.

What is that Plan? What is the great blueprint for Earth? I have
been asked this by so many people. I can only tell it in bits because
it's according to how big your bit is that I can give you the
corresponding byte. And, you see, the byte holds many countless
thousands of moments of information.

What are you ready for? I can tell you the most astounding
thing here and see it go right over your head. Why? Because it was
never meant to go into it! But you think it is! You think "you" have
to grasp it by thinking. I say you only experience it by feeling! If
I take a bite of Scott, he knows he's been off-guard, but it leaves no
mark! (That's his material, well-manufactured!) You see, if he lives
by the Laws of Manu, then he hasn't fractured what appears as his
part. But if he breaks the Law, then he suffers the stain of that
bifurcated state that is termed duality: relationships, which are the
hindrance to the Actuality of Being.

We are so involved with relationships, friendships, and families that we fail to perceive the Universal Friend, the Universal
Family, the Universal Man. It is the suggestion of the "fragment
teaching" that you have this pedigree. You're a shepherd. You're
a bloodhound. You're a Newfoundland. You're a St. Bernard. But
really, those dogs got their fame because they helped somebody over
the mountain when they couldn't use the pass out of season. When
you walk between the mountains, it's termed the Narrow Way.
One side of the mountain is always in the shadow, but you can never
be in it, unless you have realized, and then the Shadow is the State
in which you walk in the "Peace that passeth the understanding."[3]
That is how your Light is cognized. Because you can walk through
the valley of the shadow of death, but **what is death? The purity that
cannot be contaminated by the analysis of an intellectual achievement.
It has to be experienced in the Soul-fullness of Being That I AM!**

They say the world is waiting for the Sunrise. Some say a new
Messiah, some say a new Avatar, some say the hope of something
that is Real. But you know, the world is not waiting for a sunrise,

the world is waiting to be identified correctly! Do you realize, if it were not for the Sun that never sets, you would not be able to perceive the stage upon which you are acting?

The reason Scott comes in to see me in the morning in the Cedar Room is because he knows that the Temple of Eternality is supposedly structured with the Cedars of Lebanon. **What is that Temple of Eternality? That State in which no division is perceived.** As long as he is divided he will have to come to see me as I AM. When he is not divided he will see me as I feel I AM. Feeling the Being! Is it any wonder that it is a song?[4] Do you know that the great demand of the Age is the restoration of the Soul to the entire world? In Russia, wherever we go, the first thing that is asked by everyone is about the Soul. They ask me about the Soul. They don't know that for years it was my hell. Because I always had to worship HAL! (The son of IBM, the Intellectual Bombardment Movement!) I had to only identify as HAL; I didn't know where in hell I could find David![5]

David was the great symbol of Love, and, of course, Jonathan was the other aspect of the sameness coming together as Oneness. It was what? Historically thought of as the greatest love affair of all time, because no one could understand it and have it legitimized. It was so fearful to find Oneness the empowerment to what appeared as twoness. Why is that Oneness so powerful? Because the Essence of Soul is the Feeling of Being I AM, which I found after thirty-some years of slugging away at this: "What is Soul?" I never lost the energy of questioning because I never gave up the forging of it as my life. Had I just fretted over Soul, I could have been part of your violin or your guitar, but I didn't want to be played upon by "you" in case you didn't correctly pitch your woo/wu. Then you have why/wei. No wonder you need a finger pointing to the moon!

What is the purpose of a book? To hold your attention as you are wondering about who you are without questioning what you are.

If I say, "who you are," how would you say it?

Aaron S.) "I have been wondering who I am."

Exactly. "Who I am." Well, you know you are going to find it through Wonder, because "I have been wondering." *Curiosity is one of the great leaks of energy if you don't fill the hole that is causing the leak with healthy search!* If you wonder who you are, don't bother going to India. Maharshi is gone, and Nisargadatta is gone. Ramana Maharshi said, "Who am I?" I have always said, "What am I?" when there is no "who" to go with the suggestion of the owl. Hootie the Owl: "Who am I?" I think "What am I?" is more interesting because it can be done in earnest, and who may be found dead? Done in earnest, it can bear interest. Dead earnest only gives you a dividend as a legacy!

This doesn't make any sense! But it makes incredible feeling! Because it is disorientating to your logical, rational mind enslaver! Your rational mind is your great dominating factor in your life. If you can't reason a thing, you don't want it. That's when you should always take it, because That which you can't reason is beyond "you"! I AM beyond you, and that is why it is so difficult to take Me as I AM. *You can take "me" as a social counterpart to "you"; that's easy! But take my Point and it spurs you to fight, flight, or fear!* Of course, I don't mind fear at all, because then you have the Soul Factor always present to your **Earth**, to your **hearing**, and to your **fear**.[6]

What do you seek after? "What am I?" Or "What I am I?" One person came to me once and said he was so upset. He knocked on my door at about midnight. He said, "Mr. Mills, I've got to talk to you!" I said, "What for?" He said, "I don't know what's wrong with me. I just realized there are three of me!" I said, "Don't worry, you can count them!" He stared at me. I had his attention, and where your attention is, there AM I also. If I had disagreed with him, I wouldn't have had his attention, and he would have just had "himself" and "me." I said, "Don't worry, you can count them. There are so many of me, over fifty-seven varieties, but they are not bottled! They are under a Cap, but you have to know how to see that Hat!"

How many I's/eyes have you? Some say only two. I say there is only One! What's going to happen to "you," if I AM All?

Boy, oh boy! They say there is no hierarchy!? Businesses are scared to death of an hierarchy today. They are trying to put everything down into little pockets of power in order to get things done quickly, because the hierarchy is usually so slow. That's why the governments are so wasteful. The governments could not really go on existing for so long, if they didn't have all those people who just like to do paperwork! It's all that slowness that just allows the pulp to have an industry, you know.

Undirected energy is wasted energy. That's why if I am going to hit you, I just go right ahead and hit you. I don't bother wasting my time just sitting wishing I could!

What do you feel fragmentation is? The suggestion that Wholeness could be broken into parts!

Do you realize, our whole world is built upon the belief of parts? But mind you, fitly joined together. But no one can account for you. Do you realize that everyone who is going to account for the fact that you live is going to disappear? Everyone who accounts for me, they have all disappeared but one. Who says, "Really you are K.G.M."? The government wouldn't believe it, that I was K.G.M. and not G.K.M., until my mother came in and said, "He is K.G.M.!" I said, "But there has been no doubt that I am K.G.M. as far as my income tax is concerned, only as far as my old age pension; if I hadn't gotten it changed on my birth certificate to K.G.M., G.K.M. would still exist — no K.G.M.! Why didn't you think of that when you taxed me?! I wouldn't have been paying any all these years." Then, of course, they would have realized it and I suppose would have come back on me for seventy years of tax evasion because of an initial. For what? A brand! We're all marked one way or another. Some on the rump and some have hide-and-steer, hide-and-seek, and everything else!

But you see, what you're dealing with here is the exaltation of a fragment in the attempted worship of that which never could be Whole. That's why Gurdjieff said "All and Everything"; he didn't say "Every-thing and All." Being All, I can have all of Me appearing multiplied as "you." That's My lovely All-inclusive nature. I never consider you other than aspects of My own Selfhood. Everything that's beautiful I love and everything that I don't care about comes to me to give itself up, because where will it go, if it doesn't come to One who knows it isn't true. I know two and two isn't five. So anyone who believes that two and two is five, either rejoices in knowing it's four or goes on believing it's five and suffers.. my kicks, which, of course, are not wasted energy, but a boost to their freedom!

So, what happens? You don't expect to make the fragment whole; you re-identify the ornament and see the Principle Tone that is being exalted. That is termed the Fundamental Tone: "I"! You never need to worry when you realize that all there is to this "I" of time, in Essence, is "I"! Why do we say it's so easy to sing? It's just "I" clothed in different garments. [Mr. Mills sings a tone moving through the sounds "ay," "ee," and "oh."] It's all the same.

You say, "Glory, glory, hallelujah!" It's just "I" being elongated through augmentation. "Hallelujah" is just "I" augmented. **Love is just "I" clothed in the Garment that is conditionless.** That's why love, as you know it, is an imitation; it's a counterfeit, because the Love that IS is unconditional!

What is the New Year to be? You should include it in the Allness of your Being. You should allow those fragments who consider themselves the personalities of time to walk before your Light of Glorification and allow them to see the Adoration beyond that conceived by the Magi. You should allow your Tree to so shine with the auric field of Wonder so enhanced by the entire System flooding your presence with the Magnetic Force and Attraction of the Allness of God Being Real that What I AM is beyond question. And when you ask, "Who am I?" there AM I in the midst of your question. Then in the Answer, who asked the question?

Your New Year is what others will call your dance in agreement with the Rhythm that holds man in its embrace. *Remember, for a Center to be powerful, it has to be rhythmic.* The Rhythm can never be destroyed and that is just what a Satanic force will try to do. *What's a Satanic force? The force that exists on your beliefs of fragments. The Satanic force is a suggestion that there is a force opposed to the Wholeness of Being.*

When you go out of this body, as you can, what does that signify? That what Man IS can never be contained by what appears to be and isn't Real. Just because I left my body behind, went out of it for two or three hours, walked the streets with a friend and then told him the stores and everything we'd been in, didn't mean that my body wasn't. I had to come back over the rooftops to get back into it, so that I'd be in it when he appeared around the corner of the house. He thought he was going to surprise me. I said, "Hello, Francis!" He said, "How did you know?!" "Well," I said, "I've just walked with you for the past three miles." He said, "What?!" He didn't believe me. I said, "Well, I'll tell you where you've come: I've just walked with you down Calais Avenue. You came that way, didn't you, down past Dr. Miner's home?" He said, "Yes!" I said, "You went into the Boston Shoe Store, asked for a pair of shoelaces, and then you went into the fruit market, Mike Dimitri's. At the border they asked you where you were going, and you said up to see Ken Mills up on Schoodic Street."

We are so confined by the womb of thought that we do not experience the Wonder of an Unconfined State because we think conception is in form. Conception is not in form. The New Birth comes through the larynx or the voice. *You don't have to wait to be Real; your only condition is: are you **willing** to BE?* Then you will find your relationships and your relativeships all facing an **Absolute State.** What's That? **The One that is devoid of alternatives. You have no choice. As fragments, you may think you do; as the Totality, you don't!**

> You have no alternative but to love yourself as I AM,
> To Be yourself as I AM,
> To Feel the Self as I AM,
> And to see the Self as I AM
> And let others call you a Master as I AM.

What is the point of allowing yourselves the extravagant leeway of just being a student, so you can go on stewing in your duality and relativism? Or are you willing to be Real?

To will demands dynamism, vitality, and daring, which are not looked upon with too much appreciation today. *How can you rock another's boat?* **By being still!**

If you don't agree with a suggestion, how's it going to keep moving? That's how you rock the boat. In other words, you anchor it! *What is the boat?* **The unrecognized Ship of Soul.** *How do you stop a person's boat from rocking or the Ship of Soul from being in a fluctuating state?* **By being Real!**

Feeling is the essential feature of the next year. Every moment you are without Feeling, you will be devoid of Substance. Selfish feeling: you will find it the dark side of the mountain without the

Peace that passeth the understanding. *But you must extend in Feeling beyond your thought-frontiers.* Your thought is only given to you to navigate your beautiful bit of machinery. It was never meant to usurp the Throne of your Royalty of Being.

Fragmentation is what those who would control the world want to keep as part of the political arena. But people are never wise. People have never been wise. How could they be? A nation made up of people can never be wise. *"People"* is the name given to figures who are formed but *uninformed* of Being Real or Real Being. It's frightening when you consider the United States or Canada or the entire world. People think through the framework of sight that their eyes are telling them the glorious story of their supremacy. All the eyes are telling you is your ability to project your own stage setting, your own conditions under which you must work. Do you realize everything here this evening you have projected? You include it as the Festival of Celebration. I have included it as part of mine from the moment I conceived it; you put it into the house. I put it into the all-inclusive Nature of Being so that a house might appear in which you could be included!

Have you ever considered the face you see in the mirror is only seen because of the Face that's not in it? Why is it that I can hear a recording of the Singers and say, "Oh, there's Sandy!" I recognize her by her voice. "There's Dianne!" I recognize her by her voice. **All I'm hearing is a sound and I'm already figuring.** You hear my Voice and you figure "me" separate from "you." That's always the way of multiplication. *Multiplication or fragmentation depends upon separation.* Why do you think you attempt to get married and bring people together? And seldom better. No wonder they say, "For better or for worse; for rich or poor, until death do us part." I wish I had met it before I even started. I went through all those stages. Any who haven't, bless you and keep you!

Isn't it wonderful to BE? No wonder they have fig leaves! It's all such a fragment. A fig leaf is a fragment of a fig tree. What's a fig tree? It bears a figure that you call a tree with a leaf that you use to shield your possibilities so that you don't have to show them. What are your private parts? Are they fragments, or the evidence of your innate ability to be creative and co-creative to all appearances with the Divinity Unseen but formed and cognized as your Art of Living.

Your force field should be so rhythmical and so powerful that you would naturally draw all others unto you, for that is the State of a Master. He is simply Being, and everyone makes Him up.

Do you realize the university is the result of fragments? Do you realize the faculties of every university are specialized, theoretical situations, all attempting to be whole, but all filled with holes! I'm so grateful I haven't any degrees that are visible. It's so interesting to talk to people highly educated . . in their own eyes!

What seek ye after? Whom seekest thou?

Well, I've talked enough.

Erika Z.) You spoke about feeling earlier. How does one discriminate between emotion or sentiment and feeling?

Oh, those are the lower echelons of Feeling. Emotion and sentiment go hand in hand with bondage. *Feeling is the Rhapsody that allows you to be wrapped in Wonder, freed with Magic, and filled with the buoyancy becoming the Newness of Being Real.* Sentiment and emotion give you seasickness, until "I" come and then you'll scream "Eureka"! (That's Erika!) Eureka!

Nora B.) In the song, "The Bells of Christmas,"[7] there's a line, "the head does carry the Feeling. . . ." What does that mean, Sir?

"The head does carry the Feeling. . . ." Well, the head at the moment is carrying the Feeling. When it isn't carrying the Feeling, you will be the living Answer to what you call your question. "The head does carry the Feeling: I AM One. I AM One, the Only, the One called simply Divine." That's how the head carries it until IT's experienced.

I say I love Scott, I love David, I love Kathy, I love Janis, I love Katrine. I have to balance it; my God, I don't want a war here! Why? That's how they're created! The fragments all respond differently according to their parts.

Why is revelation so exciting? It's revealing. What's revealing? **Revealing allows curiosity to die.** Curiosity is the worst avenue for a waste of energy. Once upon a time, women used to be great things of curiosity. Today they're not; there's nothing curious about a woman other than the stories. There's nothing curious about a man, anymore, other than the stories. The mystery of what it is to be feminine or masculine no longer exists. It has become common. People don't exalt those qualities which each is in Totality. You go outside looking for the woman — the woman is within you; but as long as you can keep her without you, you have no obligation to her. But when she lives as a very part of your being — oh, brother! And the woman: the man doesn't live outside her; she puts him outside her. But he lives inside her as a part of her own being. But if a man lives inside of a woman, and a woman lives inside of a man, what is this "inside" and "outside"? It's funny how you go outside yourself to find what you consider the opposite of yourself in order to make yourself whole (for better or worse). And look what we do: we constantly go within and without.

I thought those were only the doors in a department store: entrance and exit. You go within and you come without. You go in with something and you come out without it!

What's the value of going to church? The value of going to church is to keep alive a Flame of Promise until all others can see how the cracker crumbles and the Fire still blazes. Then you won't just have firecrackers for a celebration. That's how Fire works!

Are there any questions? Have you any questions for 1993? Before it comes, get them answered, then 1993 won't have any question about it! If you have a question tonight, 1993 will be a question. I hope people who are celebrating tonight realize . . because if they don't, their cells are going to be screaming the false message to their wealth, to their health, to their well-being. *All celebrations should be the extolling of Reality, the Authentic, the Real.* To meet a loved one is to celebrate. To meet an unknown one is to celebrate. We don't always know just how advanced one is, but if one cognizes one as All, it's a celebration. If I hold you in the Light of what I know, it doesn't matter whether you know what I know or not. You come to see/C.

If you come to C/see, then you may be able to perceive it in a symbol of a baby in a cradle[8] suspended between Mrs. Treble Clef and Mr. Bass Clef, but loved by both. So sometimes it's up closer to Mrs. Treble Clef and playing with her kids, and some days it's down closer to Mr. Bass Clef playing with his kids. The baby is shared, but you know it always goes to D. Where is your D? Dee dum diddle is like the Narrow Way; it's always in the middle.

But it's also the signal of the Divine,
Because, you see, when the thought is raised and you hear a
     Siren in time,
It may be the ship is a'sailing between the straits of despair;
It may be that the sails are wailing and they call it the Sirens
     emblazoned, who dare
To take the fearless voyager upon the ship of his life
And he has to lash himself to the Mast of Principle in order
     to stem the attraction of the Dark Side, the Night!

What if your ship is a'sailing and you hear the wail
Of the shrouds as the Wind in its Might and its
     Omnipotence grasps your sails?
How will you steer your course becoming the Narrow Path
     of the Light
And leave the sea tormented and enter the calm, the peaceful
     Light?

What have you to find in your voyage of time?
Are you going to reap what you have sown? You will!
But you have a chance to change your seeding.
Consider your apple. Get off the barge of temptation.
Don't lash yourself. No one else will!

So many people want to feel martyred — because they're dumb![9] They are dumb! People love to feel martyred because they are dumb. **What is someone who is dumb? Numb to feeling Allness. He feels selfishness. Feeling is sel*fless*ness. Emotion and sentiment are sel*fish*ness.** And like fish, after three days it smells! You change your mood. **Every mood is selfishness dressed up.** Usually it's for a ball/bawl and you have to provide Kleenex.[10]

Have you ever noticed how selfishness always wants to cry? Selflessness is usually the evidence there is a hidden canvas at work upon which are being brushed the Wonders of Simplicity. It isn't difficult to be Real, but it takes a hell of a long time to see that. You can see it like that! [Mr. Mills snaps his fingers.]

Anyone who tells you that you have to take course after course after course to be Real is filled with expectation, because actually you can't be *made* Real. **Reality knows nothing to be made.**

Were you carried in the cradle of the deep? Or did you come in on the Zephyr of the West? Or did you come in on a wing and a prayer? Most people pray to be delivered from the dream of passing or of appearing. Why do they pray to be freed from the dream of appearing? Because they haven't dared to face disappearing. **Do you think God appears and disappears? God is the Force that allows the appearance and the disappearance to be bridged. And that's God Insight/in sight!**

What's the greatest miracle? That you can appear to be "this" and have God present! This some"thing," and the power of the Unthing present. The Great Unthing.

I say "God" and we all "become Holy." I say "you" and we drop our considerations. What if somebody called you "Godson" and it really was a contraction of "God's Son"? They would say: "Who are you?" You could say: "**I and My Father is One.**" "*Oh, what's your name?*" "**I haven't any.**" "*But what is your initial?*" "**I haven't any.**" "*What is your mark?*" "**Hi!**" It takes One to know One!

I can tell when you say "I" whether you're sure of it or you're not. I hear in a very interesting way. I hear more than I see because my hearing doesn't give me images, my sight does. It gives me "you." My hearing doesn't. My hearing allows me to hear what you really sound like and I like it. I am pleased.

Nurit O.) Mr. Mills, I have been considering Divine Idea and cognizing the corresponding identity, the object. For example, if the idea is containment, the object would be a cup, or if the idea is movement, the corresponding identity would be a vehicle. It seems there's always a purpose behind it, a purpose which translates as movement, and, therefore, there is the object or the corresponding identity.

I'm wondering if that's correct or if that's the way the mind perceives it? What is the origin or the source of purpose?

Oh, the origin and the source of purpose is the mind, but the mind must have a purpose so that its origin is perceived. **The mind** is nothing that you treat with disrespect, but you don't allow it to usurp a prerogative that it doesn't have. I AM in control of it. Most people think the mind controls them. No, not any more than the typewriter. *The computer doesn't control you; you feed the computer what you expect it to regurgitate. The mind will regurgitate what it's been fed. But it's fascinating, it will also allow that which it has never been fed, by using what it has been fed to reassemble into another structure what has not been said in the formation with which it has been codified. It alters the coding. That Which IS alters the coding of my mind. The Mind That IS allows the mind that isn't to appear to inculcate the Message That IS in contradistinction to what isn't.* It's really amazing! Amazing Grace. It really is, because that is the anointing of the Chosen Race. It's God's Race; that's why it's Grace!

What is God's Race? **A Sound Race.** And the communication will be in tones; it will not be in words. Words have come to have too many meanings, which means that we involve ourselves too much with the possibilities of language; whereas, a C is always a C, a D is a D in any Octave of Being. There is no escaping from the demand. If you're supposed to sing a C, you cannot sing a D and get away with it. But I can say, "God," and you swear I'm saying, "God," and then you might swear, "No, he isn't saying, 'God,' he's saying something else."

Jo Ann V.) Mr. Mills, I wonder where Idea originates?

It originates with "you." I have no idea that I AM!

Valerie W.) So, that is why every idea has a corresponding identity, then?

Well, if you wish to put it that way, fine. Don't make things like other things. You make so many of "you's/ewes," I have to keep shearing you.

Aaron S.) Sir, why is there a suggestion of duality?

Because you haven't questioned its source. When the source of duality is perceived to be fictitious, there won't be a suggestion of it. I see duality; I don't have to live by that. I enjoy the appearance of duality, but I don't live by that at all. I don't believe . . at all; I know! When you know you know, you know you know. Until that time you think you know, and as long as you think you know, you don't know. That's why you have to kneel before the Now, and that's how the Knowingness is open to being attained.

Dina R.) Mr. Mills, in the song "The Heraldic Message"[11] you say, "The angels and their band have been crying to be freed from bondage, held on the plane out of sight. May their promptings touch the heart. . . ." What does this mean?

The angel-hood of "you" is always claiming your attention to consider your Transcendent Nature, and that's what the angels always do. They're always calling you to consider That which you aren't . . crying. Usually the one caught in the flesh needs to be cried unto in order for the angels to get his attention. That's why your son or your daughter would cry to you. They would cry to get your attention. Well, that's what the angels do. They are that part of you which you have allowed to be etherized, therefore, not considered viable as your dressed-up situations. So, they're always crying unto you. It's a great Force Field because it's uncontaminated by your mind, but it's known to exist by its pulling at your heartstrings.

Michael S.) Mr. Mills, does Feeling have a figure?

Hi!

Michael S.) Is it correct to say, "I cognize that I feel"?

You can say it if you wish. I won't keep you in after school!

Michael S.) Can you have feeling without cognition?

Of course! I don't have to cognize I feel. I AM Feeling. There's nothing going on other than That. You describe my feeling; I don't describe it. If I embrace you, you describe "me" and say, "Oh, he's a pervert; he's hugging me and I'm different from him." Oh, it's the greatest bestowal upon you. I don't see any difference. You do! That's why I hugged you. If it bothered you, then you haven't found anything. You've been thinking you know; and thinking you know, you don't know. But if I hug a woman, if I hug Lynn, it's great as long as it doesn't go any further, and as long as you're around when I hug her. That's okay because she's the opposite. No one will think anything of that. It's just as ridiculous as hugging you and thinking that you're separate from me. I won't. I couldn't. I can't!

What does Feeling know about difference? Difference is only for the fun of it, for allowing mentality to have a corresponding identity. The only thing that goes with you is your mentality. I don't. **I don't come with "you" and I don't go with "you."** You will always be Conscious Awareness coming or going, appearing or disappearing. The only thing that comes with "you" is your mentality, and it goes with "you." What goes with "you"? The awareness that used the mentality, the Conscious Awareness that used the mentality to become the Son of God or the son of a relative. I bear no relationship to "me father" or "me mother," to "me sister" or "me brother"! I can tell you that!

Steve D.) Mr. Mills, you were speaking on Christmas of the rhythmic waves of the Unseen and of the relation between the Unseen and the seen, and you mentioned the importance of feeling in that regard. I wondered if that were one of the key elements of which you were speaking last week: that feeling could be a barometer or an indication of the extent of a correspondence between the rhythmic movement in what we call the world of the seen and the rhythm of the Unseen.

Your feeling may be described that way. Mine can't be. Mine doesn't seem to change; you may think it does. If I didn't criticize you or find fault or constantly tell you how wonderful you are, can you imagine the swings you would have?! It would be like a pendulum, swinging between last year and this year. Who wants that type of matter? What a rib! That's what you call ribbing. The past and the future: the ribs of suggestion. Hi! Hi! Hi! Hi! Within, without; without, within. Above, below, or sideways? These are all made up! Isn't it horrific when you suddenly realize you're sitting there making this all up? They made up this whole trip. They brought all the angels with them and left all the smog there![12]

Did you ever realize that before, that you're making this all up?

Aaron S.) You told me that before.

Are you beginning to see it?

Aaron S.) Tonight.

Yes. What do you call this? [Mr. Mills is pointing to his hand and then to Aaron's hand.]

Aaron S.) Form.

Yes. What's this?

Aaron S.) Form.

What's that?

Aaron S.) Form.

Do you think if you lost it there would be less of you?

Aaron S.) No.

If you lost both of your legs, would you be less Man?

Aaron S.) No.

You might appear to be. One of my friends lost both of his legs and he used to have to jump from the floor to the sofa with his arms. He got so he could leap, push himself up from the floor and land on the sofa. But you never called him less Man, although there was certainly much less form. He was a great athlete before he thought he was a fragment and caught it in the war. (The fragments blew off his legs.) A fragment is what you appear to be, but just because you don't know What IS, you feel you're less Man? You have to move as if you are totally All. This man, minus his legs, became mayor of the town, acted and lived as if he were total. He had artificial legs; he came in, took off his belt, and threw the legs on the sofa. He behaved as if he were total. He appeared to be cut off. He was never cut off from his purpose. He was never cut off from being active and fulfilling an incredible position in life. *He behaved as if he were complete.* You've got both legs, both arms, a total form, and how often do you exercise being complete? You said I told you. I'm telling you now: you're complete, but "this" couldn't contain it. All it can do is by the Grace of Presence. You have to unwrap the Present and that's how you take care of what appears as tomorrow. *If you unwrap the Present, where is the future?* I allow the future to appear. I allow the future to appear for those who want a calendar of events, but **I AM Instantaneity exemplified!**

Christopher D.) Mr. Mills, music has been known to be the way of engendering or transmitting a feeling that can't be labeled and doesn't have any way of being pulled down by a label. There is something very magical in that, by our recognizing that Power, we can also recognize the Power present right now that is available, if we stop labeling in our thought-structures this gigantic Happening or this gigantic Presence that you are emanating.

Well, the music allows you to feel the Presence. Presence is the Feeling that allows itself to be felt because it knows no other Presence to feel! That is why it is intoxicating to the one who is still in the throes of decision, because it is so thrilling to feel what isn't in throes or in the turbulence of question. It's so wonderful to feel something that is beyond that realm of conjuring. Feeling cannot be conjured. **Feeling is the authentic characteristic of the Soul Force of All-inclusiveness!**

We tend to exclude others; the best way to be is all-inclusive and others will exclude themselves. They won't be able to stand you!

Joe D.) Mr. Mills, is there an agreement of the mind with the heart before the Feeling of Being I AM can be experienced?

Well, it appears to be that way but it isn't quite so! The reason you lecture is to allow the head to receive information that cannot contradict the Divine Dictation, and the reason the heart responds is because the Essence of its rhythmic pulse is non-material. So, when the head and the heart are in agreement, then there is the natural flow of the River of Life and that is termed the Feeling of the Soul. The River of Life is the pulsating Force that allows the Power exchange between the Feeling of Being I AM and THAT I AM which is beyond question.

As long as you say "I AM" you can sit in a chair; but when you say,"I AM AM-ing," I AM creating. As soon as you declare "I AM," you must create, and that is everything *unlike* your appearance. Not *like* your appearance — *unlike* it, because I AM not in the appearance, I AM the Light to the appearance! That's why the Creativity of the AM-ing of the I is *so totally different* from the name given to it.

It's as simple as ABC and, as you know, when you have
     found the C in the cradle, after it comes D, and
     that's totally Divine.
E is for Eternality, and then comes the Father in/out of time.
G is for the Good; it's bound to be had
When you find Freedom is the answer to what is your Dad!

He said, "Freedom, my Son! Fetch me water for my
     thirst!"[13]
You ran right to the well and you gave your Self birth,
For obedience is the first Law that you must find
Enacted in your peregrinations from the head to the Heart
     Divine.

When your movement is commensurate with the rhythm of
     the "I,"
You will find how you start to sing and your song entrances
     the sky.
The Celestial Beings shall clap their wings for joy
For from the Earth there sounded a Song which Heaven
     employed!
For the Harmony shall so garment those who are given to
     utter song

That there is nothing else to Being other than the Tonality
    that e'er so long
Shall be breathed into existence as man expires in the Light
And carries with him his Fragrance; yet leaves it for those
    who would have second sight!

Those who can perceive the passing say I came so I could
    disappear,
For in my coming and my going, you have numbered all the
    years.
But in my present moment, unwrap it (the ribbons of the
    band),
And you will see in the rhythmic Utterance how I live and
    move and stand!

For I move with alacrity beyond the vestibule of your
    thoughts;
I move with ebullience and find this rippling, bubbling lot
That knows within the heart the Meaning that every lamb
    shall find
An Answer to its questing, if it is questing of Love Divine!

In this boundless Rapture, may you hear with the Words at
    hand
How they lead you to the backside of the mountain where,
    in the Light, the Great I AM stands!
What is that gleaming Present? Why, it's the Fire at work,
    you know;
You, the cracker, showing off that you, too, want to be part
    of the show!

Well, you celebrate with rapture the Wisdom of this time:
That the Divine Self was born beyond the cradle of the
    mind!
For there, in rapturous splendor, beyond the Crèche you see
    this Fact:
That the Wise Men *never* cease to Wonder, because I AM
    always a Wonder termed as THAT!
Wonder transcends curiosity and a curious story you may
    have been told.

If you have to take these bloody footsteps, well, don't be so
    bloody stupid, don't you know?
Take the Winged Messenger and keep Mercury company as
    you move
And find the Mercurian Splendor is in breathing as you
    should do!

In your movement is the Magic; in your Presence, the
    Wonder to be perceived
By those who catch the rhythmic beating of your Heart
    beyond all dreams!
What is the secret of this passage from sense to Soul? You
    find the Way?
You know it's the Tone that's sounding, unsounded, that
    you hear resplendent and claim by saying, "I have
    found the Enraptured Way!"

You've navigated the riptides of suggestion,
You have moved between the isles of thought and doubt,
And you have found the knowing Wonder
That Love is all about/a bout!

You can't knock it in, you can't knock it out!
So why bother diving in or diving without?
Just die and get it over and then you'll see this Fact:
That you're the most incredible Being allowing other
    humans to call you "Jack"!

So, you and Jill go up the hill and fetch a pail of water
But you remember "Father, Son and Basket": he just kept
    on doing it because it was no bother.
The son said, "My basket's empty, Father, and your thirst is
    not thereby quenched."
But the Father said, "Wake up, my son, don't you see the
    Wonder? Look how clean your basket is, for having
    done what you were told to do!
My thirst was only the suggestion for you to have an
    opportunity to test your own growth in attainment!"

The Father didn't have to prove anything; He only had to allow the son to see the Undivided State and then I and My Father are One Now and not shall be!

> The Hierarchy is only for reference, but the Joy is Total
> Divine!
> That's why the Herald Angels sing a Joy unto this time!
> Oh, but the Infant Holy is One who knows this Fact:
> That the Cradle of the Dawning gave the mountain back!

It no longer was a great big rock; it was just the evidence that the Earth laughed. It had to in order to put up with "you" trying to "make a go of it" on it! Did you ever try to "go" on a mountain? All you have to do is climb. It said, "Go 'round me or go over me; don't be dumb and climb me. I was only meant to allow you an opportunity to cause me to fade out as a limit and to be seen as a rippling laughter of the Creative Might in expression!"

We take everything for being solid. I could take Scott, put him in an atomic press, Aaron along with him, have all the holes squeezed out, and what's left over be on the head of a pin! Ahh! "I've got my dust to do! With my dust I've got to go and play my drums!" "With my dust I've got to play the piano." "With my dust I've got to run the store." "With my dust I've got to breed some dust!"

But what have you bred? If you can look at it correctly, it's the most incredible Self sponsoring Self. When you treat it so Lightly, you free it from thinking it's so important as the "thing" and you are allowed to see the Wonder that it really is! What's more wonderful than to see Dina and Victoria and Jo Ann here and, of course, Diamond and Richard and Terry?!

I better not tarry on six; it's got to be seven, either no one will really, really be merry! Six is reliable responsibility. Twenty-two is the Year of the Master visible! Eleven is the Invisible.

Last year was the year of reflection. It should have been such an easy year, if people had only looked in the mirror and seen their acts completed. It would have been a whole new year of released expression, instead of a whole new year under the discipline of co-operating with Principle as if it were an outside element!

The Augmentation of Authenticity

Remember, this year can never be contracted into anything other than what it is. *It demands your utmost attainment to be a success and to allow others to feel the Wonder of your Presence.*

It's been a wonderful Holiday because it has been totally whole. Love has been on the field, Substance has been evidenced, and the Wealth so great that "this" is not big enough to cope with it!

I'm so glad you were here. I hope your future is as beautiful as this Moment when you are freed from thoughts of "you" and "me" and are wrapped in the Stillness becoming Tranquility!

Good night!

December 31, 1992

1 Mary Baker Eddy, *Science and Health with Key to the Scriptures* (Boston: Trustees Under the Will of Mary Baker G. Eddy, 1934), p. 272, l. 28.
2 Ibid, p. 124, l. 14.
3 Philippians 4:7.
4 "Feeling the Being," published in Kenneth G. Mills, *Embellishments* (Toronto: Sun-Scape Publications, 1986), p. 30. This poem was set to music by Kenneth G. Mills and Christopher Dedrick for The Star-Scape Singers.
5 Mr. Mills makes reference here to *2001: A Space Odyssey*, a film by Stanley Kubrick, 1968.
6 The "ea" which numerologically represents 5+1 equaling 6, which represents reliable responsibility.
7 Words by Kenneth G. Mills, music by Kenneth G. Mills and Christopher Dedrick, recorded on *The Song — The Heart of Christmas* (Toronto: Sun-Scape Records, 1990).
8 Middle C on the music staff.
9 Mr. Mills plays on the word "martyrdom."
10 "Kleenex" is a registered trademark of the Kimberly-Clark Corporation.
11 Words by Kenneth G. Mills, music by Kenneth G. Mills and Christopher Dedrick, recorded on *The Heraldic Message* (Toronto: Sun-Scape Records, 1985).
12 Mr. Mills refers to visitors in the audience from Los Angeles.
13 See "Father, Son and Basket," in Kenneth G. Mills, *The Beauty Unfoldment* (Toronto: Sun-Scape Publications, 1977), pp. 25-27.

The Star-Scape Singers with Conductor, 1992

KENNETH G. MILLS

The spontaneous lectures of Kenneth Mills have reached thousands of people from a wide spectrum of traditions and cultures. Flowing from a singular Standpoint, these lectures offer hearers a daring new view and comprehensive practicality. In describing his speaking, Mr. Mills has said: "The Unfoldment is really a projection from another dimension or plane of consciousness, causing those prepared to hear to awaken to the Higher/Greater possibilities of living beyond the limits of three dimensions and translating what seems to be the ordinary into another level of consideration."

The life of Kenneth Mills unfolds through a deep interest in music, the arts, and education, as well as in health, architecture, fashion, landscaping, and interior design. The boundless energy, innovation, and love that characterize his multi-faceted creative expression have come forth from his unswerving fidelity to his original vow, a vow that he made within himself that he would speak of his realizations if asked about them directly. These insights have since become a continued vocalization dedicated to sharing limitless possibilities with those who question the apparent state of affairs in their lives and in the world.

Trained for twenty-five years as a concert pianist, Kenneth Mills followed an intuitive prompting to decline the offer of a world concert tour. The major turning point in his life came in 1967 when he received an identical message from two different people. Within a few weeks, an acquaintance whom he had known only slightly and a Buddhist monk whose lecture series he had just attended each told him: "You must learn to speak the Word again!"

Not entirely understanding the scope of this unusual message, Mr. Mills decided, "Since I of myself can do nothing, I will move with the statement from Psalms — 'May the words of my mouth and the meditations of my heart be acceptable in the Light of the One Altogether Lovely' — I will speak if I am asked and otherwise I will appear to speak like everyone else." Very soon thereafter, people began seeking him out to ask about their deepest questions and concerns; ultimately, the questioning became so frequent, and the numbers so many, that he turned to public lecturing to accommodate this. Since he began speaking publicly in 1968, he has given many thousands of hours of spontaneous Unfoldments.

The special genius of this man finds expression in unique and diverse forms. From Carnegie Hall to the great choral festivals of Europe, Kenneth Mills appears in concert, on radio and television with his internationally acclaimed choral ensemble, The Star-Scape Singers. He founded this ensemble in 1976 and since then has won the hearts of audiences around the world, serving as a powerful force for world harmony and unity. From China, Russia, Estonia, Lithuania, Latvia, Yugoslavia, Poland, Czechoslovakia, and across Western Europe, the invitations have come to Mr. Mills and The Star-Scape Singers for performances and broadcasts. With the principal composer, Christopher Dedrick, and others, Mr. Mills has created over 150 original choral works.

The lyrics for many of the works in The Star-Scape Singers' repertoire are taken from the poetry of Kenneth Mills. His poems are spontaneously created and given during lectures, or manifest themselves in his day-to-day activities. Over 3,000 of these spontaneous poems have been transcribed, and some of them appear in several published volumes. In response to the Spirit of these poems, New York dramatist Dr. Barry Brodie formed the Earthstage Actors and a "Theatre of Philosophy" in 1987, dedicated to performing dramatic settings of Mr. Mills' poetry and prose.

Currently, Kenneth Mills offers lectures, workshops, and seminars, and speaks with performing artists, public representatives, award-winning composers, and international figures. His meetings with members of the professional disciplines (such as teachers, designers, doctors, dramatists, musicians, dancers, singers, writers, and businesspeople) open the door to transformed insights into these fields, offering a freedom from the old views and a host of radical new ideas.

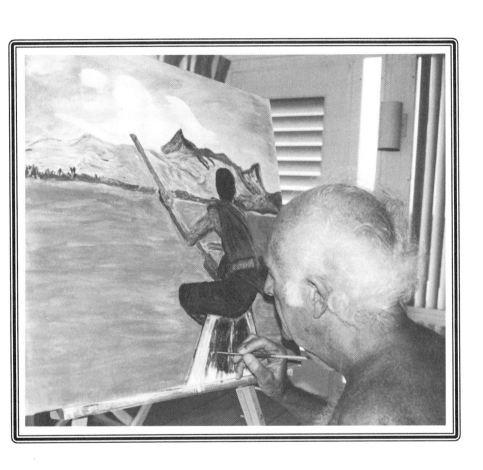

To Mr. Kenneth Mills on His Seventieth Birthday

"If there was a Birth of Wonder" –
And there has been One indeed –
How would you find the Act
And recognize the Deed?

Would you find it in St. Stephen
Or beyond the Holy Cross?
Would you venture to the Saint of Strength
And ask him for the Cause?

Would you cast beneath the lily pads,
If you had any doubt,
And find That which you're looking for
Might be a Rainbow Trout?

Or would you seek the kingdom high
And talk to birds above?
A wild Canary, Eagle gold,
A circling, cooing Dove!

You might dive beneath the shell
Of appearances to find
The secret voice of Turtle says,
"You are Divine!"

Or would you pass through Nature's realms
And land upon the stage
Of busy cities 'round the world
To come upon the page

That tells the news that's paramount
In headlines big and bold
That standing room is only found
To see the Tale unfold!

That birth of wonder could be a leaf
You find within a book
On which is etched a Face of Power
With penetrating look.

You might turn on your radio
And flick your dial just right
To find there is a Voice about
That boldly speaks of Light.

"If there was a Birth of Wonder . . ."
Why not drop the "if" of time
And know the Infinite Fact
That Wonder is Divine.

But, if you search your dictionary
Whence the meanings stem,
You'll find the Word of Wonder
Is spelled with "K-G-M"!

– Barry T. Brodie

Other Publications by
KENNETH G. MILLS

BOOKS
Given to Praise!
A Word Fitly Spoken
The New Land!

POETRY
Words of Adjustment
Surprises
Anticipations
Embellishments

TAPED LECTURES
The Beauty Unfoldment
The Newness of the Unchanging
The Seal of Approval
Near to the Fire
The Quickening Spirit of Radiance
Freedom is Found

For more information on Kenneth G. Mills or other
Sun-Scape publications and recordings, contact:

Sun-Scape Publications
65 High Ridge Road, Suite 103
Stamford, Connecticut 06905 USA
Tel. (203) 838-3775   Fax (203) 348-0216
or
Sun-Scape Publications
P.O. Box 793, Station "F"
Toronto, Ontario, Canada M4Y 2N7
Tel. (416) 470-8634   Fax (416) 470-1632